VARIORUM COLLECTED STUDIES SERIES

Astronomy and Astrology in al-Andalus and the Maghrib

Julio Samsó

Julio Samsó

Astronomy and Astrology in al-Andalus and the Maghrib

ASHGATE
VARIORUM

Published in the Variorum Collected Studies Series by

Ashgate Publishing Limited
Gower House, Croft Road,
Aldershot, Hampshire
GU11 3HR
Great Britain

Ashgate Publishing Company
Suite 420
101 Cherry Street
Burlington, VT 05401–4405
USA

Ashgate website: http://www.ashgate.com

ISBN 978–0–7546–5934–1

British Library Cataloguing in Publication Data

Samsó, Julio
Astronomy and astrology in al-Andalus and the Maghrib. – (Variorum collected studies series)
1. Astronomy, Medieval – Spain – Andalusia 2. Astronomy, Medieval – Africa, North 3. Astronomy – Spain – Andalusia – History 4. Astronomy – Africa, North – History 5. Islamic astrology – Spain Andalusia – History 6. Islamic astrology – Africa, North – History 7. Islamic astrology – History
I. Title
520.9'468'091767

ISBN 978–0–7546–5934–1

Library of Congress Cataloging-in-Publication Data

Samsó, Julio.
Astronomy and astrology in al-Andalus and the Maghrib / Julio Samsó.
p. cm. – (Variorum collected studies series; 887)
Includes index.
ISBN 978–0–7546–5934–1 (alk. paper)
1. Astronomy, Medieval – Spain – Andalusia – History – Sources 2. Astronomy, Medieval – Africa, North – History – Sources. 3. Astrology – Spain – Andalusia – History – Sources. 4. Astrology – Africa, North – History – Sources. 5. Astronomy – Spain – Andalusia – History – Sources. 6. Astronomy – Africa, North – History – Sources.
I. Title.
QB23S259 2007
520.946'8–dc22 2007022639

The paper used in this publication meets the minimum requirements of the American National Standard for Information Sciences – Permanence of Paper for Printed Library Materials, ANSI Z39.48–1984. ∞ ™

Printed and bound in Great Britain by TJ International Ltd, Padstow, Cornwall

VARIORUM COLLECTED STUDIES SERIES CS887

CONTENTS

This volume contains xiv + 366 pages

PUBLISHER'S NOTE

The articles in this volume, as in all others in the Variorum Collected Studies Series, have not been given a new, continuous pagination. In order to avoid confusion, and to facilitate their use where these same studies have been referred to elsewhere, the original pagination has been maintained wherever possible.

Each article has been given a Roman number in order of appearance, as listed in the Contents. This number is repeated on each page and is quoted in the index entries.

PREFACE

This volume offers me the opportunity to give a new life to a series of papers published between 1994 and 2004. My previous collection (articles dated during the period 1977-1994)[1] dealt exclusively with Andalusian and Alfonsine materials and this subject of study is still present here in papers I-VII. In 1994, however, after the publication of my work on the history of science in al-Andalus,[2] my colleagues at the University of Barcelona and I had the impression that we had already seen most of the available sources related to Andalusian astronomy. There was only one gap left in our exploration of these sources: that of the criticisms of Ptolemy's astronomy made, in the 12th century, by Jābir b. Aflaḥ in his *Iṣlāḥ al-Majisṭī* and I began to fill it with VII. Fortunately a far more serious effort in this direction has been made in Josep Bellver's doctoral thesis.[3]

I soon became aware of the fact that there is a wealth of unexplored information available in Maghribī sources closely related to an Andalusian tradition. One main topic is the existence of a school of Andalusian *zīj*es (astronomical handbooks with tables) in the Maghrib (13th- 14th c.) which had developed as a result of the diffusion of the astronomical theories of the great Toledan astronomer Abū Isḥāq ibn al-Zarqālluh (Azarquiel, d. 1100). These theories reached Ibn Isḥāq al-Tūnisī (fl. ca. 1193-1222) who began the compilation of a new *zīj* which was left unfinished and was the object of several "editions", prepared by indirect disciples like the anonymous Tunisian author of the compilation extant in MS Hyderabad Andra Pradesh State Library 298 (ca. 1266-1281), Ibn al-Bannā' al-Marrākushī (1256-1321) and Ibn al-Raqqām al-Tūnisī (fl. Tunis and Granada, d. 1315): the latter prepared three different "editions" of that

---

[1] *Islamic Astronomy and Medieval Spain*. Variorum, Aldershot, 1994.

[2] *Las Ciencias de los Antiguos en al-Andalus*. Mapfre, Madrid, 1992.

[3] Josep Bellver, *Críticas a Ptolomeo en el s. XII: El caso del* Iṣlāḥ al-Maŷisṭī *de Ŷābir b. Aflaḥ*. Ph.D. diss., University of Barcelona, 2006.

work. This tradition has been the main object of our research during the last fifteen years. In 1996 a Syrian post-graduate student of mine, Muḥammad ᶜAbd al-Raḥmān, presented a Ph.D. dissertation on the computation of planetary longitudes in one of Ibn al-Raqqām's *zījes*.[4] In the same year, Angel Mestres published a complete description of the contents of the Hyderabad MS and presented, three years later, a Ph.D. thesis which contained an edition and commentary of the canons of this source and a selection of the numerical tables.[5] To this one should add my own study, together with E. Millás, of the *Minhāj* of Ibn al-Bannā' (VIII),[6] whose canons had been edited by my master Juan Vernet in 1952.[7]

In the meantime I had discovered a later *zīj*, also strongly influenced by Ibn Isḥāq and by other Andalusian sources, prepared by Ibn ᶜAzzūz al-Qusanṭīnī (d. 1354) (IX) and found in it the first symptoms of a criticism of the aforementioned tradition. This led me to investigate the abandonment of this tradition in the Maghrib and its replacement by an Eastern one (XI-XIII) towards the end of the 14th c.[8] Although no precise date can be given, for example, for the introduction in the Maghrib of the *Tāj al-azyāj* of Ibn Abī l-Shukr al-Maghribī (d. 1283), it is quite interesting to remark that the three extant manuscripts of this work were copied in the Maghrib: this was the object of the research of another postgraduate student of mine, Carlos Dorce.[9]

The same kind of curiosity led me to explore a different tradition: that

---

[4] M. ᶜAbd al-Raḥmān, *Ḥisāb aṭwāl al-kawākib fī l-zīj al-Shāmil fī tahdhīb al-Kāmil*. University of Barcelona, 1996.

[5] Angel Mestres, "Maghribī Astronomy in the 13th Century: a Description of Manuscript Hyderabad Andra Pradesh State Library 298", in J. Casulleras & J. Samsó (eds.), *From Baghdad to Barcelona. Studies in the Islamic Exact Sciences in Honour of Prof. Juan Vernet* (Barcelona, 1996), I, 383-443; id., *Materials andalusins en el Zīj d'Ibn Isḥāq al-Tunisī*. University of Barcelona, 1999.

[6] See also J. Samsó & E. Millás, "Ibn al-Bannā', Ibn Isḥāq and Ibn al-Zarqālluh's Solar Theory" in J. Samsó, *Islamic Astronomy and Medieval Spain*. Variorum. Aldershot, 1994, no. X (35 pp.).

[7] J. Vernet, *Contribución al estudio de la labor astronómica de Ibn al-Bannā'*. Tetuán, 1952.

[8] M. Díaz Fajardo, *La teoría de la trepidación en un astrónomo marroquí del siglo XV. Estudio y edición crítica del* Kitāb al-adwār fī tasyīr al-anwār *(parte primera), de Abū ᶜAbd Allāh al-Baqqār*. Barcelona, 2001.

[9] C. Dorce, "The *Tāj al-azyāj* of Muḥyī al-Dīn al-Maghribī (d.1283). Methods of computation". *Suhayl*, 3 (2002-2003), 193-212; id., *El* Tāŷ al-azyāŷ *de Muḥyī al-Dīn al-Magribī*. Barcelona, 2002-2003.

of the *Almanach Perpetuum* (printed in 1496) compiled by Abraham Zacut (1452-1515) and his disciple José Vizinho and translated into Arabic by the Morisco exile al-Ḥajarī (1570- after 1640) (XIV-XVI): I was also gently pushed in this direction by Bernard R. Goldstein who, together with José Chabás, had recently published an important book on the *Almanach*. This has the obvious interest of bearing witness to the indirect introduction, in the Arab world, of the *Alfonsine Tables*, which were the main source used by Zacut. On the other hand, it was quite a surprise for me to discover that this tradition had been alive in the Maghrib until the 19th c. and that al-Ḥajarī's translation had been used not only in the Maghrib but also in Egypt and that it had even reached the Yemen.

Some of the papers reproduced in this volume have been written in accordance with the personal interests of scholars to whom they were dedicated, in their corresponding *Festschrifts*: paper I was prepared for a symposium in honour of David King (2001) and the subject was suggested to me by Sonja Brentjes who has always been enthusiastic about the social aspects of the history of science.[10] I also tried to dedicate article XI to David: I was not allowed to do so by the Journal where it was published, but I have done so now. Paul Kunitzsch's long-standing interests in star-tables led me to look for a star-table on which I could say something and this was the origin of II. One of the main interests of my master Juan Vernet was always the transmission of knowledge between East and West and this is why I prepared item VI. John North's splendid *Horoscopes and History* (London, 1986) aroused my curiosity in the study of horoscopes and I wrote paper X, dedicated to him. The same kind of interest was the origin of V. I have already mentioned Bernard Goldstein's concern with the Arabic translations of Zacut's *Almanach* and this is why XIV was published in his *Festschrift*.

My final words here should express my gratitude, first of all, to my masters who have become my friends (Juan Vernet and E.S. Kennedy) and to my friends who have taught me many things and have also become my masters (David King and John North). Thanks also to my colleagues and co-authors who have allowed me to reprint here papers in which they have collaborated: Margarita Castells (III), Honorino Mielgo (IV), Hamid Berrani (V) and María Rosa Puig, widow of my late friend Eduardo Millás (VIII). Thanks, finally, to Josep Bellver and Montse Díaz Fajardo

[10] A four-page summary was published in the Proceedings of the symposium: *Is a Social History of Andalusī Exact Sciences Possible?*. "Early Science and Medicine" (Leiden), 7 (2002), 296-299.

who have redrawn some of my figures and to Michael Maudsley (University of Barcelona) who has spent many hours correcting the English of the papers appearing here.

JULIO SAMSÓ

Barcelona
April 2007

ACKNOWLEDGEMENTS

Grateful acknowledgement is made to the following persons, journals, institutions and publishers for their kind permission to reproduce the papers included in this volume: Societat Catalana d'Història de la Ciència i de la Tècnica, Barcelona (for chapter I); Harrassowitz Verlag, Wiesbaden (II); Archives Internationales d'Histoire des Sciences, Rome (III); *Journal for the History of Astronomy*, Cambridge (IV, XI); Oxford University Press, Oxford (V); Montserrat Camps, Dean of the Faculty of Philology, University of Barcelona, Barcelona (VI, VII, XV); Cambridge University Press, Cambridge (VIII, XII); Institut für Geschichte der Arabisch-Islamischen Wissenschaften, Frankfurt (IX, XVI); Brill, Leiden (X); The MIT Press, Cambridge, MA (XIII); Blackwell Publishing Ltd, Oxford (XIV).

I

A SOCIAL APPROXIMATION TO THE HISTORY OF THE EXACT SCIENCES IN AL-ANDALUS

To David A. King.

Introduction

A social history of Andalusī exact sciences is, by definition, extremely poor due to the lack of sources. Those extant (*ṭabaqāt* and biographical dictionaries) have already been explored by G. Balty-Guesdon [1992] (from the beginning until the Almoravid invasion in 1085); M. Forcada, [1997] (general analysis of the *ṭabaqāt* from the point of view of the history of science), as well as [1999] and [2000] (Almoravid and Almohad periods); R. Puig [1983 *a* and *b*], [1984] (the Naṣrid Kingdom of Granada in Ibn al-Khaṭīb's *Iḥāṭa*). These efforts should be placed in the context or the research programme on biographical dictionaries undertaken by the Departments of Arabic Studies of the Consejo Superior de Investigaciones Científicas in Madrid and Granada. This programme begun in connection with the international project *Onomasticon Arabicum* but became later independent and produced the eleven volumes of the *Estudios Onomástico-Biográficos de al-Andalus* (*E.O.B.A.*, published by the C.S.I.C. in Madrid and Granada between 1988 and 2000). The main extant biographical dictionaries (all published and well explored) are:

- — Ibn al-Faraḍī (962-1012), *Tārīkh ᶜulamā' al-Andalus*
- — al-Ḥumaydī (1029-1095), *Jadhwat al-muqtabis*
- — Ibn Bashkuwāl (1101-1182), *al-Ṣila fī akhbār a'immat al-Andalus*
- — al-Ḍabbī (d. 1203), *Bughyat al-multamis*
- — Ibn al-Abbār (1199-1260), *Takmila li-Kitāb al-Ṣila*
- — Ibn al-Zubayr (1230-1308), *Ṣilat al-Ṣila*
- — Ibn ᶜAbd al-Malik al-Marrākushī (1237-1303), *Al-Dhayl wa 'l-takmila li-Kitābay al-Mawṣūl wa 'l-Ṣila*
- — Ibn al-Khaṭīb (1313-1374), *al-Iḥāṭa fī akhbār ahl Gharnāṭa.*

The main source for the history of the exact sciences is Ṣā'id's *Ṭabaqāt al-umam* (1068) which contains little information on biographical details. The author is interested in the scientists' production, the sciences they cultivate, the most significant places in which they lived, as well as the travels they made. His sources are mainly oral and he ignores important characters such as Ibn Muᶜādh al-Jayyānī (d. 1093). Biographical dictionaries are only interested in scientists when they also cultivate the religious sciences and the information they contain about their scientific activity is limited. Two short biographical notes on Ibn Muᶜādh (who was also a *qāḍī*) are extant: Ibn Bashkuwāl does not say a word about his scientific works; al-Ḍabbī merely calls him *faylasūf zamānihi*. A partial exception is Ibn al-Abbār (1199-1260), who is more open to this kind of activity: his *Takmila* contains the names of more than 100 scientists out of some 3000 biographies. He is the only biographer to give information about Ibn al-Zarqālluh (d. 1100), especially about his late years in Cordova. He is also interested by Ibn al-Zarqālluh's disciples Ibn al-Amīn (d. 539/1144) and Ibn al-Kammād. Ibn ᶜAbd al-Malik al-Marrākushī has an attitude similar to Ibn al-Abbār. In spite of this our main source for the biography of Ibn al-Zarqālluh is late (14th c.) and not very reliable, namely Isaac Israeli's *Yesod ha-ᶜOlam*.

Scientific schools and travels to the East

A social history of Andalusī science should deal with *scientific schools*, teaching, travels to the East, patronage and scientific professions. Ṣā'id, for example, provides enough information about Maslama's school (end of the 10th and beginning of the 11th c.) and recent studies have established the possible links between the disciples of Maslama and the development of new schools in Toledo (Ṣā'id, Ibn al-Zarqālluh) and Zaragoza (al-Mu'taman) during the *ṭā'ifa* period (1035-1085). The continuity of the Toledan school both in al-Andalus and in the Maghrib (13th-14th c.) is a well established fact.

Travels to the East are another significant topic. Vernet (1950) and Grau (1957-58) studied it in a general way (not only scientists) in a geographical area (the Ebro Valley) and established, for example, that in the 10th c. the 25% of the Andalusīs of that zone who travel go to the East, while in the 11th c. the percentage is reduced to 11%. This is one of the many symptoms of the tendency towards cultural isolation which appears in al-Andalus during the *ṭā'ifa* period: Ṣā'id has very little information about Eastern science after the end of the 10th c. and there is no evidence that important scientists such as Maslama, Ṣā'id, Ibn al-Zarqālluh or Ibn Rushd ever traveled to the East. Ibn Muᶜādh was probably an exception: there is no evidence that he ever made the *riḥla* (the standard trip to the East undertaken by somebody who pretended to become a scholar) but he seems to have priviledged sources of information. In the 15th c. we have an exceptional source, al-Qalaṣādī's *Riḥla*, which shows clearly that, in spite of having been in the Mashriq, Qalaṣādī's teachers were in the Maghrib.

Science and Religion

ᶜIlm al-Farā'iḍ and Misāḥa

Mathematics and Astronomy are sciences, not professions. There are a few professions, however, which require mathematical knowledge: *faraḍīs* and calculators, land-surveyors, teachers, artisans who make astronomical instruments, *muwaqqit*s and astrologers.

Biographical dictionaries often include *nisbas* or other kinds of denominations related to professional activities. The most frequent is *faraḍī*, but we also find *ḥāsib*, *ḥisābī, ᶜadadī*, *qassām*, *asṭurlābī*, *naqqāsh* or *munajjim*. The *ḥāsib* (and related professionals) will deal with difficult problems related to calculation in everyday life and his services will be well paid for, as he will have acquired a technical knowledge based on his reading of Euclid, Nichomacos, al-Khwārizmī, Abū Kāmil, as well as treatises on *farā'iḍ* (partition of inheritances) and *mu'āmalāt* (commercial arithmetic).

Balty-Guesdon has emphasized the importance of *farā'iḍ* in the origins of the Andalusī mathematical and astronomical school: Maslama's masters were all *faraḍī*s and Ibn Bashkuwāl calls him Faraḍī and Ḥāsib. *ᶜIlm al-Farā'iḍ* is the door through which Arithmetic became an accepted science in conservative religious circles and both disciplines were taught in the Great Mosque of Valencia by Abū Bakr ibn Juzayy (1105-1187). In fact, when *Qāḍī* Ṣā'id talks about the decay of the sciences in the time of al-Manṣūr he states that scientists only cultivated openly those sciences which were considered officially adequate such as Arithmetic, *Farā'iḍ,* Medicine and similar sciences. Out of 55 mathematicians documented by Balty-Guesdon (pp. 118, 191-192, 735) until 976, 34 were *faraḍī*s. From this list 25 were also geometers. Others were interested in Arithmetic (*ᶜilm al-ᶜadad*, *ḥisāb*) —which sometimes included Algebra—, *muᶜāmalāt* (defined above) or astronomy. Mathematical treatises unrelated to *farā'iḍ* appear for the first time during the Caliphate: such is the case of Ibn ᶜAbdūn al-Jabalī (fl. 950-980) whose *Mukhtaṣar jāmiᶜ li-wujūh al-misāḥa*, also called *Risāla fī 'l-taksīr*, is a treatise on practical geometry which gives rules for the calculation of surfaces, often equivalent to second degree equations. The study of *misāḥa* applied to the measurement of lands has obvious legal applications and it is reasonable to see in this discipline another point of contact between *fiqh* and the Sciences of the Ancients. In fact, the treatises on the use of the astrolabe, such as those written by the two disciples of Maslama, Ibn al-Ṣaffār and Ibn al-Samḥ, insist on the practical applications of the instrument for operations of land-surveying such as the measurement of distances, heights or inclinations. In the same way the treatises on agriculture (*filāḥa*) of the 11th and 12th century also describe the use of an astrolabe (probably a simplified instrument similar to the later mariner's astrolabe) for the measurement of the inclination of lands for the building of a *qanāt* (an underground canal which conducts water from a mother well until it reaches the surface).

Towards the end of the Caliphate we see the apparition of the first mathematical works which show an interest in theory, although this is also the moment in which several of the members of Maslama's school publish treatises on *muᶜāmalāt*, which do not seem to be extant, although some evidence about their possible contents can be infered from the Latin *Liber mahameleth*, studied by Sesiano (1987, 1988, 1989), and considered by Balty-Guesdon (pp. 406-407) as a textbook. The treatise states that it should be studied after Euclid's *Elements* and it refers to the interest of the study of number in itself (the source mentioned is Nichomacos' *Arithmetic*) or considered from a practical point of view, namely operations one may do with it (the source here is al-Khwārizmī's *Arithmetic*).

It seems clear, therefore, that if a social history of mathematics in al-Andalus has to be written, one should begin by an analysis of all the extant sources related to *farā'iḍ*, *muᶜāmalāt* and *misāḥa*. The problem lies in the fact that this kind of sources rarely attract the attention of historians with some rare exceptions like Sánchez Pérez who, already in 1914, edited an *aljamiado* (in Spanish, though written in Arabic script) text on *Farā'iḍ* or Djebbar (and disciples) who have become interested in the innovations introduced in this discipline by Abū 'l-Qāsim al-Qurashī (d. 1184), an author who seems to have studied and taught in Seville and established himself later in Bijāya (Djebbar, 1991). This kind of work should include a study of, for example, Ibn ᶜAbdūn's unpublished treatise on *misāḥa* (Ahmed Djebbar has prepared an edition and French translation of that text), the treatise on *Farā'iḍ* by a certain Abū 'l-Ṭāhir Muḥammad ibn ᶜAbd al-Kabīr al-Murādī, Ibn al-Jayyāb, also called al-ᶜAdadī, al-Faraḍī al-Ḥisābī, who lived between the end of the 11th c. and the middle of the 13th c. (Paris BN Ar. 7228, see Balty-Guesdon pp. 400-401), and of various works compiled in the 15th c. by the well known mathematician al-Qalaṣādī. Once this kind of work has been done, one may wonder up to what extent we will gain deeper insight into the general development of Andalusī mathematics, although we will probably obtain some information about certain mathematical branches which, like Algebra, are not well attested.

Mīqāt

In spite of the efforts of scholars such as M. Rius (2000), very little is known about *mīqāt* in al-Andalus. We know that some literature on this topic did exist: for example biographical dictionaries mention a certain Abū Bakr ᶜUbayd Allāh al-Qurashī (d. 1052), who was a *faqīh* and wrote a *Ta'līf fī awqāt al-ṣalawāt ᶜalà madhāhib al-ᶜulamā'* which seems not to be extant (Balty Guesdon pp. 429-430); on the other hand when al-Manṣūr ibn Abī ʻĀmir burned a part of the library of al-Ḥakam II, he spared the books related to the *ᶜilm awqāt al-ṣalawāt* (Samsó, 1992, p. 71). There is no secondary literature on this topic or about the visibility of the lunar crescent with the exception of the analysis of some materials extant in the *anwā'* literature (Samsó, 1983; Forcada, 1990, 1994), what is possibly a 10th c. universal table for lunar crescent visibility (King, 1987, pp. 197-207), or the treatment of this latter problem by Ibn al-Raqqām (d. 1315) (Kennedy, 1997, pp. 38-41). The *qibla* problem seems clearer in spite of the fact, underlined by Rius, that the richness of Maghribī sources on this topic shows a clear contrast with the lack of precise information about al-Andalus. It seems that Andalusī scholars were conscious of the «erroneous» orientation of the Great Mosque of Cordova towards the end of the ninth century: biographical dictionaries and *Ṣāᶜid's Ṭabaqāt* refer to the famous Abū ᶜUbayda Muslim b. Aḥmad, called *Ṣāḥib al-qibla* (d. 907 or 914), who oriented himself towards the East when he made his prayers (*yusharriqu fī ṣalawāti-hi*). Shortly thereafter a Caliph like ᶜAbd al-Raḥmān III (912-961) must have used the services of an astronomer to orientate adequately the mosque of Madīnat al-Zahrā' (the *mirāb* was oriented about 18° S of E, which is a significant improvement upon the Great Mosque of Cordova, which faces 62.4° S of E). His son, al-Ḥakam II (961-976), who was a great patron of learning, sent his astrologer, Aḥmad b. Fāris al-Munajjim (Forcada, 1996 and 2000 b), to Fuengirola (named Suhayl in Arabic texts) in order to check whether the star Suhayl could actually be seen from that location. The interest in Suhayl was probably due to the fact that this star was a *qibla*-indicator. Ḥistorical sources refer the disagreement between astronomers (*ahl al-taᶜdīl*) and architects in relation to the enlargement of the Great Mosque of Cordova under al-Ḥakam II: astronomers wished to take profit from this opportunity to attempt an impossible reorientation of the building. This seems to be the first known instance in which Cordovan astronomers seem to have played an important social role.

In spite of the fact that the first *muwaqqit*s attested in al-Andalus appear in the Naṣrid kingdom of Granada towards the end of the 13th c., more or less at the same time in which we have a reference to this kind of profession in Egypt, it is quite probable that his role and duties was fulfilled by other officers of the staff of the mosque: D.A. King (1996) has drawn our attention to the role of the muezzin in this respect in the Mashriq and probably the same could be applied to al-Andalus. I have no information, however, on muezzins dealing with the problem of the determination of the times of prayer, but Balty-Guesdon (pp. 430, 637-638; 295, 432, 654) has brought to light the fact that two astronomers who flourished towards the end of the 10th c. and in the 11th c. occupied posts in mosques and were interested in *mīqāt* problems. One of them is ᶜAlī b. Sulaymān al-Zahrāwī *al-Ḥāsib*, a disciple of Maslama, who was *imām* and *khaṭīb* in the mosque of Granada and wrote a *Risāla fī maᶜrifat saᶜat* [Balty Guesdon reads and translates *sāᶜat*] *al-mashriq*. The second one is Ziyād ibn ᶜAbd Allāh al-Anṣārī, Abū ᶜAbd Allāh (d. 1085) who was *khaṭīb* and *ṣāḥib al-ṣalāt* in the Great Mosque of Cordova. He knew astronomy and determined a new qibla for Cordova «along its great river» [Ibn Bashkuwāl no. 431, p. 189: *ᶜalà nahri-hā al-aᶜẓam*], which probably implies an Eastern orientation of the *qibla*, for the Guadalquivir flows approximately East-West.

In the 11th c., Ibn Muᶜādh al-Jayyānī (d. 1093), described the first exact solution for the determination of the *qibla* in al-Andalus (the so-called «method of the *zīj*es») (Samsó & Mielgo, 1994), but this does not seem to have brought significant consequences. The analysis of the actual orientation of mosques in al-Andalus made by M. Rius does not show any improvement in the *qibla* values used or clear political/dynastic tendencies as in Morocco. Only in four cases dated between the 10th and the 12th centuries (and this includes the aforementioned case of Madīnat al-Zahrā') the orientation reaches a maximum of 126° (from the North point), values which imply the possibility of the intervention of an astronomer.

The situation changed entirely towards the end of the 13th c. with the apparition of the first Andalusī *muwaqqit*s, who are also called *muᶜadhdhin* (?), *muᶜaddil*, or *amīn al-awqāt*: Ḥasan/Ḥusayn b. Muḥammad b. Bāṣo (d. 1316) and his son Aḥmad b. Ḥasan/Ḥusayn (d. 1310) were both *muwaqqit*s (as well as instrument makers) in the Great Mosque of Granada and the former was, according to Ibn al-Khaṭīb, «chief of time-keepers» (*ra'īs al-muwaqqitīn*) in the same mosque (Calvo, 1993). The profession was still alife in the 15th c. for Abū 'l-Ḥasan ᶜAlī b. Mūsā al-Lakhmī, known as al-Qarabāqī (d. 1440), one of the teachers of al-Qalaṣādī, was a *muwaqqit* (probably in Baza) and had a long discussion with Abū 'l-Qāsim b. Sirāj, *imām* and *muftī* in Granada, on the problem of the orientation of Andalusī mosques (Samsó, 1992, p. 413). The development of *mīqāt* might be the cause of the improvement in the orientation of mosques built in the 14th c. In M. Rius' classification, six mosques of that century reach a maximum of 124° from the North and three small mosques of the Alhambra are remarkable in this respect. If we consider that the *qibla* of Granada (calculated with modern coordinates) is 100;21°, it is surprising to see that these three mosques built during the reign of Yūsuf I (1333-1354) and Muḥammad V (1354-1359, 1362-1391) are oriented accurately: those of the Mexuar (error of 7;39° towards the South), the Rawḍa (id. 8;33°) and the Palace of Comares (id. 0;27°). The latter was built under Yūsuf I, who also built the *madrasa* of Granada in which the mosque has an orientation deviated 37;21° towards the South, probably as a result of the influence of the Great Mosque (deviation 40;57°). Together with the mosque of Madīnat al-Zahrā', we have four examples of astronomically-oriented mosques built in conection with royal palaces: political power did not want to introduce doubts in the beliefs and practices of common people by openly disapproving traditional orientations, but they felt free to do so in mosques reserved for their own use.

Teaching

Out of 55 mathematicians documented by Balty-Guesdon (pp. 401-493) before 976, in 28 instances there is mention of teaching: in some cases they taught mathematics to princes and we know that the *amīr* Muḥammad I (852-886) could easily detect errors in the public accounts (Balty-Guesdon p. 405). Mathematics and certain aspects of astronomy were accepted as part of the general curriculum of a cultivated person, as one can easily check by reading literary works like the *Risālat al-Tawābi*ᶜ *wa 'l-zawābi*ᶜ of Ibn Shuhayd (992-1035), which contains a surprisingly high number of astronomical and astrological images not easy to understand for somebody who did not have adequate training. In the first half of the 11th c. Ibn al-Kattānī educated female slaves, who were ignorant Christians, and taught them medicine, logic, philosophy, geometry, music, the use of the astrolabe, astronomy, astrology, grammar, prosody, literature and calligraphy. All this could be mere advertising and correspond to the stereotype of the Jāriyat Tawaddud of the *Thousand and One Nights* if we did not have other kinds of information about female slaves such as Lubnā (d. 984), who belonged to ᶜAbd al-Raḥmān III, was *kātiba* and had a good knowledge of *ḥisāb*. A similar case is that of the unnamed *Jāriyat al-Ḥakam*, who belonged to al-Ḥakam II and had good knowledge of astronomy, for she had learnt how to calculate planetary longitudes (*ta*ᶜ*dīl*) and the use of the astrolabe during three years (Marín pp. 640-641, 653-654). Certain kings had acquired this kind of specialised knowledge and this is the case of ᶜAbd Allāh, the last Zīrī king of Granada (1073-1090), who had his horoscope cast for the moment of his fourth anniversary in 1060 and used it competently to justify certain facts of his life in his memoires (*Ṭibyān*). In the same way, according to the *Iktifā'* of Ibn Kardabūs, al-Muᶜtamid of Seville (1069-1091) could use an astrolabe and had cast himself the horoscope of the battle of Zallāqa (1086) (Balty-Guesdon p. 315). Ibn Bassām (*Dhakhīra* VII, 167) describes also al-Qādir, the last king of Toledo, astrolabe in hand, trying to establish the propitious moment to abandon the city (1085) and leave it in the hands of Alfonso VI. During this operation he is surrounded by Christians and Muslims who laugh at him or are astonished by his ignorance. Finally, the Tunisian astronomer Ibn al-Raqqām (d. 1315) taught king Naṣr (1309-1314) how to calculate ephemerides and make astronomical instruments (Puig, 1984, pp. 71, 75). All this agrees with the ideal programme for the education of children sketched by Ibn Ḥazm (994-1064) in his *Marāṭib al-*ᶜ*ulūm*: children should learn *ḥisāb* which included ᶜ*ilm al-*ᶜ*adad*, the four operations, proportions, geometry, *misāḥa* and arithmetic. Astronomy (not astrology) should be taught from the *Almagest*, after having learned Euclid, and it should include the knowledge of eclipses, longitudes and latitudes, time reckoning, tides, *anwā'*, lunar mansions (*manāzil al-qamar*) and the constellations (Balty-Guesdon pp. 411-412, 433). We should finally remember that when the famous Abū Bakr ibn al-ᶜArabī (1075-1148) was 9 years old, he had three teachers, appointed by his father, who would teach him in his own home. One of them was a mathematician and taught him *mu*ᶜ*āmalāt,* algebra and *farā'iḍ*, followed by Euclid and its continuation until *al-shakl al-qaṭṭā*ᶜ (Menelaos' theorem). In astronomy he studied three astronomical tables and the use of the astrolabe (Balty-Guesdon pp. 409-410, 433).

Astrology, astronomy and scientific patronage

Scientific patronage is mainly in the hands of *amīrs*, caliphs and kings, who were interested in the prediction of future and, therefore, in astrology. There is, obviously, another kind of more popular astrology, for treatises on the *ḥisbat al-sūq* (policing of the market), such as that of al-Saqaṭī (fl. ca. 1200-1225), forbid astrologers to practice in markets (Chalmeta, 1967), but there is no information about these professionals, although we might guess that certain characteristic developments of Andalusī astronomy, designed to simplify the computation of planetary longitudes (equatoria, perpetual almanacs), were the result of the demands of popular astrologers who needed to sell a product (i.e. a horoscope) for a reasonable price. We are therefore restricted to the circles of power in which patronage follows the evolution of political and religious history.

The first reference to the interest of the Umayyad *amīrs* in astrology appears in the time of Hishām I (788-796) who, in spite of his religious beliefs, used the service of al-Ḍabbī (fl. c. 788 - c. 852), the first known Andalusī astrologer (Samsó, 1979 & 2001). The situation is clearer in the time of al-Ḥakam I (796-822) and, especially, under ᶜAbd al-Raḥmān II (822-852). The former had his son ᶜAbd al-Raḥmān adequately taught in the sciences of the ancients, and both *amīrs* had in their court an important group of poets-astrologers who are well attested in the sources precisely because they were poets. The recent publication of a facsimile edition of a manuscript of an important part of vol. II of Ibn Ḥayyān's *Muqtabis* (Madrid, 1999) has brought to light new information on these characters (al-Ḍabbī, Yaḥyā al-Gazāl, Ibn al-Shamir, ᶜAbbās b. Firnās, Marwān b. Gazwān etc.) for the manuscript contains an important chapter entitled *Akhbār al-munajjimīn maᶜa l-amīr* (= ᶜAbd al-Raḥmān II). The materials contained in this chapter and in the rest of the text should be analysed critically, because they are mainly concerned with an attempt by the *amīr* to control the veracity of the astrological predictions made by his astrologers in a set of anecdotes two of which, at least, are also attributed to Eastern astrologers such as Abū Maᶜshar and al-Bīrūnī. On the other hand, it seems that this introduction of astrology in the court is somehow related to the first manifestations of the *muᶜtazila* movement (Yaḥyā al-Gazāl) and of [Ḥarrānian?] Magic (al-Ḍabbī, ᶜAbbās b. Firnās). It would be worthwhile to establish whether there was an official list (*dīwān*) of astrologers who received a royal salary in a similar way to the list of poets (*dīwān al-shuᶜarā'*) or the list of physicians (*dīwān al-mutaṭabbibīn)* which existed in Cordova under al-Ḥakam II. The only hint we have of such arrangement is the fact that Ibn Saᶜīd (*Mugrib* I, 125) says that ᶜAbd al-Raḥmān II assigned to Ibn al-Shamir a double salary (*rizq*) for his poetry and his astrology (*tanjīm*). Was he the only case?.

Astrology was strongly attacked by *fuqahā'* like ᶜAbd al-Malik ibn Ḥabīb (d. 853), who tried to defend the existence of a legitimate folk-astronomy tradition (*anwā'* and *manāzil*) (Kunitzsch, 1994 & 1997). In any case the astrological tradition seems to have decayed under Muḥammad I (852-886) and his followers, until the reign of ᶜAbd al-Raḥmān III (912-961). In the turn of the 9th/ 10th c. only one astrologer is known: Ibn al-Samīna (d. 927-928), who was also competent in literary and religious sciences, as well as in medicine (Forcada, 1997, p. 215). In spite of this, it is clear that Cordovan astrologers must have continued practising their profession, for an anecdote mentioned by the poet and expert in *adab* Ibn ᶜAbd Rabbihi (860-940), shows the astrologer Ibn ᶜAzrā' and a group of colleagues trying to predict the end of a period of draught (Samsó, 1979).

Under the rule of *ḥājib* al-Manṣur (981-1002), a return to orthodoxy takes place and leads to a selective burning of the library of al-Ḥakam II, including, obviously, books on astrology. According to Ibn al-Khaṭīb, al-Manṣūr arrested, tortured and executed sooth-sayers (*mukahhinīn*) and astrologers because of their predictions about the end of his regime (the famous horoscope on the end of the Caliphate interpreted, among others, by Maslama al-Majrīṭī) (Balty-Guesdon p. 258). In spite of this, there is some evidence that there were important exceptions to this policy. Thus, among the educated people surrounding al-Manṣūr's son, ᶜAbd al-Malik al-Muẓaffar (975-1008), for the benefit of his education, Ibn Bassām (*Dhakhīra* VII, 79) includes *muᶜaddils* (?). Far more interesting is the fact that, according to Ibn Ḥayyān, Aḥmad b. Fāris al-Munajjim had studied the nativity horoscope of al-Muẓaffar when he was a child. He had never seen a horoscope with happier prospects. Ibn Ḥayyān satyrises this prediction as a result of the unhappy outcome of the life of al-Muẓaffar. Al-Muẓaffar's horoscope is not the only one and there is evidence showing that the upper classes were also interested in astrology, in spite of its official rejection. The texts preserve a part of the nativity horoscope of the famous Ibn Ḥazm in 994 and we should remember that his father occupied important posts in al-Manṣūr's administration (Samsó, 1992, pp. 78-79). The situation was not clear, however, for the astrologer Aḥmad b. Fāris felt the need to defend astrology by linking it to the religiously acceptable folk-astronomy (Forcada, 1996 and 2000).

With the arrival of the period of civil wars after the fall of the Caliphate (*fitna*) this hidden interest in astrology and astronomy reappears openly. Ibn al-Samḥ (d. 1035) leaves Cordova and goes to Granada where he is protected by Ḥabūs ibn Mākzan (1019-1038); Ibn al-Ṣaffār (d. 1035), another of Maslama's disciples, fled to Denia under the patronage of Mujāhid (ca. 1010-1045). These migrations of important astronomers to Granada and Denia pose the problem of establishing to what extent the members of Maslama's school had to leave Cordova because they had been protected by the circles of political power of the ᶜĀmirī dinasty, who could have exerted a hidden patronage: the case of Ibn al-Ṣaffār is particularly significant because Mujāhid of Denia was a *mawlā* of the ᶜĀmirīs and his kingdom was a standard place of asylum for those he had served al-Manṣūr's family.

The period of the *ṭawā'if* (ca. 1035-1085) is the golden age of astronomy and astrology, probably as a result of the development of patronage, a fact emphasized in Ṣāᶜid's *Ṭabaqāt* in comparison to the unhappy period of al-Manṣūr's dictatorship (Forcada, 1997, pp. 230-231). The great centre of astronomical learning is Toledo, where interest in astrology had already begun during the *fitna*, as we have some information about the activities of Yūsuf ibn ᶜUmar ibn Abī Thalla (d. 1043) in that city. Royal patronage reached its apex under al-Ma'mūn (1043-1075) (whose *laqab* is probably the result of a mimesis of that of the famous Abbasid caliph patron of astronomy) served by Yaḥyā b. Aḥmad b. al-Khayyāṭ (d. 1055), previously the astrologer of the Umayyad Sulaymān al-Mustaᶜīn (1009, 1013-1016) (Balty-Guesdon pp. 278-279, 643-644). Patronage was not restricted to kings for *Qāḍī* Ṣāᶜid himself financed astronomical and astrological research: we have similar information about the Banū Dhakwān family who supported the studies of the physician and astronomer Muḥammad b. Sulaymān b. al-Ḥannāṭ (d. 1045) (Balty-Guesdon pp. 283, 643-4). On the other hand the Banū ᶜAbbād of Seville also patronized the works of Ibn al-Zarqālluh when he was still living in Toledo (Samsó, 1992, p. 198) and al-Muᶜtamid (1069-1091) had at his service during twenty years the Jewish astrologer Yiṣḥaq ibn Barukh ibn Yaᶜqūb ibn al-Baliyya (1034-1093), as well as Abū Bakr al-Munajjim al-Khulānī (Balty-Guesdon pp. 315, 667-8, 693).

The arrival of the Almoravids to al-Andalus marks the beginning of a period of crisis and the disciplines most rejected by the *fuqahā'* (philosophy and astronomy) are less and less cultivated. This tendency continues under the Almohads who seem to restrict their patronage to physicians, although Ibn al-Hā'im dedicated his *al-Zīj al-Kāmil fī 'l-taᶜālīm* (ca. 1205) to the Almohad Caliph al-Nāṣir (1199-1213) and al-Nāṣir's physician, Abū Muḥammad ᶜAbd al-Malik al-Shadhūnī, was also an expert in astronomy and astrology (Forcada, 2000, p. 376). There is however a lack of interest reflected in the fact that we have absolutely no biographical information about important astronomers such as Jābir b. Aflaḥ, al-Biṭrūjī and Ibn al-Hā'im himself. In spite of this, astronomy and astrology were still cultivated in a more or less private, or even secret, way: we know, for example that Mālik b. Wuhayb, who had lived in the court of al-Muᶜtamid, cultivated secretly the sciences of the Ancients during the Almoravid period and that he had copied himself the *Almagest* and the *Kitāb al-Thamara* (Forcada, 1999, pp. 408-410). A certain improvement of the situation took place under the Almohad Caliph Abū Yaᶜqūb Yūsuf (1163-1184), who was interested in the sciences of the Ancients and had an important library for which he had confiscated the books on astronomy and astrology belonging to a certain Abū l-Ḥajjāj Yūsuf al-Mūranī (Forcada, 2000, p. 376). The situation becomes again worse under al-Manṣūr (1184-1199) and there is a short crisis after the battle of Alarcos (1195): the Caliph forbids books on logic and philosophy (*manṭiq wa-ḥikma*) and his physician Abū Bakr ᶜAbd al-Malik b. Zuhr al-Ḥafīd (1110-1198) –the son of the famous ᶜAbd al-Malik b. Zuhr– is a sort of censor, charged of the task to control that such books are not available. This period corresponds approximately to that of the persecution of Ibn Rushd whose books were burned and who was exiled to Lucena for about one and a half years (1197-1198) (Fricaud, 1997; Forcada, 2000, pp. 366-368). This does not imply, as we have seen, a complete abandonment of this kind of studies in cultivated circles: Ibn ᶜAbd Rabbihi al-Ḥafīd (ca. 1135-6 - 1205-6), who earned his living as a secretary of Almohad governors, corresponded with Ibn Rushd, in 1188-9, on astronomical matters and a passage of his *Kitāb al-Istibṣār* (written after 1188-9) shows his interest in trepidation and Sind-Hind cycles (b. Sharīfa, 1992). Another expert in the sciences of the Ancients, especially mathematics, Abū Muḥammad ᶜAbd Allāh b. Muḥammad b. Sahl al-Ḍarīr (1096-7 - 1186) lived in Baeza until 1158-9 and, according to Ibn al-Khaṭīb, the Christians of Toledo went there to learn from him (Forcada, 1999, pp. 415-418).

During the Naṣrid period of Granada we can see a renewal of the royal patronage of astronomy and astrology. In spite of the opposition of Muḥammad I (1237-1273), one of his sons, Yūsuf, was extremely interested in these disciplines and the same happened to another son of his, who was his successor, Muḥammad II (1273-1302), who attracted to his court the Murcian scientist Muḥammad al-Rīqūṭī (after the failure of Alfonso X to include him in the list of his collaborators) and the Tunisian astronomer Ibn al-Raqqām (d. 1315). The interest in astrology continued along the 14th c. in which we have the case of Muḥammad VI (1360-62) who followed the advice of his astrologer Aḥmad b. Muḥammad b. Yūsuf al-Anṣārī to chose the moment of the rebellion against Muḥammad V (1354-59, 1362-91). This astrologer also predicted the moment in which the latter sultan would recover his throne in 1362. Horoscopes were cast for the moment of the birth of members of the royal family (Ibn al-Khaṭīb transcribes data of the nativity horoscope of Muḥammad V in 1339) or to establish whether a minister would be adequate for his job: Muḥammad al-Fihrī, minister of Ismāᶜīl II (1359-60), had his horoscope cast for the moment in which he began to serve as such (Samsó, 1992, 409-412).

Conclusions

This analysis of the available information (mainly based on Balty-Guesdon, Forcada and Puig) yields results which are quite disappointing, as a result of the fact that the data are quite scattered. We have information about two scientific schools, those of Maslama and Ṣāᶜid/ Ibn al-Zarqālluh, but very little more. The information about travels to the East has only been studied in one particular area (the Ebro Valley) until the eleventh century and this is a topic which deserves a more general analysis. Balty-Guesdon has underlined the importance of *faraḍī*s and related mathematical professions, but there has been very little research on the available sources on *ᶜilm al-farā'iḍ* and we do not know for sure whether al-Khwārizmī's algebraical techniques (Gandz, 1938) were applied to *farā'iḍ* by Andalusī *faraḍīs*: the only available source (Sánchez Pérez, 1914) does not bear witness to this. *Mīqāt* is another topic in which serious efforts have been made, but the sources extant are scarce. My personal impression is that the exact sciences (including astrology) were part of the standard knowledge of an educated person, but there is very little information about the actual teaching of these disciplines. Finally, something can be said about the history of the astrological profession when it is linked to political power, but not about astrologers who worked in the market place. On the whole it is easy to see something which is obvious: there are periods of intellectual freedom in which astrology (and also astronomy) is cultivated and other periods of political and religious puritanism in which these disciplines survive in secret. On the whole, we cannot write a social history of the exact sciences mainly because mathematicians and astronomers were not socially valued professionals and the social importance which they enjoyed cannot be compared to that of *fuqahā'* and other experts in the religious sciences or even to that of physicians.

Bibliography

BALTY GUESDON, M.G. : *Médecins et hommes de sciences en Espagne Musulmane (IIe/VIIIe-Ve/XIe s.)*. Unpublished doctoral diss. presented in La Sorbonne Nouvelle in 1992. Available in microfiches in Atélier National de Reproduction des Thèses de l'Université de Lille, 1992.

CALVO, E.: *Abū ᶜAlī al-Ḥusayn Ibn Bāṣo (m. 716/1316), Risālat al-Ṣafīḥa al-ŷāmiᶜa li-ŷamīᶜ al-ᶜurūḍ (Tratado sobre la lámina universal para todas las latitudes)*, Madrid, 1993.

CHALMETA, P.: «El "*Kitāb fī ādāb al-ḥisba*" (*Libro del buen gobierno del zoco* de al-Saqaṭī)», *Al-Andalus* 32 (1967), 125-162, 359-397; 33 (1968), 143-195, 367-434.

DJEBBAR, A.: «Les activités mathématiques dans les villes du Maghreb Central (IXe - XVe siècle)». Preprint (1991), Université de Paris-Sud. Mathématiques. Bâtiment 425, 91405 Orsay.

FORCADA, M.: «*Mīqāt* en los calendarios andalusíes», *al-Qanṭara,* 11 (1990), 59-69.

FORCADA, M.: «Esquemes d'ombres per determinar el moment de les pregàries en llibres d'*anwā'* i calendaris d'al-Andalus». In J.M. Camarasa, H. Mielgo and A. Roca (eds.), *I Trobades d'Història de la Ciència i de la Tècnica*, Barcelona, 1994, pp. 107-117.

FORCADA, M.: «A New Andalusian Astronomical Source from the IV/Xth Century: the *Mukhtaṣar min al-Anwā'* of Aḥmad b. Fāris». In J. Casulleras & J. Samsó (eds.), *From Baghdad to Barcelona. Studies in the Islamic Exact Sciences in Honour of Prof. Juan Vernet*, Barcelona, 1996, pp. 769-780.

FORCADA, M.: «Biografías de científicos». In M.L. Avila & M. Marín (eds.), *Biografías y género biográfico en el Occidente Islámico. Estudios Onomástico-Biográficos de al-Andalus*, VIII (Madrid, 1997), pp. 201-248.

FORCADA, M.: «De Avempace a Averroes: la transmisión de las ciencias de los antiguos de la época taifa a la almohade». In M. Fierro y M.L. Avila (eds.), *Biografías almohades I. Estudios Onomástico-Biográficos de al-Andalus*, IX (Madrid-Granada, 1999), pp. 407-423.

FORCADA, M.: «Las ciencias de los antiguos en al-Andalus durante el período almohade: una aproximación biográfica». In M.L. Avila y M. Fierro (eds.), *Biografías almohades II. Estudios Onomástico-Biográficos de al-Andalus*, X (Madrid-Granada, 2000), 359-411.

FORCADA, M.: «Astrology and Folk Astronomy: the *Mukhtaṣar min al-Anwā'* of Aḥmad b. Fāris», *Suhayl,* 1 (2000), pp. 107-205.

FRICAUD, E.: «Les *ṭalaba* dans la societé almohade (le temps d'Averroès) », *al-Qanṭara,* 18 (1997), pp. 331-387.

GANDZ, S.: «The Algebra of Inheritance. A rehabilitation of al-Khuwārizmī», *Osiris* 5 (1938), pp. 319-391.

GRAU, M.: «Contribución al estudio del estado cultural del Valle del Ebro en el siglo XI y principios del XII», *Boletín de la Real Academia de Buenas Letras de Barcelona,* 27 (1957-58), pp. 227-272.

KENNEDY, E.S.: «The Astronomical Tables of Ibn al-Raqqām, a Scientist of Granada», *Zeitschrift für Geschichte der arabisch-islamischen Wissenschaften,* 11 (1997), pp. 35-72.

KING, D.A.: «Some Early Islamic Tables for Determining Lunar Crescent Visibility». In D.A. King and G. Saliba (eds.), *From Deferent to Equant: a Volume of Studies in the History of Science in the Ancient and Medieval Near East in Honor of E.S. Kennedy (Annals of the New York Academy of Sciences* 500), New York, 1987, pp. 185-225. Reprint in King, *Astronomy in the Service of Islam*, Variorum, Aldershot, 1993, no. II.

KING, D.A.: «On the Role of the Muezzin and the *Muwaqqit* in Medieval Islamic Society». In F. Jamil Ragep and Sally P. Ragep, with Steven Livesey (eds.), *Tradition, Transmission, Transformation. Proceedings of Two Conferences on Pre-Modern Science Held at the University of Oklahoma*, Brill, Leiden, New York, Köln, 1996, pp. 285-346.

KUNITZSCH, P.: «ᶜAbd al-Malik ibn Ḥabīb's *Book on the Stars*», *Zeitschrift für Geschichte der arabisch-islamischen Wissenschaften,* 9 (1994), pp. 161-194. and 11 (1997), pp. 179-188.

MARÍN, M.: «Mujeres en al-Andalus». In *Estudios Onomástico-Biográficos de al-Andalus* XI, (Madrid, 2000), pp. 1-784.

PUIG, R.: «Ibn Arqam al-Numayrī (m. 1259) y la introducción en al-Andalus del astrolabio lineal». In J. Vernet (ed.), *Nuevos Estudios sobre Astronomía Española en el Siglo de Alfonso X*, Barcelona, 1983, pp. 101-103.

PUIG, R.: «Dos notas sobre ciencia hispano-árabe a finales del siglo XIII en la *Iḥāṭa* de Ibn al-Jaṭīb», *al-Qanṭara*, 4 (1983), pp. 433-440.

PUIG, R.: «Ciencia y técnica en la *Iḥāṭa* de Ibn al-Jaṭīb», *Dynamis*, 4 (1984), pp. 65-79.

RIUS, M.: *La Alquibla en al-Andalus y al-Magrib al-Aqṣà*, University of Barcelona, 2000, 357 + 61 pp.

SAMSÓ, J.: «The Early Development of Astrology in al-Andalus», *Journal for the History of Arabic Science*, 3 (1979), pp. 228-243. Reprinted in J. Samsó, *Islamic Astronomy and Medieval Spain*, Variorum Reprints, Aldershot, 1994, no. IV.

SAMSÓ, J.: «Sobre los materiales astronómicos en el "Calendario de Córdoba" y en su versión latina del siglo XIII». In J. Vernet (ed.), *Nuevos Estudios sobre Astronomía Española en el Siglo de Alfonso X*, Barcelona, 1983, pp. 125-138. Reprinted in J. Samsó, *Islamic Astronomy and Medieval Spain*, Variorum Reprints, Aldershot, 1994, no. V.

SAMSÓ, J.: *Las Ciencias de los Antiguos en al-Andalus*, Madrid, Mapfre, 1992.

SAMSÓ, J. & MIELGO, H.: «Ibn Isḥāq al-Tūnisī and Ibn Muᶜādh al-Jayyānī on the Qibla». In J. Samsó, *Islamic Astronomy and Medieval Spain*, Variorum Reprints, Aldershot, 1994, no. VI (25 pp.).

SAMSÓ, J.: «Sobre el astrólogo ᶜAbd al-Wāḥid b. Isḥāq al-Ḍabbī (fl. c. 788- c. 852)». *Anaquel de Estudios Arabes*, 12 (2001), 657-669.

SÁNCHEZ PÉREZ, J.A.: *Partición de herencias entre los musulmanes del rito malequí. Con transcripción anotada de dos manuscritos aljamiados*, Madrid, 1914.

SESIANO, J.: «Survivance médiévale en Hispanie d'un problème né en Mésopotamie», *Centaurus*, 30 (1987), pp. 18-61.

SESIANO, J.: «Le *Liber mahameleth* un traité mathématique latin composé au XIIᵉ siècle en Espagne», *Actes du Premier Colloque International d'Alger sur l'Histoire des Mathématiques Arabes* (Alger, 1988), pp. 69-98.

SESIANO, J.: «Der *Liber Mahameleth* des Johannes Hispalensis», *XVIIIth International Congress of History of Science. Abstracts* (Hamburg-Munich, 1989), Q2 nº 8.

SHARIFA, M. b.: *Ibn ᶜAbd Rabbihi al-ḥafid. Fuṣūl min sīra mansiyya*, Beirut, 1992.

URVOY, D.: *Le monde des ulémas andalous du V/XI au VII/XIII siècle*, Génève, 1978.

VERNET, J.: «El Valle del Ebro como nexo entre Oriente y Occidente», *Boletín de la Real Academia de Buenas Letras de Barcelona*, 23 (1950), pp. 249-286. Reprint in Vernet, *De ᶜAbd al-Raḥmān I a Isabel II*, Barcelona, 1989, pp. 259-296.

VIGUERA, M.J.: *Los reinos de taifas y las invasiones magrebíes*, Madrid, 1992.

II

Maslama al-Majrīṭī and the Star Table in the Treatise *De mensura astrolabii*

In a recent paper Paul Kunitzsch has explicitly formulated the hypothesis of a relation between the works on the astrolabe made by Maslama al-Majrīṭī (d. 1007) and his disciples and the interest in this instrument which is clear in the early Arabic-Latin translations made in Catalonia towards the end of the tenth century[1]. The arguments in favour of this idea begin with the similarities established by Millàs[2] between the early Latin-Catalan texts on the astrolabe (for which Kunitzsch has coined the useful denomination of "Old Corpus" and Burnett of the "Early Collection") and the treatises on the construction and use of the astrolabe attributed to the ʿIraqī astrologer Māshā'allāh (fl. 762–815). Kunitzsch has proved that this attribution has no basis and that a part, at least, of the materials contained in the pseudo-Māshā'allāh's treatise derive from Maslama's school[3]; this leads us to interpret that the similarities between the pseudo-Māshā'allāh's treatises and the "Old Corpus" should be considered as a result of the use, by our early translators, of sources related to the school of Maslama. One should also remember that Maslama did important work on Ptolemy's *Planisphaerium*, to which he added a set of notes and an extra chapter[4], and that recent

1 Paul Kunitzsch, "Les relations scientifiques entre l'Occident et le monde arabe l'époque de Gerbert", in Nicole Charbonnel et Jean-Eric Iung, *Gerbert l'Européen. Actes du Colloque d'Aurillac. 4–7 Juin 1996*. Aurillac, 1997, pp. 193–203. See p. 196: "On peut penser que c'est bien le travail de Maslama et de son école sur l'astrolabe (dont le rayonnement se fit sentir jusqu'en Catalogne chrétienne) qui suscita l'intérêt des clercs latins de cette région pour cet instrument".

2 J. Millàs Vallicrosa, *Assaig d'història de les idees físiques i matemàtiques a la Catalunya Medieval*, Barcelona, 1931.

3 P. Kunitzsch, "On the authenticity of the treatise on the composition and use of the astrolabe ascribed to Messahalla", *Archives Internationales d'Histoire des Sciences* 31 (1981), 42–62. Reprinted in Kunitzsch, *The Arabs and the Stars*, Variorum Reprints. Northampton, 1989. See also J. Samsó, "Maslama al-Majrīṭī and the Alphonsine Book on the Construction of the Astrolabe", *Journal for the History of Arabic Science* 4 (1980), 3–8. Reprinted in Samsó, *Islamic Astronomy and Medieval Spain*. Variorum Reprints. Aldershot, 1994; M. Viladrich, "On the Sources of the Alphonsine Treatise Dealing with the Construction of the Plane Astrolabe", *Journal for the History of Arabic Science* 6 (1982), 167–171.

4 J. Vernet and M. A. Catalá, "Las obras matemáticas de Maslama de Madrid", *Al-Andalus* 30 (1965), 15–45 (see p. 45); reprinted in Vernet, *Estudios sobre Historia de la Ciencia Medieval*, Barcelona-Bellaterra, 1979, 241–271; English translation in J. Vernet and M. A. Catalá, "The Mathematical Works of Maslama of Madrid", in M. Fierro and J. Samsó (eds.), *The Formation of al-Andalus. Part 2: Language, Religion, Culture and the Sciences*, Ashgate, Variorum, Aldershot etc., 1998, pp. 359–379; P. Kunitzsch & R. Lorch, *Maslama's Notes on Ptolemy's* Planisphaerium *and Related Texts*. Bayerische Akademie der Wissenschaften. Philosophisch-Historische Klasse. Sitzungsberichte. Jahrgang 1994, Heft 2, pp. 1–121. See also P. Kunitzsch, "The role of al-Andalus

research[5] has discovered the existence of a short fragment of a very early translation from the Arabic of this Ptolemaic work, which seems to be related to the rest of the texts of the "Old Corpus".

Some more evidence can be found in the treatise *De mensura astrolabii* (called h' by Millàs) which explains, in a confused way, how to project stars on the rete of an astrolabe[6]. The procedure used can, however, be understood thanks to the information contained in other treatises on the same topic, such as the *Compositio astrolabii*, written towards the beginning of the eleventh century by Ascelin of Augsburg, who was aware of the contents of h'[7], Hermannus Contractus' *De mensura astrolabii*[8], and a fourth text on the construction of the instrument which was ascribed by Millás to Māshā'allāh[9], although it seems clear that this attribution is as inaccurate as that of the other two pseudo-Māshā'allāhs studied by Kunitzsch: it seems that this is another derivation from Maslama's school[10]. The method described in these texts has been analysed at least twice by J. North[11] and by M. Viladrich and R. Martí[12]. For the sake of completeness I will summarise it here and try to draw a few conclusions.

These texts also include a peculiar star table (see *Table 1*), classified as type III by Kunitzsch[13]. The coordinates used are called *latitudo* and *altitudo* in the treatise h'.

in the transmission of Ptolemy's *Planisphaerium* and *Almagest*", *Zeitschrift für Geschichte der Arabisch-Islamischen Wissenschaften* 10 (1995–96), 147–155.

5 P. Kunitzsch, "Fragments of Ptolemy's *Planisphaerium* in an Early Latin Translation", *Centaurus* 36 (1993), 97–101.

6 Millàs, *Assaig*, p. 300.

7 Charles Burnett, "King Ptolemy and Alchandreus the Philosopher: the Earliest Texts on the Astrolabe and Arabic Astrology at Fleury, Micy and Chartres", *Annals of Science* 55 (1998), 329–368 (cf. especially pp. 348–351, 353–358).

8 J. Drecker, "Hermannus Contractus Über das Astrolab", in *Isis* 16 (1931), 200–219 (see pp. 208–210). The same method appears described by Rudolf of Bruges: see Richard Lorch, "The Treatise on the Astrolabe by Rudolf of Bruges", in L. Nauta and A. Vanderjagt, *Between Demonstration and Imagination. Essays in the History of Science and Philosophy Presented to John D. North*, Brill, Leiden, 1999, pp. 55–100 (see pp. 67–69, 83, 88–89, 94); a star table with many points in common with the ones I analyse here has been edited in pp. 78–79.

9 Edited by J. M. Millás, *Las traducciones orientales en los manuscritos de la Biblioteca Catedral de Toledo*, Madrid, 1942, pp. 313–321 (cf. especially p. 319).

10 At least in the part concerning the projection of stars on the rete. Cf. Kunitzsch, "On the authenticity" p. 49, n. 35; R. Martí and M. Viladrich, "En torno a los tratados de uso del astrolabio hasta el siglo XIII en al-Andalus, la Marca Hispánica y Castilla", in J. Vernet (ed.), *Nuevos Estudios sobre Astronomía Española en el Siglo de Alfonso X* (Barcelona, 1983), pp. 9–74 (cf. especially pp. 70–71). P. Kunitzsch ("Glossar der arabischen Fachausdrücke in der mittelalterlichen europäischen Astrolabliteratur", *Nachrichten der Akademie der Wissenschaften in Göttingen. I. Philologisch-Historische Klasse*, 1982, Nr. 11, pp. 495–497) has established that the pseudo-Māshā'allāh edited by Millás is actually made up of three different texts.

11 J. North, *Richard of Wallingford. An edition of his writings with introductions, English translations and commentary*, III (Oxford, 1976), 159–161.

12 M. Viladrich and R. Martí, "En torno a los tratados hispánicos sobre construcción de astrolabio hasta el siglo XIII", in J. Vernet (ed.), *Textos y Estudios sobre Astronomía Española en el siglo XIII* (Barcelona, 1981), 79–99 (cf. especially pp. 94–96).

13 P. Kunitzsch, *Typen von Sternverzeichnissen in astronomischen Handschriften des zehnten bis vierzehnten Jahrhunderts*, Wiesbaden, 1966, pp. 23–30. Kunitzsch's type XI (*Typen* pp. 67–71) seems to be related to this table: the coordinates used are the same although they are called, in this second type, *Gradus cum quibus mediant celum* and *Gradus longitudinis ex utraque parte*. A good photograph of the table in MS Ripoll 225 can be seen in J. Vernet and J. Samsó (eds.),

The *latitudo*, which I will call α, agrees, in most of the cases, with the mediation (*mediatio coeli*, degree of the ecliptic crossing the meridian at the same time as the star), which appears in the star table compiled by Maslama towards the end of year 367/978 (Kunitzsch' type IA)[14]. The coordinate corresponding to the column *altitudo* requires an explanation which I will try to summarise here[15]:

Radius *OE*, in fig. 1, is the projection of the horary circle passing through the beginning (G) of the zodiacal sign which corresponds to a given star. From this radius *OE* we will take the first coordinate (α). The texts I am analysing give different instructions concerning the method used to measure α. Those we can read in the

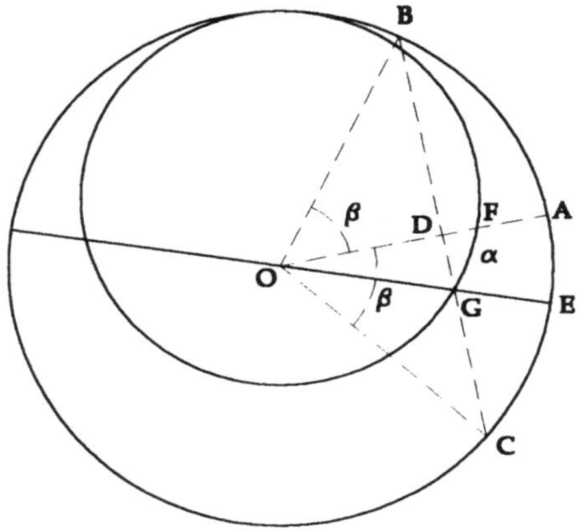

Fig. 1

treatises by Ascelin of Augsburg and by Hermannus Contractus state that angle α is measured *on the ecliptic*, which has been previously divided, from point G: we will, thus, obtain point F – also on the ecliptic – which is the star's mediation. Although

Instrumentos astronómicos en la España Medieval. Su influencia en Europa, Santa Cruz de la Palma, 1985, p. 77. Photographs of the table in two manuscripts of the treatise by Ascelin of Augsburg have been reproduced by Burnett, "King Ptolemy", pp. 366–368.

14 The complete table was also edited, from MS Paris Bibliothèque Nationale 4821, fol. 81v, by Vernet & Catalá, "Las obras matemáticas" p. 45. Kunitzsch (*Typen* pp. 15–18) also includes a Latin version which should be handled carefully, because mediations and declinations have often been displaced and transferred from one star to another. On this table see also Kunitzsch, "Two Star Tables from Muslim Spain", *Journal for the History of Astronomy* 11 (1980), 192–201. Reprinted in Kunitzsch, *The Arabs and the Stars*, no. IV.

15 The oldest version of this table seems to be the one extant in MS Paris BN 7412, fol. 5v, in which the two coordinates are named *altitudo* (= mediation) and *latitudo* (it is not the *altitudo* of MS Ripoll 225). P. Kunitzsch and E. Dekker ("The stars on the rete of the so-called «Carolingian astrolabe», in J. Casulleras and J. Samsó (eds.), *From Baghdad to Barcelona. Studies in the Islamic Exact Sciences in Honour of Prof. Juan Vernet*, Barcelona, 1996, pp. 655–672), p. 656 n. 8 suggest that it may correspond to the meridian altitude of the star for a geographical latitude of 39° (Valencia?). See below Table 3.

the text in treatise h' is not easy to understand, the projection of the stars follows immediately the explanation of the procedure for dividing the ecliptic and it is logical to assume that the version represented by h' agrees with the instructions given by Ascelin. A different technique appears in the pseudo-Māshā'allāh, which states:

> Divides circulum capricorni per 360 gradus et considerato gradu prenotato unicuique stelle pones regulam super ipsius stelle gradum in circulo capricorni et super centrum eiusdem circuli et duces lineam medium stelle notantem.

I understand here that the degree of the star is measured *on the circle of Capricorn*[16]. This would imply that we are not measuring angle α from point G to obtain F, but from E to obtain A. In both cases the man who is fabricating the astrolabe will be using a ruler and the result obtained will be identical (OGE and OFA are radii of the circle of Capricorn) but my interpretation of the procedure explained by the pseudo-Māshā'allāh has practical advantages: the circle of Capricorn is easier to divide precisely (it is larger and the divisions are equal) than the ecliptic (which is smaller and unequally divided): the methods explained in h', as well as in the related texts, for the division of the ecliptic are rather crude[17] and the accumulated error would be increased if such divisions were used to project a star. We have a reference to this difficulty in one of the two extant chapters of the treatise of Ibn al-Samḥ (d. 1035) on the construction of the astrolabe[18]: he explains the standard method used by the school of Maslama to project a star on the rete using its mediation and declination[19] and he adds that, instead of the mediation, we may use the right ascension of the mediation – the coordinate which will give point A on the circle of Capricorn – which is an "easier and more precise" result (*ashal aṣaḥḥ*). To this he adds the significant sentence: "take in the star table the [right] ascension of the degree of the mediation" (*khudh fī jadwal al-kawākib maṭāliʿ darajat al-tawassuṭ*). It seems, therefore, clear that there were star tables in which one of the tabulated coordinates was the right ascension of the mediation and that the treatise of the pseudo-Māshā'allāh contains a reference to the use of this coordinate which does not appear in star tables of type III which appear in the text immediately after.

Having established the position of point A with either one of the two methods, the second coordinate, *altitudo* (β), is measured *on the circle of Capricorn*, from point A in both the direct and retrograde sense. In this way we have:

$$AB = AC = \beta \ .$$

B is then joined to C by chord BC. The intersection of BC and OA in D determines the projection of the star and OD will be the radius of the projection of the parallel of declination of the same star. In order to check the procedure we should consider Fig. 2 in which:

16 Prof. P. Kunitzsch (letter dated 21.10.99) disagrees with this interpretation and believes that the pseudo-Māshā'allāh's text explains the same procedure as the other sources.

17 Millàs, *Assaig*, pp. 202, 315; 295; Viladrich–Martí, "Construcción" pp. 91–93.

18 M. Viladrich, "Dos capítulos de un libro perdido de Ibn al-Samḥ", *Al-Qanṭara* 7 (1986), 5–11.

19 This is why Maslama's star table gives these two coordinates for each star, as well as its longitude and latitude.

$$OD = r \tan\left(\tfrac{1}{2}(90 - \delta)\right) ,$$

r being the radius of the equator which we take as $r = 1$.

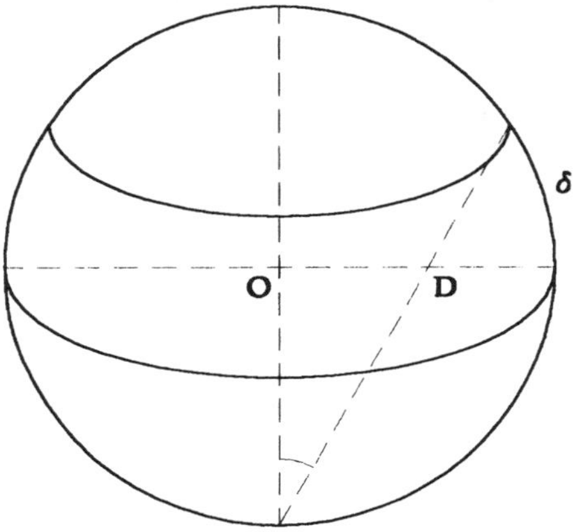

Fig. 2

On the other hand, in Fig. 1:

$$OD = R \cos\beta ,$$

where R is the radius of the circle of Capricorn, which will measure, for $r = 1$, and for an obliquity of the ecliptic $\epsilon = 23;35°$[20]:

$$R = \tan\left(\tfrac{1}{2}(90° + 23;35°)\right) = 1.527675 .$$

If we accept that:

$$OD = R \cos\beta \; = r \tan\left(\tfrac{1}{2}(90 - \delta)\right) ,$$

then:

$$\beta \; = \cos^{-1}\left((r/R) \tan\left(\tfrac{1}{2}(90 - \delta)\right)\right) .$$

We can now check the validity of this expression by recalculating with it the values of the *altitudo* in the table extant in text h'. For that purpose in *Table 1* we have:

1. Name of the star in h'.
2. Identification of the star.
3. Value of the *latitudo* in h'.
4. Value of the mediation in Maslama's star table.

20 This parameter derives from al-Battānī and it is, as we will see, the value of the obliquity used by Maslama to compute the declinations and mediations of the stars in his star table.

5. Calculated value of the right ascension of Maslama's mediation, in order to control the importance of the error the maker of the astrolabe would incur if he followed the instructions of the pseudo-Māshā'allāh, using the tabular values of column 3 (*latitudo*), measured on the circle of Capricorn and not on the ecliptic.
6. Star declination in Maslama's table.
7. Value of the *altitudo* in h'.
8. Recalculated value of the *altitudo*, for which I have used the expression:

$$\beta = \cos^{-1}((r/R)\tan(\tfrac{1}{2}(90-\delta))) ,$$

in which δ is the declination taken from column 6 and $r/R = 1/1.527675 = 0.6545894$.

My analysis of the materials in *Table 1* yields the following conclusions:

There are 27 stars in the table of text h', while Maslama's table contains only 21, 20 of which appear in h'. Only one star of Maslama's table is missing in h': *Ṭaraf dhanab al-asad* (β Leonis). Out of these 20 stars extant in both tables, the comparison between their coordinates is impossible in the case of stars 2, 7 and 24, for which Maslama's tables indicates their longitude and latitude, but not their mediation and declination. I will, therefore, limit myself to the 17 remaining stars, for which the comparison of the *latitudo* in h' with Maslama's mediation gives the following results:

- A perfect coincidence in two cases (stars 3 and 9) in which Maslama's mediation corresponds to an integer number of degrees.
- A correct rounding in 8 cases (stars 1, 10, 12, 15, 19, 21, 22, 25).
- Truncation in only one case (star 8).
- Difference of 1° (due, probably, to rounding errors or to a confusion in the transmission of the number expressed in Roman notation) in 4 cases (stars 4, 6, 11, 14).
- Difference of 2° in one case (star 20).
- Difference of 5° in one case (star 23).

I think, therefore, that there is a clear relation between the table in h' and Maslama's table in the values of the coordinate *latitudo*. There is nothing new in this respect, for this fact had already been clearly established by Kunitzsch[21].

The situation concerning the coordinate *altitudo*, however, is different. Here we can only compare the tabular values in h' with the results of a recomputation:

- We can consider rounding cases those of stars 1, 4, 9, 23 and 25. To these we may add stars 8 (h' 73;30°, but Ascelin, Hermannus and type XI 73°; rec. 73;4,59°) and 20 (h' 55°; rec. 54;28,1°). Star 19 is a special case: the tabular value is 41;30° while the recomputation yields 59;21,50°. The variants appearing in pseudo-Māshā'allāh (69°) and type XI (49°) lead me to suspect that there might have been a graphical

21 See Kunitzsch, *Typen*, type I (pp. 15–18) and type III (pp. 23–30). See also Kunitzsch, "Les relations scientifiques".

metathesis between "XLI et med." and "LIX et med.". If we accept these hypotheses, the total number of rounded values would be 8.
- Difference of 1°: 5 cases (stars 3, 6, 15, 21, 22).
- Difference of 2°: 1 case (star 14).
- Difference of 3°: 1 case (star 12).
- Difference of 4°: 1 case (star 10).
- Difference of 6°: 1 case (star 11).

The number of coincidences (13 cases out of 17 have a maximum error of 1°) makes me believe that, in the column *altitudo*, we have a set of values which depend on the star declinations appearing in Maslama's tables. My hypothesis is, then, that the values of this second coordinate are rounded figures from those taken in the corresponding columns of a star table compiled by one of the members of the school of Maslama. One should not necessarily follow the suggestion of both North[22] and Kunitzsch–Dekker[23], according to whom these values could only have been obtained by direct measurements made on an astrolabe or a drawing made to scale of the instrument[24].

In brief: I think that the star table of text h' derives from an Arabic original belonging to the school of Maslama, although not precisely from the extant star table compiled by Maslama himself which I have used for the comparison: the original table had a minimum number of 27 stars and it contained all the necessary elements to project those stars on the rete of an astrolabe. We do not know for sure whether this table contained the star longitudes and latitudes, but I believe that there was a column for the mediation – coordinate α – (and possibly the declination), as well as coordinate β (*altitudo*). The evidence furnished by MS. Paris BN, lat. 7412, fol. 5v, makes me think that the same table gave also the meridian altitude of each star for a latitude near 39° (see *Table 3*): it is unnecessary to establish a relationship between this latitude and the city of Valencia if we consider that the altitudes of this table are rounded to the nearest degree and 38;30° is a common value for the latitude of Cordova in Arabic sources. Furthermore, the extra chapter added by Maslama to his notes on Ptolemy's *Planisphaerium* contains an example for the projection on the rete of star Vega (*al-Nasr al-Wāqiʿ*, α Lyrae) by using the ecliptic degree with which the star rises and sets: the geographical latitude mentioned by Maslama is 39° and, although no reference is made to a particular place, it is clear that the Andalusian astronomer was working in Cordova and that he had no particular reason to refer to another city[25]. Finally, my interpretation of the method of projection used by the pseudo-Māshāʾallāh – in which coordinate α is measured on the graduation of the

22 North, *Richard of Wallingford*, III, 161.

23 Kunitzsch–Dekker, "Carolingian astrolabe" p. 657 n. 9.

24 Like the one studied by Kunitzsch, "Traces of a Tenth-Century Spanish-Arabic Astrolabe", *Zeitschrift für Geschichte der Arabisch-Islamischen Wissenschaften* 12 (1998), 113–120.

25 See Vernet & Catalá, "Las obras matemáticas" pp. 251 and 38; Latin translations in Kunitzsch & Lorch, "Maslama's Notes" pp. 59 and 63. See M. Comes, "La primera tabla de estrellas documentada en al-Andalus", *Actes de les I Trobades d'Història de la Ciència i de la Tècnica* ed. by J. M. Camarasa, H. Mielgo & A. Roca, Barcelona, 1994, pp. 95–109 (esp. p. 104). Maslama also uses 38;30° as a local latitude in Vernet–Catalá p. 28; in the Spanish translation (p. 43) 39;30° is a misprint.

circle of Capricorn – leads me to suggest that the hypothetical table also included a column with the right ascension of the mediation of each star.

This hypothetical table may have been compiled after the end of year 367/978 if one accepts the reference in MS Paris, BN, ar. 4821, fol. 81v, which states that Maslama's table (type Ia) derived from observations made by our astronomer in that year. This could also give us a *terminus post quem* for the star table in text h'. The argument has been used by Kunitzsch, who believes that Gerbert of Aurillac, who stayed in Ripoll between 967 and 970, could not have been aware, at that time, of the texts of the "Old Corpus" which probably reached him at a later date[26].

This hypothesis should be validated by an examination of Maslama's table (see *Table 2*) in order to verify the internal coherence of all its columns. If our astronomer made observations, its purpose would have been to determine the ecliptical longitude of some of the stars in his table. He might, however, have copied the mediation and declination of each star from a different source. It is important, therefore, to check that columns 5 (mediation) and 6 (declination) in my *Table 2* – which, as we have seen, are the coordinates related to the *latitudo* and *altitudo* of text h' – have been calculated by using the longitude of column 2 and the latitudes of column 3. Let me begin by saying that the text which accompanies Maslama's star table states that it is based on observations made towards the end of year 367/978 "according to the method of al-Battānī" (*'alā madhhab al-Battānī*). This expression can be explained by reading al-Battānī himself, who says that, in order to calculate the longitudes of the fixed stars for year 1191 of Alexander / 879–880 A. D., he made observations of a few star longitudes; one of them was Qalb al-Asad (α Leonis), for which he found 134°. The year of these observations corresponds to 1627 of Nabonassar, and Ptolemy's star catalogue is dated in year 886 of the same era (138–139 A. D.)[27]. When al-Battānī compared the longitudes of this reduced number of stars with the corresponding ones of Ptolemy's catalogue, he established that, in the period of 741 Egyptian years between 886 and 1627 of Nabonassar, the increase in longitudes due to the precession of the equinoxes amounted to 11;10°. This led him to calculate a precessional constant of 1° in 66 Egyptian years. The latitudes of his stars are the same as Ptolemy's[28].

If we compare Maslama's longitudes and latitudes for his 21 stars with those appearing in al-Battānī's table, we can establish the following facts: 1) the latitudes are the same ones except for a few mistakes; 2) the longitudes are, in most cases, the result of adding a precessional constant of 1;30° to the longitudes of al-Battānī. This implies a difference of 12;40° with the longitudes of the *Almagest*. If Maslama has established this precessional constant by observing the longitudes of a few stars, this amount of 1;30° is highly suspicious, for 1;30° in 99 years agrees too well with al-Battānī's con-

26 Kunitzsch, "Relations scientifiques" p. 199.

27 Ptolemy's catalogue is actually dated at the beginning of the reign of Emperor Antoninus, 20th of July of 137 A. D. (*Almagest* VII, 4).

28 Cf. C. A. Nallino, *Al-Battānī sive Albatenii. Opus astronomicum* I (Mediolani Insubrum, 1903), p. 124 and II (ibid., 1903), p. 144. On the other hand al-Battānī (II, 178 and ff.) reproduces a second star table in which he does not give the stars' longitudes and latitudes but mediation, declination, degree of the ecliptic which rises and sets with the star and the meridian altitude for the latitude of Raqqa. This second table is dated in 1211 of Alexander / 899–900 A. D.

stant for precession (1° in 66 years). In two cases, however – al-Ghumayṣā' (α Canis Minoris) and Qalb al-Asad (α Leonis) – the difference amounts not to 1;30° but to 1;40°, and the case of Qalb al-Asad is particularly significant because it is confirmed by other sources: we have already seen that al-Battānī states that, by observation, he determined the longitude of Qalb al-Asad to be 134° and Ibn al-Zarqālluh mentions the observation of the same star made by Maslama in 367/978, for which he obtained the longitude of 135;40°[29], precisely the same we find in our table. My impression is, therefore, that Maslama did make the observations which have been attributed to him[30]: he observed Qalb al-Asad and, probably, al-Ghumayṣā' in the aforementioned year. He obtained the precessional constant of 1;40°, for that year, and he kept it for the two stars which he had actually observed. As this value was near to that obtained through computation using al-Battānī's estimation (1;30°), this second amount was applied to the rest of the stars. It is also possible that the star table was calculated by one of his disciples who used Maslama's longitudes for Qalb al-Asad and al-Ghumayṣā', but did not dare to contradict al-Battānī's authority for the rest of the stars. We can accept, in any case, that the star table we are considering here was compiled after 978 A. D., at least in relation to the values of the star longitudes and latitudes. Columns 2 and 3 in *Table 2* reproduce the longitudes and latitudes of Maslama's table: I have added, in parentheses, the differences with al-Battānī's ecliptical coordinates.

We should now study the mediations (column 5) and declinations (column 6) in order to establish whether these values are consistent with those of the ecliptical coordinates of columns 2 and 3 and to determine, therefore, whether they derive from the "observations" of 978 A. D. To calculate the declination of each star I have used the expression:

$$\delta = \sin^{-1}(\sin\beta_s \cos\epsilon + \cos\beta_s \sin\epsilon \sin\lambda)$$

in which

δ = declination
β_s = latitude
λ = longitude
ϵ = obliquity of the ecliptic, for which I use al-Battānī's value (23;35°).

Column 6 reproduces the declinations of the table and, in parentheses, the differences, in absolute value, with the recomputations. The results obtained are surprisingly accurate in most of the cases and they allow the correction of some mistakes in the sign of the latitudes. It is clear, therefore, that the declination values are based on al-Battānī's estimation for the obliquity of the ecliptic and on the longitudes and latitudes of column 2 and 3. They can, therefore, be dated after 978 A. D.

I have continued by calculating the values of the right ascension (α_0) of each star (not included in the table) with the formula:

$$\alpha_0 = \cos^{-1}(\cos\beta_e \cos\lambda / \cos\delta)$$

using the values of δ which appear in the table. The results are reproduced in column 4.

29 J. M. Millás Vallicrosa, *Estudios sobre Azarquiel*, Madrid–Granada, 1943–50, pp. 309–310.
30 See a different interpretation in Kunitzsch, "Three star tables", p. 195, no. 12.

I have finally computed the mediation (m), for which I have used:

$$m = \tan^{-1}(\tan \alpha_0 / \cos \epsilon)$$

using, again, $\epsilon = 23;35°$. The results obtained are also consistent with the rest of the table, although they are not as precise as those of the declinations, probably due to the use of a tangent function or of the division of the values of the sign by those of the cosine.

In brief: Maslama (or one of his disciples) used both the table of declinations (for $\epsilon = 23;35°$) and the star table extant in al-Battānī's *zīj*. This agrees with the information given by Ṣā'id al-Andalusī who states that Maslama wrote a book in which he summarised how to calculate the true longitude of a planet according to the aforementioned *zīj*[31]: remnants of this version may be found among the spurious tables edited by Nallino as an appendix of his edition of al-Battānī's *zīj*[32]. In spite of this, the twenty-one-star table attributed to Maslama is original. It is the result of two different estimations of the value of precession for 978 A. D. and, as the main purpose of the table is to project the stars on the astrolabe, it contains independent computations of the mediation and declination of these stars, which are based on the previously obtained longitudes and on the latitudes of the Ptolemaic tradition, also followed by al-Battānī. It seems clear, therefore, that the star table in text h', which is based – ultimately – on the table ascribed to Maslama, must have been compiled after 978 A. D.

Acknowledgements: This paper has been written within a research programme on "Astronomical theory and tables in al-Andalus and the Maghrib between the twelfth and the fourteenth centuries", sponsored by the Dirección General de Investigación Científica y Técnica of the Spanish Ministry of Education and Culture. My gratitude to Paul Kunitzsch and Mercè Comes who revised early drafts of this paper (Kunitzsch twice) and made useful suggestions. Prof. Kunitzsch also sent me a photocopy of fol. 5v of MS Paris, BN, lat. 7412.

---

31 Ṣā'id, *Ṭabaqāt al-Umam*, ed. Ḥayāt Bū 'Alwān, Beirut, 1985, p. 169; French translation by Régis Blachère, *Kitâb Ṭabaḳāt al-Umam (Livre des Catégories des Nations)*, Paris, 1935, p. 130. I correct here, slightly, Blachère's interpretation: *ta'dīl al-kawākib* means "equation of the planets", but also "precise calculation of the planetary longitudes".

32 Nallino II, 299–307.

Table 1

The star table in the "De mensura astrolabii" (h') (Unit: degree)

1. Star name	2. Identification[1]	3. Latitudo[2]	4. Med.[3]	5. RA[4]	6. Dec.[5]	7. Alt.[6]	8. Alt.[7]
1. Alramech	al-Simāk al-Rāmiḥ (α Bootes)	[Libra] 24 [= 204]	203;52	202;4,19	24;56 N	65	65;19,11
2. Alfecat	Munīr al-Fakka (α Coronae Borealis)	[Scorpio] 16 [= 226]	–[8]	–	–	71	–
3. Alhawi	Ra'૯s al-Ḥāwī (α Ophiuchi)	[Sagit.] 24 [= 264][9]	264	263;27,28	8;30 N	57	55;39,54
4. Altair	al-Nasr al-Ṭā'ir (α Aquilae)	[Capr.] 14 [= 284]	283;18	284;27,48	6;25 N	54[10]	54;11,24
5. Delfin	al-Dulfīn (ϵ Delphini)	[Capr.] 25 [= 295]	–	–	–	59	–
6. Alferat	Mankib al-Faras (β Pegasi)	[Aquar.] 30 [= 330][11]	331;30	333;32,41	22;29 N	65	64;3,52
7. Alhcadib	al-Kaff al-Khaḍīb (β Cassiopeiae)	[Taur.] 22 [= 52][12]	–[13]	–	–	73[14]	–

1 Arabic name and modern identification
2 *latitudo* in h'
3 Mediation in Maslama's star table
4 Right ascension, modern calculation (cf. p. 511)
5 Declination in Maslama's star table
6 *altitudo* in h'
7 The same, modern calculation (cf. p. 511)
8 Maslama's table only gives the longitude and latitude of this star.
9 253° in MS Paris BN lat. 7412 and in "type XI".
10 55° in "type XI".
11 336° in "type XI".
12 42° in pseudo-Māshā'allāh, Ascelin and Hermannus. MS BN Paris 7412 has *Trutina* (= Libra) 24° (= 204°), instead of *Truta* (= Pisces) 24° (= 354°). In a private communication (21.10.99) Prof. Paul Kunitzsch tells me that Pisces is the sign needed here, while Taurus is entirely out of place and probably the result of a misunderstanding of the rare term *Truta* in MS BN Paris 7412.
13 Maslama's table only gives the longitude and latitude of this star.
14 91° in pseudo-Māshā'allāh and Ascelin. 111° in Hermannus.

Table 1 (*continued*)

1. Star name	2. Identification	3. Latitudo	4. Med.	5. RA	6. Dec.	7. Alt.	8. Alt.
8. Alrif	al-Ridf (α Cygni)	[Capr.] 29 [= 299][15]	299;44	301;55,54	42;4 N	73;30[16]	73;4,59
9. Wega	al-Nasr al-Wāqiʿ (α Lyrae)	[Capr.] 1 [= 271]	270	270	38;25 N	72	71;33,33
10. Benenas	Qā'id Banāt Naʿsh (η Ursae Maioris)	[Libra] 18 [= 198]	197;35	196;11,42	55;30 N	74	78;16,21
11. Calbagrab	Qalb al-ʿAqrab (α Scorpii)	[Scorp.] 25 [= 235][17]	234;18	231;54,5	23;5 S	14	7;53,13
12. Alcimek	al-Simāk al-Aʿzal (α Virginis)	[Libra] 8 [= 188][18]	187;30	186;52,48	5;10 S	41[19]	44;14,17
13. Algurab	al-Gurāb (γ Corvi)	[Virgo] 18 [= 168]	–	–	–	41	–
14. Alhabor	al-Shiʿrā al-ʿAbūr (α Canis Maioris)	[Cancer] 1 [= 91]	90;20	90;21,49	15;35 S[20]	32[21]	30;26,37
15. Rigel	Rijl al-Jawzā' (β Orionis)	[Gemin.] 8 [= 68][22]	68;15	66;28,32	10;29 S	39	38;6,37
16. Pantangaitot	Baṭn Qayṭus (ζ Ceti)	[Aries] 20 [= 20][23]	–	–	–	36[24]	–
17. Denebgait	Dhanab Qayṭus (ι Ceti)	[Pisces] 20 [= 350][25]	–	–	–	35[26]	–

15 289° in Hermannus; 300° in "type XI".
16 63° in pseudo-Māshā'allāh; 73° in Ascelin, Hermannus and "type XI".
17 237° in "type XI".
18 189° in "type XI". 187;30° (a surprisingly accurate value) in MS Paris BN lat. 7412.
19 29° in pseudo-Māshā'allāh; 15° in Ascelin and Hermannus; 42° in "type XI".
20 10;35 S in Maslama's table. The correction is justified below, in my analysis of Maslama's table.
21 36° in Hermannus, pseudo-Māshā'allāh and "type XI".
22 70° in "type XI"; 67° in MS Paris BN lat. 7412.
23 18° in MS Paris BN lat. 7412.
24 39° in pseudo-Māshā'allāh and in "type XI".
25 352° in "type XI".
26 36° in pseudo-Māshā'allāh, Ascelin and "type XI".

Table 1 (*continued*)

1. Star name	2. Identification	3. Latitudo	4. Med.	5. RA	6. Dec.	7. Alt.	8. Alt.
18. Denebaliz	Dhanab al-Jady, δ Capricorni	[Aquar.] 7 [= 307][27]	–	–	–	19[28]	–
19. Aldeuaran	al-Dabarān (α Tauri)	[Taur.] 27 [= 57][29]	56;34	54;13,54	14;12 N	41;30[30]	59;21,50
20. Malgeuze	Mankib al-Jawzā' (α Orionis)	[Gemin] 18 [= 78][31]	76;21	75;9,32	6;48 N	55	54;28,1
21. Algoize	al-Shiʿrā al-Ghumayṣā' (α Canis Minoris)	[Cancer]11 [= 101][32]	100;40	101;36,48	6;56 N	56	54;33,46
22. Aldiraan	Muqaddam al-dhirāʿayn (α Hydrae) ?	[Leo] 6 [= 126]	125;49	128;13,5	2;25 N	52	51;7,51
23. Calbalaze	Qalb al-Asad (α Leonis)	[Leo] 19 [= 139][33]	134;20	136;49,50	16;27 N	61[34]	60;42,31
24. Algol	Ra's al-Ghūl (β Persei)	[Taur.] 10 [= 40][35]	–[36]	–	–	71	–
25. Alhaioc	al-ʿAyyūq (α Aurigae)	[Gemin.] 3 [= 63]	62;55	60;50,25	43;50 N	74	73;48,2

27 308° in Hermannus and pseudo-Māshā'allāh; 306° in "type XI".
28 35° in pseudo-Māshā'allāh; 34° in "type XI".
29 58° in "type XI".
30 69° in pseudo-Māshā'allāh; 61° in Ascelin and Hermannus; 49° in "type XI".
31 74° in "type XI"; 76° in MS Paris BN lat. 7412.
32 107° in pseudo-Māshā'allāh, Ascelin and Hermannus; 100° in "type XI".
33 138° in Paris BN 7412, pseudo-Māshā'allāh, Ascelin, Hermannus and "type XI".
34 41° in Ripoll 225.
35 45° in pseudo-Māshā'allāh; 37° in "type XI"; 36° in MS Paris BN lat. 7412.
36 Maslama's table only gives the longitude and latitude of this star.

Table 1 (*continued*)

1. Star name	2. Identification	3. Latitudo	4. Med.	5. RA	6. Dec.	7. Alt.	8. Alt.
26. Arrucaba	al-Rukba, θ Ursae Maioris	[Leo] 19 [= 139][37]	–	–	–	75[38]	–
27. Egreget	al-Rijl (ι Ursae Maioris)	[Cancer] 26 [= 116][39]	–	–	–	72[40]	–

37 167° in "type XI".
38 76° in pseudo-Māshā'allāh and in "type XI".
39 117° in pseudo-Māshā'allāh; 114° in "type XI".
40 76° in Hermannus.

Table 2
Maslama's star table (Unit: degree)

1. Star	2. Longitude	3. Latitude[41]	4. RA[42]	5. Mediation	6. Declination
1. Ra's al-Ghūl (β Persei)	42;20 (+1;30)	+23;0 (0;0)	–	–	–
2. al-Dabarān (α Tauri)	55;20 (+1;30)	–5;10 (0;0)	54;10,36	56;34 (+ 0;4)	+14;12 (0;0)
3. Rijl al-Jawzā' (β Orionis)	62;30 (+1;30)	–31;50 (+0;20)	66;29,14	68;15 (–0;1)	–10;29 (0;0)
4. al-'Ayyūq (α Aurigae)	67;40 (+1;30)	+22;30 (0;0)	60;52,39	62;55 (–0;2)	+43;50 (0;0)
5. Mankib al-Jawzā' (α Orionis)	74;40 (+1;30)	–16 (–1;0)	75;10,4	76;21 (0;0)	+6;48 (0;0)
6. al-'Abūr (α Canis Maioris)	90;20 (+1;30)	39;10 (0;0)	90;15;46	90;20 (+0;6)	–10;35 (+5;0)[43]
7. al-Ghumayṣā' (α Canis Minoris)	102 (+1;40)	16;10 (0;0)	101:36,17	100;40 (+0;0)	+6;56 (0;0)
8. Muqaddam al-Dhirā'ayn (α Hydrae)[44]	130;20	–16	128;30,53	125;49 (–0;17)	+2;25 (+0;6)
9. Qalb al-Asad (α Leonis)	135;40 (+1;40)	–0;10 (0;0)	138;13,44	134;20 (–1;24)[45]	+16;27 (+0;22)[46]
10. Ṭaraf Dhanab al-Asad (β Leonis)	156;40 (+1;0)	11;50 (0;0)	163;5,40	161;40 (+0;1)	20;4 (0;0)
11. Qā'id Banāt Na'sh (η Ursae Maioris)	162 (+1;0)	+55 (+1;0)	164;23,9	197;35 (+0;37)	55;30 (+0;15)[47]

41 Long. and Lat.: in brackets appear the differences from al-Battānī

42 Right ascension, modern calculation (cf. p. 514)

43 M. A. Catalá ("Consideraciones sobre la tabla de coordenadas estelares", *Al-Andalus* 30 (1965), 46–47) already noted an error in the declination of this star. The correct value should be 15;35°.

44 This identification is conjectural and it follows Vernet–Catalá. The value of the mediation coincides approximately with that given by al-Battānī (125;58) to this star and the same can be said of the declination although with a different sign (Battānī –2;55). We cannot analyse the corresponding longitudes and latitudes because in the only extant MS of al-Battānī's *zīj* the folio which should contain the ecliptical coordinates of the stars of the constellation of Hydra is missing. In the *Almagest* (VIII, 1) its longitude amounts to 120° (the corresponding longitude for 978 A.D. should be 132;40° or 132;50°, not very far from the 130;20° of our table). The latitude is clearly wrong (–20;30° in the *Almagest*).

45 This is the only value of the table which, apparently, has not been calculated but copied from al-Battānī (cf. Nallino II, 178).

46 I obtain 16;24° with a latitude of +0;10° instead of –0;10°.

47 A declination of 54;30° can be obtained with a latitude of 54° (instead of 55°) and a longitude of 162° (the one of the table).

Table 2 (*continued*)

1. Star	2. Longitude	3. Latitude	4. RA	5. Mediation	6. Declination
12. al-Simāk al-A'zal (α Virginis)	188;20 (+0;30)	-2 (0;0)[48]	173;9,19	187;30 (+0;2)	-5;10 (0;0)
13. al-Simāk al-Rāmiḥ (α Bootes)	189;40 (+1;30)	31;30 (0;0)[49]	157;57,37	203;52 (+0;2)	+ 24;56 (0;0)
14. Munīr al-Fakka (α Coronae Borealis)	207;20 (+1;30)	44;30 (0;0)	–	–	–
15. Qalb al-cAqrab (α Scorpii)	235;20 (+1;30)	-4 (0;0)	231;55,2	234;18 (-0;1)	-23;5 (0;0)
16. al-Nasr al-Wāqi' (α Lyrae)	270 (+1;30)	+62 (0;0)	270	270 (0)	+38;25 (0;0)
17. al-Nasr al-Ṭā'ir (α Aquilae)	286;30 (+1;30)	+29;10 (0;0)	284;27,7	283;18 (+0;1)	+6;25 (0;0)
18. Ra's al-Ḥāwī (α Ophiuchi)	–	–	–	264	+8;30
19. al-Ridf (α Cygni)	321;50 (+1;30)	+60 (0;0)	301;58,26	299;44 (-0;2)	+42;4 (0;0)
20. Mankib al-Faras (β Pegasi)	344;50 (+1;30)	+31 (0;0)	333;33,20	331;30 (-0;1)	+22;29 (0;0)
21. al-Kaff al-Khaḍīb (β Cassiopeae)[50]	347 (-32;0)	29 (-22;40)	–	–	–

48 Positive latitude in Maslama's table; negative in that of al-Battānī. The correction is necessary to obtain the declination of the table.

49 Southern latitude in Maslama's table; northern in al-Battānī (Nallino II, 147). The correction is necessary to obtain the declination of the table.

50 The coordinates of this star are clearly corrupt in Maslama's table: see Kunitzsch, *Typen* p. 18 n. 21. M. Comes ("La primera tabla de estrellas" pp. 100–101) remarks that this is one of the several instances of confusion between β Cassiopeiae with γ Pegasi / α Andromedae. Confusion of this kind appears also in the star table of Qāsim b. Muṭarrif al-Qaṭṭān (ca. 950), as well as in Ibn al-Zarqālluh, Ibn al-Kammād, al-Marrākushī and Ibn al-Bannā'. See also M. Comes, "Deux échos andalous à Ibn al-Bannā' de Marrākush", in *Le Patrimoine Andalous dans la Culture Arabe et Espagnole*, Tunis, 1991, pp. 87–88. B. R. Goldstein and J. Chabás ("Ibn al-Kammād's Star List", *Centaurus* 38 (1996), 317–334) identify al-Kaff al-Khaḍīb with α Andromedae.

Table 3
The values of the coordinate *latitudo* in Ms Paris BN lat. 7412, fol. 5v

Recomputed values follow E. Dekker's suggestion that the *latitudo*, in this table, corresponds to the meridian altitude of the star for a local latitude of 39°. I have used the declinations of Maslama's table. No attempt at recomputation has been made in those cases in which the star does not appear in Maslama's table. Unit: degree.

1.	Alramech	77 (+1)
2.	Alfecat	81
3.	Alhawi	65 (+5;30)
4.	Altair	60;30 (+3)
5.	Delfin	60
6.	Alferat	75 (+1;30)
7.	Alhcadib	78
8.	Alrif	86 (–5)
9.	Wega	90 (+0;30)
10.	Benenas	missing in the table.
11.	Calbagrab	29 (+1)
12.	Alcimek	46 (0)
13.	Algurab	39
14.	Alhabor	36 (–4;30)
15.	Rigel	41 (+0;30)
16.	Pantangaitot	37
17.	Denebgait	38;30
18.	Denebaliz	28
19.	Aldeuaran	72 (+7)
20.	Malgeuze	58 (0)
21.	Algoize	59 (+1)
22.	Aldiraan	55 (+1;30)
23.	Calbalaze	69 (+1;30)
24.	Algol	88
25.	Alhaioc	82 (–3)
26.	Arrucaba	74
27.	Egreget	72

III

SEVEN CHAPTERS OF IBN AL-ṢAFFĀR'S LOST *ZĪJ**

MARGARITA CASTELLS, JULIO SAMSÓ

Abū-l-Qāsim Aḥmad b. ʿAbd Allāh b. ʿUmar (d. 1035), known as Ibn al-Ṣaffār, was one of the disciples of Maslama al-Majrīṭī (d. 1008) traditionally associated with the Cordovan revision of al-Khwārizmī's *zīj*. Ṣāʿid al-Andalusī states that he wrote a *Zīj mukhtaṣar ʿalā madhhab al-Sindhind* ("an abridged *zīj* according to the Sindhind school") [1]. This is probably the work quoted by Abraham b. ʿEzra in the 12th c. [2]: this latter author states that Ibn al-Ṣaffār was responsible for the change from the Persian calendar and the Yazdijird era used by al-Khwārizmī to the Muslim calendar and the *Hijra* era which appears in the Latin version of Adelard of Bath, but Ṣāʿid attributed this change to Maslama al-Majrīṭī [3]. According to Ibn ʿEzra, Ibn al-Ṣaffār corrected the position of the apogee of Saturn from 8^s 20;55° to 8^s 4;55°, which he considered to be the correct longitude in al-Khwārizmī's *zīj*, stating that the translator(?)/copyist (*ipsum qui transtulit*) had been mistaken by the similarity of the form of the 20 (*kāf*) and the 4 (*dāl*) [4]. It is clear now that this

* This paper has been the object of a thorough revision, in terms of both style and contents, by Prof. E.S. Kennedy. Further comments and corrections have also been made by David A. King and Bernard R. Goldstein. To all of them we express our gratitude. We should also mention that it was written as part of a research programme on 'Astronomical Theory and Tables in al-Andalus in the tenth and eleventh centuries', sponsored by the Dirección General de Investigación Científica y Técnica of the Spanish Ministerio de Educación y Ciencia.

1 Ṣāʿid al-Andalusī, *Ṭabaqāt al-umam*, ed. Ḥayāt bū ʿAlwān (Beirut, 1985), 171; French translation by Régis Blachère, *Kitâb Ṭabakāt al-umam (Livre des Catégories de Nations)* (Paris, 1935), 131. Other biographical references in Ibn Bashkuwāl, *Kitāb al-Ṣila* (ed. Madrid, 1886) no. 83, p. 45; Ibn Abī Uṣaybiʿa (*ʿUyūn al-anbāʾ fī ṭabaqāt al-aṭibbāʾ* [ed. Beirut, 1957], III, 63-64) follows Ṣāʿid and does not provide new information. See other references in F. Sezgin, *Geschichte des Arabischen Schrifttums*, VI (Leiden, 1978), 250-251.

2 J. M. Millás Vallicrosa, *El libro de los fundamentos de las tablas astronómicas de R. Abraham ibn ʿEzra* (Madrid, Barcelona, 1947), 75, 109-110. See also Millás' commentary, pp. 23, 50-51.

3 Ṣāʿid, ed. Bū ʿAlwān, *op. cit.*, 169; tr. R. Blachère, *op. cit.*, 130.

4 Millás remarked that the confusion is more likely to occur in Hebrew than in Arabic script. Therefore, this could be Abraham b. ʿEzra's own explanation.

correction in Saturn's apogee was an error made by Ibn al-Ṣaffār [5] which appears in Adelard of Bath's Latin translation [6]. We will try to show in this paper that there might be, at least, one other instance in which Ibn al-Ṣaffār's and Maslama's materials have been mixed in Adelard's translation.

Six chapters and the end of another from Ibn al-Ṣaffār's canons are extant in manuscript Paris, Bibliothèque Nationale heb. 1102 (fols 1ʳ-5ʳ). [7] The text is preserved in Arabic written in Hebrew script: this is not an uncommon usage and we know of a certain number of other astronomical manuscripts written in Arabic with Hebrew characters [8]. An edition in Arabic script is presented as an appendix to this article, with which we try to render accessible another Khwārizmian source which has the additional interest of being the earliest known source related to the *Sindhind* tradition extant in Arabic [9]. Furthermore, this is only the second work ascribed to Ibn al-Ṣaffār which has ever been published [10].

Our commentary will try to summarize its contents, mostly straightforward instructions for the use of the tables, and explain the very few significant new materials that appear in it. We have also included a comparison with sources other than Adelard of Bath's translation, such as the Hebrew and Latin translations of Ibn al-Muthannā's commentary on al-Khwārizmī's *zīj* [11] and the Latin

[5] See David Pingree, *The Thousands of Abū Maʿshar* (London, 1968), 50; Raymond Mercier, "Astronomical Tables in the Twelfth Century", in Charles Burnett (ed.), *Adelard of Bath. An English Scientist and Arabist of the Early Twelfth Century* (London, 1987), 92.

[6] O. Neugebauer, *The Astronomical Tables of al-Khwārizmī. Translation with Commentaries of the Latin Version Edited by H. Suter Supplemented by Corpus Christi College MS 283* (Copenhagen, 1962), 41, 99.

[7] H. Zotenberg, *Catalogue des manuscrits hébreux et samaritains de la Bibliothèque Impériale* (Paris, 1866), 203.

[8] Cf. Bernard R. Goldstein, "The Survival of Arabic Astronomy in Hebrew", *Journal for the History of Arabic Science, 3* (1979), 31-39. See especially pp. 34-35 for a discussion of another part of the same Ms. B.N. heb. 1102.

[9] A new Latin source – closely related to Ibn al-Muthannā's commentary has recently been published by Fritz S. Pedersen, "Alkhwarizmi's Astronomical Rules: Yet Another Latin Version", in *Cahiers de l'Institut du Moyen-Âge Grec et Latin, 62* (1992), 31-75.

[10] The first was his treatise on the use of the astrolabe, edited by J.M. Millás Vallicrosa, "Los primeros tratados de astrolabio en España", *Revista del Instituto de Estudios Islámicos, 3* (1955), 35-49 (of the Spanish section) and 47-76 (of the Arabic section, where the edition of Ibn al-Ṣaffār's treatise appears). A short text on the construction of a very rudimentary sundial appears ascribed to Ibn al-Ṣaffār in Ms. Medicea-Laurenziana (Florence) Or. 152: D.A. King edited it in "Three Sundials from Islamic Andalusia", *Journal for the History of Arabic Science, 2* (1978), 358-392 (reprinted in King's *Islamic Astronomical Instruments*, London, 1987). J. Casulleras ("Descripciones de un cuadrante solar atípico en el Occidente Musulmán", *Al-Qanṭara, 14* [1993], 65-87) has proved that this text derives from an older source.

[11] B.R. Goldstein, *Ibn al-Muthannâ's Commentary on the Astronomical Tables of al-Khwârizmî. Two Hebrew Versions, Edited and Translated with an Astronomical Commentary*, New Haven, London, 1967; E. Millás, *El comentario de Ibn al-Muṯannā a las Tablas Astronómicas de al-Jwārizmī*, Madrid, Barcelona, 1963.

translation of the canons written by Ibn Muᶜādh al-Jayyānī (d. 1093) for his *Tabulae Jahen* [12].

1. *On the calculation of a lunar eclipse (fols 1ʳ-1ᵛ)*

The extant part of this chapter corresponds to the end of the second version of chapter 33 of Adelard of Bath's canons [13]. This version is preserved only in two of the three extant manuscripts [14]: Millás discovered what seemed to be the Arabic original in a chapter of Ibn al-Zarqālluh's canons on the use of his *Almanac* [15], and conjectured an early diffusion of the latter work which would have been amalgamated with materials of the Khwārizmī-Maslama tradition. The existence of Ibn al-Ṣaffār's incomplete chapter implies another alternative which might also apply to the second version of chapter 37 ("How to find the aspect of the stars, in sextile or quartile or trine") [16], a situation parallel to that of chapter 33: unfortunately this version has been preserved neither by Ibn al-Ṣaffār nor by Ibn al-Zarqālluh.

In the following lines we will present a summary of the operations described in the three aforementioned sources, making a comparison between them whenever necessary. Numbers between square brackets correspond to passages of Ibn al-Ṣaffār's edition.

The texts of Adelard and Ibn al-Zarqālluh require the establishment of an opposition of the Sun and the Moon, with the latter near the ascending or descending node. One should, then, obtain the adjusted argument of latitude (*ḥiṣṣat al-ᶜarḍ al-muᶜaddala* = a_β) for the time of the true opposition (*li-waqt al-istiqbāl al-ḥaqīqī*). If the Moon is at apogee or perigee, one enters with a_β in the table of eclipses for the corresponding distance [17] and notes the digits (*aṣābiᶜ* = *a*) and minutes (*daqā'iq*) of the immersion (*suqūt*, *elciicuth/casus* = d_i) and – if such is the case – of the duration of totality (*al-makth*, *elmuht* = d_m). If the Moon is neither in its apogee nor in its perigee [18],

[12] Ed. Nuremberg, 1549. See H. Hermelink, "Tabulae Jahen", *Archive for the History of the Exact Sciences*, 2 (1964), 108-112, and J. Samsó, *Las Ciencias de los Antiguos en al-Andalus* (Madrid, 1992), 152-166.

[13] H. Suter, *Die astronomischen Tafeln des Muḥammed ibn Mūsā al-Khwārizmī in der Bearbeitung des Maslama ibn Aḥmed al-Madjrīṭī und der latein. Uebersetzung des Athelhard von Bath* (Copenhagen, 1914), 27-28; O. Neugebauer, *al-Khwārizmī*, cit., 67-68.

[14] These two manuscripts are Chartres, Bibliothèque Publique no. 214, and Madrid, Biblioteca Nacional no. 10016; this version does not appear in manuscript Oxford, Bodleian Library, Cod. Auct. F.I.9.

[15] J.M. Millás-Vallicrosa, *Estudios sobre Azarquiel* (Madrid, Granada, 1943-1950), 109-111 (Arabic) and 143-145 (Spanish translation). See also O. Neugebauer, *al-Khwārizmī*, cit., 67, n. 21.

[16] Suter, *Tafeln*, cit., 31; Neugebauer, *al-Khwārizmī*, 79-80.

[17] Suter, *Tafeln*, tables 73-76, pp. 187-190.

[18] Here begins Ibn al-Ṣaffār's extant text.

[1] note a, d_i and d_m for both distances and establish:

$$\Delta a,\ \Delta d_i \text{ and } \Delta d_m$$

which correspond to the differences between the values of a, d_i and d_m for the perigee and the apogee.

[2] With the adjusted lunar anomaly (*ḥiṣṣat al-qamar al-muᶜaddala*) as argument we enter the interpolation table [19], called *jadwal al-nisba* by Ibn al-Ṣaffār, which corresponds to the *tabula proportionis* in Adelard's translation, while Ibn al-Zarqālluh uses the expression *jadwal al-taqwīm*. We note the corresponding value (m) of the *daqā'iq al-faḍl* (*dakaicae superationum*, *minuta residui* or *dakaicae elfudhul* in Adelard, *daqā'iq al-ḥiṣaṣ* in Ibn al-Zarqālluh's text) and

[3] multiply:

$$\Delta a \times m$$
$$\Delta d_i \times m$$
$$\Delta d_m \times m$$

(Ibn al-Zarqālluh adds that m should have been divided by 60, which seems unnecessary and does not appear in Adelard's text).

[4] The products obtained in [3] are then added to the apogee (*ap*) values of a, d_i and d_m. The results are:

$E = a(ap) + \Delta a \times m$ (eclipsed digits of the lunar diameter);
$G = d_i(ap) + \Delta d_i \times m$ (minutes of arc from the beginning of the immersion to the middle of the eclipse);
$F = d_m(ap) + \Delta d_m \times m$ (minutes of arc from the beginning of totality to the middle of the eclipse).

We should remark that Ibn al-Ṣaffār departs from the terminology used in Adelard's translation: immersion corresponds, in this text, to *niṣf al-mudda* instead of *suqūṭ*, *elciicuth/casus* (in Ibn al-Zarqālluh and Adelard's canons).

[5] v being the hourly motion of the Moon, and I the interval in hours between the beginning and the middle of the eclipse, then:

$$I = (G + G/12)\ /\ v.$$

Here the analysis of the three texts gives contradictory results: on the one hand both Ibn al-Ṣaffār and Adelard talk about the hourly motion of the Moon (*ḥarakat al-qamar li-sāᶜa*, *motum lunae horarium*) while Ibn al-Zarqālluh introduces the technical term *buht*, which has exactly the same meaning. On the other hand

[19] Suter, *Tafeln*, tables 73-75, last two columns, pp. 187-189.

Adelard's text seems nearer to Ibn al-Zarqālluh when it states that the result obtained will be the interval of time between the beginning of the eclipse and the beginning of totality, if there is totality [20]. The two versions complement each other: Ibn al-Ṣaffār considers only the case of a partial eclipse, while both Adelard and Ibn al-Zarqālluh are only concerned with the total eclipse. The addition of *G/12* is standard to take into account the mean increase in elongation during the time the Moon requires to travel the arc *G*.

[6] Again, for *T* = interval of time corresponding to the phase of totality:

$$T/2 = (F + F/12) \,/\, v$$
$$T = T/2 \times 2$$

(these expressions appear, with no significant variants, in the two other sources considered);

[7] and

Total time of the eclipse from first to last contact = $I \times 2$

in agreement with our remark on the meaning of *I*, in Ibn al-Ṣaffār's text (see above no. [5]). As for the two other sources:

Total time of the eclipse from first to last contact = $I \times 2 + T$.

At this point Adelard's chapter ends.

[8] If *H* is the hour of the middle of the eclipse:

Hour of the beginning of the eclipse = $H - I$

(a passage is now missing at the end of fol. 1^r). Ibn al-Zarqālluh's text contains this rule, as well as several others to establish the different phases of the eclipse.

[9] Finally, if there is no totality, one should enter with *E* (the eclipsed digits of the lunar diameter) in the "Table of the equation of digits" (*Jadwal taᶜdīl al-aṣābiᶜ*) to obtain the number of eclipsed digits of the lunar area [21]. There is no reference to the use of this table in Ibn al-Zarqālluh's chapter.

In conclusion, we think that the chapters of Ibn al-Ṣaffār, Ibn al-Zarqālluh and Adelard of Bath derive from a common source. This would explain why Adelard's text seems, sometimes, nearer to Ibn al-Ṣaffār's chapter and, at other times, to Ibn al-Zarqālluh's *Almanac*. It is difficult to decide at this stage whether this common source is Ibn al-Ṣaffār's lost *zīj*, al-Khwārizmī's Arabic original or somebody else's

[20] Suter, *Tafeln*, 27: "ipsum est a principio eclipsis ad initium ipsius morae, si habuerit moram". J.M. Millás-Vallicrosa, *Azarquiel*, cit., 110: "fa-huwa mā marra min awwal al-kusūf ilā awwal al-makth, in kāna makthan".

[21] See Suter, *Tafeln*, table 76 (last column), p. 190 (*Partes duodecimarum lunae*).

work. The only thing which seems entirely clear to us is that there seems to be no reason to reject the second version of chapter 33 as not belonging to the set of al-Khwārizmī-Maslama's tables. The fact that we find the bulk of its contents in an Arabic text ascribed to Ibn al-Ṣaffār shows that the source used was older than Ibn al-Zarqālluh and, perhaps, contemporary to the Cordovan revision of al-Khwārizmī's *zīj*.

2. *On the determination of the longitude of a place from the centre of the Earth, used as a basis (*aṣl*) in this book (fols* 1^r-2^v*)*

This chapter, which has no equivalent in Adelard's translation, deals with a standard topic: [10] calculate a lunar eclipse for the meridian used as a basis in this book and [11] determine the difference in equal hours between the beginning or the end of the eclipse and the following midday. [12] Then, using an astrolabe, establish the difference in equal hours between the beginning or the end of the eclipse and the next local midday. [13] The difference in equal hours may be used to determine the difference in longitude. The conversion factor (15° per hour) does not appear in the edited text, for there is a short passage missing in the manuscript. There is, however, a reference to five hours which we do not understand. Another possible interpretation of this passage is that one should read *khums sāᶜa* (the fifth of an hour, *i.e.* 12 minutes) instead of *khams sāᶜāt* (five hours).

The important passage in this chapter is [14] where the text states that the table of conjunctions and oppositions in this book is computed for the meridian of Cordova. If you calculate the eclipse for this locality and add, to the local time, four equal hours and one fifth ($4;12^h$) you will obtain the time of the zero meridian (centre of the Earth, *i.e.* Arin).

The tables mentioned in the text are tables 69-72, of which the two first ones state specifically that they have been calculated "secundum medium diem / meridiem Cordubae" [22], a remark we also find in the corresponding canons [23]. By comparing this tables of mean conjunctions and oppositions with mean motion tables for the Sun and the Moon, Neugebauer established that the former were meant in Cordova local time, while the solar and lunar mean motion tables used epoch values for a meridian $4;12^h$ east of Cordova. So far, there is complete agreement between Adelard's tables and the text of Ibn al-Ṣaffār. Only one thing is new in the text we are commenting: Ibn al-Ṣaffār states clearly that the meridian placed $4;12^h$ (or 63°) to the east of Cordova is the meridian of the centre of the Earth, Arin, placed 90° east of the western prime meridian, which implies that

[22] *Ibid.*, 183-186. See the commentary by Neugebauer, *al-Khwārizmī*, 108-115.

[23] Suter, *Tafeln*, 25; Neugebauer, *al-Khwārizmī*, 61.

Cordova is also 27° east of this latter meridian, instead of the 9;20° which is the standard longitude for Cordova in sources related to the Ptolemaic geographical tradition which uses as prime meridian the meridian of the Fortunate Islands [24]. This correction – which appears quoted in many later Andalusian and Magribī sources – is also mentioned in a horoscope, dated 940 A.D. and added as an appendix to ᶜUmar b. al-Farrukhān's *Liber Universus* [25]. The horoscope in question was computed using al-Khwārizmī's *zīj* but it is difficult to establish whether it was cast before or after that date and, therefore, whether the correction in the difference of longitudes between al-Andalus and Arin should be ascribed to Maslama's school or to an earlier source.

3. *On the knowledge of the lunar parallax in longitude and the hours of parallax (fol. 2ʳ)*

This chapter is in essential agreement with the first half of chapter 34 of Adelard's canons [26], which deals both with the longitude and latitude components of parallax [27], although this latter text contains a couple of small errors which are not to be found in Ibn al-Ṣaffār. It is also very similar to a passage in Ibn al-Shāṭir's *zīj* in which he describes "a method followed by many of the ancient [people] of this science" [28]. Nothing very exciting appears in it but we summarize it for the sake of completion and also introduce a few remarks on the terminology used.

[15] One should first calculate the ascendant (λ_H) for the moment we are concerned with, the moment of the true conjunction or another one.

[16] Then we put:

$$\lambda_{90} = \lambda_H - 90^o$$

[24] E.S. and M.H. Kennedy, *Geographical Coordinates of Localities from Islamic Sources* (Frankfurt, 1987), 95. On this topic see M. Comes, "The *Meridian of Water* in the Tables of Geographical Coordinates of al-Andalus and North Africa", *Journal for the History of Arabic Science, 10* (1994), 41-51. See also J. Samsó, *Ciencias de los Antiguos*, cit., 90.

[25] David Pingree, "The *Liber Universus* of ᶜUmar Ibn al-Farrukhān al-Ṭabarī", *Journal for the History of Arabic Science, 1* (1977), 8-12.

[26] Suter, *Tafeln*, 28-29; Neugebauer, *al-Khwārizmī*, 69-71.

[27] See, for the underlying theory, E.S. Kennedy, "Parallax Theory in Islamic Astronomy", *Isis*, *47* (1956), 33-53. Reprinted in E.S. Kennedy *et al.*, *Studies in the Islamic Exact Sciences* (*S.I.E.S.* hereafter) (Beirut, 1983) 164-184.

[28] E.S. Kennedy, Nazim Faris, "The Solar Eclipse Technique of Yaḥyā b. Abī Manṣūr", *Journal for the History of Astronomy, 1* (1970), 20-38. Reprinted in *S.I.E.S.*, pp. 185-203 (see especially pp. 198-199).

and obtain the nonagesimal, that is the highest point of the ecliptic. This point is usually called by Eastern Arabic astronomers *wasaṭ samā' al-ru'ya* (visible midheaven), but our text uses the expression *wasaṭ samā' al-ṭāliᶜ* (midheaven of the ascendant) which corresponds exactly to the *horoscopi medium coelum* of Adelard's translation [29].

[17] For λ_m = the true lunar longitude and α any right ascension, let us obtain $\alpha(\lambda_{90})$ and $\alpha(\lambda_m)$ and then

$$\Delta\alpha = \alpha(\lambda_{90}) - \alpha(\lambda_m).$$

[18] With $\Delta\alpha$ as argument we enter the table of parallax and obtain the "hours of parallax" (*sāᶜāt ikhtilāf al-manẓar*) [30], which is the difference in hours between the moment for which the true lunar longitude has been calculated and the moment in which the moon is seen in that position.

[19] This results should be multiplied by the corrected (true) lunar motion in one hour (*ḥarakat al-qamar al-muᶜaddala li-sāᶜa*) and we will obtain, expressed in minutes and seconds, the lunar parallax in longitude. In this way time is converted into longitude and the geocentric distance of the Moon is taken into account.

There follows a rule to determine whether the parallax component is added or subtracted: [20] if the Moon is placed between the nonagesimal and the ascendant, the parallax should be added to the true lunar longitude [31]; [21] we subtract the parallax from the true lunar longitude when the Moon is placed between the descendant and the nonagesimal. [22] After this final operation we obtain the apparent lunar position (*mawḍiᶜ al-qamar al-mar'ī*) on the ecliptic, *i.e.* the lunar longitude corrected for parallax [32].

29 Cf. e.g. Suter, *Tafeln*, 28. Ibn al-Muthannā's Latin translation uses the expression *portio orientis* (E. Millás, *Ibn al-Muṯannā*, cit., 185; see also Goldstein, *Ibn al-Muṯhannā*, cit., 126 and 237, who translates *portion of the ascendant*). This expression is, obviously, the same as that used in the Latin translation of the canons of Ibn Muᶜādh's *Tabulae Jahen* (chapter 22): *portio ascendentis*.

30 Suter, *Tafeln*, tables 77 and 77a, pp. 191-192 (col. 2: *Horae diversitatum respectum lunae [in longitudine]*); Neugebauer, *al-Khwārizmī*, 123-126.

31 There is a small mistake in Adelard's text (Suter, *Tafeln*, 28) according to which the parallax should be added to the *hours* of the conjunction (*erit hoc productum horis coniunctionis addendum*). See also Neugebauer, *al-Khwārizmī*, p. 70, n. 7.

32 Again a mistake in Adelard's text (Suter, *Tafeln*, 28, and Neugebauer, *al-Khwārizmī*, p. 70, n. 8), according to which we obtain the *hour* of the eclipse (*horam eclipsis supra locum pro quo inquiris ex diversitate aspectus mutatam ponit*).

4. *On the determination of the lunar parallax in latitude (fols 2r-2v)*

This chapter corresponds to the second part of chapter 34 in Adelard's version [33]. Virtually the same process is followed by Yaḥyā b. Abī Manṣūr in the chapter of his *zīj* on the calculation of the solar eclipse and by Ibn al-Shāṭir in the same chapter quoted above (see § 3 above) [34]. As in the case of the parallax in longitude we start with:

[23] λ_H for the moment required.

[24] $\lambda_{90} = \lambda_H - 90^\circ$

[25] Obtain δ_{90}, the declination of λ_{90}, as well as its direction.

[26] Φ being the local latitude, put:

$\Phi - \delta_{90}$ for a northern declination. However, if $\delta_{90} > \Phi$, then $\delta_{90} - \Phi$.
$\Phi + \delta_{90}$ for a southern declination.

The [approximate] result (D) is the zenithal distance of the nonagesimal (*buʿd darajat wasaṭ samā' al-ṭāliʿ min samt al-ru'ūs*, which corresponds to what Eastern astronomers call *ʿarḍ iqlīm al-ru'ya*, latitude of the visible climate) [35].

[27] Obtain the latitude of the Moon (β), considering the Moon to be in the nonagesimal (λ_{90}). The procedure, not clearly explained in the text, does not appear in Adelard of Bath's translation, but it is the same one we find in Ibn al-Shāṭir's *zīj* and in Ibn al-Muthannā's commentary on al-Khwārizmī's *zīj* [36].

Calculate [using tables 19-20] the longitude of the lunar node (*jawzahār*, λ_n). Then subtract [37]

$$a_\beta = \lambda_{90} - \lambda_n,$$

to find a_β, the argument of latitude with which we can obtain the lunar latitude [using the last column of tables 21-26], as well as its direction [38].

[33] Suter, *Tafeln*, 28-29; Neugebauer, *al-Khwārizmī*, 70-72.

[34] See E.S. Kennedy, N. Faris, "The Solar Eclipse Technique", cit.

[35] As Neugebauer states (*al-Khwārizmī*, 72) the result would be exact if we worked with the *medium coelum* instead of the nonagesimal.

[36] See Kennedy-Faris, in *S.I.E.S.*, 32 and 34; Goldstein, *Ibn al-Muthannâ*, 89-92, 127-128, 211-212, 237-238; E. Millás, *Ibn al-Muṯannā*, 73-74, 154-156, 185-186; see also Pedersen, "Alkhwarizmi's Astronomical Rules", cit., 47, 59-60.

[37] The text says "add" (*tazīd*) which seems an obvious mistake.

[38] Ibn al-Muṯannā (as well as the Latin text edited by Pedersen) does not use tables and explains a computational procedure instead:

$$\beta = (\mathrm{Sin}_{150}\, a_\beta)\ 9/5$$

which is the result of applying the approximate rule:

$$\beta \approx \beta_{max}/150\ \mathrm{Sin}_{150}\, a_\beta$$

for $\beta_{max} = 4;30^\circ = 270'$.

[28] If the lunar latitude is northern, calculate:

$$D - \beta,$$

while if it is southern we should determine

$$D + \beta$$

which will be the [corrected] zenith distance of the Moon (D') "if you (?) [= the Moon] are in the nonagesimal" (*buᶜd al-qamar min samt al-ru'ūs law anta* [sic] *fī darajat samā' al-ṭāliᶜ*).

[29] D' is the argument with which we will enter the table (77 or 77a) for the parallax in latitude (P_β) which will be southern or northern depending on D' [*i.e.* the Moon] being South or North of the zenith.

5. *How to calculate a solar eclipse (fols 2ᵛ-4ʳ)*

The beginning of Ibn al-Ṣaffār's text ([30]-[33]) fits well with chapter 35 of Adelard of Bath's translation which is concerned only with the correction of the parallax in longitude at the place and the hour of the true conjunction [39]:

[30] Obtain an adjusted true conjunction (*al-ijtimāᶜ al-ḥaqīqī al-muᶜaddal*) which takes place during daytime and near one of the lunar nodes.

[31] Obtain the adjusted argument of latitude a_β (*ḥiṣṣat al-ᶜarḍ al-muᶜaddala*), the longitude of the ascendant (λ_H) for the moment of the true conjunction and the longitude of the nonagesimal (λ_{90}).

[32] With the longitude of the nonagesimal we obtain the hours (*sic*) of the lunar parallax in latitude (P_β), [40] as well as the longitudinal parallax (P_λ).

[33] If the place of the true conjunction (λ_c) is between the *nonagesimal* (λ_{90}) and the ascendant (λ_H), we subtract:

$$(1)\quad \lambda_c - P_\lambda$$
$$(2)\quad H_c - H_{P\lambda}$$

(H_c being the hour of the conjunction and $H_{P\lambda}$ the hours of the longitudinal parallax).

[39] Suter, *Tafeln*, 29; Neugebauer, *al-Khwārizmī*, 73.

[40] Adelard of Bath's text does not mention the lunar parallax in latitude. However, concerning the anomalous mention of the "hours" in connection with the latitudinal component of parallax, we should remark that tables 77 and 77a (Suter, *Tafeln*, 191-192) allude several times to hours in the same connection.

If λ_c is between λ_{90} and the descendant λ_{VII} we should add:

$$(3) \quad \lambda_c + P_\lambda$$
$$(4) \quad H_c + H_{P\lambda}$$

the results being the apparent position of the Moon (*mawḍiᶜ al-qamar al-mar'ī*) for (1) and (3), and the hour of the apparent conjunction (*sāᶜāt al-ijtimāᶜ al-mar'ī*) which is the hour of the centre of the eclipse (*sāᶜāt wasaṭ al-kusūf*) for (2) and (4).

From here onwards we only find occasional allusions to the complete doctrine on the solar eclipse – as explained by Ibn al-Ṣaffār – in the two additions to chapter 31, written in two different hands, which appear in the printed edition of Adelard of Bath's translation [41].

[34] P_λ is added to or subtracted from the argument of latitude of the true conjunction (a_β, obtained *supra* in [31]):

$$a_E = P_\lambda \pm a_\beta.$$

The sign will depend on the rules established in [33]. The result (a_E) will be the argument of latitude for mid-eclipse (*ḥiṣṣat al-ᶜarḍ li-wasaṭ al-kusūf*).

[35] We form

$$\lambda_{SE} = \lambda_c \pm P_\lambda/13$$

applying the same rules for the sign as in [33]. The result (λ_{SE}) will be the solar longitude for mid-eclipse (*mawḍiᶜ al-shams li-wasaṭ al-kusūf*).

$P_\lambda/13$ seems to be an attempt to calculate the value of the solar parallax in longitude based on the idea that the parallax increases as the distance diminishes. It does not seem to depend on a relation of the geocentric distances of the Sun and the Moon, as established in the *Almagest*, but rather on the relation of mean daily velocities of these two celestial bodies ($\approx$ 13:1), an approximation used by al-Khwārizmī to calculate the apparent diameter of the solar and the lunar disk [42]. However, al-Khwārizmī's tables for parallax (77 and 77a) do not give the lunar parallax but the "adjusted lunar parallax" (*i.e.* the difference between the lunar and the solar parallax) (?). It is interesting to remark that λ_{SE} is not, apparently, to be used in the rest of the computation of the eclipse.

[36] Calculate the lunar parallax in latitude as well as its sign for mid-eclipse ($P_{\beta E}$) as explained in the corresponding chapter (see above § 4). $P_{\beta E}$ will always be southern in Cordova and in any other place in which the Moon cannot cross the meridian north of the zenith.

[41] Suter, *Tafeln*, p. xx, n. 13; Neugebauer, *al-Khwarizmī*, 73-74.
[42] Neugebauer, *al-Khwārizmī*, 57-59.

[37] Multiply

$$P_{\beta E} \times 12;45.$$

This amount is to be subtracted from or added to the argument of latitude for mid-eclipse (a_E, see *supra* [34]) if P_β is southern and the conjunction takes place in the ascending node (subtraction) or the descending node (addition). If P_β is northern, we will operate with the opposite signs. The result (a_{lv}) will be the argument of latitude for the apparent position of the Moon (*ḥiṣṣat al-ʿarḍ li-mawḍiʿ al-qamar al-marʾī*), the argument used by Ibn al-Ṣaffār to determine the magnitude (*qadr*) of the eclipse:

$$a_{lv} = a_E \pm P_{\beta E} \times 12;45.$$

It seems, therefore, that Ibn al-Ṣaffār intends here to correct the argument of latitude. In fig. 1, A is the ascending node, AV an arc of the ecliptic, and AL an arc of the Moon's orbit. The Moon is at L, but as a result of latitudinal parallax, is seen in L' ($P_{\beta E} = LL'$). $\angle LAV = \beta_{max} = 4;30^o$ and we will put $\angle L'AV = i$. The correction he is introducing is:

$$AL - AL' \approx (150 \times LV \,/\, Sin_{150}\ 4;30^o) - (150 \times L'V \,/\, Sin_{150}\ i).$$

If we accept the approximation:

$$Sin_{150}\ 4;30^o \approx Sin_{150}\ i$$

then

$$AL - AL' \approx 150 \times P_{\beta E} \,/\, Sin_{150}\ 4;30^o = P_{\beta E} \,/\, Sin\ 4;30^o$$

and

$$1 \,/\, Sin\ 4;30^o = 12;44,44.$$

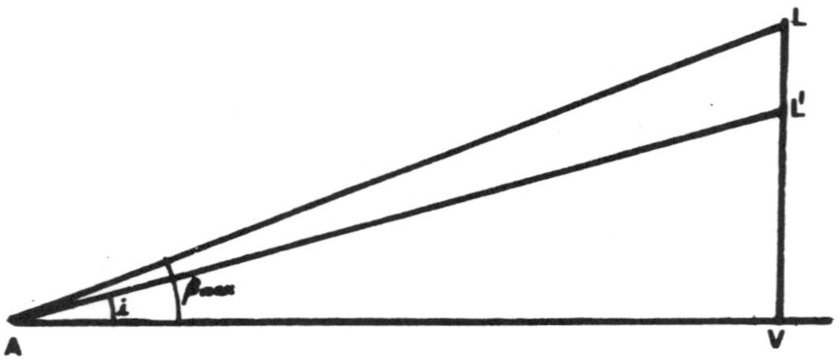

Fig. 1

[38] With a_{lv} as argument we enter the appropriate section (depending on whether the Moon is in its apogee or in its perigee) of the table of the solar eclipses [43] where we will obtain the corresponding values in D, digits (*aṣābi*ᶜ, *digiti*), and M, minutes of half duration of the eclipse (*daqā'iq niṣf al-mudda*, *dakaicae casus*). If the Moon is neither at apogee nor perigee, we will note the values of D and M for both distances and establish the two corresponding differences (Δ_D and Δ_M).

[39] Using the adjusted lunar anomaly for the true conjunction (*ḥiṣṣat al-qamar al-muᶜaddala li-l-ijtimāᶜ al-ḥaqīqī*) as argument [44], we enter the interpolation table ("table of proportion", *jadwal al-nisba*, *tabula proportionis* in Adelard's translation) [45] and obtain the corresponding values of m_f ("minutes of difference", *daqā'iq al-faḍl*, *dakaicae superationum*) and multiply:

$$m_f \times \Delta_D$$

and

$$m_f \times \Delta_M.$$

The results should be added to the corresponding values of D and M obtained from the column of the lunar apogee (D_{ap} and M_{ap}). Then

$$D_{ap} + m_f \times \Delta_D$$

will be the number of digits of the solar diameter which will be eclipsed.

[40] We take $M_{ap} + m_f \times \Delta_M = M_c$ and add to it $M_c/12$. The result should be divided by the Moon's hourly velocity [46] and we will obtain the "hours of the half duration of the eclipse" (*sāᶜāt niṣf muddat al-kusūf*). If we subtract these hours from the "hours of mid-eclipse" (*sāᶜāt wasaṭ al-kusūf*, see above [33]) we will obtain the hour of the beginning of the eclipse (*sāᶜāt ibtidā' al-kusūf*). If we add them, the result will be the hour of the end of the eclipse (*sāᶜāt tamām al-injilā'*).

[41] With the digits of the solar diameter obtained in [39] as argument, we

[43] Suter, *Tafeln*, table 78 (p. 193); Neugebauer, *al-Khwārizmī*, 126-128.

[44] Columns 6-7 of tables 73-75 (Suter, *Tafeln*, 187-189) call the argument *partitiones diversitatum*. Variant readings quoted by Suter give *aguze/ajuze elihtilef* which implies Ar. *ajzā' al-ikhtilāf*.

[45] This table has already been mentioned in [2] because it has to be used for both lunar and solar eclipses. See Neugebauer, *al-Khwārizmī*, 117.

[46] As in [5] above.

enter the "table of the equation of digits" (*jadwal taᶜdīl al-aṣābiᶜ*) [47]. The result obtained will be the number of digits of the solar disk (*jirm*) that will be eclipsed.

[42] Ibn al-Ṣaffār finally states that the Moon is in its apogee when the lunar anomaly at the moment of the true conjunction is approximately twelve signs, while it is in its perigee when the aforementioned anomaly is approximately six signs.

6. *On the equation of time (fol. 4ʳ)*

This short chapter appears, in an abridged form, within Adelard of Bath's chapter 31, which is concerned with the computation of the conjunction and opposition of the Sun and the Moon [48]. An addition, of a more elaborate character, appears in one of the manuscripts used by Suter [49]. Neither text corresponds exactly to Ibn al-Ṣaffār's chapter.

[43] If we want to convert "unequal" (*mukhtalifa, i.e.* true) days into mean days, enter with the degree [of solar longitude] as argument in the table for the equation of time (*jadwal taᶜdīl al-ayyām bi-layālī-hā*) [50], and subtract the minutes of hour which we will find in the table from the days we wanted to convert.

47 This table allows the computation of the eclipsed digits of the solar disk as a function of the eclipsed digits of the solar radius. It is table 76, cols 6-7, of al-Khwārizmī's *zīj* (Suter, *Tafeln*, 190; Neugebauer, *al-Khwārizmī*, 118). This table seems to have a Ptolemaic origin: see *Almagest* VI, 8 in the English translation by G.J. Toomer (New York etc., 1984), 308; see also the *Handy Tables* in the French translation by Halma II (Paris, 1823), 94-95 left. It appears also in al-Battānī's *zīj* (ed. by C.A. Nallino [Milan, 1907], vol. II, 89). In the Andalusian tradition we find the same table in the Toledan *zīj* (G.J. Toomer, "A Survey of the Toledan Tables", *Osiris*, *15* [1968], 113, where it is called *Tabula quantitatis tenebrarum eclipsis*), and in Ibn al-Zarqālluh's *Almanach* (Millás-Vallicrosa, *Azarquiel*, 233). There is, finally, a reference to a similar table (*Tabula mensurae solis*) in chapter XXII of Ibn Muᶜādh's canons of the *Tabulae Jahen*.

48 Suter, *Tafeln*, 25; Neugebauer, *al-Khwārizmī*, 61.

49 Suter, *Tafeln*, p. xix, n. 10; Neugebauer, *al-Khwārizmī*, 61-62 and commentary p. 65. Recent studies on the equation of time in the Islamic tradition are: E.S. Kennedy, "Two Medieval Approaches to the Equation of Time", *Centaurus*, *31* (1988), 1-8; Benno Van Dalen, *Ancient and Mediaeval Astronomical Tables: Mathematical Structure and Parameter Values* (University of Utrecht, 1993), 97-152; *id.*, "On Ptolemy's Table for the Equation of Time", *Centaurus*, *37* (1994), 97-153.

50 Tables 67-68 in Suter, *Tafeln*, 181-182. The title of the table is *Pagina examinationis dierum*. The argument receives the name of *gradus regulares* or *equales*. See Neugebauer, *al-Khwārizmī*, 107-108.

[44] In case we want to convert mean days into unequal days, the method is exactly the same but the result should be added and not subtracted.

According to these instructions, the values of the table of the equation of time mentioned by Ibn al-Ṣaffār are always negative, as in the table extant in Adelard of Bath's translation. No information is given as to the independent variable used (true or mean solar longitude): Adelard's table uses the true solar longitude [51]. This latter table is calculated to the precision of seconds and it is somewhat surprising to find that Ibn al-Ṣaffār states explicitely twice (both in [43] and [44]) that the table gives minutes but does not mention seconds [52].

7. *On the determination of the ascendant* (iqāmat al-ṭāliᶜ) *and of the twelve astrological houses (fols 4ʳ-5ʳ)*

Paragraphs [45]-[49], concerned with the determination of the ascendant during daytime and at night, as well as with the computation of midheaven, do not appear in Adelard of Bath's canons. Ibn al-Muthannā's commentary [53] alludes to the techniques used here by Ibn al-Ṣaffār but, without any doubt, the best agreement with our text can be found in Ibn Muᶜādh's canons of the *Tabulae Jahen* (chapter 16). The ultimate source is probably the *Almagest* (II, 9). [54] Ibn Muᶜādh

[51] B. Van Dalen, *Tables*, cit., p. 140, n. 156. See also B. Van Dalen, "Al-Khwārizmī's Astronomical Tables Revisited: Analysis of the Equation of Time", to appear in *From Baghdād to Barcelona. Studies in the Islamic Exact Sciences, in Honour of Prof. Juan Vernet*, ed. by J. Casulleras and J. Samsó (Barcelona [1996]).

[52] Ibn Muᶜādh's *Tabulae Jahen* have the same peculiarity (see chapter 7: *De aequatione dierum cum noctibus suis*). It seems, however, that Ibn Muᶜādh's table for the equation of time did not share with al-Khwārizmī's (in Adelard's version) the characteristic of being always negative. The Latin text of the canons states that [if you want to convert real hours into mean hours], once you have obtained the minutes of the equation as a function of the [true or mean?] solar longitude you should add them or subtract them [to the date and hour], according to what has been written above [the tabular value?] and then you will obtain the date expressed in mean time [*Et fac cum illis minutis quod supra scriptum est, de additione aut diminutione, et erit Era quam habebis, Era aequata Canonica*]. If you have mean time and want to obtain real time the sign will be the opposite to what has been written above [*Et accipe quod est in directo de minutis horarum, et fac cum eis contrarium, et quod est supra scriptum, scilicet, si fuerit super ea adde, tunc minue ea de Era, et si fuerit super ea minue, tunc adde ea super Eram, et erit hora temporalis absoluta*]. Our suspicion is that Ibn Muᶜādh used a table for the equation of time which was different from those attested in al-Andalus until the 11th century. His conversion factor was, possibly, not 15° for, in chapter 6 of his *Tabulae Jahen* he states that the times of an equal hour are 15 degrees and a small amount [*Scias quod tempora horae unius aequalis, sunt 15 gradus et res parua*].

[53] B.R. Goldstein, *Ibn al-Muthannâ*, 84-85, 209-210; E. Millás, *Ibn al-Muṭannā*, 149.

[54] See Toomer's translation, cit., 99-104.

establishes a relation between al-Khwārizmī's method of "domification" and Ptolemy [55] although he does not seem to refer to the calculation of the ascendant and midheaven but rather to the rest of the houses according to the "standard" method: such an ascription of the "standard" method to Ptolemy reappears in several Alfonsine translations [56]. [50]-[54] correspond to materials which are found in all the sources mentioned and describe the "standard" method: see, however, our remarks on [50].

A summary, with brief comments, of the contents of Ibn al-Ṣaffār's chapter follows:

[45] *Determination of the ascendant during daytime*: establish the number of hours since sunrise. If they are unequal (*muʿawwaja*) hours multiply this number by the number of [equatorial] degrees corresponding to one hour; if they are equal hours, multiply them by fifteen [57]. You will obtain the time expressed in degrees since sunrise (t).

[46] Obtain the [oblique] ascension of the solar degree [for that day], $\alpha_\Phi(S)$, and add:

$$\alpha_\Phi(S) + t.$$

[See Fig. 2 where S_0 is the position of the Sun at sunrise. After t hours, the Sun will be at S_t, and the distance S_0-S_t, will be t degrees. A_t will be the position of Aries 0° in this moment. The oblique ascension of the solar degree will be the arc between A_t and point M of the equator which crosses the horizon together with the Sun at sunrise. When we add $\alpha_\Phi(S) + t$, we obtain the arc between A_t and point Q if we establish that $MQ = t$. Q will be the equatorial degree crossing the horizon after t hours.]

[47] Look for the value $\alpha_\Phi(S) + t$ in the table of oblique ascensions. [If you do not find the exact value in the table] subtract the nearest inferior tabular value from $\alpha_\Phi(S) + t$ and find the inverse oblique ascension (α_Φ^{-1}) of the remainder, expressed in degrees of the ecliptic (*daraj al-sawāʾ* or *daraj mustawiya*). Determine to which zodiacal sign belongs the result: the corresponding degree of that sign will

[55] The relevant passage appears in chapter 25 of the Nuremberg's edition: "Illud quidem quod Alchorismus in suo libro dixit, et quod narrauit ex Ptolomeo non probo, et est ut accipias ascensiones ascendentis in regione, et ascensiones decimi in orbe recto. Deinde assumas tempora unius horae partis ascendentis, et dupla illa tempora, et quod est, est sexta arcus diei. Adde ergo illud super ascensiones decimi, et quod est, sunt ascensiones domus undecimae".

[56] J.D. North, *Horoscopes and History* (London, 1986), 34.

[57] Fifteen is represented in the text by *ṭāʾ-wāw* instead of *yāʾ-hāʾ* according to the Jewish custom which avoids, in this way, the use of the two first letters of the *tetragrammaton*.

be the ascendant. The rest of the paragraph is a set of instructions for linear interpolation to be used with a table of oblique ascensions calculated with an interval of one degree of the argument. Ibn al-Ṣaffār ends by saying that the procedure is the same as that used with a sine table.
[Clearly, the inverse oblique ascension of point *Q* will be the point of the ecliptic which will cross the meridian simultaneously with *Q*, that is the instantaneous ascendant.]

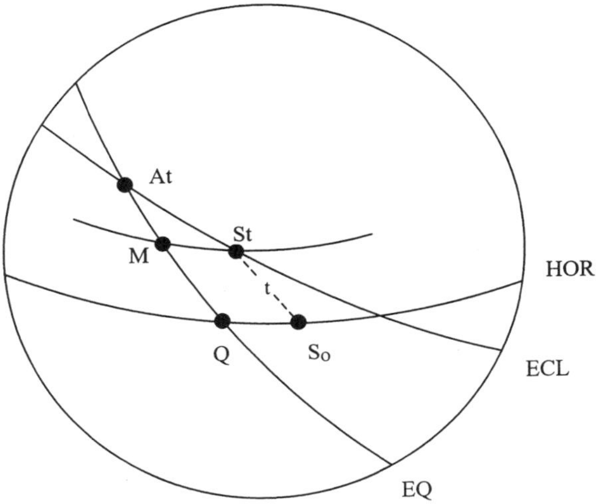

Fig. 2

[48] *Determination of the ascendant during the night*. As in [45] Ibn al-Ṣaffār determines the hour angle (*t*) since sunset. Then one should obtain the [oblique] ascension of the *naẓīr* of the solar degree, expressed in degrees and minutes, with precision (*bi-l-taᶜdīl*). The rest of the procedure is identical to what he has explained for daytime.

[49] *Determination of the House of the King (*malik*)* [upper midheaven]. Take the [oblique] ascension with which you obtained the ascendant, [an arc] the starting point of which is Aries, and look for this value in a table of right ascensions. Calculate the inverse right ascension, expressed in degrees of ecliptic longitude and the result will be the longitude of midheaven.

[He is obviously applying the well known equation: $\alpha(X) = \alpha_{\Phi}(H) - 90^o$. The table of right ascension he uses does not start, however, in Aries but in Capricorn. What he is saying, therefore, is: $\alpha(X) + 90^o = \alpha_{\Phi}(H)$.]

[50] *Determination of the House of Fortune* (saᶜāda) [XI House]. "If you want to establish the House of Fortune, take the times of the hours of the degree of the ascendant, no matter whether it is in daytime or during the night. Double them once" and add it to the [oblique] ascension you used to calculate the longitude of the ascendant and of midheaven. Find the inverse right ascension of this value. The result, expressed in ecliptic degrees, will be the degree of Fortune from the sign in which your computation ended.

[The text, the beginning of which has been translated litterally, does not state clearly that the double hour of the ascendant should be a daylight hour. The meaning of the whole sentence seems ambiguous to us and it makes us think of the possibility of interpreting "no matter whether it is in day time or during the night" as if the author of the text considered that the practising astrologer might choose freely between day and night hours of the ascendant, contrary to the standard custom. No more information will be obtained below (in [53] and [54]), where night hours of the ascendant should be required to obtain the beginning of Houses II and III. Ibn Muᶜādh, in chapter 25 of his *Tabulae Jahen*, states clearly that one should use day hours in the computation of the beginnings of Houses XI and XII and the same can be found in Adelard's translation of al-Khwārizmī's canons [58]. Ibn al-Muthannā's commentary, however, does not seem so clear in the Hebrew translation and, apparently, uses night hours (instead of day hours) in the Latin translation [59].]

[51] *Determination of the House of Misfortune* (shaqā') [XII House]. The two temporal hours are added to the right ascension of the XI House. The rest as in [50].

[52] *A check of the previous computation.* If the two temporal hours are added to the right ascension of the XII House and the result is the right ascension of the ascendant, the previous computation is correct. Otherwise, it should be repeated.

[53] *Determination of the House of Richness* (māl) [II House]. The two temporal hours should be subtracted from 60°. The remainder is added to the right ascension of the ascendant. Find the inverse right ascension of the result and we will obtain the beginning of House II.

[58] Suter, *Tafeln*, 25; Neugebauer, *al-Khwārizmī*, 76-77.

[59] B.R. Goldstein, *Ibn al-Muthannâ*, 85-86; E. Millás, *Ibn al-Muṯannā*, 150-151. This latter text seems to imply an error for, after mentioning "the times of the hours of the degree of the ascendant during the night" (*tempora horarum gradus orientis nocte*), he starts to explain the procedure to obtain the right ascension of House XI from the right ascension of House X and successively.

[See above [50]. Obviously the degrees of rotation which correspond to two day hours plus two night hours will always equal 60°. There is something missing in the corresponding passage of Ibn Muʿādh's *Tabulae Jahen* for it states "add 60° to the ascensions of House XII and the result will be the ascensions of the House II (...). Add 120° to the ascensions of House [II] and the result will be the ascensions of House III".] [60]

[54] *Determination of the House of Brothers (*ikhwa*)* [III House]. Adding the same remainder obtained in [53] to the right ascension of House II, we will obtain the right ascension of House III and operate following the same routine.

The text finishes with the sentence: "End of the canons (*risāla*) of Ibn al-Ṣaffār's *zīj*".

60 Chapter 25 of Nuremberg's edition: "Deinde adde super ascensiones duodecimae sexaginta, et erunt ascensiones domus secundae. (...) Deinde adde super ascensiones domus centum et uiginti et erunt ascensiones domus tertiae".

Fig. 3. - Ms. Paris, Biblioth

nale heb. 1102, fols 3^r and 3^v.

Appendix

In the present edition, we have transliterated the text preserved in manuscript Paris B.N. heb. 1102, fols 1-5^r, into Arabic characters.

Table 1 presents the system of transcription which has been used and tries to represent the Hebrew paleographical characteristics of the manuscript. The symbols representing the glottal stop consonant, *hamza*, and the necessary *shadda* have been added.

The edition tries to present a legible text according to principles of standard grammar. The language of the text shows good agreement with the main features of Judaeo-Arabic as analyzed in numerous studies by J. Blau [1].

Chapter headings also appear in the original, but we have used bold characters to distinguish them clearly from the text. We have added punctuation marks and divided the text into paragraphs.

Numbers between square brackets correspond to a division into sections to facilitate references in the commentary.

Square brackets have also been used for the editor's additions and comments on the manuscript. Three dots between brackets indicate the existence of a missing or an unreadable passage.

1 See, e.g., Joshua Blau, *The Emergence and Linguistic Background of Judaeo-Arabic. A Study of the Origins of Middle Arabic*, Oxford, 1965.

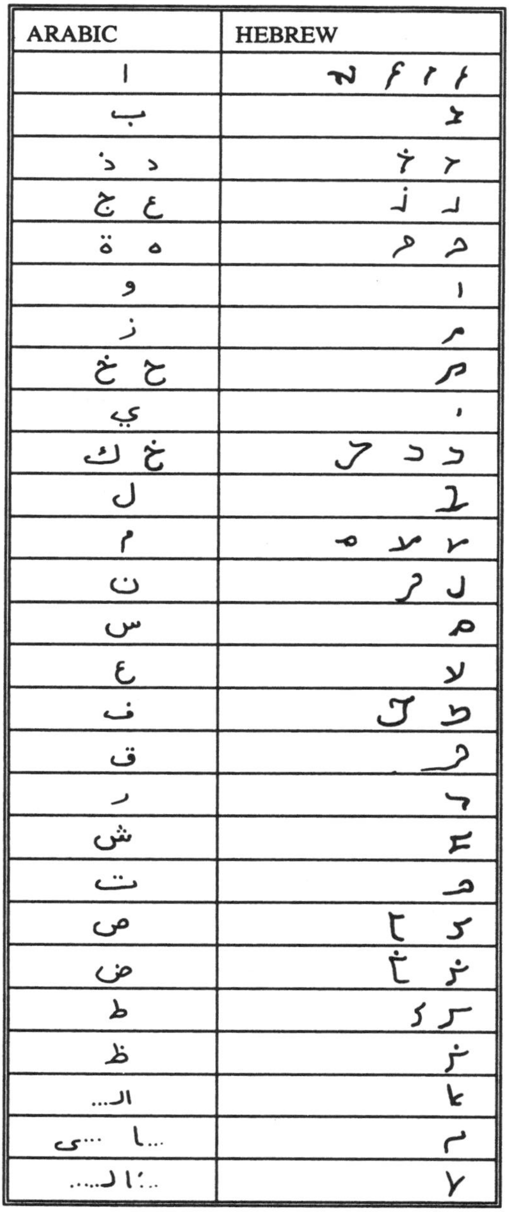
ARABIC
HEBREW
ا
ب
د ذ
ع ج
ه ة
و
ز
ح خ
ي
خ ك
ل
م
ن
س
ع
ف
ق
ر
ش
ت
ص
ض
ط
ظ
الـ...
...ـا ...ى
...ـلا...

Table 1

Arabic text

<1 r> [...] [1] فخذ ما بحيال حصّة العرض في كلّ
واحد من الموضعين واطرح أقلّ من أكثر كلّ واحد من
جنسه واعرف ما بينهما [2] ثمّ ادخل بحصة القمر المعدلّة
في سطري العدد من جدول النسبة وخذ ما بحيالها من دقائق
الفضل [3] واضرب تلك الدقائق في الفضل الذي حفظت من
الأصابع ودقائق المدّة ونصف المكث إن كنت أخذتـ[ـها]
[4] وتزيد ما اجتمع على ما كان بحيال الحصّة للعرض في
البعد الأبعد كلّ واحد على جنسه تكون ما يجتمع من
الأصابع هي أصابع الكسوف المعدلّة من قطر القمر وتكون
دقائق نصف المدّة ونصف المكث المعدلّة لوسط الكسوف
[5] ثمّ تزيد على دقائق نصف المدّة نصف سدسها وتقسم ذلك
على حركة القمر لساعة فما خرج فساعات ما من أول
الكسوف إلى وسطه [6] ثمّ تزيد على دقائق نصف المكث إن
كان مكث نصف سدسها وتقسمها على حركة القمر لساعة
فيكون نصف المدّة التي يمكث القمر أسود فاضعفها فتكون
ساعات ما يبقى القمر أسودا [كذا] [7] واضعف ساعات
نصف المدّة فيكون ذلك ما من أوّل بدء الكسوف إلى تمام
الانجلاء [8] وأسقط ساعات نصف المدّة من وسط الكسوف
فيكون ذلك أوّل ابتدائه وأسقط ساعات نصف المـ[...]

<1 v> [...] قبل [9] فإن كان الكسوف ليس له مكث
فادخل بالأصابع المنكسفة من القمر في سطر العدد من

جدول تعديل الأصابع وخذ ما بحيالها من أصابع تعديل القمر فما كان فهو أصابع ما ينكسف من جرمه إن شاء الله.

باب في معرفة أخذ طول البلد من وسط الأرض الذي وضع الاصل في هذا الكتاب عليه

[10] إذا أردت ذلك فعدّل الكسوف القمري إذا كان على نصف نهار البلد الذي وضع أصل هذا الكتاب عليه [11] واعرف بالتعديل بعد ابتداء الكسوف أو انجلائه من نصف النهار الذي يتلوه ليلة الكسوف لساعة معتدلة فإذا عرفت ذلك فاحفظه [12] ثمّ ارتقب في بلدك بالاسترلاب[1] بعد ابتداء الكسوف من نصف نهار بلدك [أ]و وقت انجلائه لساعة معتدلة [13] وخذ فضل ما بين الابتدائين من الساعات المعتدلة أو فضل ما بين الانجلائين أيهما عدّلت وارتقبه فماكان من الـ[ـساعا]ت وكسوفها فهو اختلاف ما بين بلدك وبين البلد الذي [وضع الأصل في هذا الكتاب عليه] [...] درجات إن شئت <2 r> ساعات وخمس ساعات معتدلة [14] وضعت الأصل في جدول الاجتماعات والاستقبالات التي في هذا الكتاب على نصف نهار قرطبة فإذ أكملت تعديل الكسوف على نصف نهار قرطبة فزد على وقته أربع ساعات وخمس ساعة معتدلة فإن الوقت لوسط الأرض إن شاء الله.

---

1. هكذا مكتوب بحرفي ם وת في المخطوطة.

باب في معرفة اختلاف منظر القمر في الطول وساعات الاختلاف

[15] إذا أردت أن تعرف ساعات اختلاف منظر القمر فاعرف الطالع للوقت الذي تريد معرفة ذلك إن كان وقت الاجتماع الحقيقي أو غير الاجتماع [16] وانقص من الطالع ثلاثة بروج فما بقي فهو وسط سماء الطالع [17] فادخل به في مطالع الفلك المستقيم وخذ ما بحيالها من المطالع واحفظه ثمّ ادخل أيضا بموضع القمر في مطالع الفلك المستقيم وخذ ما بحيالها من المطالع واعرف ما بينهما وبين الذي حفظت أوّلا من الدرجات فذلك ما بين موضع القمر ووسط سماء الطالع من درج معدّل النهار [18] فادخل بها في سطور العدد من جدول اختلاف المنظر وخذ ما بحيالها من ساعات اختلاف المنظر فما كان منها فهو ساعات اختلاف ما بين ذلك الوقت الذي عدّلت القمر له وبين الوقت الذي يرى فيه القمر في موضعه [19] فاضرب ذلك الساعات في حركة القمر المعدّلة لساعة فما خرج من الدقائق والثواني فهو اختلاف منظر القمر في الطول [20] ثمّ انظر فإن كان القمر فيما بين وسط سماء الطالع وبين الطالع فزد اختلاف منظر القمر على موضع القمر المعدّل [21] وإن كان القمر فيما بين الغارب ووسط سماء الطالع فانقصه من موضع القمر المعدّل [22] فما كان من موضع القمر بعد الزيادة او النقصان فهو موضع القمرالمرئي من فلك البروج إن شاء الله.

باب في معرفة اختلاف منظر القمر في العرض

[23] إذا أردت ذلك فاعرف الطالع للوقت الذي تريد معرفة ذلك إن كان وقت الاجتماع أو غير وقت الاجتماع [24] وانقص <v 2> من الطالع ثلاثة بروج فما بقي فهو وسط سماء الطالع [25] واعرف ميله وناحية الميل [26] فإن كان الميل شماليا فانقصه من عرض بلدك وإن كان جنوبيا فزد عليه فإن كان الميل أكثر من عرض البلد فانقص العرض من الميل فما كان بعد الزيادة أو النقصان فهو بعد درجة [وسط] سماء الطالع من سمت الرؤوس [27] ثمّ اعرف ما يكون من عرض القمر لو أنت في درجة وسط سماء الطالع وذلك أن تستخرج وسط الجوزهر لذلك الوقت وتزيد على درجة وسط سماء الطالع أو تعرف بما يجتمع عرض القمر لو أنت في الدرجة التي ذكرنا [28] فما كان من العرض فانظر إن كان شماليا فانقصه من البعد الذي حفظت وإن كان جنوبيا فزد عليه فما كان بعد الزيادة أو النقصان فهو بعد القمر من سمت الرؤوس لو أنت في درجة وسط سماء الطالع [29] فادخل بذلك البعد في سطر العدد من جدول اختلاف المنظر وخذ ما بحياله من اختلاف المنظر في العرض فما كان من الدقائق والثواني فهو اختلاف منظر القمر في العرض واعلم أنت متى كان البعد الذي دخلت به لتعرف اختلاف المنظر جنوبيا من سمت الرؤوس فاختلاف المنظر الذي أردت جنوبي وإن كان البعد شماليا فاختلاف المنظر الذي أردت شمالي إن شاء الله.

باب في معرفة تعديل كسوف الشمس

[30] إذا أردت معرفة كسوف الشمس فاعرف الاجتماع الحقيقي المعدّل الذي يكون نهارا والشمس قريبة من الرأس أو الذنب [31] واعرف حصّة العرض المعدّلة ثمّ اعرف الطالع لذلك الوقت واعرف منه وسط سماء الطالع [32] ثمّ اعرف من وسط سماء الطالع ساعات اختلاف منظر القمر في العرض واعرف أيضا اختلاف منظره في الطول كلّ ذلك على ما تقدّم [33] ثمّ انظر فإن كان موضع الاجتماع فيما بين وسط الطالع وبين الطالع فانقص <3 r> اختلاف المنظر في الطول من موضع الاجتماع وانقص ساعات اختلاف المنظر من ساعات الاجتماع وإن كان موضع الاجتماع فيما بين الغارب ووسط سماء الطالع فزد اختلاف المنظر في الطول على موضع الاجتماع وزد ساعات اختلاف المنظر على ساعات الاجتماع فما كان موضع الاجتماع بعد الزيادة عليه أو النقصان منه فهو موضع القمر المرئي من فلك البروج وما كان من ساعات الاجتماع الحقيقي بعد الزيادة عليها أو النقصان منها فهي ساعات الاجتماع المرئي وهي ساعات وسط الكسوف [34] وزد اختلاف المنظر في الطول على حصّة العرض للاجتماع إن كنت زدته على موضع الاجتماع أو انقصه منها إن كنت نقصته فيكون حصّة العرض لوسط الكسوف.

[35] ثمّ خذ من اختلاف المنظر في الطول جزءا من ثلاثة

عشر وزد على موضع الاجتماع إن كنت زدت اختلاف المنظر أو انقصه منها إن كنت نقصته فما كان من ذلك فهو موضع الشمس لوسط الكسوف [36] ثمّ اعرف اختلاف منظر القمر في العرض لوقت وسط الكسوف على ما تقدّم في بابه واعرف جهته وهو جنوبي أبدا في قرطبة وفي كلّ بلد لا يجوز القمر فيه الى ناحية الشمال من سمت الرؤوس [37] واضربه في اثني عشر وثلاثة أرباع فما اجتمع فاحفظه ثمّ انظر فإن كان اختلاف [المنظر] في العرض جنوبيا والاجتماع عند عقدة الرأس فانقص الذي اجتمع من الضرب من حصّة العرض لوسط الكسوف وإن كان الاجتماع عند عقدة الذنب فزده وإن كان اختلاف المنظر شماليا فاعمل بالمجتمع خلاف ذلك تزيد على حصّة العرض إن كان الاجتماع عند عقدة الرأس وإن كان عند عقدة الذنب تنقصه فما كان من حصّة العرض بعد الزيادة أو النقصان هي حصّة العرض لموضع القمر المرئي وهي التي يعرف بها قدر الكسوف [38] فادخل بها في جدول الكسوفات الشمسية

<3 v> فإن كان القمر في بعده الأبعد فادخل بها في جدول الكسوفات الشمسية للبعد الأبعد وخذ ما بحيالها من أصابع أو من دقائق نصف المدّة وإن كان القمر في بعده الأقرب فادخل بها في جداول الكسوفات الشمسية للبعد الأقرب وخذ ما بحيالها ممّا ذكرت لك فإن لم يكن القمر في أحد هذين الموضعين فخذ ما بحيال حصّة العرض في كلّ واحد من الجدولين واعرف فضل أحدهما على الآخر من كلّ واحد من الذين أخذت واحفظ الفضلتين للأصابع ولدقائق نصف

المدّة .

[39] ثمّ ادخل بحصّة القمر المعدّلة للاجتماع الحقيقي في جدول النسبة وخذ ما بحيالها من دقائق الفضل فما كان فاضربه في الفضلتين التين حفظت أعني فضلة الأصابع على الأصابع ودقائق نصف المدّة على دقائق نصف المدّة فما اجتمع من الضرب فزده على الذي كان بحيال حصّة العرض من البعد الأبعد كلّ واحد على جنسه فما اجتمع من الأصابع فهو ما ينكسف من قطر الشمس [40] ثمّ خذ دقائق نصف المدّة بعد الزيادة التي زدت عليهَا واحمل عليها نصف سدسها واقسم ما اجتمع على حركة القمر لساعة فما خرج فساعات نصف مدّة الكسوف فانقصها من ساعات وسط الكسوف فما بقي فساعات ابتداء الكسوف وزدها أيضا على ساعات وسط الكسوف فما اجتمع فهي ساعات تمام الانجلاء [41] وادخل بالأصابع التي حفظت من القطر في سطر العدد من جدول تعديل الأصابع وخذ ما بحيالها من تعديل أصابع الشمس فما كان منها فهو أصابع ما ينكسف من جرمها إن شاء الله.

[42] وتعرف إن كان القمر في بعده الأبعد إن تكون حصّة الاجتماع الحقيقي يب برجا أو أقلّ من ذلك <4 r> قليلة أو أكثر قليلة [فـ]ـيكون في بعده الأقرب إذا كانت الحصّة التي ذكرنا ستّة بروج أو أكثر منها قليلة أو أقلّ قليلة إن شاء الله.

باب في معرفة تعديل الأيام بلياليها

[43] إذا أردت أن تصرف الأيّام المختلفة [إلى الـ]ـوسطى فاعرف مكان الشمس لذلك التأريخ الذي اردت معرفة ذلك له وادخل بدرجتها في جداول تعديل الأيّام بلياليها وخذ ما بحيالها من دقائق الساعة فما كان فانقصه من أيّام التأريخ الذي معك فما بقي من الأيام والساعات فذلك أيّام وسطى لذلك التأريخ [44] وإن اردت صرف الأيّام الوسطى إلى المختلفة فاعرف أيضا مكان الشمس للتأريخ الذي أردت معرفة ذلك له وخذ ما بحيالها من دقائق الساعة في الجدول لتعديل الأيّام بلياليها وزد على ما معك من الأيام تكون مختلفة ان شاء الله.

باب في معرفة إقامة الطالع والبيوت الاثني عشر

[45] إذا أردت أن تقيم الطالع بالنهار فخذ ما مضى من النهار من ساعة وكسر إن كان كسر إلى الوقت الذي تريد ثمّ انظر إن كانت ساعاتك معوّجة فاضربها في أجزاء ساعات يومك وإن كانت ساعات مستوية فاضربها في $\overline{\text{طو}}$ فما بلغ من

الدرج[2] والدقائق فهو ما دار الفلك مذ طلعت الشمس إلى الساعة التي أردت [46] ثمّ خذ مطالع درجة الشمس وزد عليه الذي دار الفلك [47] فما اجتمع فاطلب مثله في سطر المطالع من مطالع بلدك فحيثما وجدت مثله أو ما هو أقرب إليه ممّا هو أقلّ منه فانقصه ممّا اجتمع وقوّسه وخذ ما له من سطر درج السواء واعلم من أي برج هو فما خرج لك فهو الطالع بالدرج المستوية من البرج الذي انتهيت إليه فإن كان ما بقي معك شيء فاضربه في ستين واقسمه على فضل ما بين الباب الذي صرت إليه والباب الذي أسفل منه بدرجة فما خرج لك فدقائق فزدها على درج الطالع التامّة فما اجتمع من الدرج والدقائق فهو الطالع للوقت الذي أردت وهذا هو التقويم للطالع مثل تقويم الجيب.

<4 v> [48] فإذا أردت معرفة الطالع بالليل فاضرب ما مضى من الليل من ساعة إن كانت معوّجة في أجزاء ساعات ليلتك وإن كانت مستوية ففي طو فما اجتمع فهو ما دار الفلك من درج والدقائق مذ غاب الشمس إلى الساعة التي أردت ثمّ خذ مطالع نظير درجة الشمس ودقيقتها بالتعديل كما أريتك وزد عليها الذي دار من الفلك منذ غابت الشمس إلى ساعة القياس فما بلغ فاطلب مثله في سطر المطالع و قوّسه كما عملت في مطالع النهار فما خرج فهو الطالع من البرج الذي انتهيت إليه من الدرج والدقائق إن شاء الله.

[49] وإذا أردت أن تقيم بيت الملك الذي هو وسط

---

2. هنا يظهر "من الدقائق" مشطوبا في المخطوطة.

السماء فخذ المطالع التي أقمت بها الطالع وهي من أوّل الحمل إلى درجة المطالع فاطلب مثله في سطر مطالع الفلك المستقيم فحيثما أصبت مثله فقوّسه إلى سطر درج السواء فما خرج لك فهو درجة وسط السماء من البرج الذي انتهيت إليه.

[50] فإذا أردت أن تقيم بيت السعادة فخذ أزمان ساعات درجة الطالع كان ليلة أو نهارا واضعفها مرة ثمّ زدها على المطالع التي استخرجت بها الطالع ووسط السماء فما اجتمع فاطلب مثله في مطالع الفلك المستقيم فحيثما أصبت مثله فقوّسه إلى درج السواء فما كان فهي درجة السعادة من البرج الذي انتهيت إليها.

[51] فإذا أردت أن تقيم بيت الشقاء فخذ أزمان ساعات درجة الطالع المضاعفة وزدها على المطالع التي عرفت بها السعادة ثمّ اطلب مثلما اجتمع في مطالع(3) الفلك المستقيم فحيثما أصبت مثله فقوّسه إلى درج السواء فما وجدت فهي درجة الشقاء من ذلك البرج [52] ثمّ زد الأزمان المضاعفة على المطالع التي عرفت بها الشقاء واطلب مثله في مطالع الفلك المستقيم فحيث وفد فقوّسه إلى الدرج المستوية فما خرج لك فانظر <5 r> فإن كان موافقة لدرجة الطالع فقد أصبت وصح حسابك وإن خلف فقد أخطأت فاعد الحساب.

[53] وإذا أردت أن تقيم بيت المال فخذ الأزمان المضاعفة وانقصها من ستّين درجة فما بقي فزدها على

---

3. "المطالع" في المخطوطة ولكن يبدو أن آل التعريف مشطوبا.

المطالع التي انتهيت بها إلى درجة الطالع فما اجتمع فاطلب مثله في مطالع الفلك المستقيم فحيثما أصبت مثله فقوّسه إلى درج السواء فما خرج لك فهي درجة النسب [كذا] من البرج الذي انتهيت إليه.

[54] وإذا أردت أن تقيم بيت الإخوة فخذ البقية من الستّين وزدها على المطالع التي انتهيت بها إلى درج المال فما اجتمع فاطلب مثله في مطالع الفلك المستقيم فحيثما أصبت مثله فقوسه إلى درج السواء فما خرج فهو بيت الإخوة إن شاء الله.

تمّت رسالة زيج بن الصفّار

IBN AL-ZARQĀLLUH ON MERCURY

JULIO SAMSÓ and HONORINO MIELGO

The *Libro de las láminas de los siete planetas* contains the Alfonsine Castilian translation of two books on the construction of equatoria[1] by the Andalusian astronomers Abū-l-Qāsim b. al-Samḥ (d. 1035) and Abū Isḥāq Ibrāhīm b. Yaḥyā al-Naqqāsh (d. 1100, and known as Ibn al-Zarqālluh or Ibn al-Zarqiyāl (Azarquiel)).[2] These two treatises have recently been the object of a thorough study by Mercè Comes, who has also produced reliable editions of the Arabic text of Ibn al-Zarqālluh's treatise on the use of the instrument and of the fourteenth-century Italian translations of the Alfonsine texts.[3] One item in Ibn al-Zarqālluh's book on the construction of the equatorium that has attracted a certain amount of attention from modern scholarship is its description of the method used to draw Mercury's deferent which, in this instrument, is a non-circular curve.

The construction described in the Alfonsine translation[4] is as follows (*cf.* Figure 1, not to scale):

O is the centre of the plate (and the centre of the Universe),

E is the equant point, and

A is the centre of the small circle *AE*, the locus of the centres of Mercury's deferent ("çerco leuador del centro del leuador de Mercurio").

$AE = EO = 2;21^p$.

With *A* as centre and radius 81^p, circle *BDCG* is drawn and divided into 5° arcs. Circle *BDCG* is an auxiliary circle used to divide the small circle *AE*.

With *E* as centre and radius 80^p, circle *LDHG* (the equant circle) is also drawn and divided into 5° arcs.

Following this construction, points *I*, *J*, and *K* correspond to the first three divisions into 5° arcs of circle *AE*, starting clockwise from the apse line.

Points *L*, *M* and *N* correspond to the first three divisions into 5° arcs of the equant circle *LDHG*, starting anticlockwise from the apse line.

The first three points of the curve described by Ibn al-Zarqālluh will lie on lines *EL*, *EM* and *EN* respectively. The exact points (*O*, *P* and *Q*) will be determined by placing one of the ends of a pair of dividers successively on points *I*, *J* and *K* and, with radius $49;21^p$, tracing arcs which will intersect lines *EL*, *EM* and *EN*, respectively, on points *O*, *P* and *Q*.

Ibn al-Zarqālluh then draws an arc of a circle through the three aforementioned points and thereby obtains an approximation to the first portion of the curve described by the centre of Mercury's epicycle according to Ptolemy's model.[5] He continues the process until the figure is complete (see Figure 2, drawn

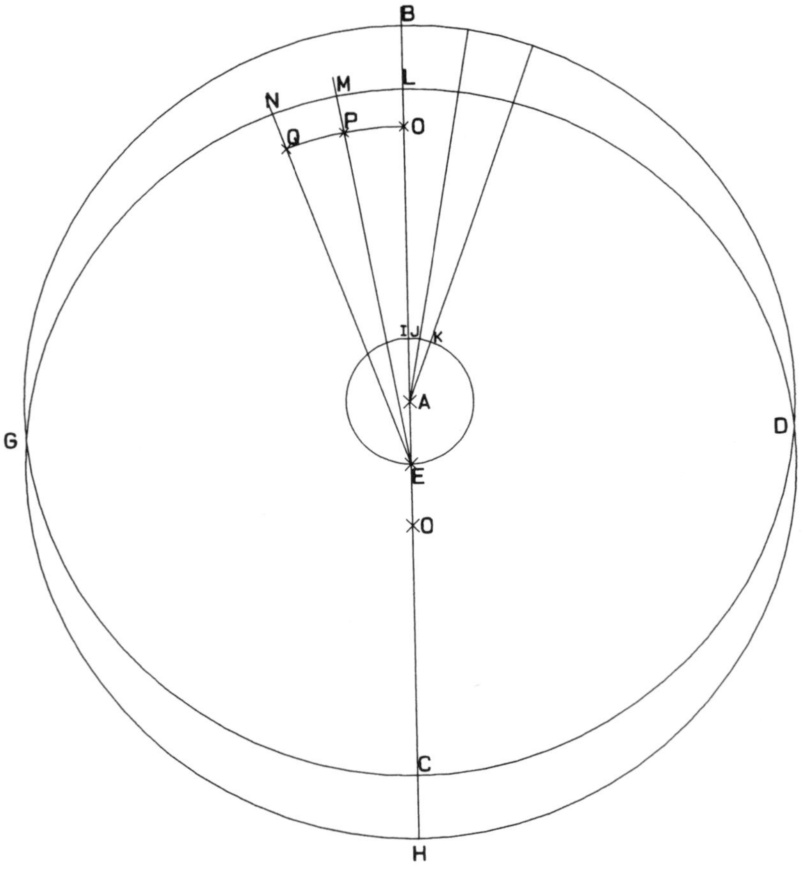

FIG. 1

to scale). The eccentricity will not be Ptolemaic: 2;21^p for a deferent radius of 49;21^p, corresponds to a normalized eccentricity of 2;51,26^p for a deferent radius of 60^p, which differs from the parameters used in the *Almagest* (3^p × 3), the *Planetary hypotheses* (2;30^p × 2 + 3^p) and the *Canobic inscription* (2;30^p × 3).[6]

The curve drawn following this procedure is described, in the Alfonsine translation of Ibn al-Zarqālluh's words, as follows: "et sera el çerco del leuador figura de taiadura menguada de las taiaduras que uienen en la figura pinnonata."[7] This passage cannot be translated without our first explaining two technical expressions which appear in it. The first is the *figura pinnonata* (*pineal figure*, shaped like a pine-cone) which attracted the attention of Willy Hartner, who considered that the oval shape of the curve resembles that of a pine-nut.[8] On the other hand, the curve is described as *bayḍī* (oval) in the Arabic text of Ibn al-Zarqālluh's

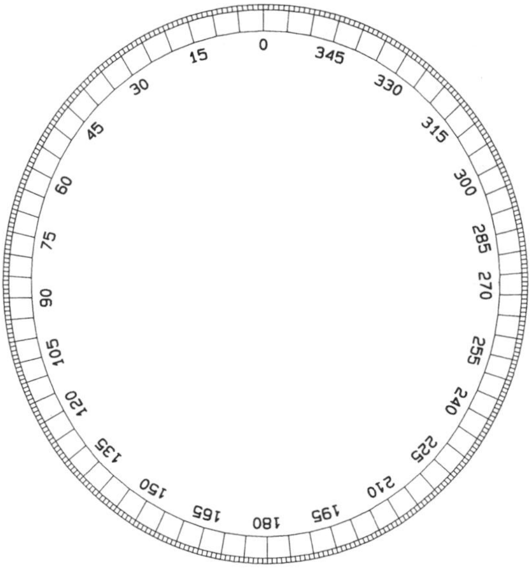

FIG. 2

book on the use of the equatorium,[9] which is a much less technical work. *Figura pinnonata* is, however, a literal translation of the Arabic *shakl ṣanawbarī* which means pineal figure but also conic figure.[10] In this sense the Alfonsine Latin (based on a previous Castilian) translation of Ibn al-Haytham's *Fī hay'at al-ᶜālam* (*On the physical structure of the world*) uses systematically *figura pinee / figura pineata / pineatum* to convey the meaning of conic figure or cone in passages in which the Arabic equivalent is *makhrūṭ* (the most common word for cone) or a term derived from this word.[11]

The second expression that deserves commentary is *taiadura menguada. Taiadura* derives from *taiar* (modern Spanish "tallar", "tajar", *cf.* French "tailler") and, therefore, means a cut or a section (Arabic *qaṭᶜ*). *Menguada* is a participle of the verb *menguar* (to diminish or reduce), and thus *taiadura menguada* is a literal translation of the Arabic *qaṭᶜ nāqiṣ* (deficient section), which is the standard Arabic expression for ellipse.[12] The translation of the aforementioned Alfonsine Castilian text is, then: "The deferent circle will have the shape of the deficient section [ellipse], of those sections which appear in the *pineal figure* [cone]."

In his famous paper first published in 1955, Hartner established that the curve described by the centre of Mercury's epicycle becomes practically identical with an ellipse when the parameters of the *Almagest* are used and that the situation does not change with Ibn al-Zarqālluh's slight modification of Ptolemaic parameters; he also stated that the Alfonsine translation of Ibn al-Zarqālluh's lost Arabic original is the first explicit description of the curve of Mercury's true deferent.[13] Now we also know that Ibn al-Zarqālluh identified this curve as an ellipse and this is the first instance, to the best of our knowledge, of the use of such a conic section in astronomy, even if the eleventh-century Toledan astronomer had no theoretical pretensions in his use of an ellipse[14] and employed it only to simplify his design of an equatorium.

A systematic attempt has been made, however, to see if a model based on an elliptic deferent could have been used to calculate the tables of equations for Mercury in Andalusian,[15] medieval Spanish[16] and Maghribī[17] astronomical tables. This would have made sense for the computation of the interpolation function (k_4 in Neugebauer's notation[18]), which — in the tradition of the *Handy tables* — cannot be calculated in a straightforward way because of the difficulty of the computation of the geocentric distance of the centre of the epicycle as a function of the true centre (and not the mean centre as in the *Almagest*). An exact method of calculation of the interpolation function leads to a sixth-degree equation, and a considerable simplification (a second-degree equation) is obtained if we assume an elliptic deferent. The results obtained have been negative: all the tables considered derive their Mercury equation tables from the *Handy tables.*[19]

Ibn al-Zarqālluh's treatise on the construction of the equatorium seems not to be the only instance in which this astronomer became interested in the study of Mercury. A surprising page written by the well-known philosopher, physicist and mathematician Abū Bakr b. Bājja (1070?–1138), usually considered to be one of the inspirers of the return to homocentric astronomy principally represented by al-Biṭrūjī (*fl.* 1185–92),[20] severely attacks both Ibn al-Zarqālluh and the famous physicist Ibn al-Haytham (945–*c.* 1040) for their criticism of Ptolemaic doctrines. This text appears in a letter addressed by Ibn Bājja to his friend the physician Abū Jaᶜfar Yūsuf b. Ḥasdāy[21] in which he explains his *curriculum studii.*[22] His criticism of Ibn al-Haytham centres on the latter's *Shukūk ᶜalā Baṭlīmūs/ Baṭlamiyūs* (*Doubts on Ptolemy*)[23] while, in the case of Ibn al-Zarqālluh, Ibn Bājja refers to an otherwise unknown short treatise on the nullity of the method used by Ptolemy to determine the position of Mercury's apogee.[24] No further information is available, but one may wonder whether Ibn al-Zarqālluh was conscious of the error Ptolemy made in establishing the line of apsides for Mercury.[25] There is however some indirect evidence that Ibn al-Zarqālluh may have made a new determination of Mercury's apogee.

An analysis of the numerical parameters underlying Ibn al-Zarqālluh's revision of the *Almanac,* calculated by the otherwise unknown Awmātiyūs, shows that they are basically Ptolemaic.[26] Table 1 displays the *Almanac*'s calculations of the planetary apogees (column 1), the longitudes of these apogees in the *Almagest* (xi, 1, 5 and 7) (column 2) and the differences between them (column 3):

TABLE 1.

Planets	*Almanac*	*Almagest*	*Almanac–Almagest*
	°	°	°
Saturn	235	233	2
Jupiter	162	161	1
Mars	117	115;30	1;30
Venus	87	55	32
Mercury	210	190	20

If we use a Ptolemaic value for precession and consider the cases of Saturn, Jupiter and Mars, column 3 seems to imply that the original work was composed between 100 and 200 years after the time of Ptolemy, that is to say in the third or fourth century. The apogees of Mercury and Venus seem, however, anomalous. We think the clue to the riddle can be found in Venus's apogee where a longitude of 87° is particularly suspicious if we remember that Ibn al-Zarqālluh established that the longitude of the solar apogee was 85;49° in observations made in 1074–75[27] and that Islamic astronomy inherited from the *Zīj al-Shāh*, from the ninth century onwards, the identification of the apogee of Venus with the solar apogee.[28] We may wonder whether Venus's apogee in the *Almanac* was 86° instead of 87°, and whether Ibn al-Zarqālluh made a new determination of the longitude of Mercury's apogee in connection with his criticism of Ptolemy's method mentioned by Ibn Bājja. This hypothesis poses serious problems for it implies that Ibn al-Zarqālluh left parts of this *Almanac* (superior planets) uncorrected, with planetary apogees calculated for the third or fourth century, but revised the tables for the inferior planets and the Sun and used apogees for his own time.[29]

If this hypothesis corresponds to the truth, in spite of all the difficulties, Ibn al-Zarqālluh's determination of the longitude of Mercury's apogee would imply a certain improvement on the one in the *Almagest*. It is a pity that Andalusian astronomers did not pay attention to a much better value extant in al-Khwārizmī's *zīj*: 224;54° for the longitude of Mercury's apogee at the beginning of the Hijra (midday, 14 July 622).[30] With the *Handy tables* we obtain, for A.D. 622 / 945 of Philip's Era, a longitude for Mercury's apogee of 194;50°, which is 30;04° below the apogee of the *Sindhind* tradition.

Acknowledgements

This paper has been written within a research programme on "Astronomical Theory and Tables in al-Andalus in the 10th and 11th centuries", sponsored by the Dirección General de Investigación Científica y Técnica of the Spanish Ministerio de Educación y Ciencia. Juan Vernet, E. S. Kennedy and John North have read a draft of this paper and offered useful suggestions. Owen Gingerich has sent to us photocopies of publications that were inaccessible to us. Our gratitude to all of them.

REFERENCES

1. For a good survey of medieval and Renaissance equatoria see Emmanuel Poulle, *Les instruments de la théorie des planètes selon Ptolémée: Equatoires et horlogerie planétaire du XIIIe au XVIe siècle* (2 vols, Geneva and Paris, 1980).
2. Manuel Rico y Sinobas, *Libros del saber de astronomía del rey D. Alfonso X de Castilla*, iii (Madrid, 1864), 241–84. On these two astronomers see Julio Samsó, *Las ciencias de los antiguos en al-Andalus* (Madrid, 1992), 80–84, 105–10, 147–52, 166–240.
3. Mercè Comes, *Ecuatorios andalusíes: Ibn al-Samḥ, al-Zarqālluh y Abū-l-Ṣalt* (Barcelona, 1991). On the basis of this study the two instruments were reconstructed by M. Comes and H. Mielgo for the exhibition "El legado científico andalusí" held in Madrid (Museo Arqueológico Nacional) in April-May 1992. Photographs of these reconstructions appear in J. Vernet and J. Samsó (eds), *El legado científico andalusí* (Madrid, 1992), 77, 211, 212. Two sets of copies of both instruments were made and they are kept in the Museo Nacional de la Ciencia y de la Técnica (Madrid) and in the Arabic Department of the University of Barcelona.
4. Rico, *Libros*, iii, 278–80. The method used to draw the curve was described by Willy Hartner in "The Mercury horoscope of Marcantonio Michiel of Venice: A study in the history of Renaissance astrology and astronomy", *Oriens-occidens* (Hildesheim, 1968), 440–95, pp. 476–7; see also Comes, *Ecuatorios*, 117–23.
5. On Ptolemy's model for Mercury see Otto Neugebauer, *A history of ancient mathematical astronomy* (Berlin, 1975), 158–82; Olaf Pedersen, *A survey of the Almagest* (Odense, 1974), 309–28.
6. On Ibn al-Zarqālluh's eccentricity see Willy Hartner's two papers reprinted in the volume *Oriens-occidens II* (Hildesheim, 1984): "Ptolemy, Azarquiel, Ibn al-Shāṭir and Copernicus on Mercury: A study of parameters" (pp. 292–312); "The Islamic astronomical background to Nicholas Copernicus" (pp. 316–25); see also Comes, *Ecuatorios*, 119–20.
7. Comes, *Ecuatorios*, 117; Rico, *Libros*, iii, 279. The Italian fourteenth-century translation states: "e sarae il cerco del leuatore figura di talliatura iscemata ouer[o] tracta delle tagliature che ue(n)gono nella figura [blank in the manuscript]" (Comes, *Ecuatorios*, 198).
8. Hartner, "Trepidation and planetary theories: Common features in late Islamic and early Renaissance astronomy", in *Oriens-occidens II*, 267–87, pp. 282, 287.
9. Comes, *Ecuatorios*, 117, 207 ("ᶜalā shakl al-bayḍa wa huwa al-shakl al-maᶜrūf bi-l-bayḍī ᶜinda-l-ᶜārifīn bi-ᶜilm al-hay'a", "with the shape of an egg, which is the shape called oval by those who know astronomy"). See J. M. Millás, *Estudios sobre Azarquiel* (Madrid and Granada, 1943–50), 459.
10. Mohammed Souissi, *La langue des mathématiques en arabe* (Tunis, 1968), 221. This Arabic equivalent was communicated to W. Hartner, before 1969, by M. Schramm: see Hartner, "Trepidation and planetary theories", 287, n. 19.
11. J. Samsó, "El original árabe y la versión alfonsí del *Kitāb fī hay'at al-ᶜālam* de Ibn al-Hayṯam", in M. Comes, H. Mielgo and J. Samsó (eds), *"Ochava espera" y "Astrofísica": Textos y estudios sobre las fuentes árabes de la astronomía de Alfonso X* (Barcelona, 1990), 115–31, pp. 124–5. The Arabic edition of Ibn al-Haytham's book has been published by Y. Tzvi Langermann, *Ibn al-Haytham's On the configuration of the world* (New York and London, 1990). The Latin Alfonsine translation has been edited by José Luis Mancha, "La versión alfonsí del Fī hay'at al-ᶜālam (De configuratione mundi) de Ibn al-Hayṭam (Oxford, Canon. misc. 45, ff. 1r–56r)" in *"Ochava Espera" y "Astrofísica"*, 133–207.
12. See Souissi, *La langue des mathématiques en arabe*, 286; J. P. Hogendijk, *Ibn al-Haytham's Completion of the conics* (New York, 1985), 399; G. J. Toomer, *Apollonius Conics: Books V to VII. The Arabic translation of the lost Greek original in the version of the Banū Mūsā* (New York, 1990), ii, 875. Our friend and colleague, Dr Roser Puig, told us that the semi-ellipses that appear in the orthographic projection of the back of the *ṣafīḥa* [*saphea*/*açafeha*] *zarqāliyya* are called, in the Alfonsine text, *linnas* [= lines] *de taias minguadas*. See R. Puig, *Los tratados de construcción y uso de la azafea de Azarquiel* (Madrid, 1987), 20–22, and "La proyección ortográfica en el *Libro de la açafeha* alfonsí", in M. Comes, R. Puig and J. Samsó (eds), *De astronomia Alphonsi Regis* (Barcelona, 1987), 127.

13. Hartner, "Mercury horoscope", 465–78.
14. Hartner, "The Islamic astronomical background to Nicholas Copernicus", 319–20.
15. We have revised the Toledan Tables (Madrid National Library manuscript 9271 and Escorial ms. O–II–10), those of Ibn al-Kammād (Madrid National Library Latin ms. 10023) and the two *zījes* of Ibn al-Raqqām (mss. Istanbul Kandilli 249, Rabat General Library 260). On Ibn al-Kammād (*fl.* 1125) and Ibn al-Raqqām (d. 1315) see Samsó, *Ciencias de los antiguos*, 320–4, 414–15, 421–7.
16. Alfonsine Tables in the edition of Emmanuel Poulle (*Les tables alphonsines avec les canons de Jean de Saxe* (Paris, 1984)); Tables of Barcelona in the edition of J.M. Millás Vallicrosa (*Las tablas astronómicas del Rey Don Pedro el Ceremonioso* (Madrid and Barcelona, 1962)).
17. *Zījes* of Ibn Isḥāq (*fl.* 1200) (Hyderabad Andra Pradesh State Library ms. 298) and Ibn al-Bannā' al-Marrākushī (1256–1321) (ms. without number in the Madrid Museo Naval).
18. Neugebauer, *op. cit.* (ref. 5), 1003.
19. We have checked the editions by Abbé Halma (Paris, 1822–25) and by William D. Stahlman ("The astronomical tables of Codex Vaticanus Graecus 1291", Ph.D. dissertation, Brown University, 1959, available through University Microfilms).
20. Samsó, *Ciencias de los antiguos*, 330–60.
21. Ibn Abī Uṣaybiᶜa, *ᶜUyūn al-anbā' fi ṭabaqāt al-aṭibbā'*, ed. by Dār al-Fikr (Beirut, 1957), iii, 82–84 and 103. The identification has already been made by Jamāl al-Dīn al-ᶜAlawī, *Rasā'il falsafiyya li-Abī Bakr b. Bājja* (Beirut and Casablanca, 1983), 77 n. 1; S. Pines, "La dynamique d'Ibn Bajja", in *L'aventure de la science: Mélanges Alexandre Koyré I* (Paris, 1964), 442–68, p. 444, notes 7 and 8.
22. The text has been edited by al-ᶜAlawī, *Rasā'il*, 77–78.
23. He quotes in particular Ibn al-Haytham's criticism of the Ptolemaic method to determine the eccentricity of Venus and Mercury: see Ibn al-Haytham's *Shukūk* in the edition by A. I. Sabra and N. Shehaby (Cairo, 1971), 29ff. This is, incidentally and to the best of our knowledge, the first instance of an allusion to Ibn al-Haytham's *Shukūk* in al-Andalus.
24. "Maqāla fī ibṭāl al-ṭarīq allatī salaka-hā Baṭlīmūs fī istikhrāj al-buᶜd al-abᶜad li-ᶜUṭārid": ᶜAlawī's edition, 78.
25. Owen Gingerich states that Ptolemy erred by about 30°: see his paper "Mercury theory from Antiquity to Kepler", first published in 1971 and reprinted in the volume by the same author, *The eye of heaven: Ptolemy, Copernicus, Kepler* (New York, 1993), 379–87. Robert R. Newton (*The crime of Claudius Ptolemy* (Baltimore and London, 1977), 278–9) reaches a similar conclusion when he says that the longitude of Mercury's apogee should be about 219° in Ptolemy's time instead of the 190° we find in *Almagest* IX,7.
26. See Marion Boutelle, "The almanac of Azarquiel", reprinted in E.S. Kennedy *et al.*, *Studies in the Islamic exact sciences* (Beirut, 1983), 502–10. This paper should be read together with the important remarks by Noel Swerdlow in *Mathematical reviews*, xli (1971), no. 5149. For a general survey of this source see Samsó, *Ciencias de los antiguos*, 166–71.
27. According to Bernardus de Virduno: see G. J. Toomer, "The solar theory of az-Zarqāl: An epilogue", in D. A. King and G. Saliba (eds), *From deferent to equant: A volume of studies in the history of science in the ancient and medieval Near East in honor of E. S. Kennedy* (New York, 1987), 513–23. This value (like many others) has been confirmed by Ibn al-Hā'im (*fl.* in Seville at the beginning of the 13th century) in his *al-Zīj al-Kāmil fi-l-Taᶜālīm* extant in the manuscript Bodleian Library Marsh ms. 618, fol. 5v: *cf.* Samsó, *Ciencias de los antiguos*, 211; see also J. Samsó and E. Millás, "Ibn al-Bannā', Ibn Isḥāq and Ibn al-Zarqālluh's solar theory", reprinted in J. Samsó, *Islamic astronomy and medieval Spain* (Aldershot, 1994), no. X, p. 9.
28. Bernard R. Goldstein, "Remarks on Ptolemy's equant model", in *Prismata: Festschrift für Willy Hartner* (Wiesbaden, 1977), 165–81.
29. A further incongruity would be raised in the case of the Sun: G. J. Toomer ("The solar theory of az-Zarqal: A history of errors", in *Centaurus*, xiv (1969), 306–36, pp. 320–1) has calculated that Ibn al-Zarqālluh uses a sidereal solar apogee in the *Almanac* the longitude of which is 79;30°: the apogee longitude 85;49° mentioned by Ibn al-Hā'im and Bernardus de Virduno is, obviously, tropical.

30. O. Neugebauer, *The astronomical tables of al-Khwārizmī: Translation with commentaries of the Latin version edited by H. Suter supplemented by Corpus Christi College MS 283* (Copenhagen, 1962), 41, 99. Raymond Mercier ("Astronomical tables in the twelfth century" in Charles Burnett (ed.), *Adelard of Bath: An English scientist and Arabist of the early twelfth century* (London, 1987), 87–118, pp. 91–92) has proved the origin of this apogee longitude: with parameters of the *Brahmasphutasiddhanta* he obtains 224;53,13° for the beginning of the Hijra.

V

WORLD ASTROLOGY IN ELEVENTH-CENTURY AL-ANDALUS: THE EPISTLE ON *TASYĪR* AND THE PROJECTION OF RAYS BY AL-ISTIJJĪ[1]

JULIO SAMSÓ AND HAMID BERRANI

1. PRESENTATION

Manuscript Escorial 939 (fols. 9v-16r) contains the only extant copy of a short work on the *tasyīr* (progression) and the projection of rays by Abū Marwān 'Abd (or 'Ubayd) Allāh b. Khalaf al-Istijjī.[2] The *risāla* is dedicated to the 'honourable minister and judge Abū l-Qāsim' (*al-Wazīr al-jalīl al-qāḍī Abū l-Qāsim*) and there seems to be no doubt regarding the identification of the dedicatee, who is the famous Abū l-Qāsim Ṣā'id al-Andalusī (1029–70). In his *Ṭabaqāt al-Umam*, Ṣā'id mentions al-Istijjī twice:[3] as one of the 'young' astronomers working in Toledo at the time of the publication of the *Ṭabaqāt* (1068) and as a man who had a sound knowledge of astrology and had written a *Risāla fī l-tasyīrāt wa-maṭāriḥ al-shu'ā'āt wa-ta'līl ba'ḍ uṣūl al-sinā'a* ('On the *tasyīrs*,

[1] The present paper has been prepared within a research programme on 'Astronomical tables and theory in al-Andalus and the Maghrib between the twelfth and the fourteenth centuries', sponsored by the Dirección General de Investigación Científica y Técnica of the Spanish Ministry of Education and Culture. Josep Casulleras and Angel Mestres have read a previous draft of this paper and made very useful suggestions. They have also provided us with unpublished research works of their own which we have used here.

[2] See Derenbourg and Renaud, 1941, pp. 54–7; Vernet, 1971, p. 746; *G.A.S.* VII, pp. 195–6. A date appears in this manuscript (fol. 34r), in the colophon of an astrological text by Mahānkard b. Mahrubān, apparently an Arabic translation from the Persian (see *G.A.S.* VII, pp. 83 and 100), where we read: 'The copy was finished on Sunday or, better, Monday (*fī yawm al-aḥad, bal al-ithnayn*) 19 Dhū l-Ḥijja 813 of the Hijra, which corresponds to 13 April 1722 of Alexander Dhū l-Qarnayn'. The 19 Dhū l-Ḥijja 813 was actually a Tuesday and the equivalent dates are 14 Nisan 1722 of Alexander and 14 April AD 1411. The years are given in Fāsī ciphers.

[3] Ṣā'id, *Ṭabaqāt*, ed. Bū 'Alwān, pp. 180, 199–200; ed. Julāmriḍā Jamshīdnizād-i Awwal, pp. 256, 273; tr. Blachère, pp.139, 153–4.

the projection of rays and the justification of some foundations of this technique'), a work which he had sent to him from Cuenca. The identification of the text extant in the Escorial manuscript with the reference made by Ṣā'id in his *Ṭabaqāt* was made by Richter-Bernburg (1987, p. 377) who noted that Ṣā'id, being a *qāḍī* in Toledo, had the right to be called *wazīr*.

Abū Marwān 'Abd (or 'Ubayd) Allāh b. Khalaf al-Istijjī was identified by Millás (1940)[4] as the mysterious *Oueidalla el sabio* who appears as the author of the eleventh-century version of the astrological *Libro de las Cruzes* translated into Castilian in the time of Alfonso X.[5] This identification should be rejected today in view of the new evidence discovered by Castells (1992): a manuscript of the *al-Zīj al-Muṣṭalaḥ* (Egypt, thirteenth century) preserved in the Bibliothèque Nationale in Paris contains a reference to a *Kitāb al-ṣulub*, the author of which would be the otherwise unknown 'Abd Allāh b. Aḥmad al-Ṭulayṭulī who is, no doubt, the *Oueidalla* of the Alfonsine translation. Our information on al-Istijjī is, therefore, limited to the references given by Ṣā'id in his *Ṭabaqāt* and to the fact that the astronomer Ibn al-Hā'im al-Ishbīlī (*fl.* 1205) mentions, in his *al-Zīj al-Kāmil fī l-Ta'ālīm*, that al-Istijjī wrote a *Risālat al-iqbāl wa-l-idbār* ('On accession and recession')[6] on the subject of the theory of trepidation, a topic of great interest for the Toledan astronomers of the eleventh century: the *Risāla fī l-tasyīrāt* states clearly (fol. 12v) that the sphere of the fixed stars is submitted to the motion of accession and recession.

Ṣā'id praised very highly the competence of al-Istijjī as an astrologer and the importance of his *risāla*. He said that he was 'one of those who have a sound knowledge of astrology and who has read the books on this subject of both ancient and modern authors. I do not know of anybody in al-Andalus either in our time or before it who has obtained such results concerning the secrets and peculiarities of this art. He is the author of an excellent epistle on the *tasyīr*s, the projection of rays, and the justification of some foundations of this technique, a topic in which he has no predecessor'.[7] An analysis of the text does not justify such praise which seems, apparently, to be based on the fact that al-Istijjī had read a good deal of eastern bibliography on the subject, that he was probably the first to have summarized it in al-Andalus, and that his 'experiments' with astrological techniques had given an extra

[4] See also Millás in *Isis*, 19 (1933), 530.

[5] On the *Libro de las Cruzes* see Vernet, 1971, and Samsó, 1979 and 1983.

[6] Bodleian Library II, 2 MS 285 (Marsh 618) fol. 4r. See, on this topic, Samsó, 1994, pp. 3 and 28.

[7] Ṣā'id, *Ṭabaqāt*, ed. Bū 'Alwān, pp. 199–200; ed. Julāmriḍā Jamshīdnizād-i Awwal, p. 273; tr. Blachère, pp. 153–4.

justification to the soundness of the *Toledan Tables* prepared by Ṣā'id and his astronomical team. It is of some interest to analyse the eastern sources mentioned by al-Istijjī in his *risāla*, most of which are also quoted by Ṣā'id in the *Ṭabaqāt*.

Such is the case of Ptolemy's *Tetrabiblos* (fol. 13r)[8] and of an unnamed book of one of the Hermes (fol. 13v) where a method for the *tasyīr* and the projection of rays was described: the identification is easy, for Ṣā'id attributes, to Hermes the Babylonian, methods for the projection of rays and for the division of the houses of the horoscope[9] which were well known in the Andalusian astrological tradition. Far more problematic is the identification of a *Kitāb al-amthāl li-l-Furs* (fol. 12r, text and margin). This ends the list of early authorities, although in al-Istijjī's text we find an interesting reference to the mistakes made by translators which might be the cause of the errors of practising astrologers (fol. 15v). A similar remark can be found in an earlier Andalusian source: the *Taṣrīf*, the great medical encyclopaedia written by Abū l-Qāsim al-Zahrāwī (d. *c.* 1013) who complains of the incomprehensible works of the ancients (Hamarneh and Sonnedecker, 1963, p. 37).

Among eastern Islamic sources we find Kanka al-Hindī (*fl.* Baghdad *c.* 775–820),[10] who is quoted in relation to the theory of Saturn–Jupiter conjunctions (fol. 11v) although this quotation—like that of Hermes—is probably indirect both in al-Istijjī and in Ṣā'id's *Ṭabaqāt*:[11] their information on both authors probably reached them through the works of Abū Ma'shar (d. 886), which they seem to know well. This latter author is, no doubt, the most important authority used by al-Istijjī, who mentions his *Kitāb al-milal wa-l-duwal*, the *Kitāb al-qirānāt* (fol. 11v), the *Mudhakkarāt*, written by his disciple Shādhān (fol. 12r), and his *al-Madkhal al-kabīr*[12] (fol. 15r): all these books are also quoted by Ṣā'id in the *Ṭabaqāt*.[13] Al-Khaṣībī, the author of a *Kitāb taḥāwīl sinī al-mawālīd* (fol. 12r, 15v), is probably al-Ḥusayn/al-Ḥasan b. al-Khaṣīb (*fl.* 844), an author praised by Ṣā'id as the author of a *zīj* and of a

[8] Ṣā'id, *Ṭabaqāt*, ed. Bū 'Alwān, p. 88; ed. Julāmriḍā Jamshīdnizād-i Awwal, p. 181; tr. Blachère, p. 72. See *G.A.S.* VII, pp. 41–6.

[9] Ṣā'id, *Ṭabaqāt*, ed. Bū 'Alwān, p. 68; ed. Julāmriḍā Jamshīdnizād-i Awwal, p. 165; tr. Blachère, p. 55. See *G.A.S.* VII, pp. 50–8.

[10] See D. Pingree, 'Kanaka', in *Dictionary of Scientific Biography*, VII (New York, 1973), pp. 222–4, and *G.A.S.* VII, pp. 95–6. A quotation from Kanka al-Hindī appears in 'Umar b. Farrukhān's *Liber Universus*, a text which apparently circulated in Cordoba in the second half of the tenth century: see Pingree, 1977.

[11] Ṣā'id, *Ṭabaqāt*, ed. Bū 'Alwān, p. 59; ed. Julāmriḍā Jamshīdnizād-i Awwal, p. 158; tr. Blachère, p. 48.

[12] See the recent edition and study by Lemay, 1995–6.

[13] Ṣā'id, *Ṭabaqāt*, ed. Bū 'Alwān, pp. 142, 144–5; ed. Julāmriḍā Jamshīdnizād-i Awwal, p. 225, 227–8; tr. Blachère, pp. 111, 112–13. See *G.A.S.* VII, pp. 139–51.

good book on nativities (*mawālīd*).[14] A similar case is that of Aḥmad b. Yūsuf al-Kātib (d. 941) whose book 'On proportion and proportionality' (*Fī l-nisba wa-l-tanāsub*) is quoted both by al-Istijjī (fol. 15v) and by Ṣā'id.[15] Al-Istijjī also quotes al-Ḥasan b. Aḥmad b. Ya'qūb al-Hamdānī (d. 946) and his book entitled *Sarā'ir al-ḥikma* (fol. 10v margin, and fol. 12r). This author appears to have been well known in al-Andalus from the time of al-Ḥakam II (961–76) and he is frequently mentioned by Ṣā'id both as a historian and as an astrologer.[16] It is clear that al-Istijjī also knew the *zīj* of al-Battānī (d. 929) (fol. 13v)—a work which had circulated in al-Andalus since the time of Maslama al-Majrīṭī and which had been used for the compilation of the *Toledan Tables*[17]—and the *Rasā'il ikhwān al-ṣafa'* (fol. 11v), a work introduced in the Iberian peninsula by al-Kirmānī (d. 1066).[18] In fact, besides the already mentioned *Kitāb al-amthāl li-l-Furs*, the only source quoted by al-Istijjī which, apparently, was unknown to Ṣā'id is a book on astrological predictions by al-Kindī (d. *c*. 870), entitled *al-Madkhal al-awsaṭ* (fol. 12r, *G.A.S.* VII, pp. 130–4).

2. NEW EVIDENCE ON THE *TOLEDAN TABLES*

Some more information on al-Istijjī, Ṣā'id, and their works can be gathered from the text of the *Risāla fī l-tasyīrāt*. First of all the author confirms Ṣā'id's remark that the *risāla* had been sent to him from Cuenca: al-Istijjī (fol. 9v) states that he is physically separated from the *qāḍī* Abū l-Qāsim and that he has decided that written correspondence will take the place of conversation and epistolary exchange that of oral discussion (*fa-innī aradtu an uqīma al-mukhāṭaba maqām al-mukāmala wa-l-murāsala badl al-munāẓara*). Their separation took place after they had reached satisfactory results in their study of the anomalies of the motions of planets and fixed stars (*ikhtilāf ḥarakāt al-kawākib al-sayyāra wa-l-thābita*). Furthermore he states (fol. 14v) that 'We have

[14] Ṣā'id, *Ṭabaqāt*, ed. Bū 'Alwān, pp. 145–6; ed. Julāmriḍā Jamshīdnizād-i Awwal, p. 228; tr. Blachère, p. 113. See Suter, 1900, no. 62 (p. 32). See *G.A.S.* VII, pp. 122–4.

[15] Ṣā'id, *Ṭabaqāt*, ed. Bū 'Alwān, p. 146; ed. Julāmriḍā Jamshīdnizād-i Awwal, p. 228; tr. Blachère, p. 113. See Suter, 1900, no. 78 (pp. 42–3). See *G.A.S.* V, pp. 288–90; VII, p. 157.

[16] Ṣā'id, *Ṭabaqāt*, ed. Bū 'Alwān, pp. 66, 113, 118, 121, 147–9, 151; ed. Julāmriḍā Jamshīdnizād-i Awwal, pp. 163, 201–2, 206, 207, 229–31, 232; tr. Blachère, pp. 53, 89–90, 93, 95, 114–16, 117. See *G.A.S.* VII, pp. 164–5.

[17] Ṣā'id, *Ṭabaqāt*, ed. Bū 'Alwān, pp. 142–3; ed. Julāmriḍā Jamshīdnizād-i Awwal, p. 226; tr. Blachère, pp. 111–12.

[18] Ṣā'id, *Ṭabaqāt*, ed. Bū 'Alwān, p. 172; ed. Julāmriḍā Jamshīdnizād-i Awwal, p. 249; tr. Blachère, p. 132.

reached, thanks to God, a perfect knowledge of the reasons (*'ilal*) of the motions of celestial bodies and we know the cause (*sabab*) which leads to its irregularity (*ikhtilāf*). We have thus acquired an authentic understanding of things which nobody knew among those whose work and reputation has reached us.' All this seems to be an allusion to the problem posed by the recension of al-Khwārizmī's *zīj* prepared by Maslama al-Majrīṭī (d. 1007):[19] this *zīj* allowed the user to compute sidereal longitudes, but it did not explain how to obtain tropical longitudes which take into account the precession of the equinoxes. In his *Ṭabaqāt* Ṣā'id insisted that Maslama perpetuated the errors of al-Khwārizmī's *zīj*, as he himself had established in his book on the *Iṣlāḥ ḥarakāt al-kawākib/al-nujūm wa-l-ta'rīf bi khaṭā' al-rāṣidīn* ('Correction of the motion of stars and information about the errors of observers').[20] Al-Istijjī, then, bears witness to the fact that Ṣā'id and his group were dedicated to astronomical research, the main result of which was the famous *Toledan Tables* which included a set of tables based on the theory of trepidation: the reference to '[our] authentic understanding of things' not reached by anybody before the Toledan group seems to be an allusion to that theory, which was to become one of the outstanding characteristics of Andalusian and Maghribī astronomy until at least the fourteenth century.

In fact, our text remarks that the *zīj*es used are corrupt (the text talks about the *fasād al-zījāt*, fol. 13v), that they contain errors (*khaṭā' al-zījāt*, fol. 14v), that none of them can be used to calculate the *nimūdār* except 'our corrected *zīj*' (*zīju-nā al-muṣaḥḥaḥ*, fol. 15r), and that—as we shall see below—the astrological techniques of the *nimūdār* and the *tasyīr*s may be used to ascertain the veracity of this set of astronomical tables (fol. 15v). This 'corrected *zīj*' mentioned by al-Istijjī should be identified with the *Toledan Tables* and the information given by our author has a certain interest for the chronology of this work: Toomer (1968) made a thorough study of its contents, showing that very little in it was original and that only the mean motion tables appear to be based on fresh observations;[21] on the other hand Richter-Bernburg (1987, pp. 375–7 and 385–90) made the obvious, and extremely important, remark that the *Toledan Tables* were not mentioned by Ṣā'id in his *Ṭabaqāt*, in spite of his own personal involvement in the compilation of the *zīj*. Richter-Bernburg's conclusion was logical: the *Toledan Tables*, partly based on Toledan observations, were the result of a hasty

[19] On this *zīj* see the recent survey by van Dalen, 1996.

[20] Ṣā'id, ed. Bū 'Alwān, pp. 146–7 and 169; ed. Julāmriḍā Jamshīdnizād-i Awwal, pp. 156, 246–7; tr. Blachère, pp. 114 and 130.

[21] Ibn al-Hā'im insists on the Toledan observations in his *Kāmil Zīj*: see Calvo, 1998a, pp. 53, 55, 86.

adaptation of the best eastern tabular materials available, and the bulk of the job was done between the completion of the *Ṭabaqāt* (1068) and Ṣā'id's death (1070). This explanation, however, is at variance with the new evidence furnished by al-Istijjī's *risāla* which, combined with the reference to this work extant in the *Ṭabaqāt*, implies that the *Toledan Tables* were compiled earlier than 1068 and before the unknown date in which al-Istijjī left Toledo and established himself in Cuenca. We are, again, left with no explanation for Ṣā'id's omission of any reference to the tables in his historical work.

3. WORLD ASTROLOGY: *TASYĪRĀT* AND SATURN–JUPITER CONJUNCTIONS

Hindu-Iranian materials strongly influenced the origins of Islamic astronomy and astrology. Among the concepts introduced we find that of the cyclical recurrence of historical events and that of very long periods of time (world-years) marked by the repetition of most unusual planetary conjunctions. Thus, in the Persian tradition, the world-year period corresponds to 360,000 solar years between two conjunctions of all planets in Aries 0°: the beginning of the present world-year took place 180,000 solar years before the Flood. A world-year is divided into smaller periods of different lengths, usually called *tasyīrāt*, *intihā'āt*, and *fardārāt* (Kennedy, 1962; Kennedy and van der Waerden, 1963; Pingree, 1968).

The first known instance of the introduction of this kind of idea in al-Andalus apparently corresponds to the second half of the tenth century, and seems to be related to the work of Maslama al-Majrīṭī and his school: John of Seville translated into Latin (*c.* 1125–40) the *Liber Universus* of 'Umar b. Farrukhān al-Ṭabarī, a short tract dealing with the astrological period called the 'mighty *fardār*', which lasted 360 years. The current mighty *fardār*, in 'Umar's lifetime, began in AD 580 and was associated with the birth of the Prophet. The interesting thing for us, in this text, is that John of Seville's translation includes a reference to the beginning of the first mighty *fardār* after 580 (580 + 360 = 940) for which a horoscope had been cast for the latitude of Cordoba, using al-Khwārizmī's *zīj* in Maslama's recension. This agrees with other evidence we have of the fact that, towards the beginning of the eleventh century, Cordoban astrologers (Maslama was one of them) made predictions based on Saturn–Jupiter conjunctions, which form the basis of shorter astrological periods frequently used in astrological history.[22] Conjunctions of Saturn and Jupiter were used by Abraham bar Ḥiyya (*fl.* 1120–45) in his *Megillat ha-megalleh* (pp. 183–252), as the basis of his astrological history of Israel and of the Jewish people.

Al-Istijjī's title mentions the terms *tasyīr* (progression) and *maṭāriḥ al-shuʿāʿāt* (projection of rays). The *tasyīr* is an astrological technique normally used to determine the length of an individual's life. This is done by establishing the length of the arc between two points of the ecliptic, usually projected on the equator: one of them (called *al-mutaqaddim* or *al-haylaj*) is often the ascendant in the horoscope, while the second (*al-thānī* or *al-qāṭiʿ*) can be a planet, a star, a house in the horoscope, or one of the astrological lots which exert a bad influence on the individual and cause his death (Schirmer, 1934; Viladrich and Martí, 1983; Yano and Viladrich, 1991). The length of the life is established by giving an equivalence in time to each degree of the equator between the two aforementioned points. As for the projection of rays, it is a related astrological technique which assumes that a planet may 'project its rays' upon another zodiacal object when the two are at a fixed distance of 60° (*tasdīs*), 90° (*tarbīʿ*), or 120° (*tathlīth*) (Kennedy and Krikorian-Preisler, 1972; Hogendijk, 1989). Al-Istijjī's *risāla* deals with both techniques, in the sense described above, but when he deals with the *tasyīrāt*, he usually uses this term with a different meaning: long and short periods of time which divide the world year and which show a gradation affecting from world events to the life of the individual.

Our author begins by describing (fols. 10v–11r) the cycles usually called, in eastern sources, *intihāʾāt*, although he does not use this term. Their motion takes place on the ecliptic (Kennedy, 1962, p. 356):

1. [The mighty world-*intihāʾ*] which moves through a zodiacal sign in 1000 years. This cycle regulates events that affect the whole world: floods, drought, periods of anarchy, wars, deposition of kings, everything concerning moral rules and laws, as well as those (prophets and kings) who dictate them. The corresponding *tasyīr* advances 0;1,48° per year (=360°/12000) (fol. 12v).

2. [The big world-*intihāʾ*] which moves through a zodiacal sign in 100 years. It affects nations and parts of the world, events related to religions and their great personages, the transfer of power from one nation to another or from one dynasty to another. The corresponding *tasyīr* advances 0;18° per year (=360°/1200) (fol. 12r).

3. [The middle world-*intihāʾ*] which moves through a zodiacal sign

[22] See Samsó, 1979, pp. 229–30, on the conjunction of year 397/1006–7 which was interpreted as announcing the end of the Caliphate.

in ten years. It affects individuals because its period is 120 years which is the natural (*ṭabīʿī*) duration of human life. In fol. 12r he adds that the portion (*ḥiṣṣa*) which corresponds to one year is 3° (=360°/120 years) and that the [standard] duration of human life is between sixty and seventy years. The reason, as explained by al-Istijjī, is clear: if one uses as *haylaj* or *mutaqaddim* the ascendant of the horoscope cast at the moment of the birth of the subject, a *tasyīr* of 3° per year will result in an arc of 180° in sixty years, which implies that the *tasyīr* has reached the descendant of the same horoscope, a most unhappy place which acts as *thānī* or *qāṭiʿ* and produces death. Another reference to the 'natural length of human life' (*al-mudda al-ṭabīʿiyya li-l-insān*) appears in fol. 12v where it is said to last seventy-five years, a period identified with the *fardārāt* of the seven planets and of the ascending and descending lunar nodes:[23] the corresponding *ḥiṣṣa* for one year amounts to 4;48° (=360°/75).

4. [The small world-*intihā'*] which moves through a zodiacal sign in one year. It corresponds to the category of anniversaries or year-transfers (*taḥāwīl al-sinīn*). Individual men are submitted each year to the influence of one zodiacal sign, which is called *burj al-dawr*, *burj al-muntahā*, and *burj al-intihā'*. This is the kind of period that affects the horoscopes of nativities as well as the study of interrogations (*masā'il*) and elections (*ikhtiyārāt*). The *tasyīr* is 1° every $12\frac{1}{6}$ days (fol. 12r).

Al-Istijjī justifies the existence of such periods—based on the numerical series 1000–100–10–1—by using numerological speculation. There is complete agreement among all men of science that the sphere of the signs (ecliptic) is divided into four parts (equinoxes and solstices) and that, as each part has a beginning, a middle, and an end, it is obvious that the ecliptic is divided into twelve parts (zodiacal signs). These divisions are considered natural while other divisions of the sphere into degrees and minutes are merely conventional and the result of a free choice. The four main parts of the sphere also correspond to the four kinds of numbers: units, tens, hundreds, and thousands, while the division of the ecliptic into twelve signs has a natural correspondence with the fact that there are only twelve names for the numbers [in Arabic]: nine correspond to the units 1–9, another to the 10, another to the 100, and the last one to the 1000.

Al-Istijjī, then, proceeds to establish a correspondence between the

[23] This is the only instance in our text at which al-Istijjī mentions the periods called *fardār*s which, as we have seen, were quoted in the appendix to the *Liber Universus* of ʿUmar ibn Farrukhān. In this system the middle *fardār* assigns 75 years to each planet and to the two lunar nodes, while the small *fardār* lasts 75 years which are distributed unequally between the planets and the nodes. See Kennedy, 1962, pp. 356–8.

four world-*intihā'āt* periods and the theory of Saturn–Jupiter conjunctions. For that purpose it is important to bear in mind the standard classification of the zodiacal signs into four triplicities, which are related to the four elements: Fire (Aries-Leo-Sagittarius), Earth (Taurus-Virgo-Capricorn), Air (Gemini-Libra-Aquarius), Water (Cancer-Scorpio-Pisces). A conjunction of Saturn and Jupiter takes place approximately every twenty years, two-thirds of a revolution (eight zodiacal signs) further along from the previous one. This is why these conjunctions tend to stay in the same triplicity. There is, however, a small advance in the triplicity of the second conjunction. Abū Ma'shar—one of the sources quoted by al-Istijjī—establishes (Kennedy, 1962, pp. 358–9) that the time between two Saturn–Jupiter conjunctions amounts to 19.848 sidereal years and that the advance in the triplicity is 2;25,17°. A change of triplicity will, therefore, require:

$$30°/2;25,17° \approx 12.39 \text{ conjunctions}$$

and

$$12.39 \times 19.848 \approx 246 \text{ sidereal years}$$

Consequently, according to Abū Ma'shar, the conjunction will have shifted through the four triplicities in:

$$246 \times 4 = 984 \text{ sidereal years.}$$

These are the kind of numbers one has to bear in mind to understand al-Istijjī's classification of Saturn–Jupiter conjunctions (fol. 11v) into:

1. The supreme conjunction (*al-qirān al-a'ẓam*) which is the time required for a shift through the four triplicities and a return of the conjunction to the same triplicity where it began. It is a period of about 1000 years and, therefore, it is similar to the category of the thousands (as the mighty world-*intihā'*).

2. The middle conjunction (*al-qirān al-awsaṭ*): it is the time which corresponds to twelve conjunctions [and, therefore, it implies a shift in the triplicity]. It belongs to the category of the hundreds (as the big world-*intihā'*).

3. The small conjunction (*al-qirān al-aṣghar*) which is the period of time between two Saturn–Jupiter conjunctions in the same triplicity. It corresponds to the category of the tens (like the middle world-*intihā'*).

4. As al-Istijjī seeks to emphasize the similarity between the two kinds of periods (*intihā'āt* and Saturn–Jupiter conjunctions) he needs something here to fill the gap corresponding to the small world-*intihā'* and, as there is nothing of the sort related to conjunctions, in the fourth place, and in the category of the units, he puts the anniversaries (*taḥāwīl al-sinīn*).

Al-Istijjī adds to the aforementioned general notions three numerical parameters which have a certain interest: he states (fol. 12r) that the portion (*ḥiṣṣa*) which corresponds to one year in the *tasyīr* of the small conjunction is 18;29°, 1;29,4° in the *tasyīr* of the middle conjunction, and 0;22,16,5° in that of the supreme conjunction. These values allow us to compute the length of the three periods which will be:

360°/18;29° = 19.477 (small conjunction)
360°/1;29,4° = 242.515 years (middle conjunction)
360°/0;22,16,5° = 969.999 years (supreme conjunction)

The period of the middle conjunction is confirmed explicitly by the text (fol. 13r) which mentions a rounded value of 242.5 years (20 years for the small conjunction). On the other hand, al-Istijjī also adds an intermediate period of sixty years (6° per year), described as the 'period of the return of the conjunction to its original place in the same triplicity where it was' (*zamān ʿawdat al-qirān ilā mawḍiʿi-hi al-aṣlī fī nafs al-muthallatha allatī huwa fī-hā*). It obviously corresponds to three small conjunctions and is considered by our author as the best natural period for casting the horoscopes of the reigns of kings.

The periods used by al-Istijjī are different from those of Abū Maʿshar quoted above. An attempt to obtain them using the parameters for the mean motion of Saturn, Jupiter, and the Sun of the *Toledan Tables* has proved to be a complete failure. We do not know, in fact, where al-Istijjī obtains his parameters.

4. ON THE METHODS FOR THE *TASYĪR* AND THE 'PROJECTION OF RAYS'

Three different astrological practices (division of the houses of the horoscope, *tasyīr*, and projection of rays) share common methods which can be difficult from a mathematical point of view and are the main object of 'mathematical astrology', a part of applied mathematics which underwent spectacular development in Islamic times. The methods for the division of the houses of the horoscope have been studied by North (1986) and Kennedy (1994 and 1996), while those used for the *tasyīr* and the projection of rays have been the object of two recent studies by Calvo (1998b) and Hogendijk (1998).[24] The problem of the projection of rays had attracted the attention of Andalusian mathematicians towards the end of the tenth century (Kennedy and Krikorian-Preisler, 1972; Hogendijk, 1989), and, in the eleventh century, Ibn Muʿādh

[24] See also Nallino, 1903, pp. 309–13.

al-Jayyānī (d. 1093) had also studied it in a highly technical way.[25] Al-Istijjī was a contemporary of Ibn Muʿādh and he was obviously interested in the topic although his approach to it does not have the same technical character. The information he gives, even though it is not original, has a certain interest, as it contains developments for which al-Istijjī seems to be one of the oldest known sources.

As for the *tasyīr*, understood as the astrological technique which has the purpose of establishing the date of a future event, it seems clear that al-Istijjī uses simple progressions on the ecliptic and not on the equator: in his classification of the different methods used, Hogendijk states that the 'simple ecliptical method' is used for the projection of rays but not for the *tasyīr*. However, we have found evidence for the use of this method in the work of the fourteenth-century Maghribī astronomer and astrologer Ibn ʿAzzūz al-Qusanṭīnī (d. Constantina 1354) (Samsó, 1997 and 1999). We may wonder, in this context, whether we are dealing here with a technique which is characteristic of Maghribī astrology. Al-Istijjī's words seem to point towards its use in earlier classical and eastern sources:

We have discovered that all those who made progressions of these principles (*jamīʿ man sayyara al-mabādiʾ*), in agreement with the categories of numbers and the periods of conjunctions, used ecliptical degrees for their progressions (*qad sayyarū-hā bi-daraj al-sawāʾ*), and not right ascensions measured in equatorial degrees which were not even used for the progression of the sign of the limit (*burj al-muntahā*) (fol. 11v).

Concerning the projection of rays, al-Istijjī seems to favour the use of the same procedure. We shall summarize here his historical information on both astrological techniques:

1. Ptolemy, author of the *Tetrabiblos*, made progressions of the indicators (*sayyara al-adillāʾ*) in the western quadrant of the sphere, in the direction opposite to that of increasing longitudes.[26] Both his progressions (*tasyīrāt*) and his projection of rays were made using oblique ascensions (fol. 13r).

The oblique ascension method for the *tasyīr* is mentioned by Ptolemy

[25] Kennedy, 1994. An edition, translation, and commentary of Ibn Muʿādh's text is currently in preparation by Josep Casulleras.

[26] This seems to refer to Ptolemy's *Tetrabiblos* 3. 10 (pp. 278–81): 'When the prorogator has been distinguished, we must still further adopt two methods of prorogation. The one, that which follows the order of the following signs, must be used only in the case of what is called the projection of rays, when the prorogator is in the orient, that is, between mid-heaven and the horoscope. We must use not only the method that follows the order of following signs, but also that which follows the order of leading signs, in the so-called *horimaea*, when the prorogator is in places that decline from mid-heaven.' Therefore, according to Robbins's interpretation, when the prorogator (*haylaj*, significator) is placed between mid-heaven and the descendant, the *tasyīr* should be

in the *Tetrabiblos* (pp. 286–7): he says that it is the usual system but that it is correct only if the celestial body or the point of the ecliptic is on the eastern horizon. The same method for the projection of rays is not mentioned by Ptolemy: Hogendijk (1998) has found it described in an appendix (probably a later interpolation) to the treatise on the use of the astrolabe by al-Khwārizmī (*fl. c.* 830) and Casulleras[27] has discovered a possible reference to it in the *al-Qānūn al-Mas'ūdī* of al-Bīrūnī.

2. The school of the Persians (*ṭā'ifa min al-furs*) made their projection of rays and their *tasyīrs* using right ascensions (fol. 13r). In fol. 14r al-Istijjī adds that if the rays of the planets are projected on the plane of the equator, right ascensions are preferable to oblique ascensions.

Hogendijk (1998) documents this method (for the projection of rays) in Andalusian sources, which ascribe it to the Persians: Ibn al-Zarqālluh (d. 1100) (Puig, 1987, p. 82) and Ibn Bāṣo (d. 1316).[28] Casulleras, again, has found a possible allusion in al-Bīrūnī's *Qānūn*. As for the *tasyīr*, the right ascension method has been found by Hogendijk (1998) in a treatise on the astrolabe by Abraham b. 'Ezra (*c.* 1090–1167). Ptolemy (*Tetrabiblos*, pp. 288–9) accepts it only when the significator is on the meridian.

3. The third reference to these methods, as given by al-Istijjī, is somewhat cryptic: 'The third school (*ṭā'ifa*) is that of the mathematicians (*muhandisūn*). When they understood, from their objectives (*min aghrāḍi-him*), that their method (*madhhabu-hum*) transformed (*radda*) the rays projected by the stars into an arc of the equator and did the same with the arcs of the *tasyīrs*, and saw in this a method attributed to one of the Hermes, they wrote mathematical books (*kutub handasiyya*) on this subject and obtained them without demonstrations which explained them and without saying why it was necessary to transform the rays of the stars and the arcs of the *tasyīr* into arcs of the equator' (fol. 13r and v).

This passage deserves a few comments: first of all the 'objectives' (*aghrāḍ*) of the mathematicians might be—following what Ibn Mu'ādh al-Jayyānī states in his treatise on the projection of rays—to establish a relationship between the division of the houses of the horoscope, the

calculated in both directions. Al-Istijjī's interpretation apparently coincides with that of Ibn Abī l-Rijāl (p. 175a) in his *Kitāb al-bari' fī aḥkām al-nujūm*: 'E la oppinion de Tolomeo e de los que con el se atorgan es que quando fuere en la .IX.ª casa e en la .VIII.ª, so atacir es contrario otrossi contra la orden de los signos. Mas los otros sabios non se atorgan en esto, si non que lo fazen derecho.'

[27] In his unpublished doctoral dissertation on Ibn Mu'ādh's treatise on the projection of rays.

[28] Calvo, 1993, pp. 199 (tr.) and 174 (Ar. text): the source of this passage seems to be the aforementioned text of Ibn al-Zarqālluh. See also pp. 92–3.

projection of rays, and the *tasyīr*, on the one hand, and the daily motion which takes place on the plane of the equator, on the other.[29] A certain confirmation of this hypothesis may be found in al-Istijjī's own remark that the only reason for the projection on the equator was that the daily motion takes place around its poles (fol. 14r). On the other hand, although the text does not explain which method is used by these mathematicians (the reference to the transformation of an ecliptic arc into an equatorial arc being too vague), the statement that it is a procedure ascribed to one of the Hermes leads us to conjecture an identification with a method which uses position circles or semicircles (Hogendijk, 1998, 6.1). A position circle, called *al-ufq al-ḥādith* ('incident horizon') in eastern sources, is a great circle which passes through the north and south points of the horizon and through another astrologically significant point on the celestial sphere. The use of position circles coincides with the attribution to Hermes of methods or techniques based in them on Andalusian sources such as Ibn al-Zarqālluh (Puig, 1987, pp. 85–6) and Ibn Bāṣo.[30] On the other hand, Hogendijk (1998, 3.1.3) has reminded us of the existence of an interesting astrolabe, made in Toledo in 1029–30, which includes two plates for the projection of rays for latitudes 38;30° (Cordoba) and 42° (Saragossa?) with position circles which intersect the equator at 6° intervals (Woepcke, 1858). To this one should add the use, by Maslama al-Majrīṭī, of the four position circles method for the approximate computation of tables for casting the rays in his revision of al-Khwārizmī's *zīj* (Hogendijk, 1989 and 1998, 4.6): the same method was presented by Ibn Muʿādh al-Jayyānī. Furthermore, Maslama's disciple Ibn al-Samḥ used position circles intersecting equal 30° divisions of the prime vertical for the computation of the houses, though not, apparently, for the *tasyīr* and the projection of rays. These latter references account for al-Istijjī's allusion to the mathematicians in the Andalusian context.

4. Our author now mentions the method of al-Battānī:

He was conscious of the error of their school (*fasād madhhabi-him*) concerning the projection of rays and, therefore, he did not pay any attention and attached no importance to it. In this respect he followed the rules of demonstrative law (*al-qānūn al-burhānī*) and operated, for the projection of rays, with ecliptical degrees when the planet had no latitude from the ecliptic. When it had latitude, the two trines and the two sextiles diverged on the ecliptic and his procedure was based on a computation which identified the place on the ecliptic where the trine and the sextile fall if the planet has ecliptic latitude. This chapter of his book is exceptional, extraordinary, and extremely brilliant. ... Al-Battānī

[29] This remark was made to us by Josep Casulleras.

[30] Calvo, 1993, pp. 90–3, 201–2 (tr.), 178–81 (Ar.).

followed their opinion in the *tasyīr* and operated (*ṣannafa*) in an approximate way (*ʿalā l-taqrīb*). What made him fall in this [error] was his lack of knowledge[31] of the meaning of *tasyīr* and the fact that he had made little research about its causes and objectives ... (fol. 13v).

Al-Istijjī refers here to chapters 54 (projection of rays) and 55 (*tasyīr*) of al-Battānī's *zīj* (Nallino, 1903, pp. 129–34, 305–17). The method used by al-Battānī for the projection of rays of a planet with no latitude is the simple ecliptical method. If the planet has latitude but we want to project its rays in a right or left quadrature, the projection will always be 90°. In the case of the trine or the sextile, the procedure used is a refinement of the simple ecliptical one and it appears in other eastern astronomical sources (Kennedy and Krikorian-Preisler, 1972, pp. 375–6; Hogendijk, 1998, 4.1): the planet is one of the vertices of a spherical right-angled triangle in which the hypotenuse is an arc of a great circle the length of which equals the aspect (60° for the sextile, 120° for the trine) and which unites the planet with the ecliptic, while the two other sides are the latitude of the planet and the length (on the ecliptic) of the projection which we want to know. Two sides being known, the third one can be determined by using more or less sophisticated procedures.

In chapter 55 al-Battānī uses, for the *tasyīr*, the hour line method, which Ptolemy (*Tetrabiblos* 3. 10, pp. 291–305) considered an approximation to the position semicircle method, and calculates an arc on the equator and not—as in the case of the projection of rays—on the ecliptic. These two facts agree with al-Istijjī's words which point to the approximate character of al-Battānī's method (approximate in relation to the exact computation according to the position semicircle method). Al-Istijjī's harsh criticism of al-Battānī, compared to his praise of his method for the projection of rays, shows that he favours the computation of both *tasyīr* and projection of rays on the ecliptic: the use of the equator is considered an error. As Hogendijk (1998, 3.1.5) has remarked, Ibn Bāṣo[32] attributes to al-Battānī a method for the computation of the *tasyīr* which is a simple variant of the one he uses for the projection of rays and we may wonder whether there was an Andalusian tradition which, in agreement with al-Istijjī's view of the problem, ascribed to al-Battānī a method for the *tasyīr* which was extrapolated from his procedure for casting the rays.

[31] *Mujmalu-hu* in the manuscript. We suggest *majhalu-hu*.

[32] Calvo, 1993, pp. 199 (tr.) and 174 (Ar.).

5. THE CALCULATION OF THE *NAMŪDĀR* AND EXPERIMENTAL ASTROLOGY

Al-Istijjī's *risāla* contains references to another astrological technique, the calculation of the *namūdār*. Its purpose is to obtain the ascendant at the moment of a nativity, the main difficulty being that of determining the hour of birth: when he describes this technique, Ptolemy (*Tetrabiblos* 3. 2, pp. 229–35; see Kennedy, 1995–6, pp. 139–44) emphasizes the errors which practitioners of astrology might commit when they use solar instruments (such as sundials) or water clocks. This is why our author, like many others, uses an indirect computation of the ascendant and remarks that, when we study the horoscope of a human nativity, 'We find that one of the cusps has a number of parts of its own sign equal to those—also of its own sign—of the planet dominating (*mustawlī*) the sign of the conjunction or of the opposition [of the Sun and the Moon] which took place before the nativity, in agreement with the procedure used to divide the signs' (fol. 10v). This information is repeated in fol. 14v and the source seems to be the aforementioned chapter of Ptolemy's *Tetrabiblos* with only one change: according to Ptolemy, with this technique we obtain the ascendant and not, as in al-Istijjī's text, one of the cusps.

A second kind of *namūdār* is ascribed by Islamic sources to Hermes. It establishes that the lunar longitude at the instant of birth is the ascendant at the instant of conception; conversely, the lunar longitude at conception is the ascendant of the nativity. Thus, if the moment of birth is known approximately and the duration of pregnancy can be established,[33] the astrologer can easily calculate the lunar longitude at the moment of conception and, consequently, he will also know the ascendant of the nativity. This procedure takes advantage of the fact that the daily rotation of the earth, which determines the longitude of the ascendant, is much faster than the motion of the Moon (Kennedy, 1995–6, pp. 140–1). Although al-Istijjī's text is not very clear, he must be referring to this second kind when he mentions the *namūdār masqaṭ al-nuṭfa* (the *namūdār* of the fall of the drop [of sperm]' (fol. 15r)[34] and when he says that these two *namūdārs*—that is, those corresponding to the techniques ascribed to Ptolemy and Hermes—do not coincide

[33] The problem of the duration of pregnancy is studied thoroughly by Ibn al-Kammād (*fl.* Cordoba, 1116): see Vernet, 1949.

[34] This passage is clarified in fol. 15v where al-Istijjī says: 'when you observe (*raṣadta*) a nativity and calculate its horoscope (*nuṣba*) with the aforementioned *zīj*, obtain the duration of pregnancy (*makth*) and the *namūdār* from the fall of the drop [of sperm]; then compare that to the *namūdār* produced by the planet dominating the degree of the [luni-solar] conjunction or opposition which took place before the nativity.'

when calculated with any *zīj* other than 'our corrected *zīj*' (*zīju-nā al-muṣaḥḥaḥ*), 'due to the correctness (*ṣiḥḥa*) in the positions of planets and of the Moon and the precision of its equation (*taʿdīl*)'. He adds that that he has written a *risāla* in which he clarifies this question (fol. 15r).

It is interesting to note that al-Istijjī refers several times to experience (*tajriba*) as a method to prove the truth of these astrological techniques and to check the validity of a *zīj*. Thus, concerning the *namūdār*, he says:

> We have experimented (*jarrabnā*) this with many nativities which had been observed (*marṣūda*) [by us] and with other useful (*mufīda*) ones which had been observed (*kānat marṣūda*) [by others]. This practice of ours met with an uninterrupted success. Then, we used this technique with other nativities whose data were not reliable (*mukhammana al-ḥirz*), we applied the *tasyīr*, and we obtained the most exact and evident indications as well as the clearest influences. In many nativities we found great differences between the degrees of the ascendants [of the horoscopes] and the correct degrees of the ascendants (fol. 15r).

In a more general way, he tells Ṣāʿid: 'When we meet, I will show you, with God's help, the collection of astronomical horoscopes (*al-nuṣab al-falakiyya*) I have gathered so that I may use them as examples (*ʿalā ṭarīq al-iʿtibār*) and you will see surprising and marvellous things' (fol. 10r). He has also experimented with the *fardārāt* of the seven planets and of the ascending and descending lunar nodes (fol. 12v) and he states clearly that

> It is convenient to know that in this *namūdār* and *tasyīr* there are indications which prove the correctness of this *zīj* of ours. Those who are ignorant of cosmology (*ʿilm al-hayʾa*), computational astronomy (*ḥarakāt al-kawākib*), and the techniques of demonstration (*mawādd al-burhān*) which lead to its verification will find [in these techniques] what will make them sure of its correction and will show them its truth (fol. 15v).

Remarks of this kind are not uncommon in other western Islamic astrological texts. Ibn Abī l-Rijāl has a chapter on the *tasyīr* in which he gives a series of examples using, apparently, authentic nativity horoscopes which might belong to a collection similar to that of al-Istijjī. On the other hand, the astrologer of Qayrawān is also the author of a lost *zīj*, which he claims is based on observations, and which he uses to justify his astrological techniques.[35] References to experimental astrology can also be found in Ibn al-Kammād's treatise on astrological obstetrics and in a treatise of the fifteenth-century Moroccan astrologer al-Baqqār (Vernet, 1971; Samsó, 1998). The most surprising case of the

[35] Ibn Abī l-Rijāl, p. 177: 'e esto auemos-lo prouado en las nuestras tablas que nos endereçamos con nuestros catamientos.'

use of experiment in astrology is that of Ibn ʿAzzūz al-Qusanṭīnī who established the existence of disagreements between actual positions of the planets and the longitudes computed with the *zīj* of Ibn Isḥāq (*fl. c.* 1193–1222) when he used *tasyīr* techniques to calculate the exact dates of known historical events, particularly the great battle of El Salado (1340), and noticed that the times calculated did not correspond to historical reality. Ibn ʿAzzūz blamed Ibn Isḥāq's tables for the mistake and, in order to correct the divergence, he made observations with an armillary sphere *c.* 745/1344: as a result he corrected Ibn Isḥāq's mean motion tables and recast the corresponding horoscopes. This time he obtained satisfactory results, once he had made the necessary corrections to the mean motion parameters deduced from observations. He then compiled his new *Muwāfiq Zīj* (Samsó, 1997 and 1999).

We have, therefore, in al-Istijjī's *risāla* some new evidence about the use of astrological techniques to verify the correctness of a set of astronomical tables and about the use of experiment to check the validity of astrological rules. It is obvious that *qāḍī* Ṣāʿid was a believer in astrology, but there is no evidence whatsoever that the *Toledan Tables* were computed for astrological reasons. Al-Istijjī's work, which is the result of the thorough reading of eastern astrological sources that were well known to Ṣāʿid, seems to be an offspring of the astronomical work made in Toledo: the tables were not only accurate in the sense that they allowed the computation of planetary positions in agreement with observation, but they were also astrologically exact. Ṣāʿid must have been very happy when he read al-Istijjī's *risāla*, and this justifies his high opinion of that short text.

LIST OF SOURCES

Bar Hiyya: Abraam bar Hiia, *Llibre revelador. Meguil.lat Hamegal.lè*. Catalan translation by J. Millḥs i Vallicrosa. Barcelona, 1929.

BGD-BCN: Josep Casulleras y Julio Samsó (eds.), *From Baghdad to Barcelona. Studies in the Islamic Exact Sciences in Honour of Prof. Juan Vernet*. 2 vols., Barcelona, 1996.

Calvo, 1993: Calvo, Emilia, *Abī ʿAlī al-Ḥusayn ibn Bāṣo (m. 716/1316), Risālat al-ṣafīḥa al-ŷāmiʿa li-yamīʿ al-ʿurūḍ (Tratado sobre la lámina general para todas las latitudes)*. Madrid, 1993.

Calvo, 1998a: Calvo, Emilia, 'Astronomical Theories Related to the Sun in Ibn al-Hāʾim's *al-Zīj al-Kāmil fī l-Taʿālīm*', *Zeitschrift für Geschichte der Arabisch-Islamischen Wissenschaften*, 12 (1998), 51–11.

Calvo, 1998b: Calvo, Emilia, 'La Résolution graphique des questions astrologiques à al-Andalus', *Histoire des mathématiques arabes: Actes du 3me colloque maghrébin sur l'histoire des mathématiques arabes, Tipaza, 1–3 Décembre 1990*. Alger, 1998, pp. 31–44.

Castells, 1992: Castells, Margarita, 'Un nuevo dato sobre el *Libro de las Cruces* en *al-Zīy al-Muṣṭalaḥ* (obra astronómica egipcia del siglo XIII)', *al-Qanṭara*, 13 (1992), 367 ff.

Derenbourg and Renaud, 1941: Derenbourg, H., and Renaud, H. P. J., *Les Manuscrits arabes de l'Escurial*. Tome II, Fasc. 3: *Sciences exactes et sciences occultes*. Paris, 1941.

G.A.S.: Sezgin, Fuat, *Geschichte des arabischen Schrifttums*: Band V, *Mathematik*. Leiden, 1974; Band VII, *Astrologie, Meteorologie und Verwandtes*. Leiden, 1979.

Hamarneh and Sonnedecker, 1963: Hamarneh, S. Kh., and Sonnedecker, G., *A Pharmaceutical View of Abulcasis al-Zahrāwī in Moorish Spain, with Special Reference to the 'adhān'*. Leiden, 1963.

Hogendijk, 1989: Hogendijk, J. P., 'The Mathematical Structure of Two Islamic Astrological Tables for "Casting the Rays"', *Centaurus*, 32 (1989), 171–202.

Hogendijk, 1998: Hogendijk, J. P., 'Progressions, Rays and Houses in Medieval Islamic Astrology: A Mathematical Classification', paper presented at the Dibner Institute Conference, *New Perspectives on Science in Medieval Islam*, held in Cambridge, Mass., 6–8 November 1998.

Ibn Abī l-Rijāl: Hilty, Gerold (ed.), *Aly Aben Ragel, El libro conplido en los iudizios de las estrellas. Traducción hecha en la corte de Alfonso el Sabio*. Madrid, 1954.

Kennedy, 1962: Kennedy, E. S., 'The World-Year Concept in Islamic Astrology', *S.I.E.S.*, pp. 351–71.

Kennedy, 1994: Kennedy, E. S., 'Ibn Muʿādh on the Astrological Houses', *Zeitschrift für Geschichte der Arabisch-Islamischen Wissenschaften*, 9 (1994), 153–60. Repr. in Kennedy, *Variorum*, no. XVI.

Kennedy, 1995–6: Kennedy, E. S., 'Treatise V of al-Kāshī's Khāqānī's Zīj: Determination of the Ascendent', *Zeitschrift für Geschichte der Arabisch-Islamischen Wissenschaften*, 10 (1995–6), 123–45. Repr. in Kennedy, *Variorum*, no. XVIII.

Kennedy, 1996: Kennedy, E. S., 'The Astrological Houses as Defined by Medieval Islamic Astronomers', BGD-BCN, II, pp. 535–78. Repr. in Kennedy, *Variorum*, no. XIX.

Kennedy, *Variorum*: Kennedy, E. S., *Astronomy and Astrology in the Medieval Islamic World*. Variorum, Aldershot, 1998.

Kennedy and Krikorian-Preisler, 1972: Kennedy, E. S., and Krikorian-Preisler, H., 'The Astrological Doctrine of Projecting the Rays', *Al-Abḥāth*, 25 (1972), 3–15. Repr. in *S.I.E.S.*, pp. 372–84.

Kennedy and van der Waerden, 1963: Kennedy, E. S., and van der Waerden, B. L., 'The World-Year of the Persians', *Journal of the American Oriental Society*, 83 (1963), 315–27. Repr. in *S.I.E.S.*, pp. 338–50.

Lemay, 1995–6: Lemay, Richard, *Abū Maʿšar al-Balhī [Albumasar], Liber introductorii maioris ad scientiam judiciorum astrorum*. 9 vols, Naples, 1995–6.

Millás, 1940: Millás Vallicrosa, José María, 'Sobre el autor del "Libro de las Cruces" ', *al-Andalus*, 5 (1940), 230–4.

Nallino, 1903: Nallino, C. A., *Al-Battānī sive Albatenii Opus Astronomicum*, I, Mediolani Insubrum, 1903. Repr. Frankfurt, 1969.

N.E.A.E.S.A.X: Vernet, J. (ed.), *Nuevos estudios sobre astronomía española en el siglo de Alfonso X*, Barcelona, 1983.

North, 1986: North, John, *Horoscopes and History*. London, 1986.

Pingree, 1968: Pingree, David, *The Thousands of Abū Maʿshar*. London, 1968.

Pingree, 1977: Pingree, David, 'The "Liber Universus" of ʿUmar Ibn al-Farrukhān al-Ṭabarī', *Journal for the History of Arabic Science*, 1 (1977), 8 ff.

Ptolemy, *Tetrabiblos*: Ed. and tr. F. E. Robbins. Loeb Classical Library. London, 1940.

Puig, 1987: Puig, Roser, *Los tratados de construcción y uso de la Azafea de Azarquiel*. Madrid, 1987.

Richter-Bernburg, 1987: Richter-Bernburg, Lutz, 'Ṣāʿid, the *Toledan Tables* and Andalusī Science', in David A. King and George Saliba (eds.), *From Deferent to Equant: A Volume of Studies in the History of Science in the Ancient and Medieval Near East in Honor of E. S. Kennedy* (=*Annals of the New York Academy of Sciences*, vol. 500, New York, 1987), pp. 373–401.

Ṣāʿid, *Ṭabaqāt*: Ṣāʿid al-Andalusī, *Ṭabaqāt al-Umam*. Ed. Ḥayāt Bū ʿAlwān. Dār al-Ṭalīʿa li-l-Ṭibāʿa wa-l-Nashr. Beirut, 1985; ed. Julāmriḍā Jamshīdnizād-i Awwal, Tehran, 1415/1995; *Kitāb Ṭabakāt al-Umam* (*Livre des catégories des nations*). French translation by Régis Blachère. Paris, 1935.

Samsó, 1979: Samsó, Julio, 'The Early Development of Astrology in al-Andalus', *Journal for the History of Arabic Science*, 3 (1979), 228–43. Repr. in Samsó, *Variorum*, no. IV.

Samsó, 1983: Samsó, Julio, 'La primitiva versión árabe del Libro de las Cruces', in *N.E.A.E.S.A.X*, pp. 149–61. Repr. in Samsó, *Variorum*, no. III.

Samsó, *Variorum*: Samsó, Julio, *Islamic Astronomy and Medieval Spain*. Variorum, Aldershot, 1994.

Samsó, 1994: Samsó, Julio, 'Trepidation in al-Andalus in the 11th Century', in Samsó, *Variorum*, no. VIII (31 pp.).

Samsó, 1997: Samsó, Julio, 'Andalusian Astronomy in 14th Century Fez: *al-Zīj al-Muwāfiq* of Ibn 'Azzūz al-Qusanṭīnī', *Zeitschrift für Geschichte der Arabisch-Islamischen Wissenschaften*, 11 (1997), 73–110.

Samsó, 1998: Samsó, Julio, 'An Outline of the History of Maghribī Zijes from the end of the Thirteenth Century', *Journal for the History of Astronomy*, 29 (1998), 93–102.

Samsó, 1999: Samsó, Julio, 'Horoscopes and History: Ibn 'Azzūz and his Retrospective Horoscopes related to the Battle of El Salado (1340)', in Lodi Nauta and Arjo Vanderjagt (eds.), *Between Demonstration and Imagination*. Leiden, 1999, pp. 101–24.

Schirmer, 1934: Schirmer, O., 'Tasyīr', in *Encyclopédie de l'Islam*, 1st edn. VIII (Paris, 1934), 729–33.

S.I.E.S.: Kennedy, E. S., Colleagues and Former Students, *Studies in the Islamic Exact Sciences*. Beirut, 1983.

Suter, 1900: Suter, H., *Die Mathematiker und Astronomen der Araber und ihre Werke*. Leipzig, 1900.

Toomer, 1968: Toomer, G. J., 'A Survey of the Toledan Tables', *Osiris*, 15 (1968), 5–174.

van Dalen, 1996: van Dalen, Benno, 'Al-Khwārizmī's Astronomical Tables Revisited: Analysis of the Equation of Time', BGD-BCN, I, pp. 195–252.

Vernet, *E.H.C.M.*: Vernet, Juan, *Estudios sobre historia de la ciencia medieval*. Barcelona-Bellaterra, 1979.

Vernet, 1971: Vernet, Juan, 'Tradición e innovación en la ciencia medieval', *Oriente e Occidente nel Medioevo: Filosofia e Scienze* (Rome, 1971), pp. 741–57. Repr. in Vernet, *E.H.C.M.*, pp. 173–89.

Vernet, 1949: Vernet, Juan, 'Un tractat d'obstetrícia astrològica', *Boletín de la Real Academia de Buenas Letras de Barcelona*, 22 (1949), 69–96. Repr. in Vernet, *E.H.C.M.*, pp. 273–300.

Viladrich and Martí, 1983: Viladrich, M., and Martí, R., 'Sobre el *Libro dell Ataçir* de los *Libros del Saber de Astronomía* de Alfonso X el Sabio', in *N.E.A.E.S.A.X*, pp. 75–100.

Woepcke, 1858: Woepcke, Franz, 'Über ein in der Königlichen Bibliothek zu Berlin befindliches arabisches Astrolabium'. *Abhandlungen der Königlichen Akademie der Wissenschaften*, 1858, pp. 1–31. Repr. in Fuat Sezgin (ed.)., *Arabische Instrumente in Orientalischen Studien. II. Astronomische Instrumente Publikationen 1858–1892* (Frankfurt, 1991), pp. 1–36.

Yano and Viladrich, 1991: Yano, Michio, and Viladrich, Mercè, 'Tasyīr Computation of Kūshyār ibn Labbān', *Historia Scientiarum*, 41 (1991), 1–16.

VI

"AL-BĪRŪNĪ" IN AL-ANDALUS

1. *The problem*[1].

J. Vernet has established the role of al-Andalus and that of the Medieval Cultures of the Iberian Peninsula in the process of transmission of Eastern Islamic Astronomy into Medieval Europe[2]. With a few rare exceptions, only those astronomical works which were known in al-Andalus were later translated into Latin, Romance languages or Hebrew and, thus, became influential in the development of European Astronomy. On the other hand, it seems clear that contacts with the East were frequent and productive between the reign of ᶜAbd al-Raḥmān II (821-852) and the fall of the Caliphate in 1031, while the period of the "petty kings" (*mulūk al-ṭawā'if*) - 1031-1086 -, even if it should be considered the Golden Age of Andalusian Astronomy, marks also the beginning of a slowing down in the arrival to the Peninsula of the Eastern astronomical production. This had two obvious consequences: on the one hand, Andalusian Astronomy acquired characteristics of its own which were, later, transmitted to the Maghrib; on the other, Andalusian isolation was, probably, the main cause of the general scientific decay, the first symptoms of which appear in the 12th c.[3].

I think we can state, in general terms, that al-Andalus was aware of the main Eastern astronomical works produced until the middle of the 10th c., but the situation is not at all clear after this date which seems to

---

[1] The present paper is the result of research undertaken within a programme on "Astronomical Theory and Tables in al-Andalus in the 10th and 11th centuries" sponsored by the Dirección General de Investigación Científica y Técnica of the Spanish Ministerio de Educación y Ciencia.

[2] J. Vernet, *La cultura hispanoárabe en Oriente y Occidente*. Barcelona, 1978. German translation, *Die Spanisch-arabische Kultur in Orient und Okzident*. Zurich and München, 1984. French translation, *Ce que la culture doit aux Arabes d'Espagne*. Paris, 1985.

[3] See J. Samsó, *Las Ciencias de los Antiguos en al-Andalus*. Madrid, 1992; a summary in English of the astronomical part in "Andalusian Astronomy: its Main Characteristics and Influence in the Latin West", in J. Samsó, *Islamic Astronomy and Medieval Spain*, Variorum Reprints, Aldershot, 1994.

be related to the reign of al-Ḥakam II (961-976), the last of the Umayyad Caliphs who had a clear policy of buying books for the royal library in the principal Oriental cities. Only a limited part of the Eastern Astronomy produced after ca. 950 reached Cordova, Toledo or Zaragoza and it is often difficult to establish clearly the list of sources available in al-Andalus[4]. One example will be sufficient: only very recently has J.P. Hogendijk been able to document the early diffusion of the *Kitāb al-Manāẓir* of Ibn al-Haytham (ca. 965-1039) a copy of which was used by king al-Mu'taman (reigned 1081-85) of Zaragoza[5]. This has, however, only advanced about 75 years the chronology of the introduction of this work which was translated into Latin by Gerard of Cremona (1114-1187). The kind of problem I am going to deal with here is different: it has often been said that the works of al-Bīrūnī (973-1048) never reached the Latin West, something which implies that, very probably, he was unknown in al-Andalus. We could make the same kind of statement about the generation of his masters, an important group of Eastern mathematicians and astronomers who were active between ca. 950 and ca. 1000, most of whom shared common working techniques and interests, kept relations between themselves and with al-Bīrūnī and took part in the "trigonometrical revolution" which took place in this period[6]. I am refering to Abū Jaᶜfar al-Khāzin (d. *ca.* 965), Abū-l-Wafā' al-Būzjānī (940-997 or 998), Abū Sahl al-Kūhī (fl. *ca.* 988), Abū Maḥmūd al-Khujandī (d. *ca.* 1000), Abū Saᶜīd al-Sijzī (fl. second half of the 10th c.), Abū Naṣr Manṣūr ibn

---

[4] See the brilliant analysis of the sources accessible to *qāḍī* Ṣāᶜid (1029-1070) by L. Richter-Bernburg, "Ṣāᶜid, the Toledan Tables and Andalusī Science", *From Deferent to Equant...in Honor of E.S. Kennedy* ed. by D.A. King and G. Saliba (New York, 1987), 373-401.

[5] J.P. Hogendijk, "Discovery of an 11th-Century Geometrical Compilation: the *Istikmāl* of Yūsuf al-Mu'taman ibn Hūd, King of Saragossa, *Historia Mathematica* 13 (1986), 43-52; "Le roi-geomètre al-Mu'taman ibn Hūd et son Livre de la Perfection (*Kitāb al-Istikmāl*)", *Premier Colloque International sur l'Histoire des Mathématiques Arabes* (Alger, 1988), 53-66; "The Geometrical Parts of the *Istikmāl* of Yūsuf al-Mu'taman ibn Hūd (11th century). An Analytical Table of Contents", *Archives Internationales d'Histoire des Sciences* 41 (1991), 207-281; "Al-Mu'taman ibn Hūd, 11th Century King of Saragossa and Brilliant Mathematician", *Historia Mathematica* 22 (1995), 1-18.

[6] See M.T. Debarnot, *Al-Bīrūnī, Kitāb maqālīd ᶜilm al-hay'a. La Trigonométrie sphérique chez les Arabes de l'Est à la fin du Xᵉ siècle*. Damas, 1985.

ᶜAlī ibn ᶜIrāq (d. before 1036), etc. The purpose of this paper is to present the hypothesis that part of the work of that school was probably known in specific scientific circles in al-Andalus in the 11th c.

2. *Ibn Muᶜādh's Spherical Trigonometry.*

This hypothesis is not new. The publication, in 1979, of the *Kitāb majhūlāt qisī al-kura* of Ibn Muᶜādh al-Jayyānī (d. 1093)[7] posed the problem of the probable Eastern sources of a complete Andalusian treatise on Spherical Trigonometry, entirely independent from Astronomy, in which the author was aware of the main novelties introduced by "al-Bīrūnī's school" towards the end of the previous century[8]. Certain details in the proofs used by Ibn Muᶜādh remind us of Thābit ibn Qurra's *Kitāb fī shakl al-qaṭṭāᶜ* as well as of passages of Abū Naṣr, Abū-l-Wafā' and al-Bīrūnī (*al-Qānūn al-Masᶜūdī*). Our author calculates a tangent table for $r = 1$, for which there are precedents in the three aforementioned Eastern authors, and computes the tangents for 89;15°, 89;30°, 89;45° and 89;59° using a method of parabolic interpolation described in Brahmagupta's *Khaṇḍakhādyaka*, a source which al-Bīrūnī knew well although he did not mention the interpolation rule[9]. Like Abū Naṣr, Ibn Muᶜādh also uses a polar triangle, although there does not seem to exist a direct link, in this respect, between the two authors[10]. On the whole,

---

[7] M.V. Villuendas, *La trigonometría europea en el siglo XI. Estudio de la obra de Ibn Muᶜāḏ, El Kitāb maŷhūlāt*. Barcelona, 1979.

[8] J. Samsó, "Notas sobre la trigonometría esférica de Ibn Muᶜāḏ". *Awrāq* 3 (1980), 60-68 (reprint in *Islamic Astronomy and Medieval Spain*). See also *Ciencias de los Antiguos* pp. 139-144.

[9] E.S. Kennedy, "The Motivation of al-Bīrūnī's Second Order Interpolation Scheme", *Proceedings of the First International Symposium for the History of Arabic Science* (Aleppo, 1978), 67-71; M. G[arcía] Doncel, "Quadratic Interpolations in Ibn Muᶜādh", *Archives Internationales d'Histoire des Sciences* 32 (1982), 68-77. The same interpolation scheme is used by Ibn Muᶜādh to calculate the sines of 0;13,56° and 80;36,58° in his *Liber de Crepusculis*.

[10] M.T. Debarnot, "Introduction du triangle polaire par Abū Naṣr b. ᶜIrāq". *Journal for the History of Arabic Science* 2 (1978), p. 132 n. 30.

our author had probably access to Eastern literature on Spherical Trigonometry - particularly an unknown treatise on the subject in which the solution of spherical triangles was systematised into 16 different cases - but he had enough personality to deal with his subject in an independent way.

3. *Ibn Muᶜādh and the "Method of the Zījes"*.

Ibn Muᶜādh also wrote a *zīj*, the *Tabulae Jahen*, in which he followed al-Khwārizmī's *Sindhind*. The canons are extant in a Latin translation by Gerard of Cremona and parts of the Arabic text are often quoted in the *zīj* of Ibn Isḥāq (fl. Tunis towards the beginning of the 13th c.)[11]. Even if this *zīj* was compiled later than the *Kitāb al-majhūlāt*, its trigonometrical part does not have the interest of the former source. Other parts of the work point, however, in the same direction. Such is the case of chapter 18, in which Ibn Muᶜādh uses the "method of the *zīj*es" for the determination of the *qibla*[12]. A certain number of Eastern authors are known to have dealt with this method, namely Ḥabash al-Ḥāsib (fl. 850), Abū-l-Wafā', Abū Sahl al-Kūhī, al-Bīrūnī - at least in three of his works (*Taḥdīd*, *Maqālīd* and *Qānūn*) -, Kūshyār b. Labbān (*ca.* 971-1029), Ibn Yūnus (d. 1009) and Ibn al-Haytham (ca. 965-1039).

The conclusions of a careful analysis of Ibn Muᶜādh's formulation compared to the other sources have a certain interest for the purpose of this paper: first of all we should reject al-Bīrūnī's *Qānūn* because it uses $r = 1$ (Ibn Muᶜādh: $r = 60$) and the final stage of the computation is different. Abū-l-Wafā' al-Būzjānī can also be disqualified for he introduces certain improvements in the calculation that are not to be found in Ibn Muᶜādh. Nothing certain can be said about the other sources: our author uses a logical, though independent, terminology to denominate the

---

[11] Gerard of Cremona's translation was printed in Nüremberg, 1549. Ibn Isḥāq's *zīj* is extant in manuscript Hyderabad Andra Pradesh State Library no 298: it was discovered by D.A. King who sent me a copy of it. On the *Tabulae Jahen* cf. H. Hermelink, "Tabulae Jahen", *Archive for the History of the Exact Sciences* 2 (1964), 108-112 and *Ciencias de los Antiguos* pp. 152-166.

[12] Both the Arabic text (from Ibn Isḥāq's *zīj*) and the Latin translation are edited in J. Samsó and H. Mielgo, "Ibn Isḥāq al-Tūnisī and Ibn Muᶜādh al-Jayyānī on the Qibla" in *Islamic Astronomy and Medieval Spain*.

four auxiliary arcs used for the computation of the *qibla*. This independence has, however, one exception: to name the fourth arc he uses, *al-masāfa mā bayn baladi-ka wa-Makka* ("distance between your locality and Mecca", Lat. *arcus spacii quod est inter regionem tuam et Metram*), which is the same as that used by al-Bīrūnī in the *Qānūn* (*al-masāfa bayn al-baladayn*) and in the *Taḥdīd* (*al-masāfa bayn al-balad wa-bayn Makka*). In this latter source, al-Bīrūnī uses the "method of the *zīj*es" to establish the distance between two localities and only Abū-l-Wafā' seems, as far as I know, to have done a similar thing. We should, therefore, consider the possibility that Ibn Muᶜādh's source might have been al-Bīrūnī's *Taḥdīd*.

This agrees with another small bit of evidence which we can gather from our sources: the method requires to establish which is the endpoint (north or south) from which the *qibla* has to be measured and which is the direction (east or west) of the *qibla*. Only two of the aforementioned authors give criteria for this purpose: Abū-l-Wafā' and al-Bīrūnī (in his three aforementioned books). The same criteria are used by Ibn Muᶜādh and, thus, the evidence points, once more, towards al-Bīrūnī's *Taḥdīd* or towards Abū-l-Wafā'. This is not the only instance in which we will find a possible link between al-Bīrūnī, the determination of the azimuth of the *qibla* and a Maghribī-Andalusī astronomer: such is the case of Ibn al-Raqqām (d. 1315) in whose treatise of Gnomonics, the *Risāla fī ᶜilm al-ẓilāl*, we find an analemma used to solve this problem which derives, ultimately, from Ḥabash al-Ḥāsib but which seems to be narrowly related to a passage of al-Bīrūnī's *al-Qānūn al-Masᶜūdī*[13].

---

[13] J. Carandell, "An Analemma for the Determination of the Azimuth of the Qibla in the *Risāla fī ᶜilm al-ẓilāl* of Ibn al-Raqqām". *Zeitschrift fur Geschichte der Arabisch-Islamischen Wissenschaften* 1 (1984), 61-72.

4. *On the division of the houses of the horoscope: prime vertical (fixed boundaries) and equatorial (fixed boundaries) methods*[14].

Our understanding of the history of the methods used to divide the houses of the horoscope has been considerably improved by John North's *Horoscopes and History*[15]. He has, for example, advanced the chronology of the fixed boundaries methods traditionally ascribed to Campanus of Novara (prime vertical) and to Regiomontanus (equatorial): according to these methods, the ecliptic is divided by six great circles which go through the North and South points of the local horizon and through equal divisions of 30° of the prime vertical or the equator, starting in both cases from the East or West point. North has established that the prime vertical method is described in al-Bīrūnī's *al-Qānūn al-Masᶜūdī* with no claim to originality, as he merely qualifies it as "The method which I prefer" (*al-ṭarīq alladhī āthartu-hu*)[16]. It is also clear, as North points out, that the method reappears in three of the Alfonsine *Libros del Saber de Astronomía*, namely the *Libro dell astrolabio redondo*[17], the *Libro de la lámina universal*[18] and the *Libro de la*

[14] This passage contains developments of many ideas presented, for the first time, by E. Calvo, "La résolution graphique des questions astrologiques à al-Andalus". To be published in the proceedings of the "Troisième Colloque International sur l'Histoire des Mathématiques Arabes".

[15] J.D. North, *Horoscopes and History*. The Warburg Institute. London, 1986.

[16] Al-Bīrūnī, *Qānūn* (Hyderabad, 1954) III, 1359-1369; North, *Horoscopes* pp. 32-33.

[17] M. Rico y Sinobas, *Libros del Saber de Astronomía del Rey D. Alfonso X de Castilla*. 5 vols., Madrid, 1863-67. II, 193 (chapter LX), where it is assigned to Hermes and Ibn al-Zarqālluh. M. Viladrich ("Una nueva evidencia de materiales árabes en la astronomía alfonsí" in *De Astronomia Alphonsi Regis*, ed. by M. Comes, R. Puig and J. Samsó, Barcelona, 1987, pp. 105-116) has established that the treatise on the use of the plane astrolabe by Abū-l-Qāsim ibn al-Samḥ is the main source used by the Alfonsine astronomers for the compilation of the part of the book related to the use of the spherical astrolabe. Chapter 60, however, has no equivalence in Ibn al-Samḥ's book: see M. Viladrich, *El "Kitāb al-ᶜamal bi-l-asṭurlāb" (Llibre de l'ús de l'astrolabi) d'Ibn al-Samḥ. Estudi i traducció*, Barcelona, 1986.

[18] Rico, *Libros* III, 72 (chapter LXIII), ascribed to Hermes.

açafeha[19]. According to this latter source Abū-l-Qāsim ibn al-Samḥ (d. 1035) knew the method and computed a table for the division of the houses according to it.

Some more evidence can be obtained if we consider two other works by al-Bīrūnī: his *Maqālīd ᶜilm al-hay'a*[20] and his *Kitāb fī istīᶜāb al-wujūh al-mumkina li-ṣanᶜat al-asṭurlāb*[21]. In both works, al-Bīrūnī claims that the prime vertical method is the result of his own invention[22] and that he had explained it in a previous book of his called *Tajrīd al-shuᶜāᶜāt wa-l-anwār*[23]. He also explains that the method is long and tedious if one has to calculate with it the longitudes of the houses, but extremely simple with an astrolabe. For that purpose he designs a special astrolabe plate: the description, as it appears in the *Istīᶜāb*, is not precise and does not include a figure, but it contains enough hints to unable us to reconstruct it (see Fig. 1, not to scale):

Let *ABGD* be the projection of the tropic of Capricorn in a

---

[19] Rico, *Libros* III, 209-211 (chapter LXIII) ascribed to Hermes. Unlike the two other Alfonsine sources, we have here the possibility to control that this chapter is not an Alfonsine interpolation because the Arabic original by Ibn al-Zarqālluh is extant: see R. Puig, *Los Tratados de Construcción y Uso de la Azafea de Azarquiel*, Madrid, 1987, pp. 84-85.

[20] Ed. Debarnot, *Maqālīd* pp. 284-291.

[21] I am using two manuscripts: Istambul Carullah 1451 fols. 24 r -24 v (which I owe to the generosity of Prof. F. Sezgin) and Tunis National Library 5540, fols. 35 r -35 v, a photocopy of which was lent to me by Emilia Calvo.

[22] *Maqālīd* ed. Debarnot pp. 284-285:

عمل تسوية البيوت على مذهبي ... فمن الواجب أن أذكر طريقا ثالثا قد تفرّدت باختراعه.

Istīᶜāb (Carullah fol. 24 r, Tunis fol. 35 r):

تخطيط الدوائر التي تحدّ البيوت الاثنا عشر على مذهبي ...ولي طريق في تسوية البيوت يختصّ بي دون غيري.

[23] This work seems to be lost: see D.J. Boilot, "L'oeuvre d'al-Beruni. Essai bibliographique". *Mélanges de l'Institut Dominicain d'Etudes Orientales* (Cairo) 2 (1955), 189-190 (no. 42).

standard astrolabe plate and *KEHMF* the projection of the equator. He

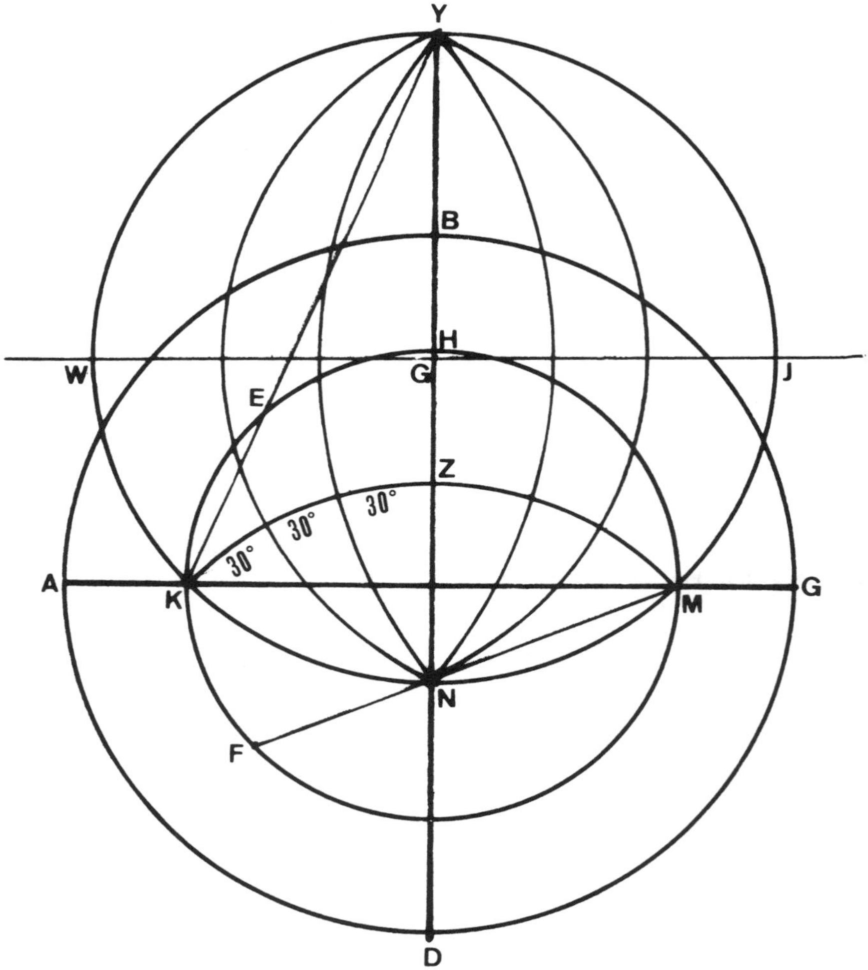

Figure 1

first determines which, among the vertical circles, is the prime vertical (*KZM*) and divides it into 30° arcs starting from the East point. The next step is to determine the centre of the projection of the horizon which he can do using the same procedure he has employed for the equatorial method (see below): from point *K* he takes arcs *KE* and *KF*, on the projection of the equator, both equal to the local latitude. Straight lines *KE* and *MF* will determine, on the meridian line, points *Y* (South point of the horizon) and *N* (North point of the horizon). *G* will be the midpoint of segment *YN* and, thus, the centre of the projection of the horizon. *WGJ*, perpendicular to the meridian line, will be the line on which we will find all the centres of the circles which will divide the ecliptic. These circles will necessarily go through points *Y* and *N* and through the 30° divisions of the prime vertical.

The situation, then, seems clear: al-Bīrūnī is the inventor of the prime vertical method, a technique which could have reached al-Andalus when he was still alife, for it was used by Ibn al-Samḥ (d. 1035)[24]. There is no evidence of the diffusion in al-Andalus of a special astrolabe plate for this purpose until the time of Ibn Bāṣo (d. 1310)[25]. Even if the methods of computation are independent we might have here the first possible instance of a diffusion of al-Bīrūnī in al-Andalus in which Ibn Muᶜādh - whose knowledge of the work of the Eastern author seems privileged - is not concerned.

With the equatorial method, John North[26] brings us back to Ibn Muᶜādh for the two Alfonsine treatises which describe it, the *Libro de las Armellas*[27] and the *Libro del Ataçyr*[28] assign it to him. In fact the method is used by this author in an appendix to his *Tabulae Jahen* entitled *Rememoratio aequationis domorum duodecim* where Ibn Muᶜādh reduces it to an algorithm which has been recently explained by J.P. Hogendijk

---

[24] See, however, the paper by E.S. Kennedy in this volume where he uses new evidence furnished by Ibn Muᶜādh's work on the projection of rays (*Maṭraḥ al-shuᶜāᶜāt*, extant in ms. Florence Medicea-Laurenziana Or. 152): Ibn al-Samḥ's method of computation is erroneous and entirely independent from al-Bīrūnī.

[25] North, *Horoscopes* pp. 60-63.

[26] North, *Horoscopes* pp. 35-38.

[27] Rico, *Libros* II, 59 (chapter XLII).

[28] Rico, *Libros* II, 309 (chapter IX).

and E.S. Kennedy. Kennedy has also found the same algorithm in the *al-Zīj al-Shāmil* of Ibn al-Raqqām (d. 1315)[29] and I suspect that some more evidence could be obtained from Ibn Muᶜādh's *Maṭraḥ al-shuᶜāᶜāt* not only because the equatorial method is used for three different astrological practices (division of the houses, *tasyīr* and projection of rays) but also because the source of the Alfonsine *Libro del Ataçyr* seems to have been precisely the *Maṭraḥ al-shuᶜāᶜāt*[30].

On the origin of the method, some more evidence can, once more, be obtained in al-Bīrūnī's *Istīᶜāb*[31] where he describes how to project an astrolabe plate which he calls *ṣafīḥat al-tasyīr* (*tasyīr* plate) although it is better known as *ṣafīḥat maṭraḥ al-shiᶜāᶜ* (plate for the projection of rays). In it we find the projection of great circles which pass through each degree of the equator as well as through the two intersections of the meridian and the horizon. According to al-Bīrūnī each one of these circles is the projection of an horizon the latitude of which is comprised between 0° and the latitude of the plate. The system described by al-Bīrūnī to project these circles is analogous to the one described before for the prime vertical method. ABGD is, again, the tropic of Capricorn (see fig. 2, not to scale), KLTM the equator, KOM the horizon for a given latitude. We take arc KE equal to the latitude and the straight line KE will determine point Y (south point of the horizon) in its intersection with the meridian line. S will be the midpoint between Y and O (north point of the horizon) and we will trace, through S, a parallel to the East-West line AG: this parallel will be the locus of all the centres of the desired circles which will pass through points Y and O as well as through equal divisions of the equator.

---

[29] On Ibn al-Raqqām's *zījes* see *Ciencias de los Antiguos* pp. 421-427.

[30] Rico, *Libros* II, 68 (chapter LII): "Este ombre a que dizen Aben-Mohat. fue gran sabio en geometría et en astrología. et fizo un libret en que fabla dell echamiento de los rayos et del atazir. et de la yguación de las .XII. casas. et mostró en él razones et pruebas que son muy acerca de la uerdat. et mostró en él otrossí cuemo deuen fazer cada una destas cosas sobredichas."

[31] Ms. Carullah fols. 15 v - 16 v.

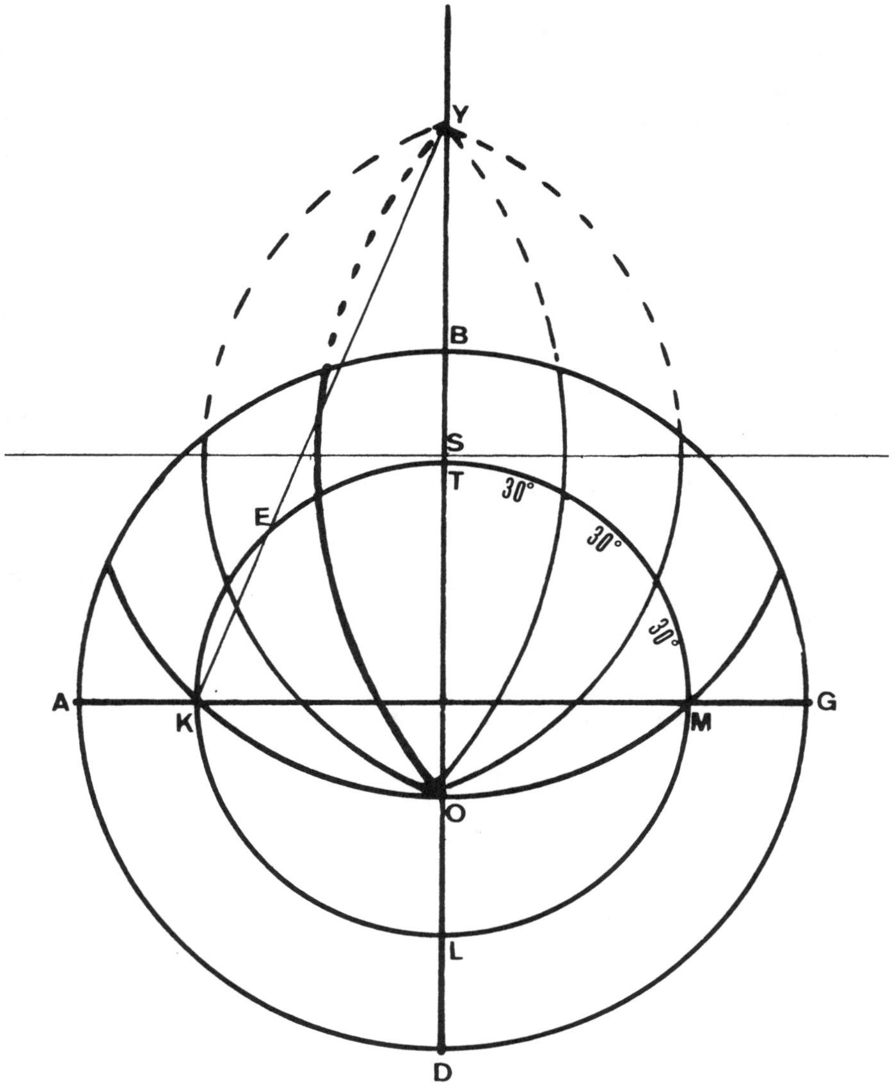

Figure 2

With minimum differences the same procedure is applied by Rabiçag (Rabbi Isḥāq b. Sīd)[32] to draw a similar plate which, combined with a standard astrolabe, has, basically, astrological uses, especially the three aforementioned ones (*tasyīr*, projection of rays and division of the houses according to the opinion of Ibn Muᶜādh)[33]: we should only remark that Rabiçag's plate contains the whole projection of the horizon while al-Bīrūnī's outer limit is, as usual in an astrolabe plate, the projection of the tropic of Capricorn.

As a conclusion, I would like to say that, in my opinion, Ibn Muᶜādh did not invent the equatorial method for the division of the houses and that, at the most and until new evidence appears, he might have applied to the solution of this problem a method which existed already for the practice of *tasyīr* and projection of rays, and he also might have discovered the algorithm he describes in the *Tabulae Jahen*. Al-Bīrūnī does not pretend, either, to have been the first to design such a plate and his words, in the *Istīᶜāb*, rather imply that he is merely describing an instrument which was fairly standard in his time. We will see in a moment that Abū Jaᶜfar al-Khāzin probably used the same sort of plate. As for al-Bīrūnī being the source of the diffusion of the equatorial method in al-Andalus, the possibility obviously exists but the evidence available is not strong enough.

5. *Andalusian equatoria and the* Zīj al-ṣafā'iḥ *of Abū Jaᶜfar al-Khāzin (d. ca. 965).*

The three earliest known equatoria are those described by the Andalusian astronomers Abū-l-Qāsim b. al-Samḥ (d. 1035), Abū Isḥāq b. al-Zarqālluh (d. 1100) and Abū-l-Ṣalt Umayya b. Abī-l-Ṣalt (*ca.* 1067-1134)[34] although this does not imply that equatoria were necessarily an

---

[32] Rico, *Libros* II, 302-304.

[33] See, on this work, M. Viladrich and R. Martí, "Sobre el *Libro del Ataçir* de los *Libros del Saber de Astronomía* de Alfonso X el Sabio". *Nuevos Estudios sobre Astronomía Española en el Siglo de Alfonso X*, ed. by J. Vernet (Barcelona, 1983), 75-100.

[34] M. Comes, *Los ecuatorios andalusíes. Ibn al-Samḥ, al-Zarqālluh y Abū-l-Ṣalt*. Barcelona, 1991.

Andalusian invention. Ptolemy himself, in his own introduction to the *Handy Tables*, gives instructions for finding the longitude of the Moon and planets by graphical constructions[35]. As for a possible Eastern origin of the instrument, the obvious candidate is Abū Jaᶜfar al-Khāzin who does not seem to have been entirely unknown in the West, for his homocentric solar model reappears in the *De reprobatione eccentricorum et epicyclorum* by Henry of Hesse or of Langenstein (1325-1397)[36]. Al-Khāzin's *Zīj al-ṣafā'iḥ* has been, until very recently only known through secondary sources (mainly quotations by Abū Naṣr Manṣūr and al-Bīrūnī)[37], to which one should add the photographs of parts of a lost astrolabe made in 1119-20 by Hibat Allāh ibn al-Ḥusayn al-Baghdādī on the basis of al-Khāzin's lost work. The *zīj* plate of this astrolabe has a ring of holes for each degree and this was interpreted by D.A. King as a trace of an equatorium added by Hibat Allāh to al-Khāzin's instrument. The plate contains also tables for determining the right ascensions of any ecliptic degree of longitude and for determining lunar and planetary latitudes[38].

New evidence has recently appeared on the mysterious *Zīj al-ṣafā'iḥ*: photocopies of five pages of a manuscript extant somewhere in India and containing a complete (?) copy of al-Khāzin's book have reached me thanks, once more, to the generosity of David King. What is interesting in these photocopies is that they contain the prologue, the index of the book and two incomplete examples of the use of the instrument described. The prologue starts with the sentence *Qāla Muḥammad b. al-Ḥusayn* ("M. b. al-Ḥ. said") which fits al-Khāzin whose complete name

---

[35] O. Neugebauer, *A History of Ancient Mathematical Astronomy* (Berlin-Heidelberg-New York, 1975) II, 990 and 1004.

[36] J. Samsó, "A Homocentric Solar Model by Abū Jaᶜfar al-Khāzin". *Journal for the History of Arabic Science* 1 (1977), 268-275 (reprinted in Samsó, *Islamic Astronomy and Medieval Spain*).

[37] See J. Samsó, "al-Khāzin" in *Encyclopédie de l'Islam* IV (Leiden-Paris, 1978), 1215-1216.

[38] D.A. King, "New Light on the *Zīj al-ṣafā'iḥ* of Abū Jaᶜfar al-Khāzin". *Centaurus* 23 (1980), 105-117. Reprinted in King, *Islamic Astronomical Instruments*. Variorum Reprints. London, 1987, no. XI.

was Abū Jaᶜfar Muḥammad b. Muḥammad b. al-Ḥusayn al-Khurāsānī. The author also states that, after having studied carefully Ptolemy's *Almagest*, he decided to trace the circles, arcs, centres, intersections etc. described in Ptolemy's models for the Sun, Moon and planets, in such a way that they would imitate the structure (*hay'a*) of the spheres of these celestial bodies, explain the reasons (*ᶜilla*) for their equations and allow the computation of their positions in longitude and latitude. Then it occurred to him[39] the possibility of making a second instrument having the same applications as the first one but using less circles and enabling him to make more accurate computations. This instrument will allow him to dispense with the use of most of the *zīj*es and will simplify the heavy task of computations. He writes his book to explain the use of the instrument, as well as the theory behind it, and he believes that he has solved most of the problems of the *Almagest*.

The vague allusions which I have summarized here seem, however, enough to conclude that the *Zīj al-ṣafā'iḥ* was a book in which the construction and use of an equatorium was described. On the other hand, the instrument was more ambitious than the extant descriptions of Andalusian equatoria which limit themselves to provide graphical solutions to the determination of solar, lunar and planetary longitudes, while it seems that al-Khāzin's instrument - like al-Kāshī's in the 15th c.[40] - also dealt with the problem of lunar and planetary latitudes. The index of the book will provide us with some extra information.

As we already knew, the book is divided into two parts (*maqāla*) and each part into chapters (*anwāᶜ*)[41]. The first *maqāla* (divided into five *anwāᶜ*) deals with the computation of the longitude and latitude of the planets using the instrument (*Taqwīm al-kawākib al-sayyāra bi-hādhihi-l-āla fī-l-ṭūl wa-l-ᶜarḍ*) although the first four *anwāᶜ* seem to be theorical

---

[39] Or to somebody else: there is an ink blot (?) in the manuscript which prevents me from reading the key word. The sentence reads: ثمّ وقع في (؟) صنعة آلة أخرى

[40] E.S. Kennedy, *The Planetary Equatorium of Jamshīd Ghiyāth al-Dīn al-Kāshī (d. 1429)*. Princeton, 1960.

[41] There is no confirmation in the index about the additional (*mulḥaqa*) *maqāla* mentioned by Abū Naṣr Manṣūr in his *Risāla fī taṣḥīḥ mā waqaᶜa li Abī Jaᶜfar al-Khāzin min al-sahw fī zīj al-ṣafā'iḥ* in *Rasā'il Abī Naṣr ilā-l-Bīrūnī* (Hyderabad, 1948 no. 3) pp. 39-49.

introductions to the problems of solar, lunar and planetary astronomy while the fifth *nawᶜ* is concerned with the construction and use of the instrument. The second *maqāla* (divided into seven *anwāᶜ*) deals with the rest of the topics of a *zīj* other than computation of the position of a planet (*maᶜrifat al-aᶜmāl al-madhkūra fī-l-zījāt baᶜd ᶜamal al-taqwīm*), namely spherical trigonometry and astronomy (sine, declination, oblique ascensions and Menelaos' theorem in the first *nawᶜ*; determination of the azimuth of a shadow, of the amount of the equator which has rotated at a given time, of the meridian line[42] and the azimuth of the *qibla*[43] in the second *nawᶜ*), parallax (third *nawᶜ*), astrological transits[44], occultation and apparition of a celestial body under the solar rays, crescent visibility, different length of day and night throughout the year, solar and lunar conjunctions and oppositions (fourth *nawᶜ*), eclipses, projection of rays and *tasyīr* (fifth *nawᶜ*). The title of the sixth *nawᶜ* is extremely interesting because it deals with the solution of all the problems posed in the five preceding *anwāᶜ* using the plates of the instrument and without any computation (*Fī maᶜrifat hādhihi-l-anwāᶜ al-khamsa min ṣafā'iḥ al-zīj bi-lā ḥisāb*). Finally, the seventh *nawᶜ* is concerned with mean motions according to two schools: that of *raṣad....*[45] *wa imtiḥān* (*Mumtaḥan zīj*, although it probably means tropical mean motions) and that of the *Sindhind* (probably sidereal mean motions).

On the whole, if one has to believe in the title of the aforementioned sixth *nawᶜ*, al-Khāzin's instrument was much more than an equatorium for it contained a whole set of graphical solutions of the standard problems solved by a *zīj*. A certain amount of confirmation can be obtained from two examples extant in my five photocopies. The first

---

[42] According to Abū Naṣr Manṣūr (*Zīj al-ṣafā'iḥ* pp. 15-33), the sixth *shakl* of the second *nawᶜ* of the second *maqāla* deals with a partially incorrect method to determine the meridian line if we know the solar degree.

[43] On the mistakes made by al-Khāzin on this topic see Abū Naṣr Manṣūr, *Zīj al-ṣafā'iḥ* pp. 33-39.

[44] On al-Khāzin's criticisms of the treatment of transits by Abū Maᶜshar, see *Al-Bīrūnī on Transits* translated by M. Saffouri and A. Ifram, with a commentary by E.S. Kennedy (Beirut, 1959), 85-87, 172.

[45] There is a blank in the manuscript.

one corresponds to the beginning of the sixth *naw*ʿ of the second *maqāla* and it deals with the obtention of sines, versed sines, arc sines and arc versed sines using the "southern plate" (*ṣafīḥat al-janūb*), which seems to contain, basically, a set of perpendiculars from the divisions of the circumference to one of the diameters. For its use this southern plate should be put on top of the others and on the plate we will place a ruler (*musaṭṭara*) which is graduated into chords (*awtār*) and versed sines (*sihām*). The second and last example appears in fol. 194 r of the manuscript[46] which is the end of the fifth *naw*ʿ of the second *maqāla* and it deals with a graphical solution to the problem of the projection of rays. My impression is that he is working with an astrolabe and with a special plate for the projection of rays which could very well be the aforementioned plate described by al-Bīrūnī and divided according to the equatorial method (see above § 4). His treatment of the sextile and trine in the eastern half is complete and I think I can make some sense out of it: he puts the alidade on the degree of longitude of the planet [in the rete] (the latitude of the planet is, therefore, not considered) and makes a mark on the intersection of the alidade with the graduated rim [of the astrolabe]. Then he moves the alidade to make it coincide with the intersection of the equator with the "arc" passing through the planet and makes a second mark also on the intersection of the alidade with the rim. He states that the angular difference between the two marks will be the equation of daylight (*taʿdīl niṣf al-nahār*), because "each one of the arcs of the plate occupy, in the corresponding place, the position of the horizon" (*kull wāḥid min qisī al-ṣafīḥa yaqūmu fī mawḍiʿi-hā maqām al-ufq*). This sentence reminds me of what al-Bīrūnī says on the "circles" of his plate for the projection of rays according to the equatorial method: each one of them is the projection of an horizon the latitude of which is comprised between 0° and the latitude of the plate. If such is the case the method can be explained in fig. 3 where:

HH' is the horizon of the plate,
QQ' is the equator,
EE' is the ecliptic,
G is Aries 0°,
K is the ecliptic degree of the planet the rays of which we want

[46] It is the only one of my five photocopies in which the folio number appears.

to project,

PB corresponds to the first position of the alidade,
B corresponds to the first mark on the rim of the astrolabe,
HAKH' is the "arc" which passes through the planet *K*,
PA corresponds to the second position of the alidade,
A corresponds to the second mark on the rim of the astrolabe.

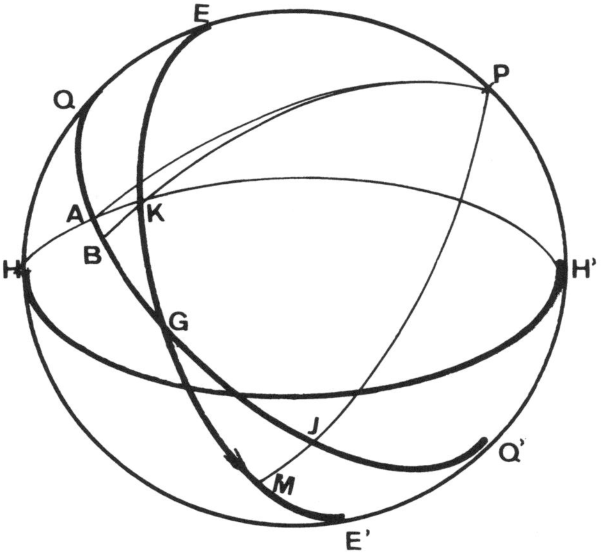

Figure 3

If we consider *HAKH'* as an horizon which the planet *K* is crossing in a given moment, *GQ'A* will be the oblique ascension of *K*, *GQ'B* its right ascension and

$$e = GQ'B - GQ'A$$

obviously equal to the equation of daylight of planet *K*.

Now, if the longitude degree of the planet belongs to a northern sign and we are dealing with a left sextile we will add:

$$60° + e/3$$

and count this amount, in the sense of the zodiacal signs, from the second mark (*A*) on the rim of the instrument. We will place the alidade at the end of this arc (*AJ*) and we will mark its intersection with the rete (*ᶜankabūt*). The corresponding degree of the ecliptic (*M*) will be the place (*mawqiᶜ*) where the rays of the left sextile fall. What we have actually done has been to find the inverse right ascension (*GM*) of the equatorial arc *GJ*[47]. The rest of the page merely gives instructions concerning the positive or negative sign of *e/3* according to the different positions of point *K* and the left or right character of the projection.

To end with this part of the paper: I think the instrument described in the *Zīj al-ṣafā'iḥ* contained an equatorium as well as a collection of graphical solutions of standard astronomical problems which included an astrolabe. The different parts of it were probably presented in special plates of the astrolabe and there were, no doubt, plates in which tabular values (mean motions, for example) were inscribed. There is no way to reach a definite conclusion on the possible influence of al-Khāzin's equatorium on the instrument designed by Ibn al-Samḥ although both have in common the fact that they were astrolabes with equatorium plates[48]. In any case the figure of al-Khāzin acquires an obvious interest for the study of this series of obscure transmissions between Eastern and Western Islam towards the beginning of the 11th c. Let us also remember the fact that al-Bīrūnī mentions al-Khāzin's *Zīj al-ṣafā'iḥ* as well as Ibrāhīm b. Sinān's *Kitāb ḥarakat al-shams* as the two standard sources where an explanation of the trepidation theory could be found and states that both sources explain the diminution of the obliquity of the ecliptic due to a motion of the poles of the ecliptic around "a point" (*ḥarakat quṭbay falak*

---

[47] The system used for the projection of rays is, therefore, slightly different from the procedure which al-Bīrūnī ascribes to Ptolemy: see E.S. Kennedy and H. Krikorian-Preisler, "The Astrological Doctrine of Projecting the Rays" in E.S. Kennedy *et al.*, *Studies in the Islamic Exact Sciences* (Beirut, 1983), 374. See also a different method described, in the 9th c., by al-Hāshimī, in which the amount added to the oblique ascension of the longitude degree of the planet is also divided by three: ᶜAlī ibn Sulaymān al-Hāshimī, *The Book of the Reasons behind Astronomical Tables* (Kitāb fī ᶜilal al-zījāt). Translation by F.I. Haddad and E.S. Kennedy, commentary by D. Pingree and E.S. Kennedy. New York, 1981, pp. 186, 323-324.

[48] I would like to draw attention to the fact that the name *Zīj al-ṣafā'iḥ* used by al-Khāzin could be related to the *ṣafīḥa zījiyya* used by Ibn al-Zarqālluh as a denomination for his equatorium. See M. Comes, *Ecuatorios andalusíes* p. 203.

al-burūj ḥawla nuqṭa)[49]. The Eastern precedents of trepidation developped by Andalusian astronomers in the 11th c. have not yet been studied[50].

6. *Velocity sectors and transits in thickness.*

Planetary sectors (*niṭāqāt*) do not seem to be a very common topic in Islamic *zījes*. Kennedy's *Survey* only mentions three *zījes* (Naṣīr al-Dīn al-Ṭūsī's *Zīj-i Īlkhānī*, al-Kāshī's *Zīj-i Khāqānī* and Ulugh Beg's *Zīj-i Sulṭānī*) containing tables of *niṭāqāt*[51] to which other three (al-Bīrūnī's *Qānūn*, Sanjar al-Kamālī's *Zīj-i Ashrafī*, Shams al-Munajjim's *al-Zīj al-Muḥaqqaq*) were added in his most important paper on the doctrine of transits[52]. Most of these sources are late but earlier direct or indirect references on sectors and transits can be found in astrological and astronomical works of the 8th and 9th c. such as those of Māshā'allāh[53], Abū Maᶜshar, Ibn Hibintā and al-Hāshimī[54]. The most complete

[49] al-Bīrūnī, *al-Athār al-Bāqiya ᶜan al-Qurūn al-Khāliya*. Ed. C.E. Sachau (Leipzig, 1923), 326; *Kitāb taḥdīd nihāyāt al-amākin li- taṣḥīḥ masāfāt al-masākin*, ed. by P. Boulgakoff in *Majallat Maᶜhad al-Makhṭūṭāt al-ᶜArabiyya* 8 (1962), 101; translation of this latter work by J. Ali, *The Determination of the Coordinates of Cities* (Beirut, 1967), p. 70; E.S. Kennedy, *A Commentary upon Bīrūnī's Kitāb Taḥdīd al-Amākin* (Beirut, 1973) p. 43.

[50] On trepidation in al-Andalus see Samsó, *Ciencias de los Antiguos* pp. 219-240 and "Trepidation in al-Andalus in the 11th century" in Samsó, *Islamic Astronomy and Medieval Spain*. Variorum Reprints, 1994. See also the papers by R. Mercier and J. Ragep in this volume.

[51] E.S. Kennedy, "A Survey of Islamic Astronomical Tables", *Transactions of the American Philosophical Society* (Philadelphia) 46, no. 2 (1956) [there is a recent reprint published in Philadelphia with no date], pp. 21, 40, 43, 45.

[52] E.S. Kennedy, "The Sasanian Astronomical Handbook *Zīj-i Shāh* and the Astrological Doctrine of 'Transit' (*Mamarr*)" in Kennedy *et al.*, *Studies in the Islamic Exact Sciences*, 319-335.

[53] See f. ex. D. Pingree, *The Thousands of Abū Maᶜshar* (London, 1968), 75-76.

[54] See Haddad, Kennedy and Pingree, *The Book of the Reasons* pp. 286-289, 295, 305, 307-308, 314-315 and the corresponding passages of the translation and Arabic text.

information on this subject is, however, given by al-Bīrūnī in his *Risālat tamhīd al-mustaqarr li-taḥqīq maᶜnā al-mamarr*[55].

Ibn Muᶜādh's *Tabulae Jahen* is the first Andalusian source in which sectors and transits are dealt with in chapter 11 of the Latin translation. The Arabic text is extant in chapter 39 of the *zīj* of Ibn Isḥāq[56] in a long quotation headed by *wa ammā madhhab al-qāḍī Ibn Muᶜādh, qāla* ("as for the method of *qāḍī* I.M., he said"). The Sun and the Moon do not retrogradate but they have a faster and a slower motion. Both reach their mean velocity (*muᶜtadil al-sayr*) when their anomaly[57] reaches the end of the first and the third sector, while their velocity is slow (*baṭī' al-sayr*) in the first and the fourth sectors (*niṭāq*), and fast (*sarīᶜ al-sayr*) in the second and third sectors. The Arabic text does not mention the value of the anomaly corresponding to the end of the first and third sectors and only states that this can be known from the corresponding table (*wa-dhālika maᶜlūm min jadwali-hi*). The Latin translation is more explicit and states the following limits (counting from the apogee):

- Sun: 92;14° and 267;46° (= 360° - 92;14°)
- Moon: 94;56° and 265;4° (= 360° - 94;56°)

These limits correspond to maximum equations of 2;14° for the Sun and 4;56° for the Moon, which are standard Indian parameters used, among many other sources, in al-Khwārizmī's *zīj* (see fig. 4). If we should take these limits seriously, they have an obvious implication: mean velocity is reached by the celestial body when the equation reaches its maximum value; if Sun and Moon reach their maximum equation at 92;14° and 94;56° from their apogee, it means that the corresponding tables in Ibn Muᶜādh's *zīj* are calculated with a Ptolemaic method and not the solution by declinations used in al-Khwārizmī's *zīj* according to which the maxi-

---

[55] Edited in *Rasā'il al-Bīrūnī* (no. 3), Hyderabad 1367/1948. See Saffouri, Adnan and Kennedy, *Al-Bīrūnī on Transits*.

[56] Manuscript Hyderabad Andra Pradesh State Library no. 298 is not foliated.

[57] *ḥiṣṣa* for the Sun, *ḥiṣṣa muᶜaddala* (corrected anomaly) for the Moon.

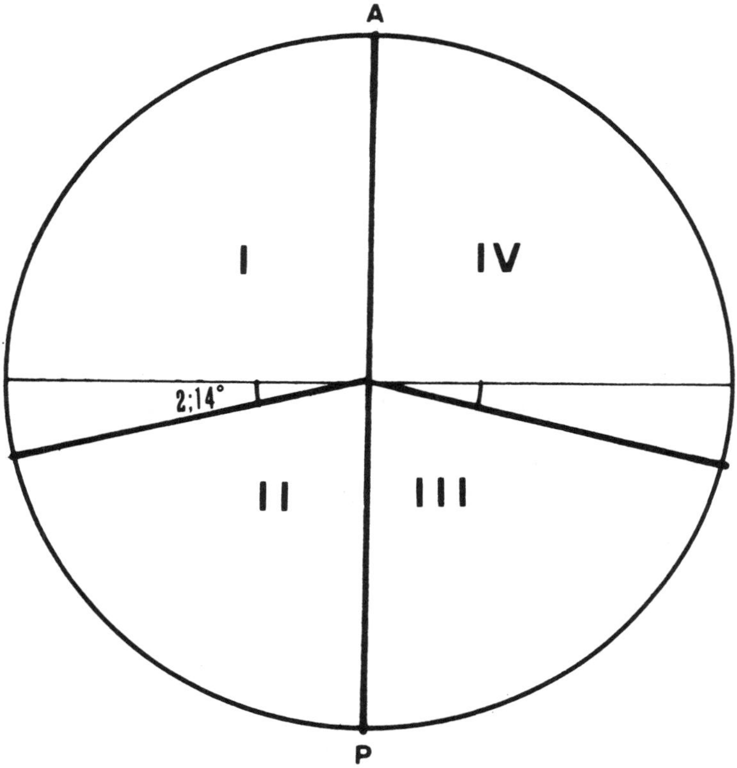

Figure 4

mum equation is reached with an anomaly of 90°[58]. On the other hand, it is clear enough from chapter 9 of the *Tabulae Jahen* that Ibn Muᶜādh uses a simplified lunar model with only one equation, but the evidence

[58] E.S. Kennedy and A. Muruwwa, "Bīrūnī on the Solar Equation" in Kennedy *et al.*, *Studies* pp. 603-612. The same implication appears in a peculiar passage of al-Hāshimī (Haddad, Kennedy and Pingree, *Book of the reasons* pp. 153 and 295-297) related to the mean solar velocity in the *Zīj al-Shāh* which is reached, according to the text also at 92;14° of the apogee in spite of the fact that it has been well established that this *zīj* used the method of sines for the computation of the solar equation, according to which the maximum value will also be reached for an anomaly of 90°.

found in the chapter we are now considering is that the model implied is an eccentric and not a concentric deferent with an epicycle. As both Arabic and Latin text state clearly:

وأمّا صعود الكواكب وهبوطها فإنّ لكلّ كوكب منها فلك أوج ثمّ لكلّ واحد من الخمسة المتحيّرة زيادة خاصّة فلك تدويره.

> *Ad sciendum uero ascensionem stellarum, et earum descensionem, est notandum quod unicuique stellae earum est orbis augis, et unicuique 5 erraticorum est additio prima orbis reuolutionis suae.*

Sun, Moon and planets have, therefore an eccentric (*falak al-awj*) but only the *five* planets have an epicycle (*falak al-tadwīr*). I know of two other uses of an eccentric model for the Moon: it appears in al-Hāshimī's *ᶜIlal al-zījāt*[59] and in the first, simplified, lunar model of Ibn al-Samḥ's equatorium[60].

Velocity sectors are also applied to the five planets. No limits are given, for both the Arabic and Latin translation state that they can be found in the corresponding tables. The sectors in the planet's deferent are analogous to those of the Sun and the Moon, while the sectors in the epicycle are obviously reversed (sectors I and IV are fast, while sectors II and III are slow). If one pretends to establish the slow or fast character of a planet at a given moment, there is no problem if the planet is in a fast or slow sector of its epicycle and the centre of its epicycle is in an equivalent sector of its deferent. The problem is posed when the epicycle and deferent sectors diverge: in that case the epicycle sector usually predominates but this can be checked by considering the actual motion of the planet in one day:

فإن أردت تحقيقها فاعلم حركة الكوكب المختلفة حينئذ ليوم واحد

This raises the question of whether Ibn Muᶜādh's *zīj* contained tables of planetary velocity.

---

[59] Haddad, Kennedy and Pingree, *The Book of the Reasons* pp. 150 and 313.

[60] Comes, *Ecuatorios andalusíes* pp. 63-65.

The text continues with a set of definitions related to the sectors on whether a celestial body is increasing (*zā'id*) or decreasing (*nāqiṣ*) in number (*ᶜadad*), computation (*ḥisāb*) and equation (*taᶜdīl*) and on whether it is ascending (*ṣāᶜid*) or descending (*hābiṭ*). The definitions and the terminology used coincide exactly with what we can read in al-Bīrūnī's *Tafhīm*[61] or *Qānūn*[62]. The most interesting part is, however, the passage in which Ibn Muᶜādh describes how to compute the transit (*mamarr*) of one planet on top of the other if both are in conjunction (*iqtirān*) or aspect (*tanāẓur*). This part seems an interpretation of Abū Maᶜshar's method as it is presented by al-Bīrūnī in his treatise on *Transits*[63]:

In this latter source there is a table of "chords" (*watar*) where each chord (w) is the result of the multiplication of the maximum equations of the centre and of the anomaly for each planet by a constant (K):

$$w = K \cdot e_{max}$$

K being 4/25 for the planets and 8/25 for the Sun and the Moon.

If we want to compare which of two planets in aspect has his transit on top of the other (= is farther away from the Earth neglecting a physical system of the world in which each one of the planets moves in his own sphere, the planetary spheres being nested one inside the other) we multiply, again, by K the actual equations of the centre and of the anomaly (e) for a given centre or anomaly and call the result "the partial chord" (*al-watar al-juz'ī*). Then we divide the "partial chord" by the "chord". The result (m) is called "minutes of transit of the celestial body in relation to the chord" (*daqā'iq mamarr al-kawkab min al-watar*):

$$m = K\,e \,/\, K\,e_{max} = e \,/\, e_{max}$$

Abū Maᶜshar operates with m directly in sectors I and III, m being the

---

[61] al-Bīrūnī, *Kitāb al-tafhīm li-awā'il ṣināᶜat al-tanjīm*. Transl. by R. Ramsay Wright (London, 1934), 110-112.

[62] al-Bīrūnī, *Qānūn* III, 1454-1455, 1458-1459.

[63] al-Bīrūnī, *Mamarr* p. 86; *Transits* pp. 95-96, 176-178. See also *Qānūn* III, 1461-1462.

magnitude of the descent of the planet from its apogee (*miqdār hubūṭi-hi min al-awj*) in the first sector[64] and the magnitude of its ascent (*miqdār ṣuᶜūdi-hi*) in sector III. As for sectors II and IV, he subtracts:

$$w - m$$

the result being the magnitude of its descent in sector II and of its ascent in sector IV.

The results obtained are rather clumsy as we can see in the graphs of figs. 5-6 where I have plotted[65] the "magnitude" (*miqdār*) function in sectors I and II (III and IV are symmetrical) for the case of the Sun in which $w = 0;42,42,36$ according to Abū Maᶜshar. Subtracting $w - m$ in sectors II and IV does not seem to have any practical application because it does not lead us to any general formulation which allows us to get rid of casuistics: each sector needs to be dealt with separately and in sectors I and II the magnitude will increase, as the planet is farther away from its apogee, while the contrary will happen in sectors III and IV.

Ibn Muᶜādh's procedure seems a modification of the method of Abū Maᶜshar. He takes the value of the equation (e) (of the centre or of the anomaly) for a given position of the celestial body (probably expressedin minutes) and multiplies it by the "root of the transit" (*aṣl al-mamarr*) (w) which can be found in the corresponding table. This implies that he is not using the unnecesary constant (K) and that he has, for w:

$$w = 60 / e_{max}$$

---

[64] Abū Maᶜshar's formulation presents certain problems due, particularly, to inconsistencies in his use of his own terminology. Thus, he states, that "when the minutes of transit equal the minutes of the chord, the transit takes place at the beginning of the second sector":

فإذا ساوى دقائق الممرّ دقائق الوتر كان ممرّه في أوّل النطاق الثاني.

which is, obviously, not true, for, at the beginning of the second sector $e = e_{max}$ and

$$m = e / e_{max} = 1$$

What Abū Maᶜshar probably means here is "the minutes of the partial chord" (*daqā'iq al-watar al-juz'ī*) instead of "the minutes of transit".

[65] I have used Benno van Dalen's programme "Table Analysis" for all these plots.

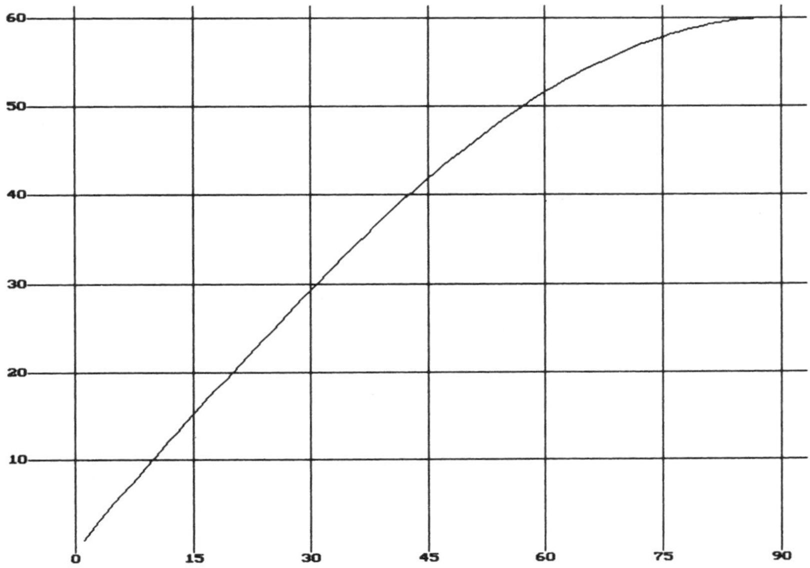

Fig. 5: Abū Maᶜshar, transits, sector I

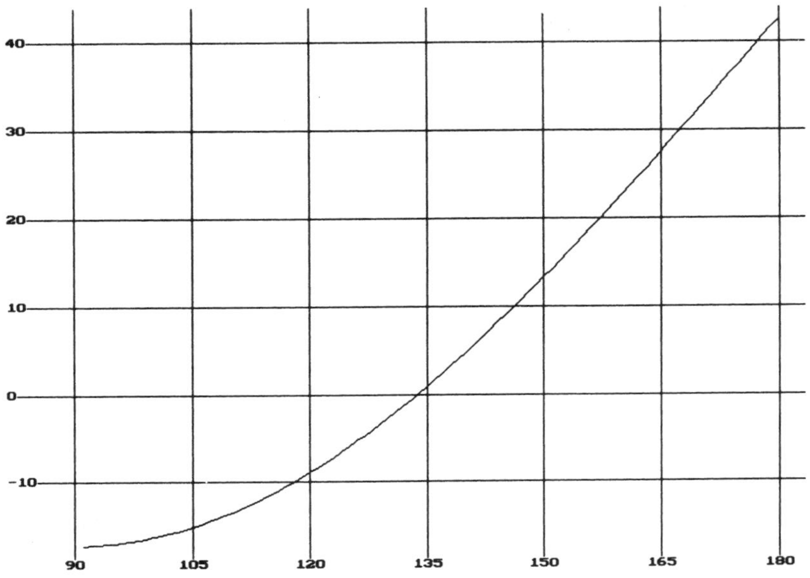

Fig. 6: Abū Maᶜshar, transits, sector II

Then he considers the argument used to obtain the equation. If it corresponds to sectors I and IV, $e \cdot w$ will be the "minutes of the transit" (*daqā'iq al-mamarr*) (*m*). If it corresponds to sectors II and III, he subtracts the result from 60:

$$m = 60 - e \cdot w$$

As an example I have plotted the corresponding function for the case of the Sun (e_{max} = 2;14°) in figs. 7-10 where we can see that Ibn Muᶜādh has succeeded in simplifying the rule to determine which of two planets transits over the other: *m* will in all cases increase, in absolute value, as the celestial body gets farther away from its apogee. For the case of the planets the values of *m* corresponding to the deferent and the epicycle will have to be considered. There is no problem if both values correspond to the same zone (ascending or descending) of both sectors. If there is disagreement, the epicycle values predominate[66]. The passage ends with a consideration of the changes of luminosity and apparent diameter of the celestial bodies: both will be reduced as the body gets nearer to its apogee, except for the case of the Moon for which light will change as a function of its elongation from the Sun. It is interesting to remark that the Latin translation mentions a table of apparent sizes[67] in which the argument is the mean centre for the Sun and the Moon and the mean anomaly for the planets: the amount tabulated is the apparent diameter for

[66] This contradicts the order of priorities in Abū Maᶜshar's *zīj*. Cf. *Mamarr* p. 88 and *Transits* p. 97.

[67] The same table is mentioned by al-Bīrūnī as extant in Abū Maᶜshar's *zīj*. Cf. *Mamarr* p. 88; *Transits* p. 98.

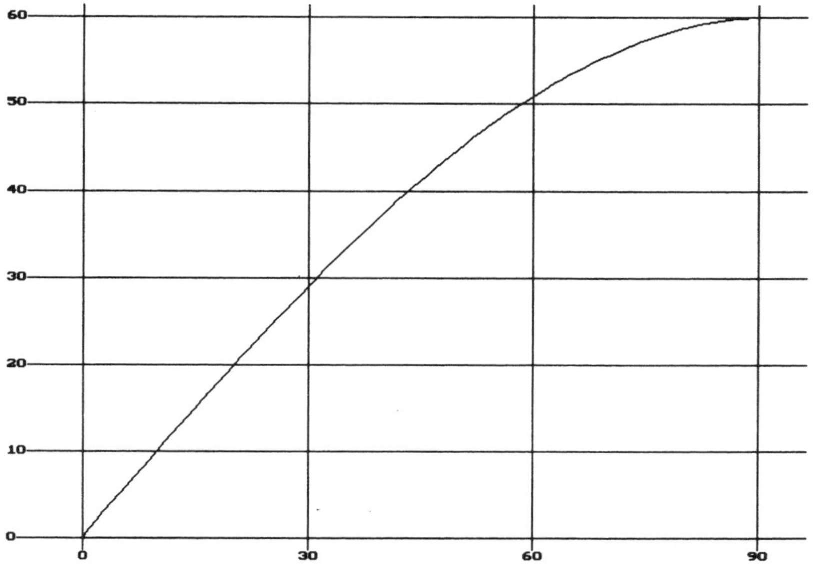

Fig. 7: Ibn Muʿādh, transits, sector I

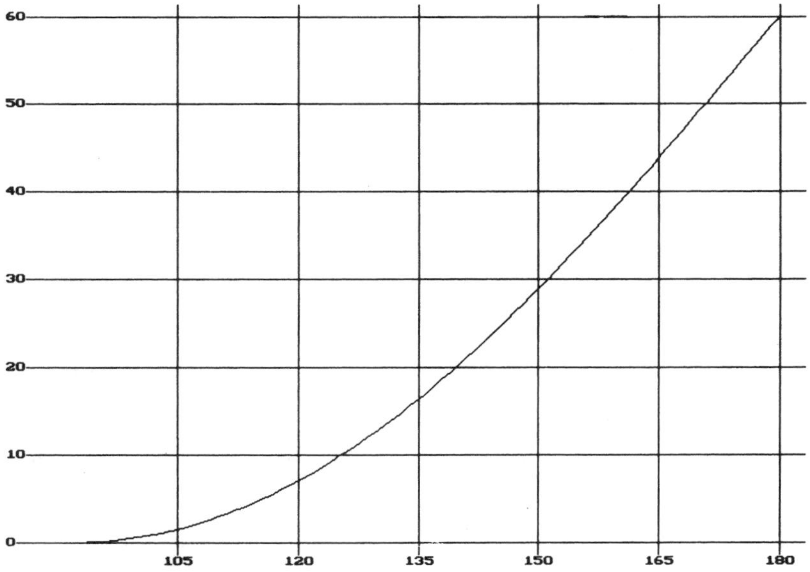

Fig. 8: Ibn Muʿādh, transits, sector II

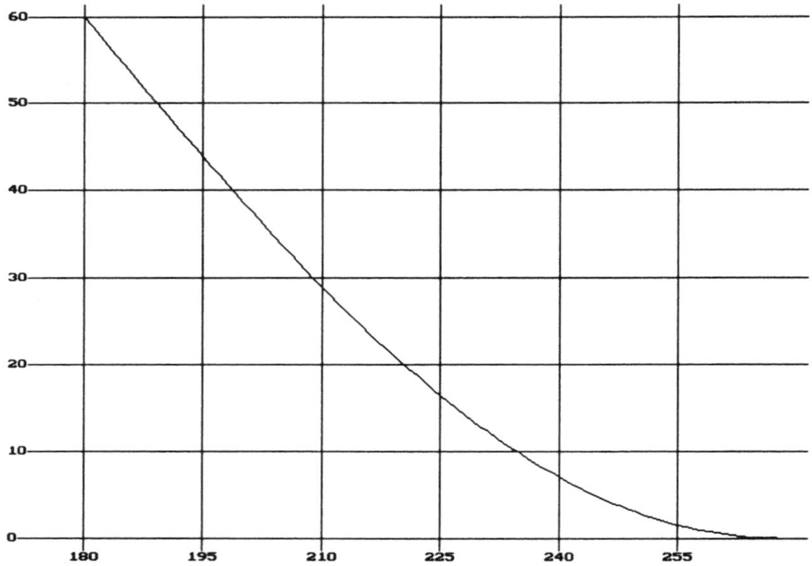

Fig. 9: Ibn Muʿādh, transits, sector III

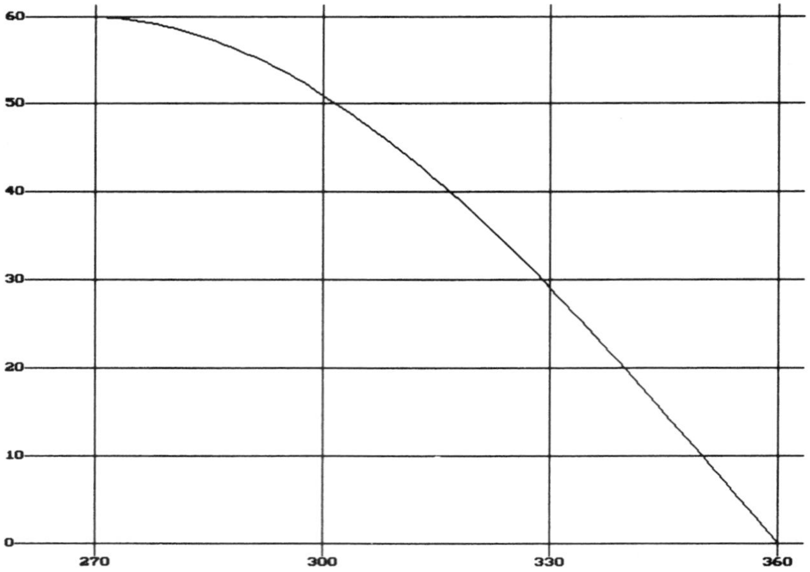

Fig. 10: Ibn Muʿādh, transits, sector IV

the planets and the apparent radius for the Sun and the Moon[68].

As a consequence, there are a lot of similarities between the treatment of velocity sectors and transits by Ibn Muᶜādh and al-Bīrūnī. The method explained by Ibn Muᶜādh to calculate whether a celestial body has its transit over another one seems an improvement of Abū Maᶜshar's procedure as explained in the *Mamarr* but it is, obviously, also possible that the actual source used by Ibn Muᶜādh was Abū Maᶜshar's lost *zīj*.

7. *Conclusions.*

No definite conclusions can be formulated from this long exposition except in one case: the fact that al-Bīrūnī states clearly that he invented the method of the first vertical (fixed boundaries) to divide the houses of the ecliptic and that the same method was known by Abū-l-Qāsim ibn al-Samḥ when al-Bīrūnī was still alife, seems to point in the direction of a transmission. This coincides with the description, in the *Istīᶜāb*, of a plate traced according to the equatorial method for the calculation of the *tasyīr* and the projection of rays, which reappears in the 13th c. *Libros del Saber de Astronomía*, while the same method is used, in the 11th c., for the division of the houses. The *Istīᶜāb* becomes, then, an essential source which should be studied carefully in order to see if other coincidences with Andalusian sources could be discovered (the orthographic projection used in the back of Ibn al-Zarqālluh's *ṣafīḥa*[69] and the construction of the spherical astrolabe as described in the Alfonsine texts are obvious candidates).

The new evidence presented on Abū Jaᶜfar al-Khāzin's *Zīj al-ṣafā'iḥ* proves that this author had designed a graphical method to determine the celestial longitude of a planet but until the whole manuscript can be studied we will not be able to establish a relation between this text

---

[68] Et nos quidem iam fecimus ad quantitates corporum 5 stellarum et 2 luminarium tabulas. Ex eis ergo extrahes quantitates stellarum, ita ut intres cum portione secunda in illas tabulas, et accipias quod est coram ea de quantitate corporali illius stellae. In duobus uero luminaribus intrabis cum portione unius earum in tabulas medietatum quantitatum duorum luminarium, et accipes quod est coram ea de medietate quantitates circuli cuiusque eorum uolueris. Et si uolueris quantitatem totius, tunc duplabis illud et erit quantitas corporis totius.

[69] See the paper by Roser Puig in this volume.

and Andalusian equatoria of the 11th and 12th c. This *zīj* has also an obvious interest concerning the origins of trepidation theory, a characteristic element in the development of Andalusian Astronomy from the 11th c. onwards.

The rest of the evidence concerns Ibn Muᶜādh al-Jayyānī whose knowledge of developments of Eastern Mathematics and Astronomy towards the end of the 10th and beginning of the 11th c. seems privileged. His Spherical Trigonometry is particularly significant and it, definitely, could not have been written without an adequate knowledge of Eastern sources on the same topic. The rest of the materials presented here (method of the *zīj*es for the determination of the azimuth of the *qibla* and his treatment of velocity sectors and planetary transits) acquire a certain strength when added to the *Kitāb al-majhūlāt*. On the whole one should underline the fact that the identification of the actual sources used by Ibn Muᶜādh becomes especially difficult because this author does not limit himself to copying his sources but introduces original developments: his use of the polar triangle in a way which is different from that of Abū Naṣr Manṣūr and his improvement of Abū Maᶜshar's technique for the computation of transits are good examples of his attitude.

Ibn al-Haytham and Jābir b. Aflaḥ's criticism of Ptolemy's determination of the parameters of Mercury

1. Presentation

Andalusian astronomers of the 11th and 12th c. seem to have felt a certain interest in the critical study of Ptolemy's model for Mercury. This is clear in the case of Ibn al-Zarqālluh who, in his treatise on the construction of the equatorium, identifies the curve traced by the centre of Mercury's epicycle with an ellipse[1] and uses a non-Ptolemaic eccentricity of 2;51,26^{p}[2]. In addition, Abū Bakr b. Bājja (1070?-1138) ascribes to Ibn al-Zarqālluh an otherwise unknown short treatise on the invalidity of the method used by Ptolemy to determine the position of Mercury's apogee (*Maqāla fī ibṭāl al-ṭarīq allatī salaka-hā Baṭlīmūs fī istikhrāj al-buᶜd al-*

[1] J. Samsó and H. Mielgo, "Ibn al-Zarqālluh on Mercury", *Journal for the History of Astronomy* 25 (1994), 289-296.

[2] On Ibn al-Zarqālluh's eccentricity see Willy Hartner's two papers reprinted in the volume *Oriens-Occidens* II (Hildesheim, Zürich, New York, 1984): "Ptolemy, Azarquiel, Ibn al-Shāṭir and Copernicus on Mercury. A Study of Parameters" (pp. 292-312); "The Islamic Astronomical Background to Nicholas Copernicus" (pp. 316-325); see also Mercè Comes, *Ecuatorios andalusíes. Ibn al-Samḥ, al-Zarqālluh y Abū-l-Ṣalt*, Barcelona, 1991, pp. 119-120.

ab^cad li-^cUṭārid)[3]. This led me, a few years ago, to conjecture whether the anomalous position of Mercury's apogee determined by M. Boutelle[4] from Ibn al-Zarqālluh's *Almanac* tables (210°, instead of the Ptolemaic 190°) was the result of new observations made by the Toledan astronomer: it is well known that Ptolemy's apogee for Mercury was inaccurate by about 30° in his own time,[5] and Andalusian astronomers were probably conscious of the fact that an entirely different - and, in fact, far more correct - longitude of Mercury's apogee appeared in al-Khwārizmī's *zīj*: 224;54° for the beginning of the Hijra (midday of 14th July 622)[6]. A different apogee - 198;24,17° for ca. 581 A.D., corresponding to the moment at which the value of precession was 0° -[7] appears in the *zīj*es of Ibn al-Bannā' (1256-

[3] See Jamāl al-Dīn al-^cAlawī, *Rasā'il falsafiyya li-Abī Bakr b. Bājja*, Beirut-Casablanca, 1983, p. 78.

[4] See Marion Boutelle, "The Almanac of Azarquiel", reprinted in E.S. Kennedy *et al.*, *Studies in the Islamic Exact Sciences* (Beirut, 1983) pp. 502-510. This paper should be read together with the important remarks by Noel Swerdlow in *Mathematical Reviews* 41 (1971), no. 5149. For a general survey of this source see J. Samsó, *Las Ciencias de los Antiguos en al-Andalus*, Madrid, 1992, pp. 166-171.

[5] See O. Gingerich, "Mercury Theory from Antiquity to Kepler", first published in 1971 and reprinted in the volume by the same author *The Eye of Heaven. Ptolemy, Copernicus, Kepler* (New York, 1993), 379-387. Robert R. Newton (*The Crime of Claudius Ptolemy*. Baltimore and London, 1977, pp. 278-279) reaches a similar conclusion when he says that the longitude of Mercury's apogee should be about 219° in Ptolemy's time instead of the 190° we find in *Almagest* IX,7.

[6] O. Neugebauer, *The Astronomical Tables of al-Khwārizmī. Translation with Commentaries of the Latin Version edited by H. Suter supplemented by Corpus Christi College MS 283* (Copenhagen, 1962) pp. 41, 99. Raymond Mercier ("Astronomical Tables in the Twelfth Century" in Charles Burnett [ed.], *Adelard of Bath. An English Scientist and Arabist of the Early Twelfth Century*, London, 1987, pp. 91-92) has proved the origin of this apogee longitude: with parameters of the *Brahmasphutasiddhanta* he obtains 224;53,13° for the beginning of the Hijra.

[7] I.e. for a moment in which tropical and sidereal longitudes were equal. According to the *Brahmasphutasiddhānta* the sidereal and tropical longitudes of the Sun were equal in year 580 and this dating appears to have been approximately followed by Ibn al-Zarqālluh who stated that the Hindu-Iranian (sidereal) and *Mumtaḥan* systems were in agreement "about

1321) and Ibn al-Raqqām (d. 1315)[8]; this appears to be a return to the Ptolemaic tradition.

Apart from the aforementioned isolated remarks, the first complete reference to an Andalusian criticism of Ptolemy's Mercury model can be found in Jābir b. Aflaḥ's *Iṣlāḥ al-Majisṭī* (fl. ca. 1150). It is interesting, however, that another important text on the same topic circulated in al-Andalus at least from the end of the eleventh century: Ibn al-Haytham's *Shukūk ᶜalā Baṭlamyūs* ("Doubts on Ptolemy") were quoted, and severely criticised, by Ibn Bājja in another passage of the same text in which he mentions Ibn al-Zarqālluh's *Maqāla fī ibṭāl*... The same work is, apparently, one of the sources used by Ibn Rushd in his *Mukhtaṣar al-Majisṭī*.[9] Ibn Bājja's passage has a certain interest and is worth translating:

> "The same attitude [as that of Ibn al-Zarqālluh] has been adopted by others who preceded him: I feel quite astonished that such is the case of Ibn al-Haytham, in spite of his fame. If you wish to consider in detail what I am telling you, read his book entitled *Shukūk ᶜalā Baṭlamiyūs*, particularly the chapter in which he explains the invalidity of the method used by Ptolemy to establish the eccentricities of Venus and Mercury, and you will get a clear idea of what I am saying. If you make a detailed study of this work, you will reach the obvious conclusion that Ibn al-Haytham only studied Astronomy in a superficial way [*min ashal al-ṭuruq*] <and that he did not assimilate in due time those things which were difficult for him, either because they confirmed his idea on the lack

40 years before the Hijra, at the moment of the Prophet's birth". Ibn al-Zarqālluh's followers Ibn al-Kammād, Ibn al-Bannā' and Ibn ᶜAzzūz have trepidation tables in their *zījes* which imply 581 A.D. as the year in which precession reached 0°. See J. Samsó, "Andalusian Astronomy in 14th Century Fez: *al-Zīj al-Muwāfiq* of Ibn ᶜAzzūz al-Qusanṭīnī", *Zeitschrift für Geschichte der Arabisch-Islamischen Wissenschaften* 11 (1997), 73-110 (see pp. 107-110).

8 See J. Samsó and E. Millás, "The computation of planetary longitudes in the *zīj* of Ibn al-Bannā', *Arabic Sciences and Philosophy* 8 (1998), 265-270.

9 See Juliane Lay, "L'*Abregé de l'Almageste*: un inédit d'Averroès en version hébraïque", *Arabic Sciences and Philosophy* 6 (1996), 23-61.

of validity of the method or because he left them aside in a careless way > [10]. He [= Ibn al-Haytham] does not belong to the group of those who have persevered in the study of this science [= Astronomy] and, in this respect, he [= Ibn al-Haytham] is farther away from it than Ibn al-Zarqālluh himself.[11]

Ibn Bājja's words have led me to consider Ibn al-Haytham's text on this topic in some detail in order to ascertain whether it might have had any influence on other Andalusian astronomers.[12] The conclusion is clearly negative, at least in relation to Jābir b. Aflaḥ[13].

2. Ibn al-Haytham on Mercury

According to Ibn Bājja, the passage in question is concerned with

[10] According to the editor al-ʿAlawī the passage in angular brackets < > is an interpolation in the text and should be suppressed.

[11] al-ʿAlawī, *Rasā'il*, pp. 77-78.

[12] The passage in question has attracted the attention of only one scholar: Don L. Voss in his unpublished doctoral dissertation (*Ibn al-Haytham's doubts concerning Ptolemy. A Translation and Commentary*) presented at the University of Chicago, Illinois, in December 1985. See two brief summaries of the contents of the *Shukūk* in A.I. Sabra, "Ibn al-Haytham", *Dictionary of Scientific Biography* VI (New York, 1972), pp. 198-99 (reprinted in Sabra, *Optics, Astronomy and Logic Studies in Arabic Science and Philosophy*, Variorum, Aldershot, 1994, no. II); George Saliba, "Arabic Planetary Theories after the eleventh century AD" in R. Rashed and R. Morelon (eds.), *Encyclopedia of the History of Arabic Science*, Vol. I (London & New York, 1996), pp. 74-82. See also Sabra, "An eleventh-century refutation of Ptolemy's planetary theory", in *Science and History: Studies in Honor of Edward Rosen, Studia Copernicana 16*, Wroclaw: Ossolineum, 1978, pp. 117-131 (reprint in Sabra, *Optics* no. XIV). This latter paper contains an English translation of Ibn al-Haytham's general criticism of the five planetary models but omits the passage which interests me here.

[13] Ibn Rushd does not mention Ibn al-Haytham's criticism in the first part of his *Mukhtaṣar al-Majisṭī* which I have been able to read in the unpublished French translation by Juliane Lay, sent generously to me by the author. We find in the *Mukhtaṣar* frequent references to Jābir's commentary, including his criticism of the Ptolemaic method for determining the position of the apse line of Mercury and Venus - on this, see below §3.

Ptolemy's method to determine the position of the centre of the eccentre of Mercury and Venus as they appear in the Almagest IX,9 (Mercury) and X,3 (Venus).[14] This method, according to Ibn al-Haytham, is invalid (*fāsid*). These centres are determined on the basis of two observations of the maximum morning and evening elongations of each planet from the mean sun whose position coincides with that of the centre of the planet's epicycle (!) according to what he [i.e. Ptolemy] asserted:

> *Wa dhālika anna-hu istakhraja kull wāḥid min hādhayn al-markazayn bi-raṣadayn li 'l-kawkab ṣabāḥī wa-masā'ī kāna al-kawkab fī kull wāḥid min-humā fī ghāyat buᶜdi-hi min mawḍiᶜ al-shams al-wasaṭ alladhī huwa markaz falak al-tadwīr ᶜalā mā qarrara-hu.*[15]

This is Ibn al-Haytham's main error in this passage and it justifies Ibn Bājja's assertion that his knowledge of Ptolemaic astronomy was, apparently, superficial: in the *Almagest* the mean motions of the centre of the epicycles of the inferior planets are the same as that of the Sun, but, although the eccentricity of Venus ($1;15^{p}$) is half that of the Sun ($2;30^{p}$), that of Mercury (3^{p}) bears no relation to the solar eccentricity and the position of the three apogees is independent: the solar apogee is placed at $65;30^{\circ}$ from the vernal equinox and it is fixed, while that of Venus is 55° and that of Mercury 190°, both moving at the same rate as the precession of the equinoxes. In neither case, therefore, can one assert - as Ibn al-Haytham says repeatedly - that the longitude of the centre of the planetary epicycle coincides with that of the mean sun, the only obvious thing being (see below figs. 3 and 6) that the line connecting the centre of the earth and the mean sun is parallel to the line connecting the equant and the centre of the planetary epicycle. It is true, however, that Islamic astronomers, from the ninth century onwards, were influenced by Hindu-Iranian astronomy

14 Ibn al-Haytham, *Shukūk* ed. ᶜAbd al-Ḥamīd Ṣabra and Nabīl al-Shāhābī, Cairo, 1971, pp. 29-32. The corresponding chapters of the *Almagest* can be read in G.J. Toomer's translation: *Ptolemy's Almagest*, Springer Verlag, New York etc., 1984, pp. 456-460, 472-474.

15 *Shukūk* ed. Ṣabra & Shāhābī pp. 29-30.

- represented, for example, by the *Zīj al-Shāh* - and introduced an important modification in the Ptolemaic model for Venus: in the Islamic tradition the apogee of the Sun is the same as that of Venus and both are subjected to the motion of precession.[16] It is understandable, therefore, that Ibn al-Haytham identifies the position of the centre of the epicycle of Venus with the mean Sun, although this cannot be considered Ptolemaic. This identification, however, does not seem to have any precedent for the case of Mercury.

I will now return to Ibn al-Haytham's text: he mentions two maximum elongations of Mercury, which are 26° (evening) and 20;15° (morning), the distance of the mean sun from the planet's apogee - which has not moved significantly in the period of time elapsed between the two observations - being, in both cases, 90°. He is, therefore, alluding to

1) an observation, made on the evening of the 4th of July 130 A.D. by a certain Theon, which yielded a maximum elongation of 26;15° (not 26° as in Ibn al-Haytham's text), the mean Sun being at 100;5°,

2) his own observation made at dawn of the 4/5th July 139 A.D. which established a maximum elongation of 20;15°[17], the mean sun being at 100;20° (*Alm.* IX, 9). As Mercury's apogee is, in Ptolemy's determination, at 190° from the vernal point, the distance between the apogee and the mean sun is, approximately, 90°.

[16] B.R. Goldstein and F.W. Sawyer, "Remarks on Ptolemy's equant model in Islamic astronomy. Appendix: On Ptolemy's determination of the apsidal line for Venus", in Y. Maeyama and W.G. Saltzer, *Prismata. Naturwissenschaft-geschichtliche Studien. Festschrift für Willy Hartner* (Wiesbaden, 1977), 165-181.

[17] Toomer, *Almagest* p. 456.

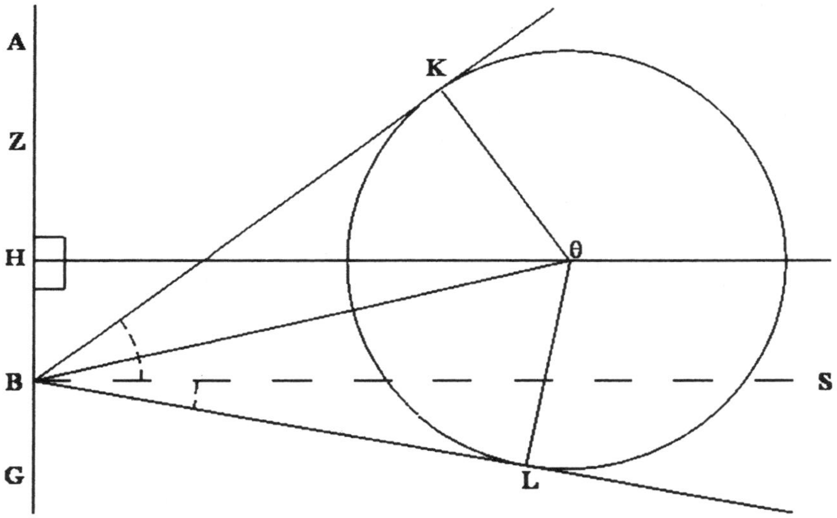

Figure 1

These observations are represented by Ptolemy with Fig. 1[18] in which AG is the apse-line, Z the centre of the eccentre, H the equant point and B the centre of the ecliptic, Θ being the centre of the epicycle. HΘ is perpendicular to AG for, in both observations, the mean Sun (S) is located at an angular distance of 90° from Mercury's apogee. Angles ∠ SBL and ∠ SBK correspond to the two maximum morning and evening elongations of the planet from the mean Sun and, obviously:

$$\angle SBL + \angle SBK = \angle \Theta BL + \angle \Theta BK$$

[18] Toomer, *Almagest* p. 457, fig. 9.6.

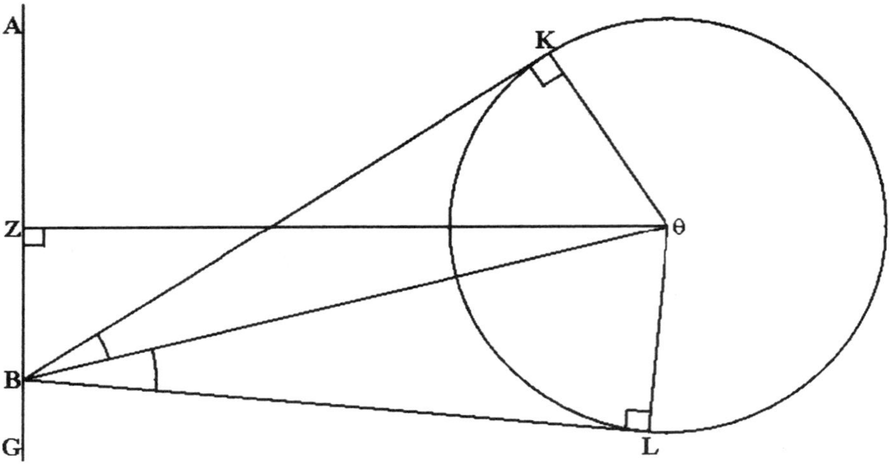

Figure 2

Fig. 2 is an attempt to reconstruct a figure which corresponds to Ibn al-Haytham's description. In it we find an important modification: the equant point (H) has disappeared from his figure and mean motion is measured from the centre of the eccentre (Z). From Z - not from the equant point as in the *Almagest* - we draw ZΘ perpendicular to AG, Θ being the centre of the epicycle in both observations[19]. Then we draw BL, BK - both tangent to the epicycle - and BΘ. The two maximum elongations correspond, according to Ibn al-Haytham, to the angle subtended by two lines: one is BΘ, which joins B, the centre of vision (*markaz al-baṣar*), with Θ, the centre of the planet's epicycle (which he identifies with the mean Sun), while the other is either BK or BL, the lines drawn from the centre of vision which are tangent to the epicycle. If the two maximum

[19] Ibn al-Haytham's text never mentions the equant point and the perpendicular is clearly drawn from the centre of the eccentre: *Wa akhraja min hādha al-markaz, aʿnī markaz al-falak al-khārij al-markaz, ʿamūdᵃⁿ ʿalā al-quṭr, wa-faraḍa markaz falak al-tadwīr nuqṭat min hādhā al-khaṭṭ* (ed. Sabra & Shahābī p. 31).

morning and evening elongations are different, the corresponding angles (∠ ΘBL and ∠ ΘBK) are also different, which implies that the two centres of the epicycles - let us call them Θ and Θ' - are at different distances from the centre of vision (B) at the times of the two observations and that the two lines tangent to the epicycles (BK and BL) have different lengths. These implications contradict the fact that, in the two aforementioned observations, the positions of the centres of the two epicycles were equal: the two lines (BΘ and BΘ', as well as BK and BL) should also be equal in both observations, and the same should happen with the lines joining the centres of the two epicycles and the points of tangency (ΘK and ΘL), and with the two angles subtended by the two radii of the epicycle (∠ ΘBK and ∠ ΘBL). Ibn al-Haytham continues with this line of argument assuming that if the centres of the two epicycles are placed, in both cases, at the end of a diameter of the eccentre perpendicular to the apse line, the two maximum and evening elongations should be equal. Ptolemy claims that the addition of the two angles ∠ ΘBK and ∠ ΘBL is equal to the addition of the maximum morning and evening elongations, something which, according to Ibn al-Haytham, is clearly absurd (*muḥāl ẓāhir al-istiḥāla*). As Ptolemy's observations do not yield the equality of angles ∠ ΘBK and ∠ ΘBL, point Θ may be the position of the centre of the epicycle in one of the two observations but not in both of them. Consequently the method used by Ptolemy is invalid, and the eccentricity obtained cannot be correct. The same remarks can be applied to the case of Venus. This implies that not all computations based on the Ptolemaic parameters for the eccentricities of Mercury and Venus are reliable, and explains the frequent divergences between computed and observed positions of these two planets. The paragraph ends with the expression of Ibn al-Haytham's lack of confidence in Ptolemy's planetary models as a whole.[20]

It is unnecessary to stress the fact that Ibn al-Haytham's criticism lies in the identification of point Θ (centre of the epicycle) with the mean Sun. As a result of his confusion he misses the role played by the equation of the centre, which justifies the difference between the maximum morning and

[20] For a complete English translation of this passage see Voss, *Ibn al-Haytham's Doubts* pp. 47-52; commentary pp. 126-131.

evening elongations from the same position of the mean Sun. This is something which will be clarified by Jābir b. Aflaḥ. I have no explanation for such a mistake which I - like Ibn Bājja - find most surprising in a scientist of the category of Ibn al-Haytham[21].

3. Jābir b. Aflaḥ on the Ptolemaic determination of Mercury's apogee

Jābir b. Aflaḥ deals with the planets in book VII of his *Iṣlāḥ al-Majisṭī*[22]. This is the famous book in which he criticises the Ptolemaic order of planetary spheres and gives an interesting - though impractical - solution to the problem of determining the apse line and the eccentricity of the superior planets[23]. In this latter instance, as in the one I am going to

[21] Recent scholarship has discussed the possibility of the existence of one or two Ibn al-Haythams: see Roshdi Rashed, *Les mathématiques infinitésimales du IXᵉ au XIᵉ siècle. Ibn al-Haytham. Vol. II*, Al-Furqān. Islamic Heritage Foundation, London, 1993, pp. 1-28, 489-538; A.I. Sabra, "One Ibn al-Haytham or two? An exercise in reading the bio-bibliographical sources", *Zeitschrift für Geschichte der Arabisch-Islamischen Wissenschaften* 12 (1998), 1-50. In spite of this, both authors seem to agree in attributing the *Shukūk* to al-Ḥasan ibn al-Haytham, the author of the *Kitāb al-Manāẓir*.

[22] I am only using MS Escorial Ar. 910 fols. 78 v - 99 v. On Jābir see Richard Lorch, "The Astronomy of Jābir ibn Aflaḥ", *Centaurus* 19 (1975), 85-107; Lorch, "The Astronomical Instruments of Jābir ibn Aflaḥ and the Torquetum", *Centaurus* 20 (1976), 11-34. Both papers have been reprinted in Lorch, *Arabic Mathematical Sciences. Instruments, Texts, Transmission*, Variorum, Aldershot, 1995 (items VI and XVI). This latter volume contains two previously unpublished papers by Lorch: "The Manuscripts of Jābir's Treatise" (no. VII) and "Jābir ibn Aflaḥ and the Establishment of Trigonometry in the West" (no. VIII). A complete list of Arabic, Hebrew and Latin manuscripts of Jābir's *Iṣlāḥ* can be found in the aforementioned book by Lorch VI, pp. 88-94 and VII, pp. 1-2.

[23] N. Swerdlow, "Jābir ibn Aflaḥ's interesting method for finding the eccentricities and direction of the apsidal line of a superior planet" in D.A. King and G. Saliba (eds.), *From Deferent to Equant. A Volume of Studies in the History of Science in the Ancient and Medieval Near East in Honor of E.S. Kennedy*, New York, 1987 (= *Annals of the New York Academy of Sciences* vol. 500), pp. 501-512; H. Hugonnard-Roche, "La théorie astronomique selon Jābir ibn Aflaḥ", in G. Swarup, A.K. Bag and K.S. Shukla, *History of Oriental Astronomy. Proceedings of an International Astronomical Union Colloquium no. 91*, Cambridge, 1987, pp. 207-208.

consider here, Jābir's criticism of Ptolemy is that of a teacher of Mathematics who considers that Ptolemy has assumed, without proof, the bisection of planetary eccentricity and considers the iterative method used by the Greek astronomer as an approximation which starts by considering that the centre of the deferent and the centre of the equant are the same point. Mathematical precision and proof seems to be Jābir's maximum aspiration, and reading the *Iṣlāḥ* leads me to believe that he was not, in any way, a practical astronomer and that he probably never made a single observation.

I will consider here Jābir's interesting criticism of the method used by Ptolemy to determine the position of the apogees of the inferior planets. He makes no reference to previous work done by either Eastern or Western Islamic astronomers. Here, as elsewhere in Jābir's book, our author seems to be unaware of any of the results obtained by those who lived and worked after Ptolemy. His purpose is at all times to present his own rewriting of the *Almagest*.

Like Ptolemy (*Almagest* IX, 6) he begins by proving that when the centre of the epicycle is placed symmetrically on either side of the apse line, the planet being - in both positions - also symmetrically on either side of the apogee of the epicycle, the angles corresponding to the equations of the centre and to the equations of anomaly will have, in both cases, the same absolute value. Therefore in Fig. 3 (which corresponds to Ptolemy's proof for the case of the superior planets and Venus)[24]:

AG is the apse line, A being the apogee,

E is the centre of the eccentre,

H is the centre of the equant,

Z is the centre of the ecliptic,

Epicycles CL (with centre at B) and NM (with centre at D) correspond to two positions of the centre of the epicycle such that $\angle$ BHA = $\angle$ DHA,

In Jābir's text L and M are two positions of the planet on epicycles CL and MN such that $\angle$ CBL = $\angle$ NDM, placed on symmetric sides of the apogee of the epicycle. On this point, Jābir's formulation is more general than that of Ptolemy for, in the *Almagest*, M and L are placed in the

[24] *Almagest* IX,6, trans. Toomer pp. 445-447; *Iṣlāḥ* MS Escorial fols. 83 r and v.

positions in which the planet attains its maximum elongation from the centre of the epicycle, so that ZL and ZM are tangents to the epicycle and BL and DM are perpendicular to ZL and ZM.

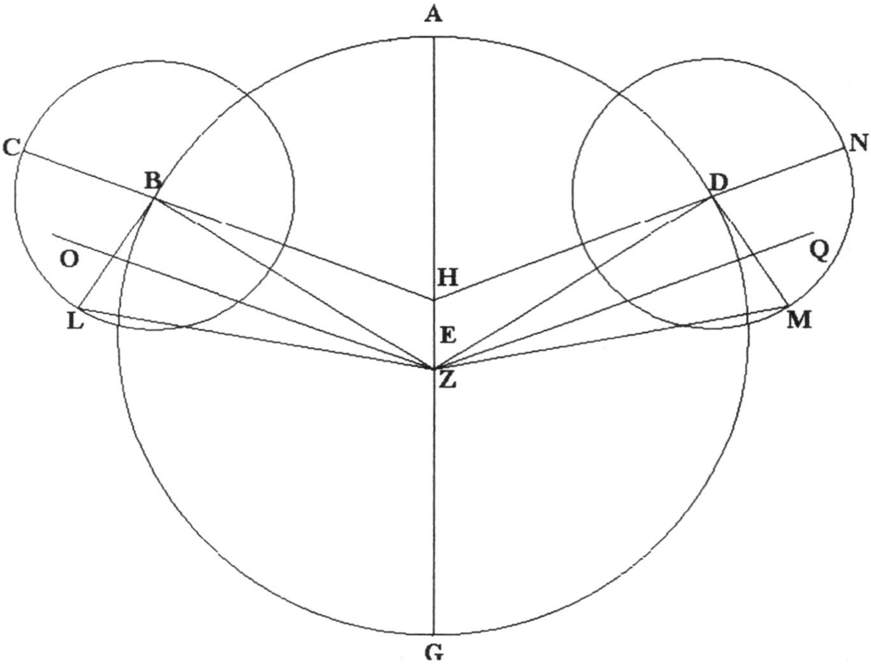

Figure 3

Both Ptolemy and Jābir seek to prove that, in the situation described, ∠ZBH = ∠ZDH (equation of the centre) and ∠BZL = ∠DZM (equation of the anomaly).

Jābir's proof follows that of the *Almagest*, with only trivial variants: he begins by stating, without proof, that DH = BH[25] and, consequently, the

[25] There is a proof in the *Almagest* which explains why Ptolemy's figure is slightly more complicated than Jābir's.

equalities of triangles $\triangle DZH = \triangle BZH$ and, therefore, that $\angle ZBH = \angle ZDH$.

In the second stage Jābir demonstrates the equality of triangles $\triangle BZL$ and $\triangle DZM$ due to the fact that $\angle ZBH = \angle ZDH$, and that $\angle CBL = \angle NDM$, from which he deduces that $\triangle LBZ = \triangle MDZ$; he has also proved that BZ = DZ and, obviously, BL = DM. Therefore $\angle BZL = \angle DZM$. Ptolemy's proof for this stage is slightly simpler for he assumes that $\angle BLZ$ and $\angle DMZ$ are right angles.

Jābir, however, proceeds one step further, for he draws lines ZO (parallel to HB) and ZQ (parallel to HD) and states that $\angle BZO = \angle DZQ$ and that $\angle OZL = \angle QZM$. No proof is given but it is easy to see that

$\angle BZO = \angle AZO - \angle AZB$

$\angle DZQ = \angle AZQ - \angle AZD$

From which we have $\angle BZO = \angle DZQ$ for

$\angle AZB = \angle AZD$, due to the equality of triangles $\angle ZBH = \angle ZDH$.

And

$\angle AZO = \angle AHB$

$\angle AZQ = \angle AHD$

$\angle AHB = \angle AHD$ by hypothesis

Therefore $\angle BZO = \angle DZQ$.

As for the equality $\angle OZL = \angle QZM$, we have that

$\angle OZL = \angle BZL - \angle BZO$

$\angle QZM = \angle DZM - \angle DZQ$

He has already proved that $\angle BZL = \angle DZM$ and we have also seen that $\angle BZO = \angle DZQ$.

Once Jābir has established this, he states that, in the case of Venus, straight lines ZO and ZQ link the centre of the Universe with the position of the mean Sun. Therefore, in this configuration, the two distances between Venus and the mean Sun will be equal, a phenomenon that can also be applied to the maximum elongations of the planet from the mean Sun.

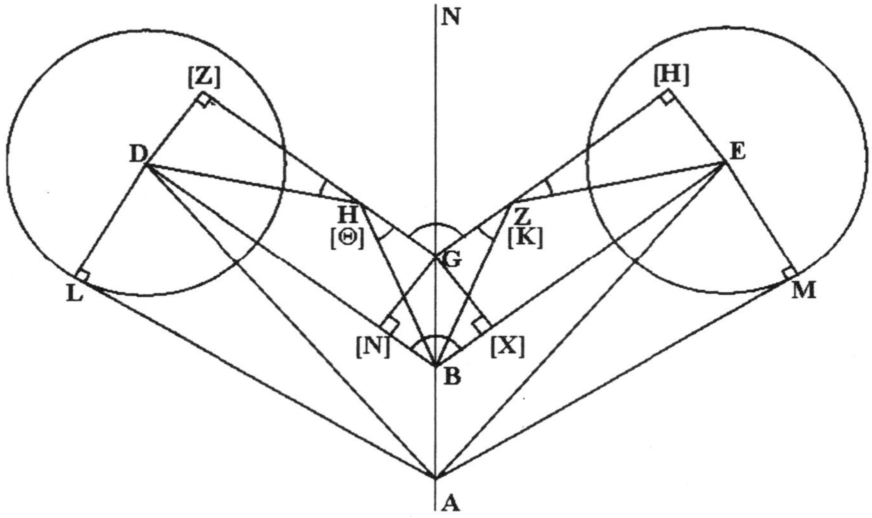

Figure 4

These trivial differences between the *Almagest* and the *Iṣlāḥ* are not so trivial in the case of Mercury[26]. Fig. 4 corresponds to the *Almagest*, and Fig. 5 is that of the *Iṣlāḥ*. In Fig. 4 letters in square brackets are those of the *Almagest* which do not appear in the figure of the *Iṣlāḥ*: for the points which are common to both figures I have added to the letters in square brackets the letters used by Jābir in Fig. 5.

In both figures:

A is the centre of the Universe

B is the centre of the equant

G is the centre of the small circle in which the centre of Mercury's deferent rotates (the *mudīr*).

DL and EM correspond to two positions of Mercury's epicycle such that

$\angle$ DBG = $\angle$ EBG

L and M are symmetrical on both sides of the apogee of the epicycle. In

[26] See *Almagest* IX, 6 (Toomer pp. 447-448); *Iṣlāḥ* fols. 83 v - 84 v.

Fig. 4, L and M correspond to maximum elongations from the centre of the epicycle and, therefore, AL and AM are perpendicular to the epicycle radii DL and EM.

GH = GZ = GB = BA and

∠ NGH = ∠ NGZ = ∠ DBG = ∠ EBG

Z, therefore, is the centre of Mercury's deferent when the centre of the epicycle is in D and H is the centre of the deferent when E is the centre of the epicycle.

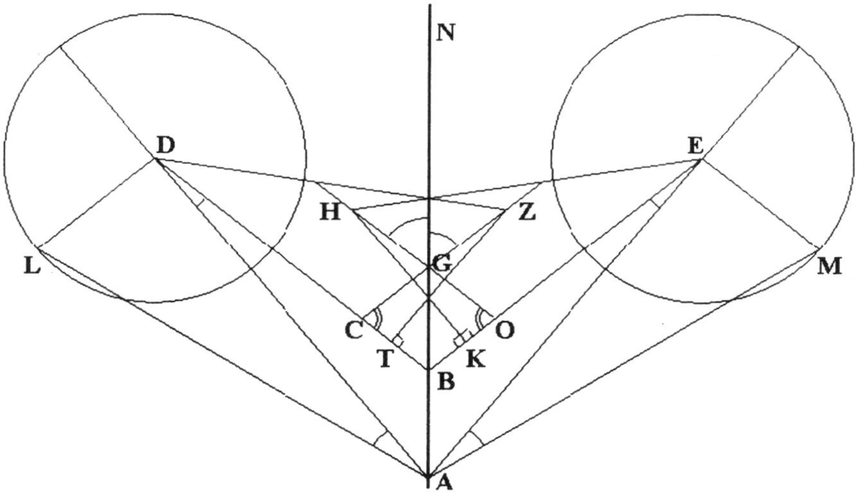

Figure 5

Both Ptolemy and Jābir seek to prove that

∠ ADB = ∠ AEB (equation of the centre)

∠ DAL = ∠ EAM (equation of the anomaly; in Fig. 4 it is also the maximum elongation of Mercury from the centre of the epicycle).

Ptolemy (Fig. 4) drops the perpendiculars:

G[N] and G[X] to BD and BE

D[Z] and E[H] to G[Z] and G[H]

He then begins by proving that right-angled triangles △GB[N] and △GB[X] are equal for they have a common side (GB) and ∠GB[N] =

∠GB[X] by hypothesis. Therefore G[N] = G[X].

As G[N][Z]D and G[X][H]E are rectangles, D[Z] = G[N] = G[X] = [H]E. Ptolemy assumes, then, that right-angled triangles △ HD[Z] and △ ZE[H] are equal because D[Z] = E[H] and HD = ZE. The latter equality is given without proof;[27] this is the basis of Jābir's criticism and the cause of his using a different approach to reach the same conclusion.

Triangles △HGB and △ZGB are also equal because they have a common side (GB), GH = GZ (by hypothesis) and ∠HGB = ∠ZGB (by hypothesis). Therefore ∠GHB = ∠GZB and, as he has just proved that ∠DH[Z] = ∠EZ[H], it is now obvious that ∠DHB = ∠BZE.

Ptolemy now deals with the equality of triangles △HDB and △ZEB in which we can see that

∠HBD = ∠GBD - ∠GBH

∠ZBE = ∠GBE - ∠GBZ

As ∠GBD = ∠GBE (by hypothesis)

∠GBH = ∠GBZ (because he has just proved the equality of triangles △HGB and △ZGB)

Therefore ∠HBD = ∠ZBE

As he has also established that ∠DHB = ∠BZE and has stated, without proof, that DH = ZE, he now assumes that BD = BE.

This allows him to prove the equality of triangles △BAD and △BAE which have

Side BA in common

∠DBA = ∠EBA (by hypothesis)

BD = BE

Therefore ∠ADB = ∠AEB (equation of the centre)

and AD = AE

Finally, right-angled triangles △ADL and △AEM are equal because DL = EM and, consequently ∠DAL = ∠EAM (maximum elongation of the planet from the centre of the epicycle).

Jābir's proof is different (Fig. 5). He joins ZD and HE (deferent radii

[27] Toomer (*Almagest* p. 448 n. 50) remarks: "Although one can see that this must be so by symmetry, the proof is quite intricate".

which correspond respectively to D and E centres of the epicycle), and extends ZG and HG until they intersect BD and BE at points C and O. From Z and H he also drops perpendiculars ZT (to BD) and HK (to BE).

As ∠ZGN = ∠GBC (by hypothesis), ∠GBC = ∠BGC and CB = GC in triangle △GBC. We can also prove, in the same way, that GO = BO [and that △GBO = △GBC (their angles are respectively equal and side GB is common to both triangles), GO being, therefore, equal to GC].

Jābir now proves that right-angled triangles △ZTC and △HKO are equal, because:

OH = CZ

[OH = OG + GH

CZ = GC + ZG

and we have just proved that OG = GC, while GH = ZG (by hyp.)]

∠ZCT = ∠HOK (△GBO = △GBC)

Therefore ZT = HK

and BK = BT

[BK = OB - KO

BT = CB - CT

and OB = CB, KO = CT]

[He then considers right-angled triangles △DZT = △EHK in which] DZ = HE (both are deferent radii) and ZT = HK. Therefore DT = EK. As he has already proved that BK = BT, BD = BE.

Jābir's demonstration now joins Ptolemy by proving (as in the *Almagest*) that △BAD and △BAE are equal and, therefore, that ∠ADB = ∠AEB (equation of the centre) and AD = AE. Finally he proves that △ADL = △AEM because DL = EM and ∠ADL = ∠AEM (by hyp.). Therefore ∠DAL = ∠EAM, *q.e.d.*

Jābir has shown a certain degree of ability by avoiding the need to prove that (in Fig. 4) HD = ZE. As a matter of fact he states[28] that, here, Ptolemy makes the mistake of considering that HD and ZE are two radii of the deferent when the centres of the epicycles are, respectively, in D and E. He could not have said, otherwise, that HD = ZE, an equality which

[28] Jābir, *Iṣlāḥ* fol. 84 v.

can only be proved if we previously demonstrate that DB = EB. To this he adds (omitting the unnecessary proof) that, as he has shown for Venus, the two distances of Mercury from the mean Sun are necessarily equal.

This first remark on Ptolemy's determination of Mercury's apogee is characteristic of Jābir's standard attitude of criticising the *Almagest* on account of what we might call his "mathematical scruples". The important part of his argument appears later[29]: Ptolemy has proved that two maximum and opposite (i.e. morning and evening) elongations of the planet from the mean Sun, which take place symmetrically in relation to Mercury's apogee, are necessarily equal. The author of the *Almagest* claims, however, that the reciprocal formulation is also true: two equal maximum and opposite elongations of the planet from the mean Sun will necessarily take place symmetrically on both sides of the apogee.[30] Jābir states repeatedly that this is not true and that a planet may have many equal maximum morning and evening elongations from the mean Sun without the planet's apogee being at the midpoint between the two positions of the centre of the epicycle.

Jābir's argument can be better explained with Fig. 6 (not in the manuscript) which corresponds to a Ptolemaic standard planetary model, like that of Venus: A is the apogee, E the centre of the equant, C the centre of the deferent and T the centre of the Universe. D_1 and D_2 are two positions of the centre of the epicycle on both sides of the apse line, P_1 and P_2 the two positions of the planet at the moment of two maximum morning elongations from the mean Sun (S_{m1} and S_{m2}). Jābir states correctly that the maximum elongation of the planet from the mean Sun ($\angle P_1TS_{m1}$ or $\angle P_2TS_{m2}$) will be equal to the angle subtended by the radius of the epicycle ($\angle r = \angle P_1TD_1$ or $\angle r = \angle P_2TD_2$) plus or minus the equation of the centre ($\eta = \angle ED_1T = \angle D_1TS_{m1}$, or $\eta = \angle ED_2T = \angle D_2TS_{m2}$). Obviously at the apogee or perigee of the deferent $\eta = 0$ and the maximum

[29] Jābir, *Iṣlāḥ* fols. 84 v - 85 r.

[30] See the interesting remarks made by Sawyer in Goldstein & Sawyer, "Remarks on Ptolemy's equant model" pp. 169-173. His observations for Venus can also be applied to the case of Mercury.

elongation will be equal to $\angle$ r.

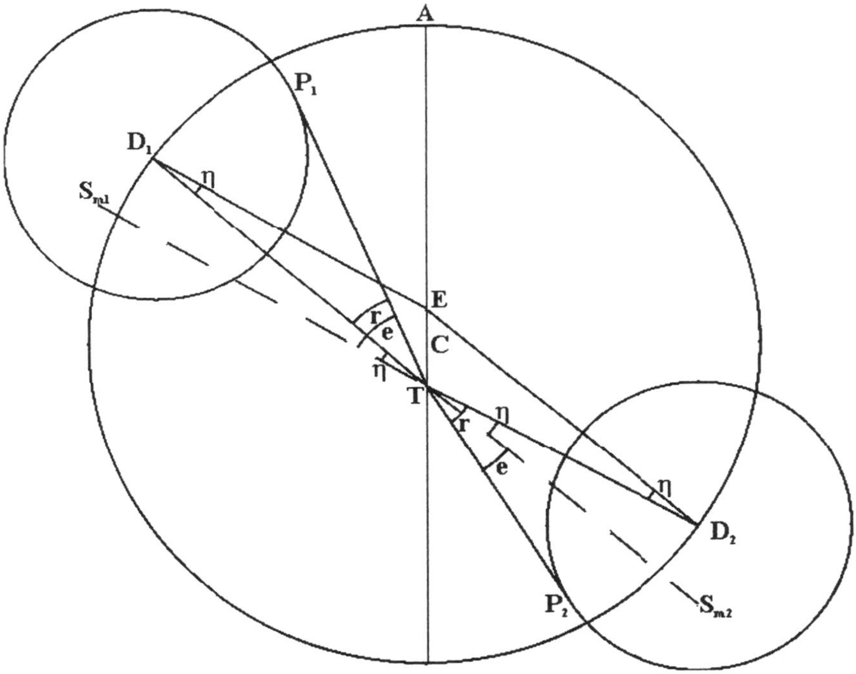

Figure 6

When the centre of the epicycle moves between the apogee and the first mean distance (in which TD = 60^p) the maximum morning elongation increases because both $\angle$ r and η increase, and η has to be added to $\angle$ r. In the same way, when the centre of the epicycle moves between the perigee and the second mean distance, the maximum morning elongation decreases because $\angle$ r decreases, while η (which has to be subtracted from $\angle$ r) increases. According to Jābir there is an unlimited number of morning elongations (*ab^cād ṣabāḥiyya ghayr mutanāhiya fī 'l-^cidda*) which have another equal morning elongation on the other side of the apse-line. If we divide the planet's deferent into four unequal quadrants determined by the apse-line and the line which joins the first and second mean distances we will have Fig. 7 in which A is the apogee, G the perigee, B and D the first and second mean distances. Each maximum morning elongation in AB will have an equal maximum evening elongation in GD (and the same can be said of BG and DA): in such cases the apogee will not be placed in the midpoint between the two positions of the centre of the epicycle. According to Jābir, in the case of Mercury Ptolemy established, by observation, that:

- 19;3° is the maximum morning and evening elongation when the centre of the epicycle is in A (apogee),
- 23;15° is the maximum morning and evening elongation when the centre of the epicycle is in G (perigee),
- 26;15° is the maximum morning elongation in B (first mean distance),
- 20;15° is the maximum evening elongation in B,
- 20;15° is the maximum morning elongation in D (second mean distance),
- 26;15° is the maximum evening elongation in D.

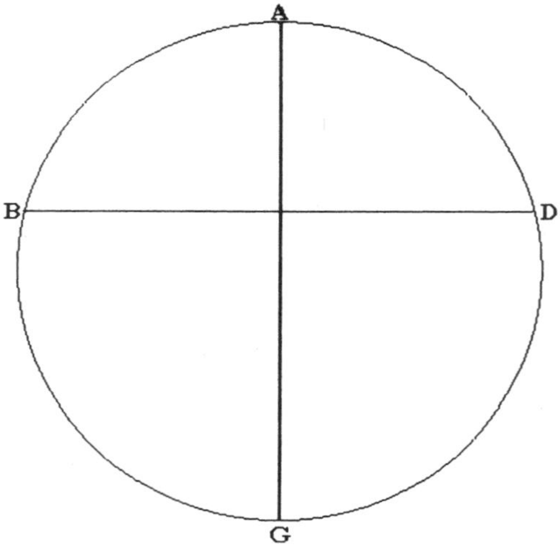

Figure 7

The aforementioned values correspond to the following four observations quoted in the *Almagest* ([3] and [4] are the same ones quoted by Ibn al-

Haytham):

Almagest	Date	Long. of Mercury	Mean solar long.	Max. elongation	Remarks
[o.1] IX,8 (Toomer 454)	2/3 Oct 134	170;12°	189;15°	19;3°	Morning
[o.2] IX,8 (Toomer 454)	5 Apr 135	34;20°	11;5°	23;15°	Evening
[o.3] IX,9 (Toomer 456)	4 Jul 130	126;20°	100;5°	26;15°	Evening
[o.4] IX,9 (Toomer 456)	4/5 Jul 139	80;5°	100;20°	20;15°	Morning

Before going further, I should make a remark: 19;3° and 23;15° correspond approximately to Mercury's maximum elongations from the mean Sun when the latter is in Ptolemy's apogee (190°) and perigee (10°), but the approximation does not seem so good for the mean distances: although the computation of the mean distance in the case of Mercury is not straightforward, Pedersen has calculated that it should be placed at 67;45° from the apogee[31]. 100;5° and 100;20° for the mean solar longitude correspond to the second mean distance which should be 190° - 67;45° = 122;15°.

Jābir also gives an equivalent list for Venus:
- 44;48° is the maximum morning and evening elongation in A,
- 47;20° is the maximum morning and evening elongation in G,
- 48;20° is the maximum morning elongation in B,
- 43;35° is the maximum evening elongation in B,
- 43;35° is the maximum morning elongation in D,
- 48;20° is the maximum evening elongation in D.

These figures correspond to

[31] O. Pedersen, *A Survey of the Almagest*, Odense, 1974, pp. 325-326; O. Neugebauer, *A History of Ancient Mathematical Astronomy*, Berlin, Heidelberg, New York, 1975, I, p. 169.

Almagest	Date	Long. of Venus	Mean solar long.	Max. elongation	Remarks
[o.5] X,2 (Toomer 471)	19/20 May 129	10;36°	55;24°	44;48°	Morning
[o.6] X,2 (Toomer 471)	18/19 Nov. 136	282;50°	235;30°	47;20°	Evening
[o.7] X,3 (Toomer 473)	18/19 Feb. 140	13;50°	325;30°	48;20°	Evening
[o.8] X,3 (Toomer 472-473)	17/18 Feb. 134	281;55°	325;30°	43;35°	Morning

As the longitude of the apogee of Venus established by Ptolemy is 55°, it is quite reasonable that Jābir should ascribe the maximum elongations corresponding to [o.5] and [o.6] to the planet's apogee and perigee respectively. The mean distance should be reached at 91;47° on both sides of the apogee[32]: therefore it should be at 55° + 91;47° = 146;47° and 360° + 55° - 91;47° = 323;13°, which agrees well with Ptolemy's maximum elongations in [o.7] and [o.8].

Jābir's analysis of these data allows him to exemplify his ideas on the subject. In the case of Mercury, the morning elongation of the planet increases between A (19°, [o,1]) and B (26°, assumed in [o.3]), and decreases between B (26°, assumed in [o.3]) and G (23°, assumed in [o.2]). Therefore we will be able to find an unlimited number of maximum morning elongations between A and B identical to other maximum morning elongations between B and G. In the same way, the maximum morning elongations decrease from G (23°, assumed in [o.2]) to D (20°, [o.4]) and we will also find another number of maximum morning elongations in this sector equal to others which take place between A and B. As each of these morning elongations will have an equal maximum evening elongation on the other side of the apse-line, one should be very careful when selecting the observations in order to establish in which of the four sectors each observation takes place, in order to determine accurately the position of the apogee.

32 See Pedersen, *Survey* p. 293.

For that purpose Jābir states the following criteria[33]:

- Between A and B the morning elongations (e_m) increase clearly, for

$$e_m = \angle r + \eta \quad [1]$$

and this is a sector in which both $\angle r$ and η increase[34].

This increase is not so conspicuous in the case of evening elongations (e_e) for

$$e_e = \angle r - \eta \quad [2]$$

- Between B and G, [1] and [2] are still valid: as $\angle r$ increases and η decreases with the motion of the centre of the epicycle towards the perigee, e_m will not increase substantially, while the growth of e_e will be clear.

- Between G and D we will have

$$e_m = \angle r - \eta \quad [3]$$

$$e_e = \angle r + \eta \quad [4]$$

As $\angle r$ will decrease while η increases with the progression of the centre of the epicycle from the perigee to the second mean distance, e_m will suffer a clear decrease, while e_e will not vary perceptibly.

- Between D and A both $\angle r$ and η diminish and, applying [3] and [4] again, we will conclude that e_m does not vary much, while e_e is notably reduced.

As a consequence, Jābir recommends making two observations of maximum morning elongations at two points of the ecliptic near to each other. If the second observation shows a clear increase of the maximum

[33] Jābir, *Iṣlāḥ* fol. 86 r.

[34] This implies that mean distances (points B and D) should coincide, approximately, with the positions of the centre of the epicycle for which the equation of the centre reaches its maximum. This is clearly not the case for Mercury. Mean distances, as we have seen, are 67;45° and 122;15°. In the tables of equations for Mercury of the *Almagest* (XI, 11, Toomer p. 553) the maximum equation of the centre is reached for an argument comprised between 90° and 96°, 264° and 270°.

elongation when compared to the first one, we may be sure that we are in sector AB. These two observations should be coupled with another two, corresponding to maximum evening elongations, in sector DA. Here the second observation should show a clear decrease of e_e in relation to the first one. Another possibility is to select two evening elongations which show a clear increase (sector BG) and two morning elongations which diminish (sector GD). In the first case half the distance between the two mean positions of the Sun will give us the planet's apogee, while in the second case we will obtain the perigee.

It is important, therefore, to make a good selection of the observations used to determine the position of the planet's apogee. A maximum elongation will be well selected (*mukhtār*) when its value increases or decreases rapidly in relation to a previous observation of the same kind. Without going into details, Jābir refers now (fol. 87 v) to an analysis of the observations used by Ptolemy to establish the longitude of the apogee in *Almagest* IX,7:

Almagest	Date	Long. of Mercury	Mean solar long.	Max. elongation	Remarks
[o.9] IX,7 (Toomer 449)	2/3 Feb. 132	331°	309;45°	21;15°	Evening
[o.10] IX,7 (Toomer 449)	3/4 June 134	48;45°	70°	21;15°	Morning
[o.11] IX,7 (Toomer 449-450)	4/5 June 138	97°	70;30°	26;30°	Evening
[o.12] IX,7 (Toomer 450)	1/2 Feb. 141	283;30°	310°	26;30°	Morning

Assuming a Ptolemaic apogee at 190° from Aries and a first mean distance placed at 67;45° from the apogee, the beginnings of the four sectors used by Jābir are:

A: 190°
B: 257;45°
G: 10°
D: 122;15°

and this explains why Jābir considers that the two first observations used by Ptolemy were well selected, for they correspond to a maximum evening elongation in sector BG ([o.9]) and to a maximum morning elongation in GD ([o.10]). The other two are not *mukhtār*, for they are a maximum evening elongation in GD ([o.11]) and a maximum morning elongation in BG ([o.12]). The same criticism can be applied to Ptolemy's selection of observations made in the third century B.C., which are:

Almagest	Date	Long. of Mercury	Mean solar long.	Max. elongation	Remarks
[o.13] IX,7 (Toomer 450)	11/12 Feb. -261	292;20°	318;10°	25;50°	Morning
[o. 14] IX,7 (Toomer 450-451)	25/26 April -261	53;40°	29;30°	24;10°	Evening
[o. 15] IX,7 (Toomer 451-452)	28/29 May -256	89;20°	62;50°	26;30°	Evening
[o.16] IX,7 (Toomer 452)	23 Aug. -261	169;30°	147;50°	21;40°	Evening
[o.17] IX,7 (Toomer 452)	29/30 Oct. -236	194;10°	215;10°	21°	Morning
[o.18] IX,7 (Toomer 452-453)	18/19 Nov. -244	212;20°	234;50°	22;30°	Morning

These six observations are used by Ptolemy in two sets of three: a maximum evening elongation of 25;50° is obtained by interpolation from [o.14] and [o.15], to match observation [o.13]. In the same way a maximum morning elongation of 21;40° is the result of an interpolation betweeen [o.17] and [o.18] to match the evening elongation of [o.16]. As the apogee obtained from these observations is 186°, the limits of the four sectors will be, in this case:

A: 186°
B: 253;45°
G: 6°
D: 118;15°

Jābir only refers to four observations out of the six mentioned by Ptolemy ([o.13]-[o.18]), for he seems to consider the two couples used to obtain a result by interpolation as two real observations. He states that two of them are well selected as they are a morning elongation in sector AB (this applies to [o.17] and [o.18]) and an evening elongation in DA ([o.16]). The two others, however, are not *mukhtār*, for they are a morning elongation in BG ([o.13]) and an evening elongation in GD ([o.14] and [o.15]).

Actually, the results obtained by Ptolemy's use of two pairs of observations in two opposite sectors do not confirm the method Jābir advocates: between [o.17] and [o.18] the morning elongation increases clearly from 21° to 22;30°, but an equivalent increase - taking into account the increment in the mean solar longitude - of the evening elongation from 24;10° to 26;30° also appears between [o.14] and [o.15]. Jābir does not say a word about this.

Jābir makes similar criticisms of Ptolemy's choice of the observations leading to the determination of the apogee of Venus. His conclusion is quite harsh: Ptolemy "has no feeling of the [real] implication of these elongations" (*inna-hu lam yash^c ur bi shay' min hādhihi 'l-ma^c ānī al-lāḥiqa fī hādhihi 'l-ab^c ād*, fol. 87 v). Ptolemy's knowledge of the subject was mistaken, but the error he made led him to a correct conclusion (*fa-kāna ^c ilmu-hu dhālika khaṭa'^an addā ilā ṣawāb*, fol. 88 r), although his determination of the apogees of Mercury and Venus was only "by accident and not by the nature of the thing itself" (*wa-kāna wujūdu-hu li-mawḍi^c al-bu^c d al-ab^c ad bi 'l-^c araḍ, lā bi 'l-dhāt*, fol. 88 r). A final casual remark is absolutely correct: Ptolemy generalised, in a rather abusive way, his conclusions about the displacement of Mercury's apogee with a velocity of 1° per century (from 186°, ca. -250, to 190°, ca. 140) to an equivalent displacement of the apogee of Venus (and of the other planets).

In brief, this interesting set of remarks made by Jābir show his mathematical ability and confirm what we already know through other indirect sources, i.e. that there was a certain awareness of the existence of an error in Ptolemy's determination of the longitude of Mercury's apogee. Jābir's criticisms have a few points in common with modern analysis of the same topic[35]. He does not offer us, however, a new set of observations or an attempt to analyse critically those made or mentioned by Ptolemy, except for a few general remarks which he does not apply to the data available to him.

ACKNOWLEDGEMENTS: This paper has been written within a research programme sponsored by the Spanish Ministry of Education. My postgraduate student Josep Bellver redrew my drawings for this paper. Juliane Lay sent me a copy of her unpublished French

[35] See Sawyer's paper mentioned above.

translation of the first part of Ibn Rushd's *Mukhtaṣar al-Majisṭī*. Prof. A.I. Sabra, Dr Richard Lorch and Dr Jamil Ragep read a draft and made suggestions and corrections. Dr Ragep made me aware of the existence of Don Voss' unpublished English translation and commentary of Ibn al-Haytham's *Shukūk* and he sent me a photocopy of the significant pages. My gratitude to all of them.

THE COMPUTATION OF PLANETARY LONGITUDES IN THE *ZĪJ* OF IBN AL-BANNĀ'

JULIO SAMSÓ and EDUARDO MILLÁS

1. IBN AL-BANNĀ' AND HIS *MINHĀJ*

The *Minhāj al-ṭālib fī ta'dīl al-kawākib* of Ibn al-Bannā' al-Marrākushī (1256-1321) is a *zīj*[1] the interest of which lies more in the changes introduced by its author in the techniques of computation of planetary longitudes than in its contents. The latter derive basically from the set of tables prepared by Abū al-'Abbās ibn Isḥāq al-Tamīmī al-Tūnisī (fl. Tunis and Marrakesh ca. 1193-1222), which survive in a unique manuscript in Hyderabad, discovered in 1978 by D.A. King.[2] The tables of Ibn Isḥāq appear to derive essentially from the Toledan astronomer Ibn al-Zarqālluh (d. 1100) and they were probably an unfinished work not accompanied originally by an elaborate collection of canons. We can identify four different "editions" of Ibn Isḥāq's tables prepared in the Maghrib in the second half of the thirteenth century:

[1] The canons were edited by J. Vernet, *Contribución al estudio de la labor astronómica de Ibn al-Bannā'* (Tetuán, 1952). On Ibn al-Bannā' see also H.P.J. Renaud, "Ibn al-Bannā' de Marrakech ṣûfî et mathématicien (XIIIe - XIVe s. J.C.)," *Hespéris*, 25 (1938): 13-42; Renaud, "Sur les dates de la vie du mathématicien arabe marocain Ibn al-Bannā'," *Isis*, 27 (1937): 216-18; Ibn al-Bannā', *Talkhīṣ a'māl al-ḥisāb*, Texte établi, annoté et traduit par M. Souissi (Tunis, 1969); *Al-maqālāt fī 'ilm al-ḥisāb li-Ibn al-Bannā' al-Marrākushī*, ed. by A.S. Sa'īdān ('Ammān, 1984;) R. Puig, "El *Taqbīl 'alā risālat al-ṣafīḥa al-zarqāliyya* de Ibn al-Bannā' de Marrākush," *Al-Qanṭara*, 8 (1987): 45-64; E. Calvo, "La *Risālat al-ṣafīḥa al-muštaraka 'alà al-šakkāziyya* de Ibn al-Bannā' de Marrākuš," *Al-Qanṭara*, 10 (1989): 21-50. This latter text has also been edited by Muḥammad al-'Arabī al-Khaṭṭābī, *'Ilm al-mawāqīt. Uṣūluhu wa manāhijuhu* (Muḥammadiyya, 1407/1986), pp. 136-74.

[2] See, for example, David A. King, "An overview of the sources for the history of astronomy in the Medieval Maghrib," *Deuxième Colloque Maghrébin sur l'Histoire des mathématiques arabes* (Tunis, 1988), pp. 125-57. See now a detailed survey of the contents of the manuscript in A. Mestres, "Maghribī astronomy in the 13th century: a description of manuscript Hyderabad Andra Pradesh State Library 298," in J. Casulleras and J. Samsó (eds.), *From Baghdad to Barcelona. Studies in the Islamic Exact Sciences in Honour of Prof. Juan Vernet* (Barcelona, 1996), vol. I, pp. 383-443.

1. An anonymous astronomer compiled, probably around 1266-1281, the collection now preserved in MS Hyderabad Andra Pradesh State Library 298. This is a monumental collection of materials which adds to the tables of Ibn Isḥāq others which the author considered were missing in the work of his predecessor, as well as a very important set of canons. Both tables and canons derive mainly from Andalusian authors and, thus, are of considerable interest in that they preserve for us sources many of which would have been otherwise lost. This "edition," however, was excessively large and was not well suited to the needs of the practising astronomer and astrologer.

2. Ibn al-Bannā' of Marrakesh prepared another "edition," in his *Minhāj*, with an entirely different structure from that of the Hyderabad manuscript: instead of an enormous accumulation of materials from different sources, this work presents a selection of Ibn Isḥāq's tables accompanied by a collection of canons, easy to understand, which makes the tables accessible for the computation of planetary longitudes. There are also some modifications of the structure of the tables, intended to make calculations easier.

3./4. The Tunisian-Andalusian astronomer Muḥammad ibn al-Raqqām (d. 1315) is the author of two *zīj*es, entitled *al-Zīj al-Shāmil fī tahdhīb al-Kāmil* (Tunis, 1280-81) and *al-Zīj al-Qawīm fī funūn al-ta'dīl wa-al-taqwīm* (Tunis and Granada, after 1280-81). The former contains the tables of Ibn Isḥāq, while the canons are, word for word, those of Ibn al-Hā'im (fl. 1205),[3] omitting, however, all the careful geometrical demonstrations introduced by this Andalusian author.[4] The *Qawīm Zīj* has not yet been thoroughly studied, but the canons are much less developed and they seem to be a simplified rewording of those of the *Shāmil Zīj*.

These facts clarify the role played by the *Minhāj*, within an Andalusian astronomical tradition which predominated in the

[3] Cf. J. Samsó, *Las Ciencias de los Antiguos en al-Andalus* (Madrid, 1992), pp. 324-6.

[4] A partial edition of this *zīj*, including a commentary and recomputation of the tables, was presented by Muḥammad 'Abd al-Raḥmān (Institute for the History of Arabic Science, Aleppo) as a doctoral dissertation (*Ḥisāb aṭwāl al-kawākib fī l-Zīj al-Shāmil fī Tahdhīb al-Kāmil li-Ibn al-Raqqām*) in the University of Barcelona (September 1996). See also E.S. Kennedy, "The astronomical tables of Ibn al-Raqqām, a scientist of Granada," *Zeitschrift für Geschichte der Arabisch-Islamischen Wissenschaften*, 11 (1997): 35-72.

Maghrib in the thirteenth century and the beginning of the fourteenth, and which was still alive in the nineteenth century.[5] This paper aims to present a study of the materials preserved in this *zīj* of Ibn al-Bannā' relating to the computation of lunar and planetary longitudes. So far the only studies on the numerical tables of the *Minhāj* are a paper by Mercè Comes[6] (on the geographical and star tables) and another on the solar tables by the present authors.[7]

2. PLANETARY MEAN MOTIONS AND POSITIONS AT EPOCH

TABLE 1 contains a list of the parameters which underlie the mean motion tables of the *Minhāj*[8] as well as those squeezed from other significant sources, namely the *Toledan Tables*[9] and the *Muqtabas zīj* of Ibn al-Kammād.[10] The parameters of the *zīj* of Abī al-Ḥasan 'Alī al-Qusunṭīnī[11] have also been added, for they often coincide with those of Ibn al-Bannā'. The first obvious remark is that the mean motion tables of Ibn al-Bannā' are the same as those of Ibn Isḥāq,[12] as preserved in MS

[5] J. Vernet, "La supervivencia de la astronomía de Ibn al-Bannā'," *Al-Qanṭara*, 1 (1980): 445-51.

[6] Mercè Comes, "Deux échos andalous à Ibn al-Bannā' de Marrākush," in *Le patrimoine andalou dans la culture arabe et espagnole* (Tunis, 1991), pp. 81-94. This paper has been discussed recently by Bernard R. Goldstein and José Chabás, "Ibn al-Kammād's star list," *Centaurus*, 38 (1996): 317-34. See, however, J. Samsó, "Andalusian astronomy in 14th century Fez: the *al-Zīj al-Muwāfiq* of Ibn 'Azzūz al-Qusanṭīnī," *Zeitschrift für Geschichte der Arabisch-Islamischen Wissenschaften*," 11 (1997): 73-110.

[7] J. Samsó & E. Millás, "Ibn al-Bannā', Ibn Isḥāq and Ibn al-Zarqālluh's solar theory," in J. Samsó, *Islamic Astronomy and Medieval Spain*, Variorum (Aldershot, 1994), no. X (35 p.).

[8] These parameters were calculated using a sexagesimal calculator and a computer programme which reconstructs the mean motion tables from a given parameter (*TAPJ*). Both were prepared by Honorino Mielgo.

[9] G.J. Toomer, "A survey of the Toledan tables," *Osiris*, 15 (1968): 5-174, p. 44.

[10] José Chabás & Bernard R. Goldstein, "Andalusian astronomy: *al-Zîj al-Muqtabis* of Ibn al-Kammâd," *Archive for History of Exact Sciences*, 48 (1994): 1-41.

[11] E.S. Kennedy & D.A. King, "Indian astronomy in fourteenth century Fez: the Versified Zīj of al-Qusunṭīnī," *Journal for the History of Arabic Science*, 6 (1982): 3-45 (see p. 10). Reprinted in D.A. King, *Islamic Mathematical Astronomy*, Variorum Reprints (London, 1986; 2nd revised edn, Aldershot, 1993).

[12] See Mestres, "Maghribī astronomy in the 13th century," pp. 412-18. These parameters have been calculated using Benno van Dalen's programme for the analysis of mean motion tables.

	Mean motion per day (unit: degrees per day)	Other sources
Solar apogee	0;0,0,2,7,10,44	Kammād: 0;0,0,2,2,14,46 Qusunṭīnī: 0;0,0,2,7,11
Head of Aries	0;0,0,54,57,17,48	Toledo/De motu: 0;0,0,52,28,37,54 Zarqālluh: 0;0,0,54,57,17,38[1] Kammād: 0;0,0,54,56,57 Qus.: 0;0,0,53,20,31
Moon: longitude	13;10,34,52,46,51,20	Khwārizmī: 13;10,34,52,46,28[2] Toledo: 13;10,34,52,48,47 Kammād: 13;10,34,52,46 Qus.: 13;10,34,52,48
Moon: anomaly	13;3,53,56,17,52,7	Toledo: 13;3,53,56,17,57 Kammād and Qus.: 13;3,53,56,19
Moon: nodes	0;3,10,46,40,59,50	Toledo: 0;3,10,46,42,33 Kammād: 0;3,10,46,41 Qus.:0;3,10,46,57,52
Saturn: longitude	0;2,0,27,46,42,52	Toledo: 0;2,0,26,35,17 Kammād: 0;2,0,25,36 Qus.: 0;2,0,27,50,55
Jupiter: longitude	0;4,59,7,36,25,12	Toledo: 0;4,59,7,37,19 Kammād: 0;4,59,6,43 Qus.: 0;4,59,7,37,54
Mars: longitude	0;31,26,31,9,5,32	Toledo: 0;31,26,32,15,17 Kammād: 0;31,26,31,40 Qus.: 0;31,26,30,0,51
Venus: anomaly	0;36,59,27,23,59,32	Toledo: 0;36,59,29,27,29 Kammād: 0;36,59,29,21 Qus.: 0;36,59,28,13,46,16
Mercury: anomaly	3;6,24,7,42,41,5	Toledo: 3;6,24,7,39,31 Kammād: 3;6,24,7,19 Qus.: 3;6,24,7,55

TABLE 1: MEAN MOTIONS

[1] This is the parameter used in the tables which correspond to the Julian and Persian calendars: see H. Mielgo, "A method of analysis for mean motion astronomical tables," in *From Baghdad to Barcelona*, I, 159-79 (see pp. 164-78).

[2] Josep Casulleras, "Las tablas astronómicas de Pedro Alfonso," in M.J. Lacarra (ed.), *Estudios sobre Pedro Alfonso de Huesca* (Huesca, 1996), pp. 349-64.

Hyderabad, and the same as the tables of the two *zīj*es of Ibn al-Raqqām.[13] In addition comparison with the other sources shows a remarkable continuity with the Andalusian tradition: the motion of the solar apogee corresponds to 1° in every 279 Julian

[13] We are using the unpublished doctoral thesis by Muḥammad ʻAbd al-Raḥmān.

years and, thus, the parameter obtained is clearly Zarqāllian in its origin[14]; the same is true of the mean motion of the Head of Aries, which derives clearly from Ibn al-Zarqālluh's *Treatise on the motion of the eighth sphere*. The lunar mean motion in longitude derives from al-Khwārizmī's *zīj* and the same parameter was used in the *Toledan Tables* and in the *Muqtabas zīj* of Ibn al-Kammād. The lunar mean motion in anomaly is, again, related to the *Toledan Tables* and to Ibn al-Kammād, while the motion of the lunar nodes is practically the same as that of the *Muqtabas*. The Toledan mean motions in longitude of Jupiter and in anomaly of Mercury seem to be reflected in the *Minhāj* of Ibn al-Bannā'. The mean motions in longitude of Saturn and Mars and the mean motion in anomaly of Venus seem to be independent of the rest of the sources and, according to the Hyderabad "edition" of the *zīj* of Ibn Isḥāq, together with the motion of the lunar nodes, they appear to be the result of research of Ibn al-Zarqālluh conducted after the completion of the *Toledan Tables*.

TABLE 2 gathers all the information in the *Minhāj* concerning the mean positions at the beginning of the Hijra. These positions have been compared with those appearing in the rest of the *zīj*es which correspond to the same tradition. The differences have been corrected to take into account the differences in geographical longitude in those cases in which the motion is fast enough to affect the radix position when there is a change of the meridian. The meridians used for this correction are:

Ibn al-Bannā': Marrakesh (21°)
Toledo: Toledo (28;30°) (Hour. diff. with Marrakesh: +30 min.)
Ibn al-Kammād: Cordova (27°) (H.d.M.: + 24 min.)
Ibn Isḥāq: Toledo (28°) (H.d.M.: + 28 min.)
Ibn al-Raqqām: Bijāya (34°) (H.d.M: + 52 min.)[15]

The mean positions at epoch in the *Minhāj* pose a few problems: Ibn al-Bannā' should have taken into consideration the fact that the equations of the centre of the Moon and the planets are displaced 13;9° (Moon), 6° (Saturn and Jupiter), and 12° (Mars); he does so, correctly, in the case of Saturn, Jupiter and Mars. In

[14] Samsó & Millás, "Ibn Isḥāq, Ibn al-Bannā' and Ibn al-Zarqālluh's solar theory," pp. 7-9.

[15] Ibn al-Raqqām's *al-Zīj al-Shāmil* gives two radix positions for the meridians of Arīn and Bijāya which are mutually coherent. Only the positions for Bijāya have been considered here.

	Aṣl (1)	Other sources (2)	Diff.(1)-(2)+ corr. hour diff. = ( )
Head of Aries	3;53,55°[1]	Zarq./Kammād:3;51,11[2]	+0;2,44°
Moon: longitude	120;47,54[3]	Toledo: 120;58,18 Kammād: 120;34,42 Isḥāq:120;32,32 Raqqām: 120;19,21	-0;10,24 -0;16,28(-0;26,52) +0;13,12 -0;13,11(+0;0,1) +0;15,22 -0;15,22 (0) +0;28,33 -0;28,33 (0)
Moon: anomaly	95;14,54 [108;23,54[4]	Toledo:108;8,39 Kammād: 108;11 Isḥāq: 108;8,39 Raqqām: 107;55,35	0;15,15 -0;16,20 (-0;1,5) 0;12,54 -0;13,4 (-0;0,10) 0;15,15 -0;15,15 (0) 0;28,19 -0;28,18 (+0;0,1)
Moon: nodes	234;19,41	Toledo:234;9,55 Kammād: 233;30 Isḥāq: 234;19;37 Raqqām: 234;19,34	+0;9,46 -0;0,4 (+0;9,42) +0;49,41 -0;0,3 (+0;49,38) +0;0,4 -0;0,4 (0) +0;0,7 -0;0,7 (0)
Saturn: longitude	116;17,17[5]	Toledo: 115;51,15 Kammād: 115;30,30 Isḥāq: 116;17,15 Raqqām: 116;17,13	+0;26,2 -0;0,3 (0;25,59) +0;46,47 -0;0,2 (0;46,45) +0;0,2 -0;0,2 (0) +0;0,4 -0;0,4 (0)
Jupiter: longitude	330;11,5 [6]	Toledo: 331;39,37 Kammād: 330:19 Isḥāq: 330;11 Raqqām: 330;10,55	-1;28,32 -0;0,6 (-1;28,38) -0;7,55 -0;0,5 (-0;8) +0;0,5 -0;0,6 (-0;0,1) +0;0,10 -0;0,11 (-0;0,1)
Mars: longitude	210;35,31[7]	Toledo: 211;24,59 Kammād: 211;27 Isḥāq: 210;37,25 Raqqām: 210;36,54	-0;49,28 -0;0,39 (-0;50,7) -0;51,29 -0;0,31 (0;52,0) -0;1,54 -0;0,37 (-0;2,31) -0;1,23 -0;1,8 (-0;2,31)
Venus: anomaly	4[4];30,43[8]	Toledo: 45;28,37 Kammād: 45;21 Isḥāq: 44;30 Raqqām: 44;29,24	-0;57,48 -0;0,46 (-0;58,34) -0;50,17 -0;0,37 (-0;50,54) +0;0,43 -0;0,43 (0) +0;1,19 -0;1,20 (-0;0,1)
Mercury: anomaly	7[3];29,6[9]	Toledo: 73;46,18 Kammād: 74;1 Isḥāq: 73;25,29 Raqqām: 73;22,23	-0;17,12 -0;3,53 (-0;21,5) -0;31,54 -0;3,6 (-0;35) +0;3,37 -0;3,37 (0) +0;6,43 -0;6,44 (-0;0,1)

TABLE 2: MEAN POSITIONS AT EPOCH

[1] 3;53,55° in M, table 34 as well as in Ibn Isḥāq (Hyderabad MS) and in Ibn al-Raqqām's two *zījes*. 3;53,25° in E, fol. 15r; 14;53,18° (?) in A, fol. 31v.

[2] J.M. Millás Vallicrosa, *Estudios sobre Azarquiel* (Madrid-Granada, 1943-50), p. 324.

[3] Ibn al-Bannā' has not taken into consideration that the equation of the centre is displaced 13;9°.

[4] Ibn al-Bannā' has corrected the displacement of 13;9° here instead of doing so with the mean position in longitude at epoch.

[5] 110;17,17° in the three MSS: we have taken into consideration that the equation of the centre is displaced 6°.

[6] 324;11,5° in the three manuscripts. The equation of the centre is displaced 6°.

[7] 198;35,31° in the three manuscripts. The equation of the centre of Mars is displaced 12°.

[8] 48;30,43° in the three MSS. The difference seems to be due to a mistake made by Ibn al-Bannā' or by somebody else: the equation of the centre of Venus is displaced 4°, but this should not affect the mean position of the anomaly at epoch.

[9] 77;29,6° in the three MSS. As in the case of Venus, there seems to be an error here. The equation of the centre of Mercury is displaced 4°, but this should not affect the mean position in anomaly at epoch.

the case of the Moon, however, the correction is applied to the mean position in anomaly at epoch, instead of the mean position in longitude. The same error appears in the mean positions in anomaly at epoch of Venus (4°) and Mercury (4°). If we disregard these mistakes, the mean positions of Ibn al-Bannā' are consistent with those of Ibn Isḥāq and Ibn al-Raqqām, with the sole exception of Mars: in this latter case, the Moroccan astronomer has introduced a correction of 0;2,31° in the positions of the other two astronomers.

3. PLANETARY APOGEES

The planetary apogees used by Ibn al-Bannā' in his *Minhāj* are:

Saturn:	7^s 29;42,45°[16]
Jupiter:	5^s 9;42,45°[17]
Mars:	4^s 2;12,45°[18]
Venus:	2^s 16;44,17°[19]
Mercury:	6^s 18;24,17°.[20]

Note that the apogees of Ibn al-Bannā' are the same as those of Ibn Isḥāq[21] and Ibn al-Raqqām.[22] Further, there is total agreement between the three sources for the apogee of the Sun/Venus. Concerning the other planets, Ibn Isḥāq rounds to the nearest minute the apogees of Jupiter (5^s 9;43°), and Mars

[16] MS M (Madrid, Museo Naval, without number), table 30; MS A (Alger 1454), fol. 43^r; MS E (Escorial 909), fol. 26^v.

[17] Cf. Vernet, *Contribución* p. 91, who follows MS E fol. 27^r. MS A fol. 45^v and MS M, table 32, give 49".

[18] 4^s 2;12,49° in MS M, table 34. See Vernet, *Contribución*, p. 92, who follows MS E fol. 28^r. The apogee of Mars seems to be missing in MS A fols. 46^r - 47^v.

[19] Ibn al-Bannā' states, in chapter 9 of his canons, that the apogee of Venus is the same as that of the Sun: see Vernet, *Contribución*, p. 34 (Ar. text) and 92 (Sp. translation). As for the solar apogee see Samsó-Millás, "Ibn al-Bannā'," pp. 7-9.

[20] See Vernet, *Contribución*, p. 34 (Ar. text) and p. 92 (Sp. tr.): the apogee of Mercury is placed at a fixed distance of 4^s 1;40° from the solar apogee.

[21] See Mestres, "Maghribī astronomy in the 13th century," p. 412. The only exception is the apogee of Mercury, which seems corrupt in the Hyderabad MS (6^s 14;43).

[22] In his *al-Zīj al-qawīm fī funūn al-ta'dīl wa-al-taqwīm* (MS Rabat, General Library 260; fragments of this same *zīj* can also be found in our MS M). The same values appear also in his *al-Zīj al-shāmil fī tahdhīb al-Kāmil* (MS Istanbul, Kandilli 249), studied by Muḥammad 'Abd al-Raḥmān. Mercury's apogee is the same as that of Ibn al-Bannā'.

(4^s 2;13°), while Ibn al-Raqqām does the same with all planets except Venus.[23]

TABLE 3 compares the positions of the apogees of Ibn al-Bannā' with those of a series of tables which form the basis of the Andalusian-Maghribī astronomical tradition: Ptolemy's *Almagest*[24] (positions for the time of Ptolemy, ca. 120-140 A.D.), the *Handy Tables* of Theon of Alexandria[25] (positions calculated for year 951 of Philippos, that is 628 A.D.), al-Battānī's *zīj*[26] (for year 1191 of Alexander, 879 A.D.), al-Khwārizmī's *zīj* (Hijra, 622 A.D.)[27] the *Toledan Tables*[28] (Hijra?), Ibn al-Kammād's *al-Zīj al-Muqtabas*[29] (Hijra?) and the *Alfonsine Tables*[30] (Hijra). A glance at TABLE 3 shows that Ibn al-Bannā's apogees are entirely independent of those in al-Khwārizmī's *zīj*, while it is obvious that the apogees of Saturn and Mars derive clearly from the Ptolemaic tradition, which is represented here by the *Almagest*, the *Handy Tables* and al-Battānī's *zīj*. The difference in the position of the apogees of Jupiter shows that al-Battānī's *zīj* is, probably, the actual source used by Ibn Isḥāq and Ibn al-Bannā'.

The apogee of Venus is the same as that of the Sun, and this agrees with the Hindu-Iranian tradition according to which the centre of the planet's epicycle is always placed in the direction of the mean Sun.[31] The position which appears in the *Minhāj* and in the Hyderabad manuscript of Ibn Isḥāq's *zīj* is very near to the one appearing in Ibn al-Kammād's *al-Zīj al-Muqtabas* (78;19,13°) and we established elsewhere[32] that these positions

[23] With the exception of Venus and the Sun, we find the same set of planetary apogees in the *zīj* of Abū al-Ḥasan 'Alī al-Qusunṭīnī: see Kennedy & King, "Indian astronomy in fourteenth century Fez," p. 10.

[24] See G.J. Toomer, *Ptolemy's Almagest* (New York, Berlin, Heidelberg, Tokyo, 1984).

[25] See W.D. Stahlman, *The Astronomical Tables of Codex Vaticanus Graecus 1291*, available through University Microfilms. Ann Arbor, Michigan, microfilm no. 62-5761.

[26] Ed. and Latin translation by C.A. Nallino, *Al-Battānī sive Albatenii Opus Astronomicum*, 3 vols. (Mediolani Insubrum, 1899, 1903 et 1907).

[27] O. Neugebauer, *The Astronomical Tables of al-Khwārizmī. Translation with Commentaries of the Latin Version edited by H. Suter supplemented by Corpus Christi College MS 283* (Copenhagen, 1962), pp. 41, 99.

[28] Toomer, "Toledan tables," p. 45.

[29] Chabás & Goldstein, "Muqtabis," p. 33.

[30] Cf. E. Poulle, *Les Tables alphonsines avec les canons de Jean de Saxe* (Paris, 1984).

[31] B.R. Goldstein, "Remarks on Ptolemy's equant model in Islamic astronomy," *Prismata. Festschrift für Willy Hartner* (Wiesbaden, 1977), pp. 165-81.

[32] Samsó & Millás, "Ibn Isḥāq, Ibn al-Bannā'...," pp. 7-9.

Planet	Almagest	Handy Tables	Khwārizmī	Battānī	Toledo	Kammād	Alfonso
Saturn	+6;42,45°	+1;48,45°	-45;12,5°	-4;45,15°	-1;7,15°	+1;4,15°	-2;53,38°
Jupiter	-1;17,11	-6;11,11	-12;49,15	-4;45,15	-4;47,11	+1;21,49	-3;7,0
Mars	+6;42,45	+1;48,45	-6;11,15	-4;45,15	+0;22,45	+2;31,45	-2;12,9
Venus	+21;44,17	+16;50,17	-4:30,43	-5;29,43	-1;5,43	-0;1,4	-3;53,46
Mercury	+8;24,17	+3;30,17	-26:29,43	-3;3,43	+0;54,17	+0;3,17	-1;27,57

TABLE 3: DIFFERENCES BETWEEN THE LONGITUDES OF THE PLANETARY APOGEES IN IBN AL-BANNĀ' AND IN THE REST OF THE SOURCES

were calculated on the basis of the solar observations made by Ibn al-Zarqālluh in 467 H./1074-75, taking into account the precession of the equinoxes and the Zarqāllian theory on the motion of the solar apogee. We do not know the origin of the longitude of Mercury's apogee in Ibn al-Bannā' and Ibn al-Raqqām (198;24,17°): the fact that the difference between this position and that of Ibn al-Kammād amounts to 0;3,17° only suggests the possibility of a Zarqāllian origin.[33]

If we consider, for example, the difference of 4;45,15° between the longitudes of the apogees of the superior planets in al-Battānī's *zīj* and in the *Minhāj*, our first impression is that this amount corresponds to the difference in precession calculated for the epoch used in the *Minhāj* (Hijra) and the time of al-Battānī's determination of the longitudes of the apogees (879 A.D.). The results obtained on the basis of this hypothesis are unremarkable: using the trepidation tables extant in the *zīj*es of Ibn Isḥāq and Ibn al-Bannā' we have calculated that the precession for the beginning of the Hijra amounts to 0;42,12° and we obtain 4;49,35° for year 879. The difference, then, will be 4;7,24°, which does not correspond to the aforementioned 4;45,15°. Nothing conclusive can be said, at present, about this difference. The situation is entirely different if we consider the difference of 6;42,45° for the time of Ptolemy, which corresponds exactly to the negative value of precession calculated by Ibn al-Zarqālluh for the time of Ptolemy (139 A.D.), with his third model of trepidation.[34] On the other hand, Ibn al-Zarqālluh also

[33] This hypothesis contradicts the one formulated in J. Samsó and Honorino Mielgo, "Ibn al-Zarqālluh on Mercury," *Journal for the History of Astronomy*, 25 (1994): 289-96.

[34] See J. Samsó, "Trepidation in al-Andalus in the 11th century," in J. Samsó, *Islamic Astronomy and Medieval Spain*, Variorum (Aldershot, 1994), no. VIII, p. 25.

calculates with his third model that the positive value of precession for the time of al-Battānī (883 A.D.) amounts to 4;52,56°, which is not far from our 4;45,15°. The conclusion is clear: the apogees of the superior planets, in the *Minhāj* of Ibn al-Bannā', have not been calculated for the beginning of the Hijra but rather for a radix date in which the value of precession was 0° (581 A.D. according to Ibn al-Zarqālluh). In other words, these apogees are sidereal, not tropical apogees for the beginning of the Hijra. This is confirmed by the actual phrasing which we find in the references to the apogees in the tables of the equations of the centre of the *Minhāj*: while in the case of the Sun the text states clearly that the solar apogee was at 76;44,17° at the beginning of the Hijra,[35] for the three superior planets, the *Minhāj* establishes that the longitudes of the apogees mentioned at the head of the table are "the fixed distance of its apogee from the point of the Head of Aries, measured on the ecliptic" (*bu'd awjihi 'an nuqṭat ra's al-Ḥamal fī falak al-burūj ḥaythu kāna abadan*). This is not the first instance of an idea of this kind in the *Minhāj*: Mercè Comes[36] noted, a few years ago, that the star table in the *zīj* of Ibn al-Bannā' was also calculated for a moment in which the value of precession was 0°. One final remark, implicit in everything we have said so far, should be made: while the apogees of the three superior planets are sidereally fixed, those of Venus and Mercury are affected by the motion of the solar apogee. This seems clear if we consider that the apogee of Venus is the same as that of the Sun, while the apogee of Mercury is always kept at a fixed distance of 4^s 1;40° from the solar apogee.

We have, therefore, a set of apogees which are clearly related to the Zarqāllian tradition in several ways. There is no clear evidence, however, that Ibn al-Zarqālluh extended the motion of the solar apogee to the inferior planets although there would have been a certain logic in his doing so, especially in the case of Venus. We should now review here what happens with the rest of the Andalusian tradition. Ibn al-Kammād (fl. 1116), for example, states clearly that his planetary apogees correspond to the beginning of the Hijra and that the motion of the solar apogee affects all the planets, and not only the inferior ones as in the

[35] E fol. 15^r; A fol. 31^v; M fol. 12^v.
[36] Mercè Comes, "Deux échos andalous à Ibn al-Bannā'."

case of Ibn al-Bannā'. Thus, we read in chapter 9 of the Latin translation of his *Muqtabas zīj*:

Differentia in aptatione augium. Cum volueris hoc extrahe singulos motus augis quem admodum praedictum est ad tempus quod volueris et *adde ipsos super auge cuiuslibet planete* qui augis planetarum positus est in capite tabularum cuiuslibet planete *ad principium annorum seductionis* et quod postea inde exierit erunt auges aptatos pro tempore illo pro quo numerasti.[37]

The same doctrine (i.e. keeping all the planetary apogees at a fixed distance from the solar apogee) is followed by Ibn al-Hā'im (fl. 1205)[38] and Ibn Isḥāq (fl. ca. 1193-1222): in the case of the latter, there is clear evidence of the doctrine in chapter 14 of the canons of the Hyderabad manuscript, which is confirmed by the tables and can, therefore, be safely ascribed to Ibn Isḥāq himself.[39] As for Ibn al-Raqqām (d. 1315), his attitude changes: his earlier *Shāmil zīj* follows literally the text of Ibn al-Hā'im while in his *Qawīm zīj* he seems to be in complete agreement with Ibn al-Bannā'.[40] Finally, during the fourteenth century, both the *Muwāfiq Zīj* of Ibn 'Azzūz al-Qusanṭīnī (fl. Fez 1318-1354)[41] and the *Tables of Barcelona*[42] follow in this subject, as in many others, the example set by Ibn al-Kammād. All this evidence,

[37] See MS Madrid, Biblioteca Nacional 10023, fol. 14ᵛ. We have used a provisional edition of this text prepared by Angel Mestres and other undergraduate students as a part of a course on Latin Paleography given by Dr. Mercè Viladrich. The italicization is ours.

[38] *Al-Zīj al-Kāmil fī al-Ta'ālīm*, MS Bodleian Marsh 618, fol. 34ᵛ. This text does not state clearly which are the planets affected by the motion of the apogee, but it defines the meaning of *awj mu'addal* ("corrected apogee"): "Obtain the mean motion of the apogee for any moment, using any era (*ta'rīkh*) you wish. Add the result to the radix position for the beginning of the era. You have obtained, then, the position of the corrected apogee (*awj mu'addal*) on the ecliptic, that is to say its distance from the point of the Head of Aries for that moment." The question becomes absolutely clear if we read the chapters in which Ibn al-Hā'im describes the procedure to calculate the true longitude of the planets: there, both for the superior (fol. 37ʳ⁻ᵛ) and for the inferior planets (fol. 38ʳ), he says that the *awj mu'addal* has to be subtracted from the mean longitude of the planet.

[39] Mestres, "Maghribī astronomy in the 13th century," pp. 394-5 and 412.

[40] We are using here Muḥammad 'Abd al-Raḥmān's unpublished doctoral dissertation. The manuscripts used are Istanbul Kandilli 249 (*Shāmil*, fols. 13ʳ and 14ᵛ) and Rabat General Library 260 (*Qawīm*, pp. 15-16).

[41] See J. Samsó,"Andalusian astronomy in 14th century Fez," pp. 82-3.

[42] J.M. Millás Vallicrosa, *Las tablas astronómicas del rey Don Pedro el Ceremonioso. Edición crítica de los textos hebraico, catalán y latino con estudio y notas* (Barcelona, 1962), pp. 128, 147 and 190; on these tables see now J. Chabás, "Astronomía andalusí en Cataluña: las Tablas de Barcelona," in *From Baghdad to Barcelona*, pp. 477-525.

and very especially the attitude of Ibn al-Hā'im – who is a strict follower of the doctrines of Ibn al-Zarqālluh – points in the same direction: Ibn al-Zarqālluh probably believed that all planetary apogees were kept at a fixed distance from the solar apogee, and it was probably Ibn al-Bannā' who restricted the doctrine to the case of the inferior planets.

4. THE TABLES OF THE EQUATIONS OF THE CENTRE

We have established elsewhere[43] that Ibn al-Bannā' seems to be the first Western Islamic astronomer to use displaced equations of the centre (η). This technique of computation was well known in the Islamic East from the ninth century onwards[44]: it enabled the preparation of tables in which the equation was always positive, simply by adding a constant ($k \geq \eta_{max}$) to each tabular value of the equation. To compensate for this addition the same constant k was subtracted from the mean longitude of the centre of the epicycle at epoch (the astronomical date of the beginning of the Hijra, midday of 14th July 622 A.D., in the case of Ibn al-Bannā'). Thus, for

- c_m mean longitude of the centre of the planetary epicycle measured from the apogee,
- c_v true longitude of the centre of the planetary epicycle measured from the apogee,
- η equation of the centre,

we have:

$c_v = c_m \mp \eta\ (c_m)$ [1]

[43] Samsó & Millás, "Ibn Isḥāq, Ibn al-Bannā'...," pp. 18-26.

[44] Cf. E.S. Kennedy and H. Salam, "Solar and lunar tables in early Islamic astronomy," in E.S. Kennedy, Colleagues and Former Students, *Studies in the Islamic Exact Sciences* (Beirut, 1983), pp. 108-13; E.S. Kennedy, "The astronomical tables of Ibn al-A'lam," *Journal for the History of Arabic Science*, 1 (1977): 13-23; E.S. Kennedy, "Al-Bīrūnī's Masudic Canon," in *Studies*, pp. 573-95; D.A. King, "A double argument table for the lunar equation attributed to Ibn Yūnus," *Centaurus*, 18 (1974): 129-46 (reprint in King, *Islamic Mathematical Astronomy*, Variorum (London, 1986; 2nd edn, Aldershot, 1993); C. Jensen, "The lunar theories of al-Baghdādī," *Archive for the History of the Exact Sciences*, 8 (1971-72): 321-8; G.A. Saliba, "The double-argument lunar tables of Cyriacus", *Journal for the History of Astronomy*, 7 (1976): 41-6; Saliba, "The planetary tables of Cyriacus," *Journal for the History of Arabic Science*, 2 (1978): 53-65; Saliba, "Computational techniques in a set of late Medieval astronomical tables," *Journal for the History of Arabic Science*, 1 (1977): 24-32.

an expression in which $\eta(c_m)$ is negative for c_m in the interval $0° \leq c_m \leq 180°$, and positive for c_m in the interval $180° \leq c_m \leq 360°$.

If we take the minimum integer number k such that $k \geq \eta_{max}(c_m)$, we may write [1] in the following way:

$$c_\upsilon = c_m - k + k \mp \eta(c_m) \text{ [2a]}$$

Here we have a new expression for c_υ, with a new argument and a new equation of the centre, and we may call:

- the new argument $c'_m = c_m - k$
- the new equation $\eta'(c'_m) = \eta'(c_m - k) = k \mp \eta(c_m)$

The new function of the equation of the centre will be:

$$c_\upsilon = c'_m + \eta'(c'_m) \text{ [2b]}$$

We may tabulate the expression $\eta'(c'_m) = k \mp \eta(c_m)$ as the new equation of the centre. As a result we obtain a displaced table where the tabular values of the new equation of the centre will always be positive because we have chosen $k \geq \eta_{max}(c_m)$ and this fact simplifies the calculation of c_υ.

To take into account the new argument $c'_m = c_m - k$, we may displace as well the column of the arguments and use the new one $c'_m = c_m - k$.[45] This will be a negative displacement while the former one was a positive one. This is done by Ibn al-Bannā' in the tables of the equation of the centre of all planets, the only exception being that of the Moon, in which only the equation (not the argument) is displaced. This is due to the fact that the same argument is used for another lunar table which cannot be displaced.

The displacement of the argument implies that the function is no longer symmetrical about 180° but rather around point S (see Fig. 1), placed before the old point of symmetry (180°) at an angular distance equal to the displacement, k, of the arguments. Thus, the argument that corresponds to this new point of symmetry, S, is $c'_{mS} = 180° - k°$. Then, any two points (B and D in Fig. 1), whose angular distances from S are equal but of opposite sign ($SB = a°$ and $SD = -a°$ in Fig. 1), will have the same equation. In fact (Fig. 1):

[45] Cf. Samsó-Millás, "Ibn Isḥāq, Ibn al-Bannā'...," p. 20.

Fig. 1

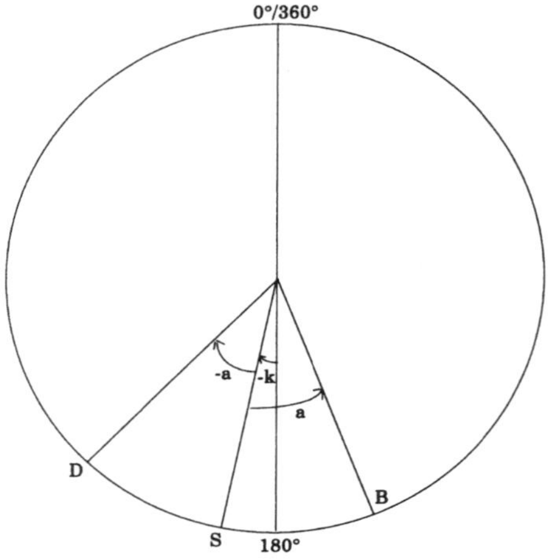

For B:

- the argument is $c'_{mB} = 180° - k + a$
- and the equation is

$$\eta'_B\,(c'_{mB}) = \eta'_B\,(180° - k + a) = k - \eta_B\,(180° + a)$$

For D:

- the argument is $c'_{mD} = 180° - k - a$
- and the equation of the centre is

$$\eta'_D\,(c'_{mD}) = \eta'_D\,(180° - k - a) = k - \eta_D\,(180° - a)$$

But taking into account that for $\eta\,(c_m)$ the point of symmetry is 180°, we have

$$\eta_B\,(180° + a) = \eta_D\,(180° - a)$$

and thus: $\eta'_B\,(c'_{mB}) = \eta'_D\,(c'_{mD})$

which implies that the equations of *B* and *D* are identical and that $S(180° - k°)$ is the point of symmetry of the tables displaced in equation and in argument.

In TABLE 4 we present the values of the maximum equations (both displaced and not displaced), of the minimum equations (displaced) and the value of the displacement used by Ibn al-Bannā'. The values of the maximum equations are the same as those used by Ibn Isḥāq and Ibn al-Raqqām. They are Ptolemaic in the cases of Mars, Mercury and the Moon. In the case of Venus we are, here, in a situation similar to that of the apogee: the equation of the centre of this planet is the same as that of

Planet	Maximum equation	Minimum equation	Displacement	Max. eq. without displacement	Eccentricity[1]
Saturn	11;48° (261°-264°)	0;12° (83°-88°)	6°	5;48°	3;2,30ᵖ
Jupiter	11;41° (257°-265°)	0;19° (83°-91°)	6°	5;41°	2;59ᵖ
Mars	23;25° (253°-255°)	0;35° (81°-83°)	12°	11;25°	6ᵖ
Venus	5;51° (265°-270°)	2;9° (82°-85°)	4°	1;51°	0;58ᵖ
Mercury	7;2° (259°-263°)	0;58° (89°-93°)	4°	3;2°	3ᵖ
Moon	26;18° (114°)	0;0° (216°)	13;9°	13;9°	10;19ᵖ (R=49;41ᵖ)

TABLE 4: EQUATIONS OF THE CENTRE

[1] The eccentricities of Saturn, Jupiter and Venus were obtained by Muḥammad ʻAbd al-Raḥmān, in his aforementioned doctoral dissertation, after checking all the values of the corresponding tables in the three aforementioned *zījes*. He used the computer programme PTA ("Planetary Tables Analysis") prepared by Honorino Mielgo.

the Sun. The maximum value 1;51° used by Ibn al-Bannā', Ibn Isḥāq and Ibn al-Raqqām seems to be a slight correction of the maximum solar equation calculated by Ibn Isḥāq (1;49,35,56, 42°), using Ibn al-Zarqālluh's solar model with variable eccentricity.[46] In spite of this, 1;51° for the maximum equation of the Sun and Venus is a problematic parameter. The corresponding eccentricity is 0;58,8ᵖ for Venus, and twice that amount (1;56,16ᵖ) for the Sun: if we calculate the corresponding date with Ibn al-Zarqālluh's model, we will obtain 1113, a date which cannot correspond to Ibn Isḥāq, but which fits the time of Ibn al-Kammād whose *Muqtabas zīj* uses a maximum solar equation of 1;52,44°.[47] We should acknowledge, finally, that we know nothing about the origin of the new eccentricities used by the three Maghribī astronomers for Saturn and Jupiter.

[46] This table of the solar equation (no. 30-32 of Ibn Isḥāq's *zīj*) bears the following title: *Jadwal ākhar bi-ta'dīl al-shams al-murakkab li-Ibn Isḥāq bi-naṣṣ al-Zarqālluh lā bi-jadwalihi* ("Second table of the solar equation, calculated by Ibn Isḥāq following [Ibn] al-Zarqālluh's instructions, not his tables"). Table 27 of this same *zīj* attains a maximum value of 1;49,7° and it has been calculated "according to the opinion of Ibn Isḥāq" (*'alā ra'y Ibn Isḥāq*). See Mestres, "Maghribī astronomy," p. 414.

[47] Chabás & Goldstein, "Muqtabis," pp. 4-10.

5. THE TABLES OF THE EQUATION OF ANOMALY

5.1 *The "planetary" method*

We calculate the equation of anomaly (γ) with a Ptolemaic table which follows the tradition of the *Handy Tables* according to the following method, which we denominate *planetary*.[48]

a) When the true centre (c_v, mean longitude of the centre of the epicycle from the planetary apogee) is comprised between 0° (apogee) and the position in which the centre of the epicycle is at the mean distance from the centre of the Earth, i.e. this distance equals the deferent radius (R), then the equation of anomaly is:

$$\gamma(\alpha_v, c_v) = c_6(\alpha_v) - c_5(\alpha_v)\, c_{4a}(c_v) \; [3]$$

In this expression:

- α_v is the true anomaly of the planet.
- $c_6(\alpha_v)$ (column 6 in a general table of equations in the *Almagest*) is the equation of anomaly for the mean distance, which we can also symbolise with γ_R.
- $c_5(\alpha_v)$ (column 5) is the difference between c_6 (= γ_R) and the equation of anomaly when the centre of the epicycle is on the apogee (maximum distance between the centre of the epicycle and the centre of the Earth equal to $R + e$, e being the eccentricity). This latter function can, thus, be represented by γ_{R+e}. We have, then:

$$c_5(\alpha_v) = \gamma_R - \gamma_{R+e} \; [4]$$

Thus, c_5 is a function of just one variable: α_v, the true anomaly.

- c_{4a} is an interpolation function for intermediate positions of the centre of the epicycle between the apogee and the mean distance from the centre of the Earth. Its argument is the true centre of the planet. We calculate this function with the following expression, the result being given in minutes:

$$c_{4a}(c_v) = [max\gamma_R - max\gamma(c_v)] \,/\, [max\gamma_R - max\gamma_{R+e}] \; [5]$$

[48] Olaf Pedersen, *A Survey of the Almagest* (Odense, 1974), pp. 291-2, 309, 325-8; Otto Neugebauer, *A History of Ancient Mathematical Astronomy* (Berlin, Heidelberg, New York, 1975), vol. I, pp. 183-90, vol. II, pp. 1002-4.

b) When c_v is comprised between the mean distance and 180° (perigee):

$$\gamma(\alpha_v, c_v) = c_6(\alpha_v) + c_7(\alpha_v)\, c_{4b}(c_v) \ [6]$$

an expression in which $c_6(\alpha_v)$ is defined as before. As for the rest of the functions:

- $c_7(\alpha_v)$ (column 7) tabulates the difference between the equation of anomaly for the minimum distance, i.e. the perigee (γ_{R-e}), and the equation of anomaly for mean distance (γ_R). Therefore:

$$c_7(\alpha_v) = \gamma_{R-e} - \gamma_R \ [7]$$

- $c_{4b}(c_v)$ is the second half of the interpolation function, for positions of the centre of the epicycle located between the mean distance from the centre of the Earth and the perigee, and it is calculated with the following expression, the result also being given in minutes:

$$c_{4b}(c_v) = [max\gamma(c_v) - max\gamma_R] \, / \, [max\gamma_{R-e} - max\gamma_R] \ [8]$$

In his *Minhāj*, Ibn al-Bannā' uses the aforementioned procedure for the computation of the equation of anomaly of Mars, Venus and Mercury. It is interesting, however, to analyse his terminology:

- c_m is called *al-markaz al-awwal* ("the first centre"),
- c_v is called *al-markaz al-mu'addal* ("corrected centre"),
- $c_6(\alpha_v)$ corresponds to the column entitled *al-mufrad* ("singular"),
- $c_5(\alpha_v)$ is *al-bu'd al-ab'ad* ("apogee"),
- $c_7(\alpha_v)$ is *al-bu'd al-aqrab* ("perigee"),
- c_{4a} and c_{4b} are called *daqā'iq nisbat inḥirāf al-kawkab* ("minutes of the ratio of the planet's deviation"). This column is divided into two parts – marked with the mentions *ab'ad* ("far") and *aqrab* ("near") – which correspond exactly to the two functions described.[49]

We should mention here that the functions *mufrad* and *bu'd* are together in a single table entitled *Jadwal ta'dīl al-...* ("Table of the equation of..."). As these two functions are not displaced, Ibn al-Bannā' uses the standard symmetries and tabulates only 180 values for each function. The *daqā'iq*, on the other hand, appear in the table of the equation of the centre (*ta'dīl al-markaz*),

[49] For all this terminology see Vernet, *Contribución*, p. 34, for example (Mars).

Planet	Computation method	*e* (centre)	*e* (anomaly)	*r* (epicycle)
Saturn	Lunar	$3;2,30^p$	$3;25^p$ (Pt.)	$6;30^p$ (Pt.)
Jupiter	Lunar	$2;59^p$	$2;45^p$ (Pt.)	$11;30^p$ (Pt.)
Mars	Planetary	6^p (Pt.)	6^p (Pt.)	$39;30^p$ (Pt.)
Venus	Planetary	$0;58^p$	$1;15^p$ (Pt.)	$43;10^p$ (Pt.)
Mercury	Planetary	3^p (Pt.)	3^p (Pt.)	$22;30^p$ (Pt.)
Moon	Lunar	$10;19^p$ (Pt.) (R= $49;41^p$)	$10;19^p$ (Pt.) (R= $49;41^p$)	$5;15^p$ (c_5) (Pt.) $5;9,41^p$ (c_4) (R= $49;41^p$)

TABLE 5: EQUATIONS OF THE ANOMALY (COMPUTATION METHODS AND PARAMETERS USED FOR THE ECCENTRICITIES AND EPICYCLE RADII)

which – as we have seen – is a displaced function. For that reason Ibn al-Bannā' has to give 360 values and repeats the series of *daqā'iq* twice (in spite of the fact that this function is not displaced). This has a certain utility for checking erroneous values in the manuscripts.

The parameters employed – see TABLE 5 – are Ptolemaic and derive from the tradition of the *Handy Tables*. There is only one inconsistency worth mentioning, and which is quite common in Islamic *zīj*es – we even find it in al-Battānī. We have already seen that Ibn Isḥāq, Ibn al-Bannā' and Ibn al-Raqqām calculate the equation of the centre of Venus with an eccentricity of $0;58^p$. However, when the three Maghribī astronomers copy the table of the equation of anomaly of Venus from a source belonging to the Ptolemaic tradition, they are actually using another eccentricity ($1;15^p$), which underlies the corresponding table of the *Handy Tables*. We have, then, two different eccentricities used for calculating the position of the same planet.

5.2 *The "lunar" method*

5.2.1 **The Moon**

The tradition of the *Handy Tables* uses a different procedure for the calculation of the equation of anomaly of the Moon.[50] The final computation is, in all cases:

$$\gamma(2f, \alpha_v) = c_4 (\alpha_v) + c_5 (\alpha_v)\, c_6 (2f) \quad [9]$$

[50] Pedersen, *Survey*, pp. 195-9; Neugebauer, *H.A.M.A.*, I, 93-8 and II, 988-9. The symbols c_4, c_5 and c_6 correspond to the columns in the *Almagest*.

Where $2f$ is the double mean elongation,

- α_v is the true lunar anomaly,

- c_4 (α_v) is the equation of anomaly at the syzygies (γ_R), in which the centre of the epicycle is placed at its maximum distance from the Earth (R).

- c_5 (α_v) is the difference, for a given α_v between the equation of anomaly for the quadratures $(\gamma_{R\text{-}2e})$ – where the centre of the epicycle is placed at its minimum distance (R-2e) from the Earth – and the equation of anomaly for the syzygies (γ_R).

- c_6 $(2f)$ is the interpolation function which corresponds to the expression:

$$c_6(2f)= [max\gamma(2f) - max\gamma_R] \;/\; [max(\gamma_{R\text{-}2e} - \gamma_R)] \quad [10]$$

the result given in minutes.

This method is also used by Ibn al-Bannā', who adds certain corrections which appeared in Eastern Islamic Astronomy as early as the ninth century or which were introduced by Ibn al-Zarqālluh in the eleventh.[51] We are not going to deal with this topic here but we would like to add a few precisions on the tables of Ibn al-Bannā' for the computation of the equation of anomaly of the Moon:

The terminology used by our author is the same as in the case of Mars and the inferior planets, although, obviously, Ibn al-Bannā' has made an adaptation of the meaning of the technical terms he is using. The function $c_4(\alpha_v)$ is called *al-mufrad*, while $c_5(\alpha_v)$ receives the name of *al-bu'd al-aqrab*. These two functions appear together in the same table and the number of calculated values is 180, as these functions are not displaced. The interpolation function (c_6 $(2f)$) is called *daqā'iq al-nisba* and it appears in the same table as the equation of the centre, which has been displaced: as in the case of Mars, Venus and Mercury, we have here 360 values and, consequently, the series of values of *daqā'iq* appears repeated twice.

The concepts of *al-bu'd al-aqrab* and *daqā'iq al-nisba* derive from the tradition of the *Handy Tables* and the underlying parameters are Ptolemaic: $10;19^p$ for the eccentricity and $5;15^p$ for the radius of the epicycle (the deferent radius being $49;41^p$). The case of the column *al-mufrad* is completely different: its maximum is 4;56° (5;1° in the *Almagest*, the *Handy Tables*,

[51] Cf. Vernet, *Contribución*, pp. 31-2 (Arabic text) and 87-9 (Spanish translation). On the Zarqāllian correction cf. Samsó, *Ciencias de los Antiguos*, pp. 218-19.

al-Battānī and the *Toledan Tables*). 4;56° is a maximum value which has an Indian origin and appears in the *Khandakhadyaka* and other similar sources,[52] in the *Zīj al-Shāh* and, within Islamic astronomy, in al-Khwārizmī (for $2f = 90°$), Abū Ma'shar, Māshā'allāh, Ibn Hibinta etc.[53] Besides, if we analyse the Andalusian-Maghribī tradition, we find the same maximum value in a table calculated with a Ptolemaic method in the *Tabulae Jahen* of Ibn Mu'ādh al-Jayyānī (d. 1093),[54] Ibn Isḥāq (max. 4;55,59°), the *Alfonsine Tables* (max. 4;56°) and Ibn al-Raqqām (max. 4;55,59°).[55] We should also note that the tabular values of Ibn al-Bannā' are those of Ibn Isḥāq rounded to minutes, and that those appearing in the *Alfonsine Tables* seem to have been computed in an independent way. From all this we can deduce that Ibn al-Bannā' is using, for this function, an epicycle radius of $5;9,41^p$ (deferent radius $49;41^p$), instead of the $5;15^p$ used for the other functions related to the computation of the equation of anomaly.

5.2.2 Saturn and Jupiter in the *Minhāj*

Ibn al-Bannā' uses the Ptolemaic Lunar method for the computation of the equation of anomaly of Saturn and Jupiter.[56] For these two planets, *al-mufrad* (m) corresponds to the equation of anomaly at the apogee (γ_{R+e}), while the *daqā'iq al-bu'd* (b) correspond to the difference between the equation of anomaly at the perigee and at the apogee ($\gamma_{R-e} - \gamma_{R+e}$). These two functions appear together in the same table, which contains 180 calculated values.

If we remember the definitions of the "planetary" functions c_5, c_6, and c_7 (see above 5.1), we can easily establish:

$$m = c_6 - c_5 = \gamma_R - (\gamma_R - \gamma_{R+e}) = \gamma_{R+e} \quad [11]$$

$$b = c_5 + c_7 = (\gamma_R - \gamma_{R+e}) + (\gamma_{R-e} - \gamma_R) = \gamma_{R-e} - \gamma_{R+e} \quad [12]$$

[52] Cf. F.I. Haddad, E.S. Kennedy and D. Pingree, *The Book of the Reasons behind Astronomical Tables (Kitāb fī 'ilal al-zījāt) by 'Alī ibn Sulaymān al-Hāshimī* (New York, 1981), pp. 167, 210, 220, 300, 308, 313.

[53] D. Pingree, *The Thousands of Abū Ma'shar* (London, 1968), pp. 47-8; Kennedy *et al.*, *Studies in the Islamic Exact Sciences*, pp. 329 and 349.

[54] J. Samsó, *Ciencias de los Antiguos*, p. 157.

[55] Cf. also B.R. Goldstein, "Lunar velocity in the Middle Ages: A comparative study," *From Baghdad to Barcelona*, I, 184-5.

[56] See, for example, for Saturn, Vernet, *Contribución*, pp. 33-5 (Arabic text) and 91-3 (Spanish translation).

We can also see easily the Ptolemaic character of the underlying parameters of the two columns. Ibn al-Bannā' has calculated them by adding or subtracting columns c_5, c_6, and c_7 in a table derived from the tradition of the *Handy Tables*. In TABLES 6 and 7 we can see samples of *m* and *b* for Saturn and Jupiter compared to c_5, c_6, and c_7 that we copy from the *zīj* of al-Battānī, to which we have added the variant readings of Ibn Isḥāq's *zīj*. When these variant readings have an asterisk, this implies that Ibn Isḥāq's values agree with *m* and/or *b* of Ibn al-Bannā' much closer than those of al-Battānī. An examination of TABLES 6 and 7 leads us to the conclusion that Ibn al-Bannā' used Ibn Isḥāq's equation table, or a similar one, for Saturn. We cannot, however, conclude the same for Jupiter.

Ibn al-Bannā's tables of the equation of anomaly also contain an interpolation function resembling the lunar c_6 (*2f*). This function, expressed in minutes, is called *daqā'iq nisbat al-ikhtilāf* (*d*) ("minutes of the ratio of the variation") and it appears in the same table as the equation of the centre of Saturn and Jupiter which, as we have already seen, are displaced. As in other similar cases Ibn al-Bannā' repeats this table and provides us with 360 values. The final formula (*al-murakkab*) of the equation of anomaly of these two planets is, according to the canons of Ibn al-Bannā':

$$\gamma = m + b\, d \quad [13],$$

whence we can easily conclude that, like in the case of the lunar c_6 (*2f*), we have, here:

$$d\,(c_v) = [max\gamma(c_v) - max\gamma_{R+e}] \;/\; [max(\gamma_{R-e} - \gamma_{R+e})] \quad [14]$$

and we can use the following values:

- For Saturn:

$$max\gamma_{R+e} = max\ m = 5;53°$$
$$max\gamma_{R-e} = max\ (m + b) = 6;37°$$

- For Jupiter:

$$max\gamma_{R+e} = max\ m = 10;34°$$
$$max\gamma_{R-e} = max\ (m + b) = 11;35°$$

If we recompute both *d* tables with [14] and the aforementioned parameters, the results obtained can be considered correct, but not remarkable. On the other hand we cannot imagine Ibn

	Mufrad (c_6-c_5)	c_6	c_5	c_7	*Bu'd* (c_5+c_7)
1	0;6°	0;6°	0;0°	0;0°	0;0°
5	0;28	0;30	0;2	0;2	0;4
10	0;57	1;0	0;3	0;3	0;6
15	1;23	1;28	0;5	0;6	0;11
20	1;51	1;57	0;6	0;8	0;14
25	2;17	2;24	0;7	0;10	0;17
30	2;42	2;50	0;8	0;11	0;19
35	3;6	3;15	0;9	0;13	0;22
40	3;30	3;40	0;10	0;15 (Isḥ. 0;14)	0;25
45	3;52	4;3	0;11	0;16	0;27
50	4;13	4;26	0;13	0;18	0;31
55	4;32	4;46	0;14	0;19	0;33
60	4;49 (+1')	5;5 (Isḥ. *5;4)	0;15	0;20	0;35
65	5;6	45;22	0;16	0;20	0;36
70	5;20	5;37	0;17	0;21	0;38
75	5;31	5;49	0;18	0;21	0;39
80	5;41 (+1')	5;59	0;19 (Isḥ.*0;18)	0;22	0;40 (-1')
85	5;48	6;7	0;19	0;22	0;41
90	5;52 (-1')	6;12	0;19	0;23	0;42
95	5;53°	6;13°	0;20°	0;24°	0;44°
100	5;51	6;12	0;21	0;24	0;45
105	5;48	6;9	0;21	0;25	0;46
110	5;42	6;2	0;20	0;24 (Isḥ.*0;25)	0;45 (+1')
115	5;33	5;53	0;20	0;24	0;44
120	5;22	5;41	0;19	0;23	0;42
125	5;7	5;25	0;18	0;22	0;40
130	4;49	5;6	0;17	0;21	0;39 (+1')
135	4;29 (+1')	4;45	0;17 (Isḥ.*0;16)	0;20	0;36 (-1')
140	4;6	4;21	0;15	0;18	0;33
145	3;41	3;55	0;14	0;16	0;30
150	3;13	3;25	0;12	0;14	0;26
155	2;45	2;55 (Isḥ. 2;54)	0;10	0;12	0;22
160	2;15	2;23	0;8	0;10	0;18
165	1;42 (-1')	1;48	0;5 (Isḥ. *0;6)	0;8	0;14 (+1')
170	1;8 (-1')	1;13	0;4 (Isḥ. *0;5)	0;6	0;11 (+1')
175	0;35 (-1')	0;38	0;2 (Isḥ. *0;3)	0;3	0;6 (+1')
180	0;0	0;0	0;0	0;0	0;0

TABLE 6: *MUFRAD* AND *BU'D* FOR SATURN

	Mufrad (c_6-c_5)	c_6	c_5	c_7	*Bu'd* (c_5+c_7)
1	0;10°	0;10°	0;0°	0;0°	0;0°
5	0;47	0;49	0;2	0;2	0;4
10	1;34	1;37	0;3	0;3	0;6
15	2;19	2;24	0;5	0;6	0;11
20	3;4	3;11	0;7	0;8	0;15
25	3;49	3;57	0;8	0;9	0;18 (+1')
30	4;32	4;42	0;10	0;11	0;21
35	5;14	5;26	0;12	0;13	0;25
40	5;56	6;9	0;13	0;14	0;27
45	6;34	6;49	0;15	0;16	0;31
50	7;11	7;28	0;17	0;19	0;34 (-2')
55	7;46	8;4	0;18	0;20	0;38
60	8;17	8;37	0;20	0;22	0;42
65	8;46	9;8	0;22	0;24	0;46
70	9;13	9;36	0;23	0;25	0;48
75	9;35	10;0	0;25	0;27	0;52
80	9;55	10;21	0;26	0;29	0;55
85	10;12 (+1')	10;38	0;27	0;30	0;57
90	10;24	10;51	0;27	0;31	0;58
95	10;33	11;1 (Isḥ. 11;0)	0;28	0;31	0;59
100	10;34°	11;3°	0;29°	0;32°	1;1°
105	10;33	11;2	0;29	0;32	1;1
110	10;25	10;55	0;30	0;33	1;3
115	10;12	10;42	0;30	0;33	1;3
120	9;54	10;23	0;29	0;33	1;2
125	9;31	10;0	0;29	0;32	1;1
130	9;2	9;30	0;28	0;31	0;59
135	8;27 (-1')	8;55 (Isḥ. 8;57)	0;27	0;30	0;57
140	7;48	8;13	0;25	0;29	0;54
145	7;3	7;26	0;23	0;25	0;48
150	6;13	6;34	0;21	0;22	0;43
155	5;18	5;36	0;18	0;19	0;37
160	4;20	4;35 (Isḥ. 4;34)	0;15	0;16	0;31
165	3;18	3;29	0;11	0;12	0;23
170	2;14 (+1')	2;21	0;8 (Isḥ. *0;7)	0;9	0;16 (-1')
175	1;6	1;11	0;5	0;5	0;9 (-1')
180	0;0	0;0	0;0	0;0	0;0

TABLE 7: *MUFRAD* AND *BU'D* FOR JUPITER

al-Bannā' painfully calculating *max* γ (c_v) with Ptolemaic parameters when this value is implied in the "planetary" functions c_{4a} and c_{4b}. As we have already seen (5.1):

$$c_{4a}(c_v) = [max\gamma_R - max\gamma(c_v)]/[max\gamma_R - max\gamma_{R+e}] \quad [5]$$

Substituting in expression [5] the aforementioned parameters and also:

$max\gamma_R$ = 6;13° (Saturn)[57]
$max\gamma_R$ = 11;3° (Jupiter)[58]

we will obtain:

$$c_{4a}(c_v) = [6;13° - max\gamma(c_v)] \,/\, 0;20° \quad [15] \text{ (Saturn)}$$

and

$$max\gamma(c_v) = 6;13° - 0;20°\, c_{4a}(c_v) \quad [16] \text{ (Saturn)}$$

By substituting in expression [14], we will obtain:

$$d(c_{4a}) = [0;20° - 0;20°\, c_{4a}(c_v)]/\, 0;44° = [0;20°\, (1 - c_{4a}(c_v))] \,/\, 0;44° \quad [17] \text{ (Saturn)}$$

This solves the problem of the computation of the first part of $d(c_v)$ (between the apogee and the middle distance) as a function of $c_{4a}(c_v)$ which can be read directly in a Ptolemaic table. On the other hand, it is easy to see that [17] implies an arithmetical progression with an increase of 0;27,16 (0;20°/0;44°) every time that $c_{4a}(c_v)$ increases one unit.

We can find, for Jupiter, the equivalent expressions:

$$max\gamma(c_v) = 11;3° - 0;29°\, c_{4a}(c_v) \quad [18] \text{ (Jupiter)}$$

$$d(c_{4a}) = [0;29° - 0;29°\, c_{4a}(c_v)]/\, 1;1° = [0;29°\, (1 - c_{4a}(c_v))] \,/\, 1;1° \quad [19] \text{ (Jupiter)}$$

This implies an arithmetical progression with a constant increase of 0;28,31 (= 0;29°/1;1°) every time that $c_4(a)$ is increased in one unit.

[57] It is the *standard* value in the tradition of the *Handy Tables*. If we use Ibn al-Bannā's tables, we would have:

(6;37° + 5;53°)/ 2 = 6;15°

We do not use this value because the results obtained are clearly worse.

[58] As in the case of Saturn, it is the *standard* value of the tradition of the *Handy Tables*. With the *zīj* of Ibn al-Bannā', we would have:

(10;34° + 11;35°) / 2 = 11;4,30°.

Here also the results obtained would be worse with this value.

c_v	c_4a	$d(c_4a)$	c_v	c_4b	$d(c_4b)$
5°	60'	0'	88°	1'	28'[1]
10	59	0	90	3	30 (+1')
15	57	1	95	8	32
20	55	2	100	13	34
25	53	3	105	17	36(+1')
30	51	5 (+1')	110	21	40(+1')
35	48	6 (+1')	115	25	41
40	46 Isḥ. 45(?)	8 (+2')	120	30	44
45	42	10 (+2')	125	33	45
50	38 Isḥ. 39	12 (+2')	130	37	47(-1')
55	34 Isḥ. 35	13 (+1')	135	42	49(-1')
60	30	14	140	45	52
65	25	16	145	49	54
70	20	20 (+2')	150	51	56(+1')
75	14	22 (+1')	155	54	57
80	8	25 (+1')	160	57	58(-1')
85	3	26	165	58	59
87	1	27	170	59	60
			175	60	60
			180	60	6C

TABLE 8: INTERPOLATION FUNCTION (d) FOR SATURN

[1] Our starting point for this column is the value of $d(c_4b)$ calculated exactly with expression [22], for $c_4b = 1$. The result is 27;49'.

As for the second part of the function (between the middle distance and the perigee) our starting point will be $c_{4b}(c_v)$. Substituting the corresponding values in expression [8], we will obtain:

$$c_{4b}(c_v) = [max\gamma(c_v) - 6;13°]/0;24° \quad [20] \text{ (Saturn)}$$

and

$$max\gamma(c_v) = 6;13° + 0;24°\, c_{4b}(c_v) \quad [21] \text{ (Saturn)}$$

Finally

$$d(c_{4b}) = [0;20° + 0;24°\, c_{4b}(c_v)]/\, 0;44° \quad [22] \text{ (Saturn)}$$

This time the underlying arithmetical progression has a ratio of 0;32,44 (= 0;24°/ 0;44°).

c_v	c_4a	$d(c_4a)$	c_v	c_4b	$d(c_4b)$
5°	60'	0'	88°	1'	29'[1]
10	60	0	90	2	30
15	59	1 (+1')	95	6	32
20	57	2 (+1')	100	11	35 (+1')
25	55	2	105	16	37
30	53	3	110	21	39
35	50 (Isḥ. 49)	5	115	25	41
40	47	6	120	30	44
45	43	8	125	35	46 (-1')
50	39	9 (-1')	130	39	49
55	34 (Isḥ. 35)	12	135	43	51
60	30	14	140	46	53
65	25	17(+1')	145	49	54
70	19	19	150	52	56 (+1')
75	14	21	155	54	57
80	8	24	160	56	58
85	3	26(-1')	165	58	59
88	0	28	170	59	60
			175	60	60
			180	60	60

TABLE 9: INTERPOLATION FUNCTION (*d*) FOR JUPITER

[1] Our starting point for this column is the value of $d[c_4b]$ calculated exactly, with expression [24], for $c_4b = 1$. The result is 29;3'.

For Jupiter:

$$max\gamma(c_v) = 11;3° + 0;32° \ c_{4b}(c_v) \ [23] \ \text{(Jupiter)}$$

$$d(c_{4b}) = [0;29° + 0;32° \ c_{4b}(c_v)] \ / \ 1;1° \ [24] \ \text{(Jupiter)}$$

which implies an arithmetical progression with a ratio 0;31,29 (= 0;32°/ 1;1°) for every increase of one unit in the function $c_{4b}(c_v)$.

TABLES 8 and 9 contain a sample of functions $d(c_{4a})$ and $d(c_{4b})$ for Saturn and Jupiter, as they appear in the *zīj* of Ibn al-Bannā'. Minutes between round brackets correspond to the differences between tabular and recomputed values using the following ratios:

- Saturn: $d(c_{4a})$ (+ 0;27°) and $d(c_{4b})$ (+0;33°)
- Jupiter: $d(c_{4a})$ (+ 0;28°) $d(c_{4b})$ (+0;31°)

Tabular values of c_{4a} and c_{4b} have been taken from al-Battānī's *zīj* and we have noted the variant readings which appear in the *zīj* of Ibn Isḥāq.

4. CONCLUSIONS

Ibn al-Bannā's *Minhāj* seemed to be extremely important a few years ago when we began studying its solar tables in which we found echoes of the lost work of Ibn al-Zarqālluh. This importance has diminished, in our opinion, since we have had access to Ibn Isḥāq's *zīj*, as it appears in the Hyderabad manuscript, generously made available to us by David King. This is, no doubt, the main source used by Ibn al-Bannā', who does not seem to have introduced anything new in the work of his predecessor. Ibn al-Bannā' has prepared an "edition" by selecting among Ibn Isḥāq's numerical tables and writing a collection of clear and simple canons.

We have also found in the *Minhāj* a few formal novelties which tend to facilitate the computation procedures: displaced tables for the equation of the centre and use of the "lunar method" to calculate the equation of anomaly of Saturn and Jupiter. We do not need to emphasize the advantages of displaced equations, which allow computation without having to remember the positive or negative sign of the equation, for they have clearly been studied for the Eastern astronomical tradition. Concerning the "lunar" method for Saturn and Jupiter, it is obvious that a simple expression such as [13] has a general value and the calculator does not need to have in mind the position of the mean centre (c_m) in order to choose between expressions [3] and [6] for the computation of the equation of anomaly, as he has to with the "planetary" method. On the other hand, there is good reason for the use of this method for Saturn and Jupiter and not for the rest of the planets: their epicycles are smaller than those of Mercury, Venus and Mars and the resulting inaccuracies of the method will be slighter.

Finally, the analysis of the planetary tables of the *Minhāj* leads us to identify, once more, the essential characteristics of the Andalusian-Maghribī astronomical school: al-Battānī's influence, which began to be felt in the middle of the eleventh century when it appeared in the *Toledan Tables* (let us remember here the apogees of Saturn, Jupiter and Mars); influence of the tables of planetary equations in Theon's *Handy Tables* which we find everywhere in the *Minhāj*; influence of the works of Ibn al-Zarqālluh on the Sun and the Moon which appear here with the motion of the solar apogee, extended to the inferior planets, and the Zarqāllian correction of Ptolemy's lunar model which we have not analysed here in detail because it has been the object of previous studies and will be dealt with in more detail in a forthcoming paper by our colleague Roser Puig. We should, furthermore, ask ourselves whether this Maghribī tradition conserves what is left of a set of planetary tables compiled by Ibn al-Zarqālluh between the completion of the *Toledan Tables* (before 1068 A.D.) and his own death (1100). The mean motion tables are particularly suspect because the radices for epoch are given by Ibn Isḥāq for the longitude of Toledo; the difference of 6;42,45° between the apogees of Ibn al-Bannā' and those of the *Almagest* (in the case of Saturn and Mars) has been traced back to a Zarqāllian source, while the apogee of Venus – like that of the Sun – has the same origin. Can we ascribe the same origin to the apogee of Mercury? Pushing the matter further, could this also be the origin of the new eccentricities of Saturn and Mars?

ACKNOWLEDGEMENTS: This paper has been written within a research programme on "Astronomical theory and tables in al-Andalus and the Maghrib between the twelfth and the fourteenth centuries," sponsored by the Dirección General de Investigación Científica y Técnica of the Spanish Ministry of Education and Culture. David King, who has many things in common with Abū 'Ubayda Muslim b. Aḥmad al-Laythī (d. 907), deserves our gratitude for the time he has spent revising this paper and correcting our English style.

IX

ANDALUSIAN ASTRONOMY IN 14TH CENTURY FEZ: *AL-ZĪJ AL-MUWĀFIQ* OF IBN ʿAZZŪZ AL-QUSANṬĪNĪ

1. *Ibn Isḥāq and the Andalusian tradition in Maghribī zījes.*

What we know about Andalusian influence on Maghribī astronomy begins in the 13th century when Abū l-ʿAbbās Ibn Isḥāq al-Tamīmī al-Tunisī (fl. Tunis and Marrakesh ca. 1193-1222), prepared a set of tables which survive in a unique manuscript in Hyderabad, discovered in 1978 by D.A. King[1]. This manuscript was copied in Ḥimṣ (Syria) in 1317 A.D. An edition of the whole set of canons and an analysis of the numerical tables is being prepared in Barcelona by Angel Mestres[2]. Ibn Isḥāq's work occupies a central position in the successive development of Maghribī *zīj*es: it seems clear that he compiled a set of tables (nos. 6-58 of the manuscript) for the computation of planetary longitudes, eclipses, equation of time, parallax and, probably, solar and lunar velocity. These tables, in which Andalusian influence seems predominant, were not accompanied by an elaborate collection of canons although they contained some kind of instructions for the use of a few tables.

These tables, with a very limited number of canons, were completed by an unknown astronomer probably around 665-680 H./1266-1281. He was the compiler of the set of canons which we find in the manuscript and which he took from Andalusian sources (Ibn al-Hāʾim, Ibn al-Kammād, Ibn Muʿādh, an otherwise unknown Ibn al-Bayṭār and al-Sabtī) as well as more conventional sources (al-Khwārizmī,

[1] See f. ex. David A. King, "An Overview of the Sources for the History of Astronomy in the Medieval Maghrib". *Deuxième Colloque Maghrébin sur l'Histoire des Mathématiques Arabes.* Tunis, 1988, pp. 125-157.

[2] See a detailed survey of the contents of the manuscript in A. Mestres, "Maghribī Astronomy in the 13th century: a Description of Manuscript Hyderabad Andra Pradesh State Library 298" in J. Casulleras and J. Samsó (eds.), *From Baghdad to Barcelona. Studies in the Islamic Exact Sciences in Honour of Prof. Juan Vernet* (Barcelona, 1996), I, 383-443.

the *Mumtaḥan Zīj*, al-Battānī and several astrological works of Mūsā ibn Nawbakht, Abū Maʿshar and Ibn Abī-l-Rijāl). Our unknown astronomer also added the numerical tables which he considered were missing in Ibn Isḥāq's early set. His sources are, again, Ibn al-Kammād and Ibn al-Hāʾim as well as others like the *Mumtaḥan Zīj*, Ṭumṭum al-Hindī and pseudo-Maslama ibn Aḥmad al-Majrīṭī (astrological tables probably linked to the *Picatrix* tradition), Abū Maʿshar, the *Sindhind* of Brahmagupta, Ibn al-Bayṭār, al-Qallās, and Ibn Muʿādh. To all this our unknown compiler adds an important collection of tables calculated by himself which includes an *almanac* (the term *al-mannākh* is used in the text) in the Zarqāllian tradition, as well as many other tables of unknown source.

This anonymous astronomer was not the only "editor" of the tables of Ibn Isḥāq, for his late contemporary Ibn al-Bannāʾ of Marrakesh (1256-1321) prepared another "edition" – in his *Minhāj al-ṭālib li-taʿdīl al-kawākib* – with an entirely different structure from that of the Hyderabad manuscript: instead of a monumental collection of materials from different sources it presents a selection of Ibn Isḥāq's tables accompanied by a collection of canons, easy to understand, which makes the *zīj* accessible for the computation of planetary longitudes. This is accompanied by some modifications of the structure of the tables, which are intended to make calculations easier (displaced equations of the centre for the Sun, Moon and planets; computation of the equations of anomaly of Jupiter and Saturn in the same way as that used for the Moon in the Ptolemaic tradition)[3].

Another contemporary of the two aforementioned authors prepared two further editions of Ibn Isḥāq's tables: the Tunisian-Andalusian astronomer Muḥammad ibn al-Raqqām (d. 1315) is the author of two *zījes*, entitled *al-Zīj al-Shāmil fī tahdhīb al-Kāmil* and *al-Zīj al-Qawīm fī funūn al-taʿdīl wa-l-taqwīm*. The former was composed in 1280-81 in Tunis: the canons are, word for word, those of Ibn al-Hāʾim[4]

[3] Ibn al-Bannāʾ's canons have been edited and translated into Spanish by J. Vernet, *Contribución al estudio de la labor astronómica de Ibn al-Bannāʾ*. Tetuán, 1952; the solar tables have been analysed by J. Samsó and E. Millás, "Ibn al-Bannāʾ, Ibn Isḥāq and Ibn al-Zarqālluh's Solar Theory" in J. Samsó, *Islamic Astronomy and Medieval Spain*. Variorum. Aldershot, 1994, no X (35 pp.). On his tables for the computation of planetary longitudes a paper by the same two authors is under preparation.

[4] Cf. J. Samsó, *Las Ciencias de los Antiguos en al-Andalus* (Madrid, 1992), 324-326.

after suppressing all the careful geometrical demonstrations introduced by the Andalusian author of the beginning of the thirteenth century; the numerical tables are those of Ibn Isḥāq[5]. The *Qawīm Zīj* has not yet been thoroughly studied but the canons are much less developed and they seem to be a simplified rewording of those of the *Shāmil Zīj*. There seem to be no great novelties in the numerical tables although some of them are adapted to the geographical coordinates of Granada, as a result of Ibn al-Raqqām's arrival in this city in the time of Muḥammad II (1273-1302): with this author, then, a collection of Andalusian materials exported to Tunis one century earlier returned to al-Andalus.

To the four aforementioned *zīj*es one should add a fifth one, prepared by Abū l-Ḥasan ʻAlī ibn Abī ʻAlī al-Qusanṭīnī (fourteenth century), who was active in Fez: its canons were written in verse so that they could easily be learnt by heart. This work, which has been studied in detail[6], has the obvious interest of being the only known document extant in Arabic in which the planetary theory is Indian and not Ptolemaic, although the influence of Ibn Isḥāq and Ibn al-Bannā' continues to be present (trepidation, mean motion tables, longitudes of the solar and planetary apogees).

2. *Ibn ʻAzzūz al-Qusanṭīnī and his "Muwāfiq Zīj".*

Abū l-Ḥasan ʻAlī ibn Abī ʻAlī al-Qusanṭīnī is not the only Constantinian astronomer active in Fez in the fourteenth century: Ahmed Djebbar[7] called attention to the existence of a new *zīj*, entitled *al-Zīj al-Muwāfiq*, extant in manuscript D 2461 of the Bibliothèque Générale

[5] A partial edition of this *Zīj*, including a commentary and recomputation of the tables, was presented by Muḥammad ʻAbd al-Raḥmān (Institute for the History of Arabic Science, Aleppo) as a doctoral dissertation (*Ḥisāb aṭwāl al-kawākib fī 'l-Zīj al-Shāmil fī Tahdhīb al-Kāmil li-Ibn al-Raqqām*) in the University of Barcelona (September 1996).

[6] E.S. Kennedy and David A. King, "Indian Astronomy in Fourteenth Century Fez: the Versified Zīj of al-Qusunṭīnī", *Journal for the History of Arabic Science* 6 (1982), 3-45; reprinted in D. A. King, *Islamic Mathematical Astronomy*. Variorum. London, 1986. no VIII.

[7] A. Djebbar, "Quelques éléments nouveaux sur l'activité mathématique arabe dans le Maghreb Oriental (IXe-XVIe s.)". *Deuxième Colloque Maghrébin sur l'Histoire des Mathématiques Arabes*. Tunis, 1988, pp. 67-68.

de Rabat (hereafter RGL). According to a note, written by a certain *faqīh* and *muʿaddil* Sīdī Muḥammad ibn Abī Yaḥyā[8] (Djebbar reads ibn Abī l-Khayr) al-Ḥabbāk, which appears on page 355 of this manuscript[9] the author of the work appears to be Abū l-Qāsim ibn [al-Ḥajjāj] ʿAzzūz [al-Qusanṭīnī, d. Constantina 755/1354][10]. A second copy of the same *zīj* is also extant in manuscript 8772 of the Ḥasaniyya Library (hereafter RHL) in which the name of the author has been omitted[11]. Al-Ḥabbāk's note in RGL also states that Ibn ʿAzzūz had

[8] Mathematician and astronomer from Tlemcen who died in 867/1463: See H. Suter, *Die Mathematiker und Astronomen der Araber und ihre Werke* (Leipzig, 1900), no. 435, p. 177. See also D.A. King, *A Survey of the Scientific Manuscripts in the Egyptian National Library* (Winona Lake, Indiana 1986), p. 140, F28; and Driss Lamrabet, *Introduction à l'Histoire des Mathématiques Maghrébines*. Rabat, 1994, p. 117 no. 445.

[9] The manuscript is paginated, not foliated. The *Muwāfiq Zīj* occupies pp. 355-463.

[10] The only source which mentions him appears to be Abū l-ʿAbbās Aḥmad b. Ḥasan b. ʿAlī b. al-Khāṭīb, known as Ibn Qunfudh al-Qusanṭīnī, *al-Wafayāt*, ed. by ʿĀdil Nuwayhiḍ (Beirut, 1978), p. 358, no. 755. See also ʿA. Nuwayhiḍ, *Muʿjam aʿlām al-Jazāʾir min ṣadr al-Islām ḥattā al-ʿaṣr al-ḥāḍir* (Beirut, 1980), p. 231. Ibn Qunfudh states that he was a *faraḍī*, a *Mālikī faqīh* and an expert in other sciences. He wrote a summary (*mukhtaṣar*) on *Farāʾiḍ* (partition of inheritances) as well as other works. I owe this information to the kindness of Prof. Fuat Sezgin.

[11] Muḥammad al-ʿArabī al-Khaṭṭābī, *Fahāris al-Khizāna al-Ḥasaniyya. III: al-Riyāḍiyyāt, al-Falak wa-Aḥkām al-Nujūm wa l-Jughrāfiyā*. Rabat, 1983, pp. 288-289. I owe a photocopy of this manuscript to the generosity of Prof. Aḥmad Shawqī Bīnbīn, Keeper of the Ḥasaniyya Library. The manuscript contains 51 folios and has been paginated, starting with the second page, using the so-called *Rūmī* or Fez ciphers. On this system of numeration the most recent survey is Ana Labarta and Carmen Barceló, *Números y cifras en los documentos arábigohispanos*. Córdoba, 1987.

Mònica Rius (Arabic Department, University of Barcelona) attracted my attention to a paper by Muḥammad al-Mannūnī ("Maktabat al-Zāwiya al-Ḥamzawiyya. Ṣafḥa min tārīḫi-hā". *Tiṭwān* 8 [1963], 97-177, see pp. 155-157) who has identified the existence of excerpts from the first chapters of this same *zīj* (geographical coordinates, chronology, solar model) in ms. 80 of the Zāwiya Ḥamzawiyya of Ait Ayache (pp. 198-202). An incomplete microfilm is extant in Rabat's General Library: I owe a copy of it to the late Keeper of the RGL Prof. Muḥammad b. Sharīfa, to whom I would like to express my gratitude. The excerpt might be longer: the text preceding this passage in the *majmūʿ* is Ibn Ḥabīb's *Kitāb fī 'l-nujūm:* Paul Kunitzsch ("ʿAbd al-Malik ibn Ḥabīb's Book on the Stars" in *Zeitschrift für Geschichte der Arabisch-Islamischen Wissenschaften* 9 [1994], 161-194), who has published an edition of this latter work, has observed that Ibn Ḥabīb's text ends abruptly on p. 195, and that pp. 196-197 are missing in the microfilm. The two missing pages might contain the end of Ibn Ḥabīb's book and the beginning of the quotation from the *Muwāfiq Zīj*.

written another *zīj*, called *al-Zīj al-Kāmil*, in 718/1318-19 and Djebbar adds that the Ṣubayḥiyya Library in Salé keeps a third work by Ibn ʿAzzūz entitled *Risāla fī adwār al-nayyirayn* (ms. 509/2). On the other hand the second book (*al-maqāla al-thāniya*) of a fourth astronomical work, the *Kitāb al-Fuṣūl fī jamʿ al-uṣūl* is extant in ms. 1110 of the Ḥasaniyya Library also in Rabat[12]: this second book is concerned with year transfers (*taḥwīl al-sinīn*), conjunctions and oppositions, and it contains ten chapters (*fuṣūl*) and a conclusion. Chapter 3 of this same *maqāla* is also preserved in ms. D 2128 of Rabat's General Library (pp. 42-44): it deals with year transfers and what they imply for kings, citizens and their situations[13].

The prologue of the *Muwāfiq Zīj*[14] contains a certain amount of interesting information on its author who reminds us of the important observations made in his time by the "unique" *faqīh* Abū l-ʿAbbās Aḥmad ibn Isḥāq al-Tūnisī. Most of his contemporaries use his cycles of planetary motions (*adwār ḥarakat al-kawākib*) in the [mean motion tables of] their *zīj*es[15]. Modern astronomers have, however, observed with their own eyes (*bi-l-mushāhada al-ʿiyāniyya*) the existence of disagreements and errors [with the amounts calculated with the tables] which affected the times of the conjunctions of the superior planets, the velocity of the motion of Mars, and the stations and retrogradations of Venus and Mercury. Ibn ʿAzzūz himself established the existence of such disagreements when he calculated the *tasyīr* of the significators (*adilla*) of conjunctions, eclipses and their ascendants to determine the time of events of the past (*fī l-mudad al-khāliya*) and, especially, the great battle which took place in the days of the *amīr al-muʾminīn*

Added in proof: Prof. Sezgin informs me that Prof. Kunitzsch has been able to obtain photographs of the two missing pages of the Ait Ayache manuscript. The text of Ibn ʿAzzūz begins on the ten last lines of p. 197. See the paper by P. Kunitzsch in this volume of the *Zeitschrift*.

12 Khaṭṭābī, *Fahāris*, pp. 367-368. See also Lamrabet, *Mathématiques Maghrébines*, p. 101.

13 Prof. Aḥmad Tawfīq, Keeper of Rabat's General Library, sent me photocopies of ms. D 2461. Mònica Rius, during a short stay in Rabat, obtained for me a photocopy of p. 355 of this same ms. and discovered the short text by Ibn ʿAzzūz in ms. RGL D 2128. My gratitude to both of them.

14 See RGL p. 357; RHL p. 2 is practically illegible in my photocopy.

15 This is true, as we have seen, in the case of the anonymous compiler of the Hyderabad ms. as well as in the case of Ibn al-Bannāʾ and Ibn al-Raqqām.

and Caliph of the Lord of the Worlds (*khalīfat Rabb al-ʿālamīn*)[16] in Faḥṣ Ṭarīf [battle of El Salado] in the month of Jumādā I of 741 H. [7 Jumādā I 741/ 30 October 1340]. The calculated times did not correspond to historical reality and he considers that the tables in use were responsible for the mistake. Therefore, in order to correct the divergence (*ikhtilāf*) existent in the famous *zīj*, he based his correction on extremely careful and precise observations made with the instrument called the armillary sphere (*dhāt al-ḥalaq*). Then he divided the *ikhtilāf* [i.e. the difference between calculated and observed positions] by the number of "star revolutions" (*adwār nujūmiyya*) between the observation of Ibn Isḥāq and the beginning of year 745 H. [1 Muḥarram 745/ 15 May 1344][17]. Ibn ʿAzzūz used geometrical demonstrations, reasonable measurements and numerical ratios (*bi-barāhīn handasiyya wa-maqāyīs ʿaqliyya wa-nisab ʿadadiyya*) and found that the result obtained from the division by the revolutions of the motions (*mā kharaja la-nā min adwār al-ḥarakāt bi-l-taqsīm*) was consistent with the result obtained from the observation "between the two of them" (?) (*muwāfiqan li-mā kharaja la-nā bi l-raṣad mā bayna-humā* [*sic*])[18] except for a small approximation which has no importance in this "art" (*ṣināʿa*). Then, taking into account the differences obtained, he cast the horoscopes of the conjunctions and total eclipses according to the system used in this *zīj* (*ʿalā madhhab waḍʿ hādhā l-zīj*) and, using again *tasyīr* techniques, obtained the times of known historical events such as the fall (*intiqāl*) of the Almohads, the establishment of

[16] Abū l-Ḥasan ʿAlī, sultan (731/1331-752/1351) of the dynasty of the Banū Marīn of Fez.

[17] The date 17 Rabīʿ I 745 appears quoted in an example for the calculation of the solar longitude (RRL p. 9; RGL p. 363, Ḥamzawiyya pp. 201-202). A note in the margin of p. 357 of ms. RGL states that this was the year of a conjunction of the two inferior planets (*qirān al-sufliyyayn*) in the sign of Aquarius, according to what was said by the author himself in his book *al-Ḥurūz fī sharḥ al-rumūz* (see below). Bryant Tuckerman, *Planetary, Lunar and Solar Positions. A.D. 2 to A.D. 1649 at Five-day and Ten-day Intervals* (Philadelphia, 1964) does not give any conjunction of Venus and Mercury in 745/1344-45, but there was a conjunction of Saturn and Jupiter in Aquarius 19° the 17th Dhū l-Qaʿda 745/ 22 March 1345. I obtain the same result with the *Alfonsine Tables*.

[18] The expression *muwāfiqan li-mā kharaja la-nā bi l-raṣad* ("in agreement with what we obtained from observation") appears to give some sense to the incomplete title of the *zīj*: Ibn ʿAzzūz states, at the end of his introduction (RGL p. 358; RHL p. 3), that he has named his work *al-Zīj al-Muwāfiq* and adds *wa-Allāhu al-muwaffiq li-l-ṣawāb* ("and God gives success to what is right").

the kingdom of the Banū Marīn [in Fez] as well as other events which took place in this period. The author himself explained all this in his book (*maqāla*) entitled *al-Ḥurūz fī sharḥ al-rumūz* ("Protections to interpret signs"). The *radices* (*uṣūl*) [of his mean motions] were established for the meridian of Fez, the latitude of which is 33;40° while its longitude from the western meridian is 25°.[19]

This passage from Ibn ʿAzzūz' introduction, which I have summarised here, has the obvious interest of describing a most peculiar "experimental" method used to correct the tables of Ibn Isḥāq: our author has used these latter tables to calculate the expected time of a known historical event using *tasyīr* techniques, the main purpose of which is precisely the prediction of the moment when a future event will take place. As he seems to be concerned only with important happenings, such as the battle of Faḥṣ Ṭarīf, he works with [Saturn-Jupiter] conjunctions and with eclipses. The results obtained were not satisfactory and Ibn ʿAzzūz made a series of observations with an armillary sphere, probably in Fez c. 1344, the purpose of which must have been the determination of the longitudes of the sun, moon and planets at the moment of the observation and the comparison between the observed and the computed positions using the tables of Ibn Isḥāq. The difference (*ikhtilāf*) thus obtained was, then, reduced to time and the resulting time difference was divided by the number of revolutions undertaken by each planet between the time of Ibn Isḥāq's observations (Ibn ʿAzzūz does not give a precise date) and the year 1344. The result of all this process must have been a small correction in the mean motion parameters used by Ibn Isḥāq and by the majority of Maghribī astronomers: we will see that no correction has been introduced in the equation tables. The new mean motion tables thus established have been used to calculate the time of past historical events obtaining, this time, good agreement between prediction and historical fact.

The rest of this paper does not aim to present an elaborate study of the whole *zīj* but rather to give an outline of some features which have attracted my attention, most of them related to the problem of the survival of Andalusian materials in Maghribī astronomical sources.

[19] Cf. E.S. and M.H. Kennedy, *Geographical Coordinates of Localities from Islamic Sources*. Frankfurt, 1987, p. 118: this pair of coordinates appears only in two *zīj*es by Muḥyī al-Dīn al-Maghribī and in an anonymous list, probably from the Ottoman period, in a manuscript in the Ẓāhiriyya Library in Damascus. Mercè Comes reminds me that these two coordinates appear in the geographical table of Ibn al-Raqqām's *al-Zīj al-Shāmil*.

3. *Mean motion parameters.*

We should look for confirmation of my interpretation of the prologue of the *Muwāfiq Zīj* in its mean motion tables. The corresponding parameters have been calculated using Honorino Mielgo's programme[20]. As the tables for *majmūʿa* and *mabsūṭa* years are often incompatible, the parameters corresponding to both sets of values have been noted in TABLE 1[21]. For the sake of comparison, the column "Other sources" gives the mean motion parameters used in the *Toledan Tables*[22], in the tables of Ibn al-Kammād[23], Ibn Isḥāq[24], Ibn al-Bannā'[25], Ibn al-Raqqām[26] and, in two instances, in the *al-Zīj al-Kāmil fī-l-taʿālīm* by Ibn al-Hā'im al-Ishbīlī (fl. ca. 1205)[27]. All the members of this school follow Ibn al-Zarqālluh in their use of the

[20] H. Mielgo, "A Method of Analysis for Mean Motion Astronomical Tables", *From Baghdad to Barcelona* I, 159-179. This programme gives the maximum and minimum possible values for the parameter: in TABLE 1 I give the mean between these two extreme values.

[21] RHL p. 59, RGL p. 408 (Saturn); RHL p. 84, RGL p. 412 (Jupiter); RHL p. 89, RGL p. 415 (Mars); RHL p. 90, RGL p. 419 (Venus); RHL p. 99, RGL p. 423 (Mercury).

[22] G.J. Toomer, "A Survey of the Toledan Tables", *Osiris* 15 (1968), p. 44.

[23] José Chabás & Bernard R. Goldstein, "Andalusian Astronomy: *al-Zîj al-Muqtabis* of Ibn al-Kammâd". *Archive for History of Exact Sciences* 48 (1994), 1-41.

[24] See A. Mestres, "Maghribī Astronomy in the XIIIth c." These parameters have been calculated using Benno van Dalen's programme for the analysis of mean motion tables.

[25] These parameters were calculated by Eduardo Millás as the groundwork for our study of the computation of planetary longitudes in Ibn al-Bannā's *Minhāj*. The manuscript used was a copy of Ibn al-Bannā's *Minhāj* extant in the Museo Naval in Madrid (ms. with no number). A sexagesimal calculator and a computer programme which reconstructs the mean motion tables from a given parameter (*TAPJ*), both prepared by Honorino Mielgo, were used.

[26] I am using the unpublished doctoral thesis by Muḥammad ʿAbd al-Raḥmān, who used Mielgo's programme for the analysis of mean motion tables. As with the parameters of the *Muwāfiq Zīj* the values quoted in TABLE 1 correspond to the mean between the maximum and minimum values given by the programme. ʿAbd al-Raḥmān has edited critically Ibn al-Raqqām's mean motion tables and he has proved that these tables are the same as in the *zīj*es of Ibn Isḥāq and Ibn al-Bannā': the small differences found between the three sets of parameters are due to the different methods of calculation used by Mestres, Millás and ʿAbd al-Raḥmān.

[27] Samsó, *Ciencias de los Antiguos* pp. 324-326.

theory of trepidation and of a solar model with variable eccentricity. On the other hand, it seems that the motion of the solar apogee established by Ibn al-Zarqālluh affects the planetary apogees also: they all move together keeping their relative distances fixed[28].

My conclusions are:

a) The mean motions of the head of Aries, of the Sun, of the Moon (longitude) seem to derive from a common Andalusian tradition. The solar mean motion implied in the table for the excess of revolution (92;20,45) is slightly different from that of the table for the mean motion of the Sun and is very near to one of the values used by Ibn al-Hā'im (92;21,45).

b) No conclusions can be drawn from the table of the mean motion of the centre of the solar eccentric due to the corrupt state of the table for the *majmū'a* years.

c) The mean motion of the lunar nodes seems related to those established by Ibn al-Kammād or by Ibn Isḥāq. In a private letter, J. Chabás remarks that the fact that Ibn al-Kammād and Ibn 'Azzūz use the same radix position for the lunar node (see TABLE 2) seems to imply that the actual source used by Ibn 'Azzūz is probably Ibn al-Kammād.

d) The mean motions of the apogees, Saturn, Jupiter and Mars (longitude), as well as Venus (anomaly) could be original or the result of a small correction of the parameter used by Ibn Isḥāq.

e) The mean motions in anomaly of the Moon and Mercury seem to derive from Ibn al-Kammād.

4. *Mean positions at epoch*

TABLE 2 collects all the information in the *Muwāfiq Zīj* concerning the mean positions at the beginning of the Hijra. These positions have been compared to those appearing in the rest of the *zīj*es which correspond to the same tradition. The differences have been corrected to take into account the differences in geographical longitude in those cases in which the motion is fast enough to affect the radix position when there is a change of the meridian. The meridians used for this correction are:

[28] A. Mestres, "Maghribī Astronomy in the 13th c." pp. 394-395.

Muwāfiq: Fez (25°)[29]
Toledo: Toledo (28;30°)(Hour. diff. with Fez: +14 min.)
Kammād: Cordova (27°) (H.d.F.: + 8 min.)
Isḥāq: Toledo (28°) (H.d.F.: + 12 min.)
Bannā': Marrākush (21°) (H.d.F.: - 16 min.)
Raqqām: Bijāya (34°) (H.d.F: + 36 min.)[30]

An analysis of the last column in TABLE 2 shows that, if we disregard the obvious errors, Ibn Isḥāq, Ibn al-Bannā' and Ibn al-Raqqām seem to use the same radix positions at all times. As for the rest, the positions are not identical, with the exception, perhaps, of the lunar mean positions in longitude which could be the same for the *Muwāfiq Zīj* and the rest of the sources, with the only exception of the *Toledan Tables.*

5. *Solar and planetary apogees at epoch*

TABLE 3 gives, again, all the available information concerning the positions of the apogees at epoch, comparing it with the data from the rest of the *zīj*es considered. In this case, the *Muwāfiq Zīj* seems to get its values from Ibn al-Kammād: it is easy to see that this is the case of the apogees of Saturn, Venus and the Sun if we accept that there is an error of -1' in the position of the solar apogee. As for the apogees of Jupiter, Mars and Mercury, the values present in Ibn al-Kammād's *al-Zīj al-Muqtabas* seem to be rounded to the nearest minute and they present a systematic difference of -0;0,30° with respect to the values of the *Muwāfiq Zīj*: my impression is that Ibn ʿAzzūz obtained his apogees from another of the *zīj*es of Ibn al-Kammād in which the values were rounded to the nearest half minute.

As for the other sources it seems that Ibn Isḥāq, Ibn al-Bannā' and Ibn al-Raqqām share a common source (which in the case of the superior planets is al-Battānī) although there are differences in rounding values: the positions of the apogees of Sun and Venus derive clearly

[29] It is remarkable to observe that practically all mean motion tables extant in both manuscripts state that they have been computed for the *latitude* of Fez which is 33;40°.

[30] Ibn al-Raqqām's *al-Zīj al-Shāmil* gives two radix positions for the meridians of Arīn and Bijāya which are mutually coherent. Only the positions for Bijāya have been considered here.

from the values established by Ibn al-Zarqālluh at a much later date than the observations which led to the computation of the *Toledan Tables*[31].

6. *Solar, lunar and planetary equations.*

Nothing new appears in the tables of the lunar and planetary equations which follow the tradition of the *Handy Tables* and use Ptolemaic parameters with the only exception of Venus, whose maximum equation of the centre is 1;59°, like that of al-Battānī.

The case of the Sun is somewhat different: the *zīj* contains a standard table of the solar equation[32] with an approximation of minutes and a maximum of 1;52°, apparently lower than Ibn al-Zarqālluh's (1;52,42°) or Ibn al-Kammād's (1;52,44°) values, but higher than those used by Ibn Isḥāq (1;49,7°) and Ibn al-Raqqām (1;47,51°). A quick check shows, however, that this table derives from the solar equation table in Ibn al-Kammād's *Muqtabas*, but that the tabular values have been truncated, not rounded. We are, therefore, in the same situation as in the *Tables of Barcelona* or in the *zīj* of Ibn al-Waqār[33]. Interestingly, like Ibn al-Kammād, Ibn ʿAzzūz uses a maximum solar equation that is different from the maximum equation of the centre of Venus and that this author also follows al-Battānī in using 1;59° for the maximum equation of the centre of Venus[34]. It seems, therefore, quite possible that the actual source used by Ibn ʿAzzūz for his equation tables was Ibn al-Kammād's *Muqtabas*.

Our *zīj* contains a second table related to the solar equation the title of which is *Taʿdīl markaz al-falak al-khārij al-markaz li l-shams li-iṣlāḥ al-taqrīb* (Table of the equation of the centre of the solar eccentric for the correction of the approximation)[35]. This table computes two functions for arguments between 1° and 180°: the first is called *taʿdīl* (equation) and reaches a maximum of 0;37,19° for an argument of 94°; the second has the title of *daqāʾiq mushtaraka*

[31] See Samsó and Millás, "Ibn al-Zarqālluh's Solar Theory" pp. 7-9.

[32] RHL p. 11; RGL p. 365.

[33] José Chabás, "Astronomía andalusí en Cataluña: las Tablas de Barcelona", *From Baghdad to Barcelona* I, 489-494.

[34] Chabás-Goldstein, *Muqtabis* pp. 32-33.

[35] RHL p. 33; RGL p. 383.

(common minutes) and decreases monotonically from 60' (for an argument of 1°) to 0' (for an argument of 180°). We should remember here that all Andalusian and Maghribī *zīj*es have in common Ibn al-Zarqālluh's solar model with variable eccentricity and that, as we have seen in § 3, the *Muwāfiq Zīj* contains a table of the mean motion of the centre of the solar eccentric. It is, then, easy to recognize in our *ta'dīl* the function called *al-zā'id al-mujarrad* by Ibn Isḥāq, *ikhtilāf al-markaz* by Ibn al-Bannā' and Ibn al-Raqqām and *minuta diversitatis centri* in the Latin version of Ibn al-Kammād's *al-Zīj al-Muqtabas*, the maximum values being 0;36,51° for Ibn Isḥāq, Ibn al-Bannā' and Ibn al-Raqqām, and 0;37,20° for Ibn al-Kammād. In all these cases the function tabulated is the difference between the value of the solar equation for a maximum eccentricity and the solar equation for a minimum eccentricity ($\eta_{max} - \eta_{min}$) for a given mean centre (λ). On the other hand, the column corresponding to the *daqā'iq mushtaraka* corresponds to the *daqā'iq nisbat al-ikhtilāf* or *daqā'iq nisbat ikhtilāf al-markaz* (*minuta associalia* in Ibn al-Kammād): it is an interpolation function (m) which, combined with a table giving the solar equation for a minimum eccentricity (η_{min}) and the aforementioned ($\eta_{max} - \eta_{min}$) allows us to obtain a good approximation to the actual value of the solar equation (η) for a given mean centre and for a given position of the centre of the eccentric (c)[36]:

$$\eta(\lambda,c) = \eta_{min}(\lambda) \pm m(c) \cdot [\eta_{max} - \eta_{min}](\lambda)$$

Our *zīj*, however, does not contain a table of η_{min}. What, then, is the use of the two functions tabulated ($\eta_{max} - \eta_{min}$ and m)? The answer can be found in the chapter on the *iṣlāḥ al-taqrīb*[37] which raises the problem of casting an horoscope for an anniversary when a long time has passed between the actual birth of the newborn or the conjunction and the moment of the anniversary: with Ibn al-Zarqālluh's solar model with variable eccentricity, the actual eccentricity may have changed when a long span of time is involved and, consequently, the period of return of the Sun to the same true longitude may be different from its return to the same mean longitude. The text explains an approximate procedure for such a case, which is exactly the same we find in a chapter of Ibn al-Kammād's *al-Kawr 'alā l-dawr* translated

[36] See two detailed descriptions in G.J. Toomer, "The Solar Theory of az-Zarqāl. A History of Errors", *Centaurus* 14 (1969), 306-336; and Samsó-Millás, "Ibn al-Zarqālluh's Solar Theory" pp. 15-35.

[37] RHL p. 34 and RGL pp. 383-384.

by Johannes de Dumpno as a kind of appendix to his translation of the canons of Ibn al-Kammād's *Muqtabas*[38]. The correspondence is so narrow that I believe that Ibn ʿAzzūz is giving us, here, the actual Arabic text of Ibn al-Kammād:

1. You should calculate the [oblique] ascension of the ascendant (α_φ) for the time of the return of the Sun to the same mean longitude it had at the moment of the radical event: call it "the first preserved" (*al-maḥfūẓ al-awwal*).

2. Then you obtain the value of c (i.e. the position of the centre of the solar eccentric) for the two moments involved, using the corresponding mean motion table, and look in the table the *daqāʾiq mushtaraka* (m) for each one of the two values of c (c' and c''). Then you put:

$$\Delta m = m(c') - m(c'')$$

3. Using the mean longitude of the Sun measured from its apogee (λ) as argument you enter the table of the *taʿdīl* and obtain:

$$\Delta\eta = [\eta_{max} - \eta_{min}](\lambda)$$

Then you multiply $\Delta m \cdot \Delta\eta$ and, thus, obtain the increase or decrease of the solar equation between the time of the radical event and the time of the anniversary due to the change of eccentricity. The result should be divided by the solar velocity (*buht*, v_s) and we will obtain the time (t) required by the Sun to travel the distance represented by ($\Delta m \cdot \Delta\eta$):

$$t = (\Delta m \cdot \Delta\eta)/v_s$$

t will be expressed in hours and fractions of an hour. By multiplying $t \cdot 15$, we express t in time degrees. Ibn ʿAzzūz, then, divides the result by 60 (?) and calls it "the second preserved" (*al-maḥfūẓ al-thānī*) ($\Delta\alpha_\varphi$). The oblique ascension of the ascendant at the moment of the anniversary will be:

$$\alpha_\varphi + \Delta\alpha_\varphi$$

where $\Delta\alpha_\varphi$ can be positive or negative.

As a conclusion of this part one may wonder why Ibn ʿAzzūz showed such interest in introducing a small correction in the computation of the ascendant of an anniversary while the value he uses for the maximum solar equation (1;52°) corresponds roughly to the end of the 11th c. and not even remotely to the middle of the 14th c., if one uses a solar model of variable eccentricity and any collection of parameters documented in the Andalusian-Maghribī tradition.

[38] See ms. 10023 of the Biblioteca Nacional (Madrid), fols. 18v-19r. I have used a provisional edition of this text prepared by Angel Mestres and other undergraduate students as a part of a course on Latin Paleography given by Dr. Mercè Viladrich.

7. *Almanac cycles*

Ibn ʿAzzūz seems interested in the quick computation of solar, lunar and planetary longitudes. For that purpose he explains the use of *goal-years*, cycles which – in the case of the planets – comprise an entire number of Julian years in which the planet makes an entire number of revolutions in longitude and in anomaly. These cycles were used in the *Almagest*[39] with the exception of the period for Jupiter which is 83 Julian years instead of the 71 mentioned in the *Almagest*: this period of 83 years was also used by Ibn al-Zarqālluh for the calculation of his *Almanac*[40] and the Hyderabad manuscript of the *zīj* of Ibn Isḥāq contains tables which use these cycles for the computation of the longitudes of the three superior planets[41]. Like Ptolemy, Ibn ʿAzzūz aims to give, for each planet, the correction (*ikhtilāf*) to introduce, in each cycle, for its motion in longitude and in anomaly, as well as the displacement of its apogee and the correction of the solar longitude[42]. All the pertinent data are summarized in TABLE 4 where the "corrections" quoted in the *zīj* have been recalculated (recomputed values appear between square brackets []) using the mean motion parameters squeezed from the *majmūʿa* years. Only in two instances (the increase in anomaly of Mars and Mercury, both marked with an asterisk *) has the mean motion obtained from the *mabsūṭa* years been used. In spite of several errors, my impression is that Ibn ʿAzzūz calculated these *ikhtilāfāt* using his own mean motion tables, approximating to the precision of seconds and truncating the results.

The case of the Moon stands apart. No cycle of this kind seems to have been known in Antiquity and when Ibn al-Zarqālluh deals with the problem of the computation of the lunar longitude in his *Almanac* he tries only to simplify the calculation of the mean motions of the

[39] O. Neugebauer, *A History of Ancient Mathematical Astronomy*. Springer Verlag. Berlin - Heidelberg - New York, 1975. See I, 150-152.

[40] See M. Boutelle, "The Almanac of Azarquiel" in *Centaurus* 12 (1967), 12-19, reprinted in E.S. Kennedy, Colleagues and Former Students, *Studies in the Islamic Exact Sciences* (Beirut, 1983), 502-510; See also Samsó, *Ciencias de los Antiguos*, 166-171. Both Jupiter periods (71 and 83 years) appear mentioned in Babylonian goal-year texts: See Neugebauer, *H.A.M.A.* I, 441 ff.

[41] Mestres, "Maghribī Astronomy in the 13th c." pp. 429-430.

[42] See RHL p. 37 and RGL p. 364 (Sun); RHL p. 37, 75 and RGL p. 387 (planets); RHL p. 37, RGL p. 388 (lunar node).

Moon in longitude (using the Metonic cycle of 19 years) and in anomaly (a cycle of 180 years), and adds to this a standard set of tables of Ptolemaic equations[43]. Quite recently, the astronomical tables of Jacob ben David Bonjorn (= Yomṭob) of Perpignan (fl. 1361) have been studied[44] and this author himself states in his canons that his predecessors were able to establish cycles allowing the determination of the true longitude of a planet which can be read directly on the table taking care only to add or subtract an equation after the completion of the first cycle of each planet. As Bonjorn remarks, no such effort has been made for the easy computation of true syzygies, and he gives a table of *true syzygies* for the period March 1361 - February 1391. This table gives the hour and minute of the conjunction or opposition for Perpignan and uses a period of 31 Egyptian years, 9 days, 23;34,11 hours (almost 11325 days) which is equivalent to 383.5 synodic months and contains, therefore, 767 consecutive syzygies. It has been believed, until now, that this period had been discovered by Bonjorn himself but we will have to reconsider this hypothesis in view of the new evidence furnished by the *Muwāfiq Zīj* of Ibn ʿAzzūz[45]. Ibn ʿAzzūz talks about a lunar cycle of 11324 days equivalent to

31 lunar years, 11 months and 14 days (= 11323.8667 d.)
or 31 solar years and 1 day (= 11323.75 d.)

The *ikhtilāf* in lunar longitude in this period amounts to $6^s\ 2;13,33^\circ$ (RGL p. 386) or $6^s\ 2;0,33^\circ$ (RHL p. 38; RGL p. 389). It is easy to see that we cannot obtain either of these results using the two parameters computed from the mean motion tables in longitude for *majmūʿa* or *mabsūṭa* years (see TABLE 1)

$$13;10,34,52,47,21,18\ (\textit{majmū`a}) \cdot 11324 = 360 \cdot n + 5^s\ 2;59,5,28^\circ$$

$$13;10,34,52,46,52\ (\textit{mabsūṭa}) \cdot 11324 = 360 \cdot n + 5^s\ 2;57,33,18^\circ$$

[43] J.M. Millás Vallicrosa, *Estudios sobre Azarquiel* (Madrid - Granada, 1943-50), 76-78, 117-119, 166-173.

[44] José Chabás, "Une période de récurrence de syzygies au XIVe siècle: le cycle de Jacob ben David Bonjorn", *Archives Internationales d'Histoire des Sciences* 38 (1988), 243-251; J. Chabás, "The Astronomical Tables of Jacob ben David Bonjorn", *Archive for History of Exact Sciences* 42 (1991), 279-314; J. Chabás, "L'influence de l'astronomie de Lévi ben Gershom sur Jacob ben David Bonjorn", Gad Freudenthal (ed.), *Studies on Gersonides. A Fourteenth-Century Jewish Philosopher-Scientist* (Brill. Leiden - New York - Köln, 1992), pp. 47-54; Josep Chabás, *L'Astronomia de Jacob ben David Bonjorn*. With the collaboration of Antoni Roca and Xavier Rodríguez. 271 pp. Barcelona, 1992.

[45] RHL p. 38; RGL pp. 386-389.

According to the text, the corresponding *ikhtilāf* in lunar anomaly amounts to 0;55,45° and in solar longitude 2;1°. As before, neither of these results can be obtained with a cycle of 11324 days. A perfect agreement in two cases is obtained if we use a cycle one day longer (11325 days) which will give us

– *ikhtilāf* in lunar longitude: 13;10,34,52,47,21,18° · 11325 = 360 · n + 6^s 2;13,33,0°

– *ikhtilāf* in lunar anomaly: 13;3,53,56,18,53,14° · 11325 = 360 · n + 0;55,54,25°

– *ikhtilāf* in solar longitude: 0;59,8,11,28,19° · 11325 = 360 · n + 2;1,5,19°

The small difference in the amount corresponding to the lunar anomaly can easily be solved if we restore the text into 0;55,[5]5°.

As a conclusion: Bonjorn's cycle appears attested in a Maghribī source dated approximately 741/1340-41, while Bonjorn's tables use 1361 as their *radix* date. It seems clear to me that Ibn ʿAzzūz did not discover the cycle but rather took it from somebody else, copied the number of entire days and forgot about a fraction which amounts to almost another day. It is impossible to guess who discovered the cycle although more information can, possibly, be gathered from another of the works of Ibn ʿAzzūz, the *Risāla fī adwār al-nayyirayn*, extant in ms. 509/2 of the Ṣubayḥiyya Library in Salé. Bonjorn was, apparently, the first to make an extensive use of this cycle for the computation of his table of syzygies and thus contributed to its diffusion in Europe.

8. *Solar, lunar and planetary velocities*

The *Muwāfiq Zīj* has tables of solar[46] and lunar[47] velocities (*buht*) which contain nothing new: they are the same as in the *zīj*es of al-Khwārizmī and of Ibn al-Kammād, among other sources[48]. Far

[46] RHL pp. 13, 78-79; RGL pp. 365, 446-447.

[47] RHL p. 62, 66-68; RGL p. 399, 442-444.

[48] Chabás & Goldstein, "Muqtabis", pp. 10-13. See also B.R. Goldstein, "Solar and Lunar Velocities in the Alfonsine Tables", *Historia Mathematica* 7 (1980), 134-140; B.R. Goldstein, "Lunar Velocity in the Ptolemaic Tradition" in P.M. Harman and Alan E. Shapiro (eds.), *The Investigation of Difficult Things. Essays on Newton and the History of the Exact Sciences in Honour of D.T. Whiteside* (Cambridge,

more interesting is the fact that Ibn ʿAzzūz repeatedly mentions[49] tables for planetary velocities (*buht*) used to calculate the exact moment of a conjunction. His *zīj* contains tables of daily velocities (*al-ḥaraka al-mukhtalifa*) for each planet[50]. These tables tabulate two functions:

a) the velocity of the centre of the epicycle on its deferent using as an argument the true centre (*markaz*) (v_1).

b) the velocity of the planet on its epicycle as a function of its true anomaly (*ḥiṣṣa*) (v_2).

These planetary velocity tables are the same as those edited by Goldstein, Chabás and Mancha[51] on the basis of manuscripts of the Alfonsine tradition: on the other hand the tables appear described in the Castilian canons of the first version of the *Alfonsine Tables* as well as in the canons of Jean de Lignères. Even the terminology used coincides: the *mouimientos diuersos* of the Alfonsine text, or the *motus diuersus* of Jean de Lignères correspond exactly to the *ḥaraka mukhtalifa* of Ibn ʿAzzūz. All variants from the edition by Goldstein, Chabás and Mancha, even those which are obvious errors, will be found in TABLE 5 where it is clear that the two manuscripts form a group, independent from the two other groups found in Latin manuscripts by the three aforementioned authors. The authors of that remarkable study stated that "No other table of planetary velocity has been located in a medieval astronomical text in Arabic, Hebrew, Greek or Latin"[52], which is absolutely true as the table extant in the *Muwāfiq Zīj* is the same one. They also suggested "an ultimate Arabic (or possibly Hebrew) origin" of the table[53] and I agree with them in view of the new evidence given here: obviously the *Muwāfiq Zīj* of Ibn ʿAzzūz is a later source than the *Alfonsine Tables*, but the astrologer from Fez is here, as often elsewhere, copying from an earlier source.

1992), 3-17; J. Chabás and B.R. Goldstein, "Nicholaus de Heybech and His Table for Finding True Syzygy", *Historia Mathematica* 19 (1992), 265-289; B.R. Goldstein, "Lunar Velocity in the Middle Ages: a Comparative Study", *From Baghdad to Barcelona* I, 181-194.

[49] RHL pp. 74, 88, 94, 99; RGL pp. 407, 414, 418, 422, 426.

[50] RHL p. 82, RGL p. 411 (Saturn); RHL p. 87, RGL p. 414 (Jupiter); RHL p. 92, RGL p. 418 (Mars); RHL p. 98, RGL p. 422 (Venus); RGL p. 426 (Mercury).

[51] B.R. Goldstein, J. Chabás and J.L. Mancha, "Planetary and Lunar Velocities in the Castilian Alfonsine Tables", *Proceedings of the American Philosophical Society* 138 (1994), 61-95.

[52] Goldstein, Chabás, Mancha, "Planetary and Lunar Velocities" pp. 61, 62.

[53] Goldstein, Chabás, Mancha, "Planetary and Lunar Velocities" p. 63.

A thorough study of the Andalusian-Maghribī tradition of *zīj*es will, in the future, shed some light on the problems posed by the *Alfonsine Tables*[54]. I can, also, furnish some limited evidence showing that the aforementioned planetary velocity set of tables is not necessarily an isolated case:

1. A passage of Ibn Muʿādh's Jayyān (= Jaén) *zīj*, preserved in the Hyderabad manuscript of the *zīj* of Ibn Isḥāq, dealing with velocity sectors and transits in thickness (see below § 9) mentions the possibility of considering the planetary daily velocity (*ḥarakat al-kawkab al-mukhtalifa ... li-yawm wāḥid*) in order to solve the problem of the slow or fast character of the motion of the planet when, for example, the centre of the epicycle is on a fast sector while the planet is on a slow sector of the epicycle[55].

2. Ibn al-Hāʾim (fl. 1205), in his *al-Zīj al-Kāmil fī-l-taʿālīm*, deals carefully with the determination of the points of station for each planet and, in order to calculate the displacement of the centre of the epicycle in a given period of time, suggests multiplying "days and hours by the unequal motion of the centre in one day corresponding to that place in the eccentric" (*ḥarakat al-markaz al-mukhtalifa li-yawm wāḥid fī dhālika l-mawḍiʿ min al-khārij*)[56]. Ibn al-Raqqām copies this passage in chapter 47 of his *al-Zīj al-Shāmil* and insists on the idea of planetary velocity in chapter 126 of the same *zīj*, in which he explains how to calculate the velocity of the Sun, Moon or of the planets by computing their true position for midday of one particular date and, then, for midday of the following date. The difference between the two positions will be the "unequal motion" (*al-masīr al-mukhtalif*) of the planet for that particular date.[57]

In both instances the references do not seem to make much sense unless a table of planetary velocity is implied. On the other hand, when Ibn al-Hāʾim refers to the unequal motion of the centre of the

[54] The unpublished Ph.D. dissertation of Muḥammad ʿAbd al-Raḥmān on Ibn al-Raqqām's *al-Zīj al-Shāmil* shows, for example, that chapter 52 of the *Libro de las Taulas* (cf. M. Rico y Sinobas, *Libros del Saber de Astronomía* vol. 4 [Madrid, 1866] p. 181) on the projection of rays seems a literal translation of chapter 113 of the *al-Zīj al-Shāmil*: once again, Ibn al-Raqqām (d. 1315) is later than Alfonso X, but both probably used the same Arabic source.

[55] J. Samsó, "«al-Bīrūnī» in al-Andalus", *From Baghdad to Barcelona* p. 604.

[56] Ms. Bodleian Library Marsh 618 fol. 63 r.

[57] I am using, again, the unpublished doctoral dissertation by Muḥammad ʿAbd al-Raḥmān.

deferent he seems to be alluding to a table similar to the one we already know.

9. *Ibn Muʿādh on transits and planetary equations*

The *Muwāfiq Zīj* deals in detail with the astrological problem of transits in thickness and considers the "states" (*ḥālāt*) of planets, that is to say whether they are "ascending" (*ṣāʿid*), "descending" (*hābiṭ*), "fast" (*asraʾ*), "slow" (*abṭaʾ*), "increasing" (*zāʾid*) or "decreasing" (*nāqiṣ*) in "number" (*ʿadad*), "computation" (*ḥisāb*), or "equation" (*taʿdīl*), and whether, in a conjunction or another aspect, a planet is "dominant" (*mustaʿlī*) on another[58]. Concerning the last "state" (*istiʿlāʾ*), our text states that when two planets are in conjunction or aspect the *istiʿlāʾ* will be in favour of the planet nearer to its own apogee. In order to establish this with precision (*taḥqīq*), he calculates the equation of the Sun, that of the Moon, or the equation of the centre of the planet (e) and multiplies it by the "root of the transit" (*aṣl al-mamarr*) (w) appearing in the "table of the sphere of apogee" ($e \cdot w$). Then he considers the anomaly (*ḥiṣṣa*) of the Sun or of the Moon, and the "centre" (*markaz*) of the planet (c): $e \cdot w$ will be the *daqāʾiq al-mamarr* ("minutes of transit") for $0° < c < 90°$ or $270° < c < 360°$. As for $90° < c < 270°$, to calculate the *daqāʾiq al-mamarr* he will subtract $60 - e{\cdot}w$.

These instructions are repeated in the case of the planets for the equation of anomaly, using, this time, the *aṣl al-mamarr* of the "sphere of the epicycle". The planet with the fewer minutes of transit will be in the dominant position.

The source of this passage in the *Muwāfiq Zīj* is Ibn Muʿādh's *Tabulae Jahen*, where the question is dealt with in exactly the same way in chapter 11 of the Latin translation (ed. Nüremberg, 1549) and in chapter 39 of the Hyderabad manuscript of the *zīj* of Ibn Isḥāq, where it appears in a long quotation headed by *wa ammā madhhab al-qāḍī Ibn Muʿādh, qāla* ("as for the method of *qāḍī* Ibn Muʿādh, he said"). Neither source transcribes the table of the "roots of the transit" and, therefore, when I first considered these passages in the two latter

[58] RHL pp. 71-73; RGL pp. 406-407. On all these questions see al-Bīrūnī, *Kitāb al-tafhīm fī awāʾil ṣināʿat al-tanjīm*. Translation by R. Ramsay Wright (London, 1934), 110-112; *Al-Bīrūnī on Transits* translated by M. Saffouri and A. Ifram, with a commentary by E.S. Kennedy. Beirut, 1959.

sources[59], I conjectured that Ibn Muʿādh was correcting the method for the computation of the *istiʿlāʾ* described by Abū Maʿshar and that the "root of the transit" had to be:

$w = 60 / e_{max}$

where e_{max} was the maximum equation of the centre or that of the anomaly for each planet. This conjecture is confirmed by the *Muwāfiq Zīj* which transcribes the "Table of the minutes of transit" (*Jadwal daqāʾiq al-mamarrāt*)(see TABLE 6)[60]. Although Ibn ʿAzzūz does not mention the name of Ibn Muʿādh, I have no doubt about the origin of the table because the calculated maximum equations correspond to what was to be expected in the tables of Jaén: the maximum equations of al-Khwārizmī. Slightly anomalous values, due to inadequate roundings, have been marked with an asterisk * and I have added, between square brackets [], the actual values which yield al-Khwārizmī's maximum equations. One should also note that, as stated by Ibn Muʿādh in his *Tabulae Jahen*, the Moon has no epicyclic equation, and an eccentric model for the Moon is used by our author.

10. *Other tables showing Andalusian influence*

Many tables other than those mentioned so far seem to have an Andalusian origin or to be related to al-Khwārizmī's *zīj*, the influence of which was predominant in Andalusian astronomy. I will try to give, here, a short summary of a few facts of this kind which I have been able to establish:

10.1 al-Khwārizmī: I have already mentioned the tables for the computation of solar and lunar velocities (see § 8) – although these tables also appear in Ibn al-Kammād's *zīj* which could, therefore, be the actual source used by Ibn ʿAzzūz – and Ibn Muʿādh's tables to calculate the "minutes of transit" (§ 9). One should add here:

– Tables for the computation of planetary latitudes[61] which are the same as those appearing in al-Khwārizmī's *zīj*[62].

[59] J. Samsó, "«al-Bīrūnī» in al-Andalus" pp. 601-611.

[60] RHL pp. 406; RGL p. 79.

[61] RHL p. 83, RGL p. 411 (Saturn); RHL p. 88, RGL p. 414 (Jupiter); RHL p. 93, RGL p. 418 (Mars); RHL p. 97, RGL p. 422 (Venus); RGL p. 426 (Mercury): this latter table is missing in RHL.

[62] H. Suter, *Die astronomischen Tafeln des Muḥammed ibn Mūsā al-Khwārizmī*

10.2 Ibn al-Zarqālluh: I have already mentioned the name of the eleventh century Toledan astronomer in relation to the motion of the solar apogee applied by the Maghribī tradition to the planetary apogees (§ 3), Ibn 'Azzūz' longitudes of the apogees of the Sun and Venus (§ 5), the solar model with variable eccentricity (§ 6) and the almanac period of 83 years for Jupiter (§ 7). We also have:

– The value for the obliquity of the ecliptic (23;33°) used, for example, in a table which gives (90° ± δ) for each degree of longitude in order to facilitate the computation of the solar meridian altitude[63]. The same obliquity is used in the table of solar declination[64].

– Lunar model with a movable equant point which follows the displacement of the solar apogee. The maximum value of the correction to apply to the mean lunar longitude is 0;24°.[65]

– Table for the computation of the ascensional difference for any latitude[66]: the maximum value is 2;10,40° in RHL (pp. 59-60) and 2;10,44° in RGL (p. 439). Ibn al-Zarqālluh[67] has the same table with a maximum of 2;10,46°.

10.3 Ibn al-Kammād: his influence has already appeared in the tables of the mean motions in anomaly of the Moon and Mercury (see § 3), the mean position in longitude of the Moon at epoch (§ 4), the positions of the solar and planetary apogees at epoch (§ 5), the solar, lunar and planetary equations as well as the table of the equation of the centre of the solar eccentric for the "correction of the approximation" and the actual procedure for such correction (§ 6). Apart from these, one should add:

– The table for the computation of the "equation of trepidation"[68] with a maximum of 9;59° as in the *al-Zīj al-Muqtabas*[69], Abū l-Ḥasan

in der Bearbeitung des Maslama ibn Aḥmed al-Madjrīṭī und der latein. Uebersetzung des Athelhard von Bath. Kobenhavn, 1914, pp. 138-167.

63 RHL p. 13; RGL p. 440.

64 RHL pp. 15-26; RGL pp. 366-377.

65 RHL p. 45; RGL p. 391. See Samsó, *Ciencias de los Antiguos* pp. 218-219.

66 O. Neugebauer and O. Schmidt, "Hindu Astronomy at Newminster in 1428", reprinted in O. Neugebauer, *Astronomy and History. Selected Essays* (Springer Verlag. New York, Berlin etc., 1983) pp. 425-432.

67 J.M. Millás Vallicrosa, *Estudios sobre Azarquiel* (Madrid - Granada, 1943-50) p. 225.

68 RHL p. 11; RGL p. 365.

69 Chabás and Goldstein, "Muqtabis" pp. 24-27.

'Alī (or Abū 'Alī al-Ḥasan) al-Marrākushī's *al-Mabādi' wa l-ghāyāt*[70], and the *Tables of Barcelona*[71] among other sources.

– Tables of stations and retrogradations (*al-istiqāma wa l-rujū'*) of planets[72]: only four values are given for each planet as in Ibn al-Kammād's *zīj*[73] although, as stated by Chabás and Goldstein, the same values appear in al-Khwārizmī's *zīj* and in the *Toledan Tables.*

– Table giving the coordinates (longitude, latitude and the planet related to it due to its *mizāj* or temperament) of 30 stars[74]. See *Appendix.*

10.4 Ibn al-Raqqām:

– RGL (pp. 438-439) contains two tables of oblique ascensions and length of seasonal hours for the latitude of Granada (the name of the city is mentioned explicitely) which is 37;10°. This extremely precise value for the latitude of Granada seems to have been established by Ibn al-Raqqām after his arrival in that city[75]: his *al-Zīj al-Qawīm* preserves exactly the same two tables copied by Ibn 'Azzūz[76].

11. *Tables computed for the latitude of Fez*

A certain number of tables depend on the geographical coordinates of Fez (see § 2) which implies that they are the result of Ibn 'Azzūz' own work or that they were copied from another Fāsī source. Obviously,

[70] J.J. Sédillot, *Traité des instruments astronomiques des arabes composé au treizième siècle par Aboul Hhassan Ali, de Maroc.* Paris, 1834 (reprint Frankfurt, 1984), p. 131.

[71] J.M. Millás Vallicrosa, *Las Tablas Astronómicas del rey Don Pedro el Ceremonioso.* Madrid - Barcelona, 1962, pp. 194-195. On this problem see, recently, Raymond Mercier, "Accession and Recession: Reconstruction of the Parameters", *From Baghdad to Barcelona* I, 299-347; Mercè Comes, "The Accession and Recession Theory in al-Andalus and the North of Africa", *From Baghdad to Barcelona* I, 349-364.

[72] RHL p. 82, RGL p. 409 (Saturn); RHL pp. 86-87, RGL p. 413 (Jupiter); RHL p. 92, RGL p. 418 (Mars); RHL p. 97, RGL p. 422 (Venus); RGL p. 426 (Mercury, table missing in RHL).

[73] Chabás and Goldstein, "Muqtabis" p. 33.

[74] RGL p. 427. This table does not appear in RHL.

[75] Samsó, *Ciencias de los Antiguos* pp. 422-423.

[76] Ms. 260 of the Rabat General Library pp. 87 (length of the seasonal hours for the latitude of Granada) and 164-165 (oblique ascensions).

the mean motion tables have radices calculated for Fez (see § 4). Other examples are:

– A table giving the solar altitude and shadow projected by a gnomon of 12^d for hours 1-6 corresponding to the entry of the Sun in the twelve signs of the Zodiac[77]. The values corresponding to the solar meridian altitude for Aries 0° (56°), Cancer 0° (80°) and Capricorn 0° (32°) seem to imply a latitude of 34° and an obliquity of the ecliptic of 24°.

– A series of 12 tables (one per each zodiacal sign) which give (apart from right ascensions, solar declination and the equation of time), oblique ascensions, length of a seasonal hour, half the day arc and the division of the astrological houses II-VI as a function of the degree of the ascendant[78]: these latter tables depend on latitude and 33;40° for Fez is quoted explicitly. RGL also contains a second set of twelve tables for the computation of the projection of rays for the latitude of Fez[79]: they include the same aforementioned tables of oblique ascensions and length of seasonal hours.

12. *Conclusions*

The *Muwāfiq Zīj* of Ibn ʿAzzūz al-Qusanṭīnī is an astronomical source which has, in my opinion, an obvious interest and deserves a detailed study. Its first point of interest is the prologue which explains a most peculiar and unorthodox method used by the author to correct the mean motions in the *zīj* of Ibn Isḥāq: the results obtained by the recomputation of the mean motion parameters seem to confirm the words of Ibn ʿAzzūz for, in the case of the three superior planets – precisely those which would attract the attention of an astrologer interested in important events – they are independent from Ibn Isḥāq's mean motions and imply, therefore, a break in the Maghribī tradition represented by the compiler of the Hyderabad manuscript, Ibn al-Bannāʾ and Ibn al-Raqqām.

On the other hand, Ibn ʿAzzūz, like his predecessors, preserves Andalusian materials: in several cases I have been able to notice the echo of the astronomical works of Ibn al-Kammād which appear in a

[77] RHL p. 12; RGL p. 366.

[78] RHL pp. 15-26; RGL pp. 366-377.

[79] RGL pp. 428-437.

proportion which seems to be higher than customary in Maghribī astronomy. Sometimes the information brought by the *Muwāfiq Zīj* is particularly interesting: this is the case of the set of planetary equations of Ibn Muʿādh, for it is the first time we have confirmation of the not unexpected fact that he used al-Khwārizmī's maximum equations. Still more important are the tables of planetary velocities and the new lunar cycle: the fact that the former were used by the Alfonsine astronomers points in the direction of an Andalusian source and the same could, probably, be said of the lunar cycle, although I am not so sure in this latter case.

	Majmū'a	Mabsūṭa	Other sources
Apogees	0;0,0,2,7,15	Corrupt table	Kammād: 0;0,0,2,2,14,46 Isḥāq: 0;0,0,2,7,10,31 Bannā': 0;0,0,2,7,10,44 Raqqām: 0;0,0,2,7,10,2,30
Head of Aries	0;0,0,54,57,16,30	0;0,0,54,57,18,17,30	Toledo/De motu: 0;0,0,52,28,37,54 Zarqālluh: 0;0,0,54,57,17,38 (Jul. and Pers. cal.)[80] Kammād: 0;0,0,54,56,57 Isḥāq: 0;0,0,54,57,18,1 Bannā': 0;0,0,54,57,17,48 Raqqām: 0;0,0,54,57,15,5
Sun: mean motion	0;59,8,11,28,19	0;59,8,11,28,26,30	Toledo: 0;59,8,11,28,27 Kammād: 0;59,8,9,21,15 Isḥāq: 0;59,8,11,28,26,22 Bannā': 0;59,8,11,28,26,24 Raqqām: 0;59,8,11,28,26,21
Sun: Excess of revolution (92;20,45°) Solar m.m. implied: 0;59,8,11,28,44,54 Solar year implied: 365 d. 6;9,23 h. 365;15,23,27,30 j.			Zarqālluh: 92;24° Kammād: 93;36° Hā'im: 92;21,45° [81] Raqqām: 92;33,22,30°
Centre of the solar eccentric	0;0,1,5,36,5	0;0,1,3 (table in a very bad shape)	Hā'im: 0;0,1,3,41,21,48,25 (Jul. cal.) 0;0,1,3,41,21,51,46 (Pers. cal.) 0;0,1,3,41,22,32,32 (Lunar cal.) Isḥāq: 0;0,1,3,41,21 Bannā': 0;0,1,3,41,21,50,8,52 Raqqām: 0;0,1,3,41,21,52,46

Moon: longitude	13;10,34,52,47,21,33	13;10,34,52,46,52,30	Khwārizmī: 13;10,34,52,46,28[82] Toledo: 13;10,34,52,48,47 Kammād: 13;10,34,52,46 Isḥāq: : 13;10,34,52,46,53 Bannā’: 13;10,34,52,46,51,20 Raqqām: 13;10,34,52,46,51,40
Moon: anomaly	13;3,53,56,18,53,29	13;3,53,56,18,53,29	Toledo: 13;3,53,56,17,57 Kammād: 13;3,53,56,19 Isḥāq: 13;3,53,56,17,51 Bannā’/Raqqām: 13;3,53,56,17,52
Moon: nodes	0;3,10,46,41,3,30	0;3,10,46,40,58,30	Toledo: 0;3,10,46,42,33 Kammād: 0;3,10,46,41 Isḥāq: 0;3,10,46,40,58,42 Bannā’: 0;3,10,46,40,59,50 Raqqām: 0;3,10,46,40,59,30
Saturn: longitude	0;2,0,26,31,14	0;2,0,26,30,46,42,30	Toledo: 0;2,0,26,35,17 Kammād: 0;2,0,25,36 Isḥāq: 0;2,0,27,46,44,53 Bannā’: 0;2,0,27,46,42,52 Raqqām: 0;2,0,27,46,42,49
Saturn: longitude	0;2,0,26,31,14	0;2,0,26,30,46,42,30	Toledo: 0;2,0,26,35,17 Kammād: 0;2,0,25,36 Isḥāq: 0;2,0,27,46,44,53 Bannā’: 0;2,0,27,46,42,52 Raqqām: 0;2,0,27,46,42,49
Jupiter: longitude	0;4,59,7,37,35	0;4,59,7,37,57	Toledo: 0;4,59,7,37,19 Kammād: 0;4,59,6,43 Isḥāq: 0;4,59,7,36,25,41 Bannā’: 0;4,59,7,36,25,12 Raqqām: 0;4,59,7,36,24,34,54

Mars: longitude	0;31,26,30,53,59,10,30	0;31,26,30,53,51,30	Toledo: 0;31,26,32,15,17 Kammād: 0;31,26,31,40 Isḥāq: 0;31,26,31,9,5,59 Bannā': 0;31,26,31,9,5,32 Raqqām: 0;31,26,31,9,5,31,37
Venus: anomaly	0;36,59,29,25,21	0;36,59,29,25,27,33	Toledo: 0;36,59,29,27,29 Kammād: 0;36,59,29,21 Isḥāq: 0;36,59,27,23,59 Bannā': 0;36,59,27,23,59,32 Raqqām: 0;36,59,27,23,59,31,28
Mercury: anomaly	3;5,2,51,2,17	3;6,24,7,20	Toledo: 3;6,24,7,39,31 Kammād: 3;6,24,7,19 Isḥāq: 3;6,24,7,42,34 Bannā': 3;6,24,7,42,41,5 Raqqām: 3;6,24,7,42,46,5

TABLE 1: *Mean motions*
Unit: degrees per day

[80] See H. Mielgo, "A Method of Analysis" pp. 164-178.

[81] On the different values ascribed to Ibn al-Hā'im see Muḥammad ʿAbd al-Raḥmān, "Ibn al-Hā'im's *zīj* did have astronomical tables", *From Baghdad to Barcelona* pp. 365-381 (in Arabic, with a summary in English).

[82] Josep Casulleras, "Las tablas astronómicas de Pedro Alfonso", M.J. Lacarra (ed.), *Estudios sobre Pedro Alfonso de Huesca* (Huesca, 1996), 349-364.

	Aṣl (1)	Other sources (2)	Diff.(1)-(2)+ corr. hour diff. = ( )
Head of Aries	3;51,21	Zarqālluh/Kammād: 3;51,11	+0;0,10
		Isḥāq/Bannā'/Raqqām: 3;53,55	-0;2,34
Sun	113;21,56	Toledo: 113;41,11	-0;19,15 -0;0,34(-0;19,49)
		Kammād: 113;20,30	+0;1,26 -0;0,20(+0;1,6)
		Isḥāq: 113;21,14	+0;0,42 -0;0,30(+0;0,12)
		Bannā': 113;22,23	-0;0,27 +0;0,39(+0;0,12)
		Raqqām: 113;20,14	+0;1,42 -0;1,29(+0;0,13)
Centre of the solar eccentric	84;40,0	Kammād: 83;40,31	0;59,29
		Isḥāq/Bannā'/Raqqām: 83;40,53	0;59,7
Moon: longitude	120;39,5	Toledo: 120;58,18	-0;19,13 -0;7,41(-0;26,54)
		Kammād: 120;34,42	+0;4,23 -0;4,24(-0;0,1)
		Isḥāq: 120;32,32	+0;6,33 -0;6,35(-0;0,2)
		Bannā': 120;47,54	-0;8,49 +0;8,47(-0;0,2)
		Raqqām: 120;19,21	+0;19,44 -0;19,46(-0;0,2)
Moon: anomaly	108;8,4	Toledo: 108;8,39	-0;0,35 -0;7,37(-0;8,12)
		Kammād: 108;11	-0;2,56 -0;4,21(-0;7,17)
		Isḥāq: 108;8,39	-0;0,35 -0;6,32(-0;7,7)
		Bannā': 108;23,54	-0;15,50 +0;8,43(-0;7,7)
		Raqqām: 107;55,35	+0;12,29 -0;19,36(-0;7,7)
Moon: nodes	233;30	Toledo: 234;9,55	-0;39,55 -0;0,2(-0;39,57)
		Kammād: -126;30 (=233;30)	0 -0;0,1 (-0;0,1)
		Isḥāq: 234;19;37	-0;49,37 -0;0,2(-0;49,39)
		Bannā': 234;19,41	-0;49,41 +0;0,2(-0;49,39)
		Raqqām: 234;19,34	-0;49,34 -0;0,5(-0;49,39)

Saturn: longitude	115;32,2	Toledo: 115;51,15	-0;19,13 -0;0,1(-0;19,14)
		Kammād: 115;30,30	+0;1,32 -0;0,1(+0;1,31)
		Isḥāq: 116;17,15	-0;45,13 -0;0,1(-0;45,14)
		Bannā': 116;17,17	-0;45,15 +0;0,1(-0;45,14)
		Raqqām: 116;17,13	-0;45,11 -0;0,3(-0;45,14)
Jupiter: longitude	330;20,18	Toledo: 331;39,37	-1;19,19 -0;0,3(-1;19,22)
		Kammād: 330: 19	+0;1,10 -0;0,2(+0;1,8)
		Isḥāq: 330;11	+0;9,18 -0;0,3(+0;9,15)
		Bannā': 330;11,5	+0;9,13 +0;0,3(+0;9,16)
		Raqqām: 330;10,55	+0;9,23 -0;0,7(+0;9,16)
Mars: longitude	211;7,57	Toledo: 211;24,59	-0;17,2 -0;0,18(-0;17,20)
		Kammād: 211;27	-0;19,3 -0;0,11(-0;19,14)
		Isḥāq: 210;37,25	+0;30,32 -0;0,18(+0;30,14)
		Bannā': 210;35,31	+0;32,26 +0;0,58(+0;33,24)
		Raqqām: 210;36,54	+0;31,3 -0;0,47(0;30,16)
Venus: anomaly	45;22,53	Toledo: 45;28,37	-0;5,44 -0;0,22(-0;6,6)
		Kammād: 45;21	+0;1,53 -0;0,12(+0;1,41)
		Isḥāq: 44;30	+0;52,53 -0;0,18(+0;52,35)
		Bannā': 44;30,43	+0;52,10 +0;0,25(+0;52,35)
		Raqqām: 44;29,24	+0;53,29 -0;0,55 (0;52,34)
Mercury: anomaly	73;54,57	Toledo: 73;46,18	+0;8,39 -0;1,48(+0;6,51)
		Kammād: 74;1	-0;6,3 -0;1,2(-0;7,5)
		Isḥāq: 73;25,29	+0;29,28 -0;1,33(+0;27,55)
		Bannā': 73;29,6	+0;25,51 +0;2,4(+0;27,55)
		Raqqām: 73;22,23	+0;32,34 -0;4,40(+0;27,54)

TABLE 2: *Mean positions at epoch*
Unit: degree

Planet	Longitude (1)	Other sources (2)	Diff.(1)-(2)
Sun	76;44,21°	Toledo: 77;50	-1;5,39
		Kammād: 76;45,21	-0;1,0
		Isḥāq/Bannā'/Raqqām 76;44,17	+0;0,4
Saturn	238;38,30	Toledo: 240;5	-1;26,30
		Kammād: 238;38,30	0;0
		Isḥāq/Bannā': 239;42,45	-1;4,15
		Raqqām: 239;43	-1;4,30
Jupiter	158;21,30	Toledo: 164;30	-6;8,30
		Kammād: 158;21,0	+0;0,30
		Isḥāq/Raqqām: 159;43	-1;21,30
		Bannā': 159;42,45	-1;21,15
Mars	119;41,30	Toledo: 121;50	-2;8,30
		Kammād: 119;41,0	+0;0,30
		Isḥāq/Raqqām: 122;13	-2;31,30
		Bannā': 122;12,45	-2;31,15
Venus	76;45,21	Toledo: 77;50	-1;4,39
		Kammād: 76;45,21	0;0
		Isḥāq/Bannā'/Raqqām: 76;44,17	+0;1,4
Mercury	198;21,30	Toledo: 197;30	+0;51,30
		Kammād: 198;21,0	+0;0,30
		Isḥāq: 194;43	+3;38,30
		13(?)[83]	+4;8,30(?)
		Bannā'/Raqqām: 198;24,17	-0;2,47

TABLE 3: *Apogees at epoch*
Unit: degree[83]

[83] See, on this anomalous value, the remarks by A. Mestres, "Maghribī Astronomy in the XIIIth. c.", p. 412 n. 51.

Planet	Cycle	Increase in the planet's longitude	Increase in longitude of the apogee	Increase in solar longitude	Increase in anomaly
Saturn	21550 d. (59 Jul. yrs.)	0;58,45° [0;58,45,18°]	0;12,41° [0;12,41,44°]	11^{S} 29;52,0° [11^{S} 29;52,0,20°]	11^{S} 28;53,15° [11^{S} 28;53,15,2°]
Jupiter	30317 d. [mss. 30316] (83 Jul. yrs.)	11^{S} 29;4,48° [11^{S} 29;3,59,35°]	0;17,[5]1° [0;17,51,37°]	0;41,52° [0;41,52,34°]	1;47,4° [1;37,53,0°]
Mars	28855 d. (79 Jul. yrs.)	0;56,29° [0;56,30,12°]	0;16,[5]9° [0;16,59,56°]	11^{S} 29;[4]4,16° [11^{S} 29;44,17,2°]	0;1,12,13° [11^{S} 28;47,48,51 *, equivalent to -1;12,11]
Venus	2920 d. (8 Jul. yrs.)	11^{S} 27;[5]8,[3]7° [11^{S} 27;58,38,18°]	0;1,43° [1;43,13°]	***********	0;15,13° [0;15,11,54°]
Mercury	16802 d. (46 Jul. yrs.)	0;11,47° [0;11,48,32°]	0;9,53° [0;9,53,54°]	***********	11^{S} 2[8];47,3° [11^{S} 28;47,1,34 *]
Sun	1461 d. (4 Jul. yrs.)	11^{S} 29;58,27° [11^{S} 29;58,27,21°]	0;0,51 [0;0,51,39°]	***********	***********
Moon	1132[5] d. (mss. 11324) (31 Jul. yrs. + [3] d.)	6^{S} 2;13,33° [6^{S} 2;13,33,0°]	***********	2;1° [2;1,5,19°]	0;55,45° [0;55,54,24°]
Lunar node	6793 d. (18 Jul. yrs. + 7 months + 7 d.)	11^{S} 29;59,15° [11^{S} 29;59,15,25°]	***********	***********	*********

TABLE 4: *Almanach cycles*

	Saturn		Jupiter[84]		Mars		Venus		Mercury	
(1)	(2)	(3)	(4)	(5)	(6)	(7)	(8)	(9)	(10)	(11)
6	*	5;37	*	9;0	*	*	*	*	*	51;15
12	*	5;30	4;33	*	*	*	*	*	*	*
18	*	*	4;34	*	*	*	*	*	*	50;35
24	*	*	*	8;13	*	*	57;16	*	*	*
30	*	*	4;37	8;6	*	*	*	*	*	*
36	*	*	*	*	*	*	*	*	*	*
42	*	*	4;40	*	*	10;36	*	*	56;56	47;50
48	*	*	4;42	7;14	*	10;23	57;44	*	*	45;50
54	*	3;48	*	*	*	10;15	*	*	57;20	*
60	*	*	*	*	*	10;3	*	14;34	*	*
66	*	*	*	*	*	*	*	*	*	*
72	*	2;52	*	*	*	*	58;23	*	*	*
78	*	*	*	4;15	*	*	*	*	58;34 (+)	*
84	*	*	*	3;10	*	*	*	13;15	58;58 (+)	*
90	*	*	*	H:2;10 G:2;1	*	*	59;5	12;40	*	24;0
96	*	*	*	*	*	*	*	*	*	*
102	*	*	*	*	*	*	59;31	*	*	*
108	*	-1;14	*	*	32;50	*	*	*	*	*
114	*	-1;54	*	*	*	*	*	*	59;2 (+)	-3;0

120	*	-2;30	*	*	34:10	*	*	*	*	*
126	*	*	*	*	*	*	*	5;0	*	*
132	*	-3;30	*	*	35;30	*	H:60;33 G:60;43	-2;0	*	*
138	*	*	*	*	36;6	H:-3;18 G:-3,58	*	H:-4;5 G:-3;5	*	*
144	*	-5;10	*	*	*	*	60;47	*	*	-58;0
150	*	-5;30	*	*	*	*	*	-13;10	*	-21;0 (+)
156	*	-5;55	*	*	*	-20;20	*	-20;50	61;36	*
162	*	-6;20	*	*	*	*	*	*	*	*
168	*	*	*	*	*	*	*	*	*	*
174	*	*	*	*	*	*	*	*	*	*
180	*	-7;10	*	13;10	38;30	H:* G:-53;30	*	*	62;0	*

TABLE 5: *Planetary velocities.*

This table presents the variant readings of mss. RHL (indicated here with an H) and RGL (indicated here with a G) in relation to the edition prepared by Goldstein, Chabás and Mancha (1994), pp. 90-92. When a variant reading is not accompanied by H or G, the manuscripts agree. An asterisk (*) implies the absence of variant readings. Obviously erroneous variants are marked with (+).

[84] Both mss. omit the indication of retrograde motion (*rājiʿ*) in the case of Jupiter.

Planet	Roots of the transit in the spheres of the apogees	Calculated maximum equations of the centre	Roots of the transits in the spheres of the epicycles	Calculated maximum equations of anomaly
Sun	26;52'	2;14° (Khw. id)	0'	
Moon	[12];10'[85]	4;55,53° (Khw. 4;56°)	0'	
Saturn	*6;58' [6;58,36']	8;36,45° (Khw. 8;36°)	10;28'	5;43,57° (Khw. 5;44°)
Jupiter	11;46'	5;5,57° (Khw. 5;6°)	*5;31' [5;31,17']	10;52,34° (Khw. 10;52°)
Mars	5;21'	11;12,54° (Khw. 11;13°)	*1;29' [1;28,51']	40;26,58° (Khw. 40;31°)
Venus	26;52'	2;14° (Khw. id)	*1;16' [1;16,18']	47;22,6° (Khw. 47;11°)
Mercury	14;53'	4;1,53° (Khw. 4;2°)	*2;47' [2;47,27']	21;33,25° (Khw. 21;30°)

TABLE 6: *Ibn Muʿādh's roots of transits and maximum planetary equations.*

85 12;10' appears in ms. RHL.

APPENDIX

On the epoch of the star table of Ibn al-Kammād and Ibn ʿAzzūz

The star table in the *Muwāfiq Zīj* corresponds precisely to Kunitzsch's *Typ.* XV[86]. The star longitudes are those of Ibn al-Kammād[87] with an increase of 0;10° or 0;11°, which implies that the difference with Ptolemaic longitudes amounts to 6;48° or 6;49° instead of the 6;38° of Ibn al-Kammād. Goldstein and Chabás have just published an excellent study of Ibn al-Kammād's star table[88] in which they state, as in their previous article on Ibn al-Kammād's *Muqtabas*[89], that this table gives the longitudes of the stars for the beginning of the Hijra. Personally, I do not think the situation is so clear. The star table in the *Minhāj* of Ibn al-Bannāʾ - which is a variant of Ibn al-Kammād's table - was studied by Mercè Comes[90], who suggested that the star longitudes were calculated for a time in which the value of precession was 0°. The same could be said for the rest of the sources considered here: the terminology used is standard in Western *zīj*es and Ibn al-Kammād's table bears the title *Tabula longitudinum stellarum fixarum a puncto capitis Arietis in circulo signorum ab initio essentiali*. This *initium essentiale* is the translation of *al-mabdaʾ al-dhātī* used by Ibn al-Bannāʾ and it is just the moving Head of Aries in a trepidation model, which is the origin of sidereal longitudes[91]. The other expression which often appears in Ibn al-Kammād's Latin text is the *initium/ principium naturale*, which translates *al-mabdaʾ al-ṭabīʿī* (the vernal equinox, which is the origin of tropical longitudes). This terminology

[86] Paul Kunitzsch, *Typen von Sternverzeichnissen in astronomischen Handschriften des zehnten bis vierzehnten Jahrhunderts*. Wiesbaden, 1966, pp. 99-102.

[87] Chabás and Goldstein, *Muqtabis*, pp. 34-35.

[88] Bernard R. Goldstein and José Chabás, "Ibn al-Kammād's Star List", *Centaurus* 38 (1996), 317-334.

[89] Chabás and Goldstein, "Muqtabis", pp. 34-35.

[90] Mercè Comes, "Deux échos andalous à Ibn al-Bannāʾ de Marrākush", in *Le patrimoine andalous dans la culture arabe et espagnole* (Tunis, 1991), 81-94.

[91] The title of the star table in the *Muwāfiq Zīj* states that the stellar longitudes are calculated from "the point of the Head of Aries" (*min nuqṭat raʾs al-Ḥamal*) (RGL p. 427). On the other hand, there are several references in this *zīj* to longitudes which are *dhātiyya* (sidereal) or *ṭabīʿiyya* (tropical).

is clearly explained in the canons of the *Minhāj* of Ibn al-Bannā'[92] who talks of *darajāt dhātiyya* and *darajāt ṭabī'iyya* and the same interpretation should be given to the corresponding passage of Abū l-Ḥasan 'Alī al-Marrākushī's *al-Mabādi' wa-l-ghāyāt*[93]. It seems, therefore, that Ibn al-Kammād's stellar longitudes are sidereal (the same could be said on the table of Ibn 'Azzūz). If an epoch has to be asigned to these tables, it must be a date in which the value of precession was 0, which corresponds to argument 0° or 180°. Thus (see TABLES 1 and 2), in the case of Ibn al-Kammād we will have:

$$n = 3;51,11° / 0;0,0,54,56,57° \approx 15146 \text{ days}$$

and in the case of Ibn 'Azzūz:

$$n = 3;51,21° / 0;0,0,54,57,18,17° \approx 15155 \text{ days.}$$

15146 days before the beginning of the Hijra (JD 1948438) correspond to 24.1.581 (JD 1933292), while, in the case of Ibn 'Azzūz, the corresponding date will be the 15.1.581 (JD 1933283). Year 581 corresponds approximately to 41 years before the Hijra and it is reasonable to relate this date to a remark by Ibn al-Zarqālluh, in his book on the motion of the fixed stars, according to which tropical (calculated with the *Mumtaḥan* tables) and sidereal longitudes (calculated with the Indian and Iranian systems) were in agreement "about 40 years before the Hijra, at the moment of the Prophet's birth"[94]. The chronology of the Prophet's birth is not at all clear and Ibn al-Zarqālluh seems to be misinterpreting a tradition according to which Muḥammad would be about 40 years old when he began his mission: it is easy to identify such a beginning with the Hijra and to forget his first years of religious activity in Mecca[95]. On the other hand, Ibn

[92] Vernet, *Contribución*, p. 46 of the Arabic text: the passage is missing in the Spanish translation. The terms *dhātī* (sidereal) and *ṭabī'ī* (tropical) are also defined in chapter 43 of Ibn Isḥāq in the Hyderabad ms.: I owe this information to Angel Mestres.

[93] See the facsimile edition of ms. 3343 of the Ahmet III Library in Istanbul: published by the Institut für Geschichte der Arabisch-Islamischen Wissenschaften (Frankfurt, 1984), I, pp. 42-45. French translation in Sédillot, *Traité* pp. 126-131.

[94] Goldstein & Chabás, "Ibn al-Kammād's Star List" p. 324; see also my paper, "Trepidation in al-Andalus in the 11th century" in J. Samsó, *Islamic Astronomy and Medieval Spain* (Variorum, Aldershot, 1994) no. VIII, p. 22.

[95] See the article "Muḥammad" by F. Buhl, updated by A.T. Welch, in *Encyclopédie de l'Islam* VII (Leiden - New York, Paris, 1993), p. 364. Mercè Comes reminds me that this anomaly is corrected by Ibn al-Hā'im in his *al-Zīj al-Kāmil fī 'l-ta'ālīm* (ca.

al-Zarqālluh is following, here, the *Brahmasphutasiddhānta*[96] according to which the sidereal and tropical longitudes of the Sun were equal in year 580. All this information points in the same direction: Ibn al-Kammād and Ibn 'Azzūz are using a table for the mean motion of the argument of trepidation which is narrowly related, both in its basic parameter and in its radix position for the beginning of the Hijra, to the Zarqāllian tradition. The fact that Ibn al-Zarqālluh states[97], in his first model of trepidation, that the value of precession in the time of Ptolemy was -6;38° cannot be independent of the 6;38° added to the Ptolemaic longitudes in Ibn al-Kammād's star table (and in many others studied by Goldstein and Chabás).

It is interesting, however, to check these conclusions against Ibn al-Kammād's trepidation table, which is exactly the same as that of Ibn 'Azzūz. The obvious conclusion will be that, with this table, Ibn al-Kammād is not following the same tradition as with his star table. I have shown elsewhere that the date probably used by Ibn al-Zarqālluh for "the time of Ptolemy" was the year 139 A.D., which corresponds to a determination of the longitude of Regulus made by the Alexandrian astronomer precisely in this year (*Almagest* VII, 2). If we use the 30.6.139 (JD 1772008) as the exact date, we will see that 161284 days will pass until the 24.1.581 (JD 1933292). We can, then, calculate the value of precession for that date. The argument will be:

$$161284 \cdot 0;0,0,54,56,57^\circ = 41;1,47^\circ$$

In Ibn al-Kammād's table for the equation of trepidation, the value which corresponds to an argument of 41° is 7;57°. B.R. Goldstein has made me aware of the fact that this value (like the preceding one) is an obvious mistake and that the *Tables of Barcelona* contain a variant reading (6;57°) which is much better[98]. I can now add that the same variant reading (6;57°) appears in both manuscripts of the *Muwāfiq*

1205; see ms. Bodleian Library Marsh 618, fol. 24 r) where he states that the Prophet's birth took place 50 lunar years before the Hijra (which allows 10 years for his preaching in Mecca), and that at that time the Head of Aries was on the equator, tropical and sidereal longitudes were the same and the obliquity of the ecliptic had attained approximately its mean value (23;43°) and was diminishing.

[96] See R. Mercier, "Studies in the Medieval Conception of Precession", *Archives Internationales d'Histoire des Sciences* 26 (1976), 204-209.

[97] See Samsó, "Trepidation", 12-16; Mercier, "Accession and Recession" pp. 338-340.

[98] Chabás & Goldstein, "Muqtabis", p. 25.

Zīj[99]. We have, therefore, a precession of -6;57° for the time of Ptolemy, a value which is different from the -6;38° of the star table. This amount, calculated with Ibn al-Kammād's trepidation table, is confirmed by Ibn al-Hā'im's *Kāmil Zīj*[100]. Ibn al-Hā'im, who criticises severely Ibn al-Kammād's deviations from Zarqāllian orthodoxy, calculates the same value but he uses the Zarqāllian anomaly of 119;2°, which agrees well with the -40;58,30° for the time of Ptolemy mentioned by Ibn al-Zarqālluh in his third model. For this anomaly he obtains a precession of -6;57°, a value which is confirmed by his following remark that this is 15' higher than the value used by Ibn al-Zarqālluh [in his third model] (6;42,45°). It is interesting to notice, however, that -6;57° is also a result obtained, for the time of Ptolemy, by Ibn al-Zarqālluh himself in his second model of trepidation[101].

In the case of Ibn al-Kammād we have, therefore, a star table which seems clearly related to Ibn al-Zarqālluh's first model (-6;38°) and a trepidation table which gives, for the time of Ptolemy, a precession of -6;57° which appears in the second model: this seems to confirm Chabás and Goldstein's hypothesis according to which Ibn al-Kammād's table would have been calculated with Ibn al-Zarqālluh's second model.

Acknowledgements: This paper has been written within a research programme on "Astronomical theory and tables in al-Andalus and the Maghrib between the twelfth and the fourteenth centuries". The very elaborate remarks made by B.R. Goldstein and J. Chabás on a previous draft of this paper have saved me from making a certain number of silly mistakes. David King has corrected my English prose and offered useful suggestions. Aḥmad Shawqī Bīnbīn, Aḥmad Tawfiq and Muḥammad b. Sharīfa have sent to me photocopies or microfilms of the manuscripts used in this study. Fuat Sezgin and my postgraduate student Mònica Rius have provided me with information which was unavailable in Spain. My gratitude to all of them.

[99] RHL p. 11; RGL p. 365.

[100] Ms. Marsh 618, fol. 5 v.

[101] Both values (anomaly of 40;58,30° and precession of -6;57°) appear in J.M. Millás Vallicrosa, *Estudios sobre Azarquiel*, Madrid - Granada, 1943-50, p. 318.

X

Horoscopes and history: Ibn ᶜAzzūz and his retrospective horoscopes related to the battle of El Salado (1340)

1. *Presentation*

I recently published a preliminary analysis of the *Muwāfiq Zīj* of Abū l-Qāsim ibn [al-Ḥajjāj] ᶜAzzūz [al-Qusanṭīnī, d. Constantina 755/1354].[1] In it I summarized the author's prologue in which he states that modern astronomers have been able to establish that the positions of the planets calculated with the *zīj* of Ibn Isḥāq (fl. Tunis and Marrakesh ca. 1193-1222)[2] were in disagreement with observations.[3] Ibn ᶜAzzūz was himself able to establish the existence of such disagreements when he calculated the *tasyīr*[4] of the significators of conjunctions, eclipses and their ascendents to determine the time of events of the past and, especially, the great battle of El Salado [Faḥṣ Ṭarīf] which took place in the days of the Mārinid sultan Abū l-Ḥasan ᶜAlī, (731/1331-752/1351) in the month of

---

[1] See J. Samsó, "Andalusian Astronomy in 14th Century Fez: *al-Zīj al-Muwāfiq* of Ibn ᶜAzzūz al-Qusanṭīnī", in *Zeitschrift für Geschichte der Arabisch-Islamischen Wissenschaften* 11 (1997), 73-110. Our author is mentioned by Ibn Qunfudh al-Qusanṭīnī, *al-Wafayāt*, ed. by ᶜĀdil Nuwayhiḍ (Beirut, 1978), p. 358, no. 755. See also ᶜA. Nuwayhiḍ, *Muᶜjam aᶜlām al-Jazā'ir min ṣadr al-Islām ḥattā al-ᶜaṣr al-khāḍir* (Beirut, 1980), p. 231. Ibn Qunfudh states that he was a *faraḍī* (expert in partition of inheritances) and a jurist belonging to the school of Mālik b. Anas, and was also proficient in other sciences. He wrote a summary (*mukhtaṣar*) on *Farā'iḍ* (partition of inheritances) as well as other works. I owe this information to the kindness of Prof. Fuat Sezgin.

[2] See A. Mestres, "Maghribī Astronomy in the 13th century: a Description of Manuscript Hyderabad Andra Pradesh State Library 298" in J. Casulleras and J. Samsó (eds.), *From Baghdad to Barcelona. Studies in the Islamic Exact Sciences in Honour of Prof. Juan Vernet* (Barcelona, 1996), I, 383-443.

[3] See also, on this topic, J. Samsó, "An Outline of the History of Maghribī Zijes from the end of the Thirteenth Century", *Journal for the History of Astronomy* 29 (1998), 93-102.

[4] See O. Schirmer, "Tasyīr", in *Encyclopédie de l'Islam*, first edition, VIII (Paris, 1934), pp. 729-733; Michio Yano and Mercè Viladrich, "Tasyīr Computation of Kūshyār ibn Labbān", *Historia Scientiarum* 41 (1991), 1-16.

Jumādā I of 741 H. [7 Jumādā I 741/ 30 October 1340]. The times calculated did not correspond to historical reality, and Ibn ᶜAzzūz blamed Ibn Isḥāq's tables for the mistake. Therefore, in order to correct the divergence, he made observations with an armillary sphere ca. 745/1344: as a result he corrected Ibn Isḥāq's mean motion tables and cast again the corresponding horoscopes. This time, he obtained adequate results, once he had made the necessary corrections to the mean motion parameters deduced from observations. He then compiled his new *Muwāfiq Zīj*.

This is quite a peculiar example of an experimental method in which the data are obtained from using astronomical and astrological criteria. Some more information on Ibn ᶜAzzūz' techniques can be obtained through an analysis of the materials contained in another of his works: his *Kitāb al-Fuṣūl fī jamᶜ al-uṣūl*, of which the second book (*maqāla*) is extant in ms. 1110 of the Ḥasaniyya Library in Rabat (RHL hereafter).[5] Chapter 3 of this same book is also preserved in ms. D 2128 of Rabat's General Library (pp. 42-44).[6] Manuscript RHL 1110 (copy finished the 13th of Dhū l-Qaᶜda 1281/ 9th April 1865) contains the aforementioned part of Ibn ᶜAzzūz' work in fols. 62 v-177 r. It is quite an extensive astrological work in which the author quotes two other works of his, about which I have no information: the *Madkhal al-ṣināᶜa ᶜalā madhhab al-jamāᶜa* ("Introduction to the Art [of Astrology] according to the opinion of the majority") (fol. 72 v), and *Maqālat al-Zuḥal* ("The book of Saturn") (fol. 121 v)[7]. The authorities quoted are early and they include

---

[5] Muḥammad al-ᶜArabī al-Khaṭṭābī, *Fahāris al-Khizāna al-Ḥasaniyya. III: al-Riyāḍiyyāt, al-Falak wa-Aḥkām al-Nujūm wa l-Jughrāfiyā*, Rabat, 1983, pp. 367-368. See also Driss Lamrabet, *Introduction à l'Histoire des Mathématiques Maghrébines*, Rabat, 1994, p. 101. I owe a microfilm of this manuscript to the generosity of Prof. Aḥmad Shawqī Bīnbīn, Keeper of the Ḥasaniyya Library and to the interest and skill of my postgraduate student Hamid Berrani who spent some time in the Rabat libraries looking for materials on Ibn ᶜAzzūz: he is preparing a critical edition with commentary and recomputation of the numerical tables in the *Muwāfiq Zīj*.

[6] This identification was made by Mònica Rius, during a short stay in Rabat. She provided me with a photocopy of these pages.

[7] Ibn ᶜAzzūz is also the author of a second *zīj*, entitled *al-Zīj al-Kāmil*, which was compiled in 718/1318-19 and does not seem to be extant. The Ṣabīḥiyya Library in Salé keeps a *Risāla fī adwār al-nayyirayn* (MS 509/2), which I have been able to read in a photocopy obtained by Hamid Berrani. This latter work is concerned with the 11325-day lunar cycle (cf. Samsó, *Muwāfiq* pp. 86-88) but it contains no more information than the *Muwāfiq Zīj*.

a *Kitāb ahl Bābil* ("Book of the people of Babylon", fol. 66 v)[8], Hermes, Ptolemy's *Tetrabiblos* (fol. 64 v), and pseudo-Ptolemy's *Centiloquium* (fol. 143 v). Among the Islamic authors we find a certain Ibn Ṭāriq, author of a *Kitāb al-Mithālāt* (fol. 64 v, 65 r): he is probably the early Abbasid astronomer Yaᶜqub b. Ṭāriq, to whom Ṣāᶜid al-Andalusī attributes a *Kitāb al-maqālāt fī mawālid al-khulafā' wa l-mulūk wa quᶜūd man lam yuᶜraf mawlidu-hu* ("Book of the predictions concerning the nativities of Caliphs and Kings and the accession to the throne of those whose date of birth is unknown"),[9] considered spurious by Pingree.[10] We also have Saᶜīd b. ᶜAlī (Sind b. ᶜAlī), author of a *Kitab al-manāḥis wa l-saᶜādāt* ("On good fortunes and misfortunes") (fol. 64 v)[11] as well as the famous Abū Maᶜshar of whom the *Kitāb al-Mudhākarāt* ("Memorabilia") (fol. 65 r) - written by his disciple Shādhān -, the *Kitāb al-qirānāt* ("On conjunctions") and the *Kitāb al-asrār fī l-milal wa l-duwāl* ("Secrets related to religions and states") - probably another title for the *Kitāb al-qirānāt* - are quoted (fol. 101 r). Among more recent authors we have Abū l-ᶜAbbās b. al-Kammad (fl. 1116), author of a *Kitāb mafātiḥ al-asrar al-falakiyya* ("The keys of astronomical secrets") (fol. 66 r)[12] and Ibn al-Bannā' al-Marrākushī (1256-1321) (fol. 101 r). To these names one should add an otherwise unknown Yaḥyā b. Mak.r, author of a *Kitāb al-musallaṭayn (?) fī (?) l-tajārib* (fol. 66 r).

This second and last book (*al-maqāla al-thāniyya*) of the *Kitāb al-Fuṣūl fī jamᶜ al-uṣūl* ends with an appendix (*khātima*), composed of a single chapter (*faṣl*) in which Ibn ᶜAzzuz states (fol. 170 r) that he is

---

[8] B.L. van der Waerden, "The 'Babylonians' and the 'Persians'", in Y. Maeyama und W.G. Saltzer (eds.), *Prismata. Festschrift für Willy Hartner* (Wiesbaden, 1977), pp. 431-440.

[9] Ṣāᶜid al-Andalusī, *Ṭabaqāt al-Umam*. Ed. Ḥayāt Bū ᶜAlwān (Beirut, 1985), p. 151; ed. Djulāmriḍā Djamshīdnizād-i Awwal (Tehran, 1415/1995), 232 (who notes a variant reading *Kitāb al-Mithālāt*); French translation by Régis Blachère (Paris, 1935), p. 117. A *Kitāb al-Mithālāt* is also attributed to Yaᶜqūb b. Ṭāriq by Abū Maᶜshar: cf. F. Sezgin, *Geschichte des Arabischen Schrifttums* VII (Leiden, 1979), pp. 101-102.

[10] David Pingree, "The Fragments of the Works of Yaᶜqūb ibn Ṭāriq", *Journal of Near Eastern Studies* 27 (1968), 97-125 (see p. 123).

[11] Sezgin, *G.A.S.* VII, pp. 119-120.

[12] An extant fragment of this work was published in Catalan translation by my master Juan Vernet, "Un tractat d'obstetrícia astrològica" in Vernet, *Estudios sobre historia de la ciencia medieval* (Barcelona-Bellaterra, 1979), 273-300.

going to cast the horoscope (*nuṣba*) of the [Saturn and Jupiter] conjunction that marks the transfer [*intiqāl*] of those great conjunctions to the triplicity of air, in Libra (1305). He adds that he will also cast a horoscope of the preceding conjunction of the Sun and the Moon (*ijtimā*ᶜ). Both remarks are inaccurate: we will see that, in agreement with standard practice, the manuscript reproduces the horoscope of the vernal equinox before the Saturn-Jupiter conjunction (HOROSCOPE 2) and the horoscope of the preceding solar-lunar *opposition* (HOROSCOPE 1) (fols. 171 v - 172 r). Ibn ᶜAzzūz comments that the conjunction took place at 17° of the beginning of Libra and, more specifically at 16;4,31° (fol. 173 r): in my recomputation,[13] the true sidereal conjunction took place on 2 Dec. 1305 at 9 p.m. At that time we have (recomputation):

Saturn 196;18,49
Jupiter 196;18,32

Horoscopes 1 and 2 are accompanied by an elaborate commentary (fols. 170 r - 177 r) of which I will not give a detailed survey in this paper: it is not easy to understand and it requires an edition and commented translation. I will, however, refer to some aspects of that commentary which are concerned with Mathematical Astrology. The subject seems appropriate for an essay written in honour of a scholar like John North, who has taught us how to analyze historical horoscopes and has provided us with a computer programme which is extremely useful for the equalization of the houses.[14]

The interesting part of the commentary begins in fol. 172 v where Ibn ᶜAzzūz reminds the reader that, in the second chapter (*faṣl*) of the same book, he has explained the importance of using a *zīj* as accurate as possible and which is based on observations which are near, in time, to

---

[13] Using a computer programme in which the parameters of the *Muwāfiq zīj* (established in Samsó, *Muwāfiq*) had been introduced. The skeleton of this programme was prepared a few years ago by Prof. E.S. Kennedy for the *Toledan Tables*. Later it was revised by Dr. Honorino Mielgo and, very recently, by Josep Casulleras who has introduced Ibn ᶜAzzūz' parameters as well as a few improvements.

[14] John North, *Horoscopes and History*, London, 1986. I hope John North will forgive me for plagiarizing the title of his book.

the date of the horoscope.[15] The present work is based on the *Muwāfiq Zīj*, which depends on observations made in 745 H [1 Muḥarram 745/ 15 May 1344] which was the year of a conjunction of the two superior planets at the beginning of Aquarius.[16] Although not fully developed, there are references in our text to an horoscope corresponding to the moment of the preceding spring equinox (24 March 1344), which I will call HOROSCOPE 4 (see below §4).

Following his presentation of his materials (fol. 172 v) Ibn ᶜAzzūz reminds the reader that in the prologue of the aforementioned *zīj* he said that he had tested (*ikhtabarnā*) it, after observation and detailed study (*baᶜd al-raṣad wa l-taḥqīq*) with the *tasyīr* of the indicators of the conjunctions, eclipses and anniversaries of the universal *promissors* or *anairetes* (*al-qawāṭiᶜ al-kulliyya*), checking that they were in agreement with symptoms of unexpected events and the times in which those took place. He studied especially the battle of Faḥṣ Ṭarīf/ El Salado which took place in Jumādā I 741 H [actually 7 Jumadā 741/ 30 October 1340], which corresponds to 1651 of Alexander's era. The vernal equinox of the year of the battle was in 739 (complete years), 8 (months), 24 days, 7 (hours) and 14 (minutes) after Hijra, which in the *ᶜajamī* calendar corresponds to 1650 (years), 5 (months), 24 (days), 7 hours and 14

---

[15] See also fol. 66 v: after a long period of time errors are accumulated. The idea of a *zīj* being useful only for a limited period of time appears frequently in western Islamic astronomy beginning with Ibn al-Hā'im (fl. 1205) who insists on the idea of the validity of a *zīj* during a period of about forty years only (see Emilia Calvo, "Astronomical Theories Related to the Sun in Ibn al-Hā'im's *al-Zīj al-Kāmil fī l-Taᶜālīm*", in *Zeitschrift für Geschichte der Arabisch-Islamischen Wissenschaften* 12 (1998), 51-111, especially p. 75) and, thus, reacts against Ibn al-Kammad who sought to compile a *zīj* valid for all times (*al-Amad ᶜalā l-abad*): see José Chabás & Bernard R. Goldstein, "Andalusian Astronomy: *al-Zîj al-Muqtabis* of Ibn al-Kammād", *Archive for History of Exact Sciences* 48 (1994), 1-41.

[16] According to B. Tuckermann, *Planetary, Lunar and Solar Positions. A.D. 2 to A.D. 1649 at Five-day and Ten-day Intervals* (Philadelphia, 1964), there was a conjunction of Saturn and Jupiter in Aquarius 19° the 17th Dhū l-Qaᶜda 745/ 22 March 1345. Using a computer programme based on Ibn ᶜAzzūz' parameters I find a sidereal conjunction seven hours after midday on the 24th February 1345 which actually takes place in the beginning of Aquarius (302;56,27°). This was the conjunction which was interpreted as announcing the Black Death of 1348 and which was analysed by Levi ben Gerson: B.R. Goldstein and D. Pingree, "Levi ben Gerson's Prognostication for the Conjunction of 1345", *Transactions of the American Philosophical Society* (Philadelphia) vol. 80, part 6 (1990).

(minutes) after Alexander's epoch.[17] We also have incomplete references to an horoscope cast for that moment, which I will call HOROSCOPE 3 (see below §3).

2. *Horoscopes 1 and 2*
2.1 *The dates of the two horoscopes*

Horoscopes 1 and 2 correspond to the last opposition of the Sun and the Moon before the vernal equinox of the year (1305) of the Saturn/ Jupiter conjunction (fol. 171 v) and to the vernal equinox of that year (fol. 172 r). The former states clearly that it has been cast according to the observation (*raṣad*) of Ibn ᶜAzzūz and that it corresponds (fol. 171 r) to a date and hour expressed, in *abjad* notation in the following way:

703 - 7 - 12 - 7 - 58 (or 258 instead of 7-58)

It is easy to establish, using the mean planetary longitudes of the horoscope itself, that this corresponds to 703 complete years, 7 months and 13 (not 12) days after the Hijra, although there is disagreement with the actual hour which cannot be 7;58^h after midday. The hour according to the different celestial bodies involved, with the exception of Saturn (5^s 27;26,54°, which is clearly erroneous for it implies more than 2 days and 12 hours less than the others), should be:

Sun	12;43^h
Moon	12;31^h
Jupiter	10;58^h
Mars	12;14^h

Since the Moon is the fastest moving of these bodies it seems logical to give priority to the lunar mean position, and the horoscope has been recomputed for 12;30^h after midday of the 14th Shaᶜbān 704 H./ 11th March 1305 (JD 2197779). A quick comparison with the recomputed positions obtained with the *Muwāfiq zīj* programme shows the following results for 13 hours after midday of the aforementioned date.

---

[17] According to my *Muwāfiq Zīj* computer programme the vernal equinox took place on the 23rd March 1340 A.D./ 24th Ramaḍān 740 H./ 23rd Adhār 1651 of the era of Alexander, between the seventh and the eighth hour after midday. The date is correctly given (with the difference of one day).

Planet	Mean longitude		Sidereal true longitude	
	Text	Recomp.	Text	Recomp.
Sun	346;31,45	346;32,59	348;23,45	348;24,58
Moon	173;10,53	173;26,48	168;23,45	168;39,14
Saturn	177;26,54	177;31,58	184;6,22	185;8,35
Jupiter	168;20,30	168;20,32	167;56,?	167;56,16
Mars	194;2,52	194;3,55	208;32,21	208;36,2
Venus	346;31,45	346;32,59	8;37,56	8;39,53
Mercury	346;31,45	346;32,59	340;31,57	340;39,55
Asc. node	2[3]2;50[18]	232;55,2	-	-

HOROSCOPE 1: 11 March 1305, 13^h after midday

Planet	Mean longitude		Sider. true longitude	
	Text	Recomp.	Text	Recomp.
Sun	358;9,59	358;10,18	0;0,1	0;0,18
Moon	328;45,16	328;49,4	334;14,58	334;19,19
Saturn	177;55,[3]8	177;55,38	184;6,22	184;13,44
Jupiter	169;19,23	169;19,19	166;27,9	166;26,31
Mars	200;14,30	200;14,40	208;26,11	207;36,2
Venus	358;9,59	358;10,18	23;7,23	23;7,17
Mercury	358;9,59	358;10,18	2;59,15	2;54,53
Asc. node	232;17	232;17,32	-	-

HOROSCOPE 2: 23 March 1305, at 8 p.m.

As for the second horoscope (vernal equinox), the date and hour appear in the horoscope itself (fol. 172 r) as

[18] 222;50 in the manuscript. The correction is obvious, for the longitude of the descending node is 52;50.

703 - 7 - 26 (read 25) - 7 - 10, after the Hijra
1615 - ? - 23 (read 22) - 7 - 53, after Alexander's epoch.

The first date corresponds to the 26th of Shaᶜbān of 704 H., and the second to the 23th Adhār (which implies that the number of complete months was 5) of 1616 of the Seleucid era and to the 23th of March of 1305 A.D. (JD 2197791). The two dates agree on the hour (7) though not on the minute (10/53), and 53^m seems a better reading. The agreement is fairly good with the results obtained with the computer for the aforementioned date at 8 hours after midday.

2.2 *The cusp longitudes*

The dates seem to be well established and the planetary longitudes appear to be well computed. The cusp longitudes pose more problems. Thus, for HOROSCOPE 1 (11 March 1305) we have:

I	252;23	VII	72;23
II	291;38	VIII	105;17 (*sic*!)
III	321;38 (58?)	IX	141;58 (*sic*!, 38/58)
IV	358;56	X	178;56
V	25;22	XI	201;38 (*sic*!)
VI	51;29	XII	231;18 (*sic*!, 29/18)

It is obvious that there are mistakes in the longitudes of the beginnings of houses II-VIII, III-IX, V-XI and VI-XII, for the longitude difference between opposite houses should be 180°. The following is an attempt to reconstruct the "correct" values:

I	252;23	VII	72;23
II	2[85];38	VIII	105;[38]
III	321;38	IX	141;[3]8
IV	358;56	X	178;56
V	25;22	XI	20[5];[22]
VI	51;[18]	XII	231;18

Using North's programme *Horosc*,[19] an obliquity of the ecliptic of

[19] North, *Horoscopes*, pp. 202-218.

23;33,30° (Ibn ᶜAzzūz actually uses 23;33° in his *zīj*) and a solar longitude of 348;23,45°, one can establish that 1) the method used for the equalization of the houses is the so-called *standard*; 2) the hour for which the horoscope was cast is 0;38,44^h after midnight (which agrees well with the 12;30^h after midday established previously; 3) the latitude implied lies between 36;44,58° and 37;12,27°, the mean value being 37;3,40°. My guess is that this horoscope was cast for latitude 37;10°, established by Ibn al-Raqqām for Granada: Ibn ᶜAzzūz takes from Ibn al-Raqqām a table of oblique ascensions for this city calculated for the aforementioned latitude. The differences between the "corrected" values of the cusp longitudes (I-VI) and the ideal values calculated with North's programme for latitude 37;10° are:

I	252;23
II	2[85];38 (0;0,53)
III	321;38 (0;1,41)
IV	358;56 (-0;4,43)
V	25;22 (0;29,25)
VI	I51;[18] (1;51,46)

After establishing this hypothesis, a second problem remains. Both horoscopes give the planetary positions twice: in one they appear within the horoscope itself, with the longitudes truncated to degrees or minutes; in the other in the margins of the horoscope, approximated to seconds and with further details about the computation which are explained below in §2.3 and reproduced in the *Appendix*. The planetary positions included in the first horoscope appear in the following way:

IV	358;56°	
	Sun	348°
	Mercury	340°
V	25;22°	
	Venus	8;37°
VI	51;29°	
	DescNode	52;50°
X	178;56°	
	Moon	168;23°
	Jupiter	167°
XI	201;38° (corr. 20[5];[22]°)	
	Mars	[20]8;30°
	Saturn	5^s ? (corr. 6^s 4°)

XII 231;18°
AscNode 222;50°

We can see, therefore, that the longitudes of Mercury, Venus, the Moon, Jupiter and Saturn precede the beginning of the corresponding houses by as much as 20°. John North has analyzed horoscopes in which the beginnings of the houses are replaced by points preceding them by five or eight degrees,[20] but this horoscope seems to exceed all known limits in this respect. I have no explanation for such an anomaly, except that of an error in the copying of the manuscript.

In the second horoscope (23 March 1305), the houses are:

I	210°	VII	30°
II	242;32°	VIII	62;32°
III	273;14°	IX	93;14°
IV	305;17°	X	125;17°
V	332;12°	XI	152;32°
VI	1;52°	XII	181;52°

There are no inconsistencies here and, again using North's *Horosc*, we can see that the standard method has been used; the hour is 20;30,40^h after midnight. The hour calculated on the basis of the mean planetary longitudes was 7;53^h after midday and the latitude implied lies between 39;6,45° and 40;3,53° (the mean value being 39;46,50°). My guess is, here, that this second horoscope was computed for the latitude of Toledo (latitude 39;54° in the canons of the *Toledan Tables*). The manuscript cusp longitudes of houses I-VI and the differences as regards the ideal values recomputed with North's programme are:

I 210°
II 242;32° (-0;31,8°)
III 273;14° (-0;50°)
IV 305;17° (-0;2,27°)
V 332;12° (-0;14,30°)
VI 1;52° (0;45,56°)

in which the longitude for the beginning of house VI could easily be

[20] North, *Horoscopes and History* pp. 1, 6, 45, 47, 72, 111, 112.

corrected into 1;[1]2 (the symbols for 10 and 50 are easy to confuse in Arabic script), the difference, then, being - 0;4,4.

In this second horoscope the planetary positions included in the diagram of the horoscope itself are in the houses in which they should be, with the exception of the Sun:

I	210°	
	AscNode	232;17°
V	332;12°	
	Moon	334;14°
VI	1;52°	
	Mercury	2;59°
	Sun	0;0,0°
	Venus	23;7°
VII	30°	
	DescNode	52;17°
XI	152;32°	
	Jupiter	166;27°
XII	181;52°	
	Saturn	184;6,22°
	Mars	208;26°

Whatever the case may be we have two horoscopes related to the same battle between King Alfonso XI of Castile and Yūsuf I, the Naṣrid sultan of Granada, who had obtained the help of Abū 'l-Ḥasan ᶜAlī, sultan of the Banī Marīn. There is a certain logic in realizing that Ibn ᶜAzzūz has cast HOROSCOPE 1 for Granada, the capital of the Banū Naṣr, and HOROSCOPE 2 for Toledo, which he undoubtedly considers to be the capital of the Castilian king. These two are not, however, the only latitudes used by Ibn ᶜAzzūz in his analysis of the situation. Using HOROSCOPE 2 as his radical horoscope, he directs (*tasyīr*) its ascendent according to four different types of *tasyīr* (see below §5) one of which is the "middle cycle" (*al-dawr al-awsaṭ*) *tasyīr*, which advances 5° per year and 0;25° per month (fol. 173 v). On the basis of a difference in time of 35 solar years and 7 months between 23 March 1305 and 30 October 1340 (the date of the battle) and an ascendent 210° in the radical horoscope, he operates

$$5^\circ * 35 + 0;25^\circ * 7 = 177;55^\circ$$

which he rounds to 178°.

Ibn ᶜAzzūz adds to this that we should direct (*tasyīr*) the degree of the ascendent expressed in ascensions: if we take the oblique ascension of the first minute of Scorpio (210°, the ascendent of the radical horoscope), add to it 178° (the middle cycle *tasyīr*) and subtract 360° from the result, the result will be an arc of *tasyīr* 34;6,19°.

This implies that the oblique ascension of 210° is 216;6,19° and that we should be able to establish the latitude which corresponds to that oblique ascension. Using an obliquity of the ecliptic of 23;33°, the right ascension of 210° will be:

$$\alpha_0\ (210°) = \tan^{-1}(\tan\lambda\cos\epsilon) = 207;53,26°$$

The ascensional difference (e) will be

$$e = \alpha_\phi - \alpha_0 = 216;6,19° - 207;53,26° = 8;12,53°$$

The declination (δ) of 210° being 11;31,26°, we may write

$$\phi = \tan^{-1}(\sin e / \tan\delta) = \tan^{-1}(\sin 8;12,53° / \tan 11;31,26°) = 35;1,22°$$

Next, he seems to obtain the inverse oblique ascension of 34;6,19°:

$$\alpha_\phi^{-1}\ (34;6,19°) = 49;6,28°$$

which is one of the *qawāṭiᶜ al-aṣliyya* (radical promissors).

We can proceed as before to calculate the corresponding latitude:

$$\alpha_\phi\ (49;6,28°) = 34;6,19°$$

$$\alpha_0\ (49;6,28°) = \tan^{-1}(\tan\lambda\cos\epsilon) = \tan^{-1}(\tan 49;6,28°\cos 23;33°) = 46;37,47°$$

$$e = \alpha_\phi - \alpha_0 = 12;31,28°$$

for $\delta\ (49;6,28°) = 17;34,48°$

$$\phi = \tan^{-1}(\sin e / \tan\delta) = \tan^{-1}(\sin 12;31,28° / \tan 17;34,18°) = 34;23,23°$$

which is not far from the 35° obtained previously. Apparently, Ibn ᶜAzzūz is using neither of the two latitudes for which he has cast his two horoscopes: 37;10° (Granada) and 39;54° (Toledo). My guess is that he might be using the latitude of the place of the battle which took place near Tarifa, slightly to the south of Algeciras, for which Arabic sources give latitudes comprised between 35;50° and 36;30°.[21]

2.3 *The computation of the planetary longitudes*

HOROSCOPES 1 and 2 offer an unusual number of details about the computation of planetary longitudes. For each planet they give its sidereal true longitude but also the *wasaṭ* (mean longitude), the *markaz thānī* or second *markaz* (the distance of the centre of the epicycle from the corrected planetary apogee, as seen from the centre of the Earth) and the *ḥiṣṣa thāniyya* or second anomaly (true anomaly measured from the true apogee of the epicycle). The details of the manuscript values as well as the recomputation made by hand using Ibn ᶜAzzūz' *Muwāfiq Zīj* will be found in the *Appendix*: values shown in parentheses ( ) correspond to differences between manuscript values and recomputations, while values shown in square brackets [ ] are my own recomputations. For each successive step of recomputation I have used the corresponding manuscript values, not the recomputed ones. This means, for example, that I have obtained the mean anomaly of the superior planets from the manuscript values of the mean positions of the Sun and the planet. Also, the

recomputed *second markaz* = manuscript *wasaṭ* - [recomp. corrected apogee] - [recomp. equation of the centre]

and that the

planet's true longitude = manuscript *second markaz* + [recomp. corrected apogee] + [recomp. equation of the anomaly]

The results obtained with my recomputations are rarely the same as the manuscript values but they were worth calculating in order to detect gross errors. Such is the case, for example, with the values for the second *markaz* and the second anomaly of Jupiter which have been exchanged in

---

[21] E.S. & M.H. Kennedy, *Geographical Coordinates of Localities from Islamic Sources* (Frankfurt, 1987), p. 19.

HOROSCOPE 2. In other cases I have given corrected readings of the manuscript values (always inside square brackets and with a footnote which indicates the manuscript actual values) in cases in which the alphanumerical Arabic system of notation (*abjad*) offers enough justification for a correction.

Ibn ᶜAzzuz' planetary apogees are sidereal and they are kept at a fixed distance from the sidereal solar apogee. This implies that their positions are displaced at a rate of $0;0,0,2,7,15^\circ$ per day, which corresponds approximately to the solar apogee's own motion as established by Ibn al-Zarqālluh (d. 1100).[22] The same doctrine is followed by Ibn al-Hā'im (fl. 1205), Ibn Isḥāq (fl. ca. 1193-1222) as well as by Ibn al-Raqqām (d. 1315) in his *Shāmil zīj*. Ibn al-Bannā' restricted the motion of the solar apogee to the inferior planets and he was followed, in this respect, by Ibn al-Raqqām in his *Qawīm zīj*.[23] In order to establish the position of the planetary apogees in both horoscopes, the obvious starting point is to analyze the information given by the manuscript itself on the solar apogee. Thus, in HOROSCOPE 1, we have:

Wasaṭ of the Sun: $11^s\ 16;31,45^\circ\ (+0;0,1^\circ)$

In the same horoscope the *wasaṭs* of Venus and Mercury contain mistakes:

Wasaṭ of Venus: $11^s\ \mathit{11};31,45^\circ$
Wasaṭ of Mercury: $11^s\ 16;3\mathit{8},45^\circ$[24]

The solar *markaz* of the manuscript is $8^s\ 27;19,31^\circ$, from which we can recalculate the longitude of the apogee (λ_A):

$$\lambda_A = 11^s\ 16;31,45^\circ - 8^s\ 27;19,31^\circ = 2^s\ 19;12,14^\circ$$

The radix position of the solar apogee being $2^s\ 16;44,21^\circ$[25] we can establish that the displacement of the solar and the planetary apogees since

---

[22] See J. Samsó & E. Millás, *Ibn al-Bannā', Ibn Isḥāq and Ibn al-Zarqālluh's Solar Theory*. "Islamic Astronomy and Medieval Spain" (Variorum, Aldershot, 1994), nº X.

[23] See J. Samsó & E. Millás, *The computation of planetary longitudes in the* zīj *of Ibn al-Bannā'*, "Arabic Sciences and Philosophy" 8 (1998), 259-286.

[24] On top of the 38' there is a correction in the manuscript which I read as 31'.

[25] Samsó, *Muwafiq*, p. 102.

epoch has been:

$2^s\ 19;12,14^\circ - 2^s\ 16;44,21^\circ = 2;27,53^\circ$

This result can be checked against the information contained in HOROSCOPE 2, where we have:

Wasaṭ of the Sun:	11^s 28;29,59°
Wasaṭ of Venus:	11^s 28;9,59°
Wasaṭ of Mercury:	11^s 28;9,7°

Here the best reading is the one the manuscript gives for Venus: 11^s 28;9,59° (-0;2,11°). If we use, here also, the solar *markaz* 9^s 8;57,45° we will obtain the same value as in the previous horoscope for the longitude of the solar apogee:

$\lambda_A = 11^s\ 28;9,59^\circ - 9^s\ 8;57,45^\circ = 2^s\ 19;12,14^\circ$

We can, therefore, be sure that the displacement of the solar and the planetary apogees since epoch has been 2;27,53°. The positions of the planetary apogees, calculated from the radix values given by Ibn ᶜAzzūz in his *Muwāfiq Zīj*:

Saturn	7^s 28;38,30° + 2;27,53° = 8^s 1;6,23°
Jupiter	5^s 8;21,30° + 2;27,53° = 5^s 10;49,23°
Mars	3^s 29;41,30° + 2;27,53° = 4^s 2;9,23°
Venus	2^s 16;45,21° + 2;27,53° = 2^s 19;13,14°
Mercury	6^s 18;21,30° + 2;27,53° = 6^s 20;49,23°

The apogee of Venus at epoch in the *Muwāfiq Zīj* (2^s 16;45,21°) derives from the apogees of the Sun and Venus in Ibn al-Kammād's *Muqtabas Zīj*, while Ibn ᶜAzzūz' solar apogee (2^s 16;44,21°) seems related to the tradition of Ibn Isḥāq, Ibn al-Bannā' and Ibn al-Raqqām (2^s 16;44,17°). I have used this position of Venus' apogee in my recomputation and this gives a better agreement with the manuscript value of the second *markaz* in HOROSCOPE 2, while the value of the solar apogee (2^s 16;44,21°) is better in the case of HOROSCOPE 1.

2.4 *Planetary latitudes*.

Surprisingly enough, HOROSCOPE 2 gives the values for the latitudes of the Moon, Saturn, Jupiter, Mars and Venus, though not Mercury. As for HOROSCOPE 1, the latitudes for the Moon and planets do not appear in the manuscript although they are announced and there is an empty space left to inscribe them. The manuscript latitude values in HOROSCOPE 2 are as follows (the differences between the manuscript values and my recomputations are added in parentheses):

Moon	[4];58,28°[26]	(0;0,56°)
Saturn	4;1[3],11°[27]	(0;0,5°)
Jupiter	2;27,27°	(-0;0,34°)
Mars	0;30,18°	(0;2,45°)
Venus	2;16,8°	(0;2,45°)

I have recomputed the lunar and planetary latitudes using Ibn ᶜAzzūz' *Muwāfiq Zīj*. In it, the table for the computation of lunar latitude is Ptolemaic and uses a value of 5° for β_{max}.[28] The tables for planetary latitudes derive from al-Khwārizmī's *zīj*.[29] The latitude is divided into two components, for the first of which (*nisba*) the argument is the second anomaly while for the second (β_2) the argument is the distance to the nearest node. The final formula to compute the latitude of the planet is:

$$\beta = nisba * \beta_2$$

It is easy to see that the values of β_2 are identical to those of the corresponding function in al-Khwārizmī's *zīj*. As for the *nisba*, Ibn ᶜAzzūz' function is the reciprocal of the corresponding one in al-Khwārizmī (β_1):

$$nisba = 60 / \beta_1$$

---

[26] 1° in the manuscript.

[27] 18' in the manuscript.

[28] *Muwafiq Zīj* MS Rabat Ḥasaniyya Library (RHL) 8772, p. 59 and Rabat General Library (RGL) D2461, p. 398.

[29] *Muwāfiq Zīj* RHL p. 83, RGL p. 411 (Saturn); RHL p. 88, RGL p. 414 (Jupiter); RHL p. 93, RGL p. 418 (Mars); RHL p. 97, RGL p. 422 (Venus); RGL p. 426 (Mercury): this latter table is missing in RHL. See H. Suter, *Die astronomischen Tafeln des Muhammed ibn Mūsā al-Khwārizmī in der Bearbeitung des Maslama ibn Aḥmed al-Madjrīṭī und der latein. Uebersetzung des Athelhard von Bath*. Kobenhavn, 1914, pp. 138-167.

which agrees with al-Khwārizmī's final formula for planetary latitude, which is:

$$\beta = \beta_2 / \beta_1$$

Ibn ᶜAzzūz' planetary nodes are kept at a fixed distance from the sidereal "corrected" apogees (*al-awj al-muᶜaddal*) which implies, obviously, that they are also affected by the motion of the apogees. The distances mentioned in the *Muwāfiq Zīj* are:

Saturn	140°
Jupiter	70°
Mars	90°
Venus	0°
Mercury	180°

The distances for the superior planets are the same as those of the *Almagest* (XIII,6). Ptolemy, however, considers that the nodal line for Mercury and Venus is perpendicular to their apsidal line and that the distances between the apogee and the node are 90° for Venus and -90° for Mercury. We have here a clear disagreement with the distances stated by Ibn ᶜAzzuz who, in the case of Venus, states very clearly *Wa-amma jawzahar al-Zuhra, fa-mawḍiᶜ awji-hā al-muᶜaddal huwa jawzaharu-hā* ("As for the node of Venus, the position of its corrected apogee is its node"). We have no way to check the nodal distance for the case of Mercury, because no latitude is given for that planet in our horoscope. In the case of Venus, however, a latitude of 2;13,23°, which is not far from the 2;16,8° of the text, has been recomputed by using an argument of latitude of

79;13,14° (apogee) - 90° = 349;13,14°

There seems, therefore, to be a mistake in the distances between the nodes and the apogees for the inferior planets of the *Muwāfiq Zīj*.

3. *Horoscope 3: the spring equinox of the year of the battle of El Salado (23 March 1340)*

In fol. 173 v - 174 r we find a reference to the horoscope of that spring equinox: the ascendent was 196;50°; Mars was in Taurus 13° in the second house from the Sun and in the VIII house of the horoscope: the recomputed longitude of Mars is 43;4,46° and, the ascendent being 196;50°, for any latitude comprised between 33;40° (Fez) and 39;54° (Toledo), house VIII will begin at about 49°, very near to the position of Mars and the Sun will be in house VI, approximately two houses away from Mars. The text goes on to say that Venus (recomputed position 7;27,36°) is in its *wabāl* (detriment), which should be Scorpio during the night and Aries in daytime. Here Ibn ᶜAzzūz seems to have in mind Aries, in spite of the fact that the hour of the horoscope is roughly 7 p.m., which would be after sunset. Venus is in house VI (beginning at about 345°).

4. *Horoscope 4: the spring equinox of 1344 (24 March 1344)*

In fol. 174 r Ibn ᶜAzzūz refers to the horoscope of the spring equinox of the year in which he made his observations: the event took place 743 [complete years], 10 [complete months], 9 [complete days], 7 [hours], 56 [minutes] after epoch. The equivalent Islamic date is, then, 10th Dhu l-Qaᶜda 744/ 24 March 1344 A.D. and the information given in our text for the planetary positions (inside square brackets the computer recalculations for 8 p.m.) is:

Saturn	Capricorn 25° [294;49,0°]
Moon	Cancer 24° [113;11,39°]
Mars	Gemini 13° [72;48,24°]

The text adds that the ascendent is Libra 27;45° and that Mars is in house VIII (for any latitude comprised between 33;40° (Fez) and 39;54° (Toledo), house VIII will begin at about 60°). The indicators predict sudden death, illness in the throat and epidemic diseases. He then refers to the Saturn-Jupiter conjunction of 1345 which took place in Aquarius 3° (recomputed 302;56,27°), and indicated earthquakes and destruction of houses. The moment of the conjunction is also given as 744 [years], 9 [months], 21 [days] and 2 [hours] (?) after epoch (22nd Shawwāl 745 H./25th February 1345 A.D.).[30] The end of the conjunction took place in the same year 10 m., 2 d., 13 h., 14 m. (3rd Dhu l-Qaᶜda 745 H./7th March 1345 A.D.). I do not understand the criteria used by Ibn ᶜAzzūz to fix the end of the conjunction: the recomputed values of the longitudes of Saturn (304;10,1°) and Jupiter (305;23,46°) are more than 1° apart on

---

[30] As we have seen in §1, the recomputed conjunction took place one day earlier: 24 February 1345.

7 March 1345, but the same happens on the 6th and the 5th of March.

5. *The different kinds of* tasyīr *used by Ibn ᶜAzzūz*

The ascendent in HOROSCOPE 2 (210°) is his significator (*dalīl*, usually called *al-mutaqaddim* or *al-haylaj*) and the period of time which corresponds to the *tasyīr* (35 solar years and 7 months between the spring equinox of year 1305 and the date of the battle, 30 October 1340) is known. Ibn ᶜAzzūz seeks to calculate which are the promissors (the planets, stars, or points of the ecliptic which were responsible for the catastrophe), according to the different kinds of *tasyīr* he uses. The promissor is usually called *al-thānī* (the second) or *al-qāṭiᶜ* (cutter), which corresponds to the Castilian-Alfonsine term *taiador*.[31] With the sole exception of his use of oblique ascensions in the calculation of the "middle cycle" (*al-dawr al-awsaṭ*) *tasyīr*, the rest of the techniques used by Ibn ᶜAzzūz are extremely simple, being based on simple progressions on the ecliptic.[32] Thus, our author calculates four different kinds of *tasyīr* according to what his earlier explanation in the fourth chapter (*faṣl*) of this same book (fols. 124 r and v):

---

[31] M. Viladrich and R. Martí, "Sobre el *Libro dell Ataçir* de los *Libros del Saber de Astronomía* de Alfonso X el Sabio", in J. Vernet (ed.), *Nuevos Estudios sobre Astronomía Española en el Siglo de Alfonso X* (Barcelona, 1983), pp. 75-100.

[32] Jan P. Hogendijk ("Progressions, Rays and Houses in Medieval Islamic Astrology: A Mathematical Classification", paper presented at the Dibner Institute Conference *New Perspectives on Science in Medieval Islam*, held in Cambridge, Mass. in November 6-8 1998) classifies the different methods for the division of houses, *tasyīr* and projection of rays and includes this simple ecliptical method among those used for the projection of rays but not for the *tasyīr*. The oblique ascension method for the *tasyīr* is mentioned by Ptolemy in the *Tetrabiblos*: he says that it is the usual system but that it is correct only if the celestial body or the point of the ecliptic is on the Eastern horizon. On the other hand, in fol. 122 r of this same work, Ibn ᶜAzzūz states that, for the calculation of the *tasyīr*, the correct method is that of Ptolemy and Hermes and that it is the method followed by modern authors in spite of its approximate character. Ptolemy describes, in his *Tetrabiblos*, the use of the "position semicircle" - whose endpoints are the North and the South points of the horizon - and the equator for the *tasyīr* (equatorial method), although he actually uses an approximation (Hour Line method). The equatorial method is also ascribed to Hermes by Andalusian sources, and this seems to be the reason for Ibn ᶜAzzūz' attribution of the same method - which he apparently does not use - to Ptolemy and Hermes.

5.1 "Small cycle" (*al-dawr al-aṣghar*): from the ascendent of the radical horoscope, with a rate of motion of 30° per year, 2;30° per month and 0:5° per day. It is also called *burj al-intihā'* and it corresponds to the "small world *intihā'*" of Eastern astrologers.[33] The amount (fol. 172 v) will be:

$$210^\circ + 35 \text{ years} * 30 + 2;30^\circ * 7 \text{ months} = 3 * 360^\circ + 180^\circ + 17;30^\circ$$

The *intihā'* in the moment of the battle will take place at 17° of the beginning of Libra (fol. 173 r), which is also the degree of the true Saturn-Jupiter conjunction (see above §1) and the degree of the ascendent of the spring equinox of the year of the battle (1340) (see above §3).

5.2 "Middle cycle" (*al-dawr al-awsaṭ*) which corresponds to a period of 72 years. It is also called *al-tadbīr al-firdārī*. It moves 5° per year, 0;25° per month and 0;0,50° per day. See above §2.2. For the spring equinox of the year of the battle we have:

$$210^\circ + 5^\circ * 35 = 360^\circ + 25^\circ$$

and, for the actual date of the battle:

$$25^\circ + 0;25^\circ * 7 = 27;55^\circ$$

Ibn ᶜAzzūz looks here for one of the *qawāṭiᶜ* (promissors), which he identifies with the lot of the kingdom (*sahm al-mulk*), which should be taken from Saturn to the Sun and then subtracted from the ascendent. In HOROSCOPE 2 Saturn's longitude is 184°, the Sun is at Aries 0° and the ascendent is 210°. Apparently he implies

$$210^\circ - 184^\circ = 26^\circ$$

5.3 A *tasyīr* of one degree per year. This cycle corresponds to the "small world *tasyīr*" or "small *qisma*" of Eastern astrologers[34], although they refer the motion to the equator rather than the ecliptic: in 35 years

---

[33] E.S. Kennedy, "The World-Year Concept in Islamic Astrology", in Kennedy *et al.*, *Studies in the Islamic Exact Sciences* (Beirut, 1983), 351-371 (see p. 356); David Pingree, *The Thousands of Abū Maᶜshar* (London, 1968), pp. 60, 65.

[34] Kennedy, "World year" p. 355; Pingree, *Thousands* pp. 59, 65.

we have 35° which are added to the 210° of the ascendent:

$$210° + 35° = 245°$$

245° is the longitude of the star *Shawlat al-ᶜAqrab* which is one of the *qawāṭiᶜ* (promissors). *Shawlat al-ᶜAqrab* is λ Sco, for which the star-catalogue of the *Almagest* gives a longitude of 237;30°. This star does not appear in the star table of the *Muwāfiq Zīj*: all the stars in that table have Ptolemaic longitudes increased by 6;48°. Ibn ᶜAzzūz, therefore, should assume a longitude for that star of:

$$237;30° + 6;48° = 244;18°$$

To this Ibn ᶜAzzūz adds that the *sahm al-saᶜd* (usually *sahm al-saᶜāda, pars Fortunae*) is 184;14°. This can be confirmed in HOROSCOPE 2 in which we have:

- Longitude of the Sun:	0;0°
- Longitude of the Moon:	334;14°
- Ascendent:	210°

The *pars Fortunae* should be:

$$334;14° + 210° - 360° = 184;14°$$

This coincides with the position of Saturn (184;6,22°). The *pars Fortunae* is the *sahm al-naḥs* (Lot of misfortune).

5.4 The "great cycle" (*al-dawr al-akbar*) or *al-tasyīr al-ṭabīᶜī*, which lasts 120 years, considered to be the natural (*ṭabīᶜī*) duration of human life. The rate of motion is, thus, 3° per year, 0;15° per month and 0;0,30° per day. We have, then, for the date of the spring equinox (fol. 173 v):

$$210° + 35 * 3° = 315°$$

and with these 315° we reach the star *al-Ḥūt al-Janūbī* in Aquarius, which is one of the *qawāṭiᶜ* (promissors). Ibn ᶜAzzūz probably refers to *Fam al-Ḥūt al-Janūbī* (*α Piscis Austrinus*) the longitude of which, in the *Almagest*, is 307°. For our author, its longitude should be:

307° + 6;48° = 313;48°

5.5 The *tasyīr* of the conjunctions (*tasyīr al-qirānāt*)

Ibn ᶜAzzuz states that he has explained the *tasyīr al-qirānāt* in the fifth chapter (*faṣl*) of this same book, but I cannot find any such explanation. He says that we should calculate where the conjunction of the change of triplicity takes place [at Libra 16°, which belongs to the airy triplicity], and obtain its distance from the triplicity of water [i.e from the beginning of Scorpio]. The distance from Scorpio is 1[4]° [= 210° - 196°]. The conjunction will stay in Libra, between the two changes of triplicity, 239 years.[35] We divide 360° by 239 years, the result being 1;30,23° (1;50,28° according to the manuscript, but the mistake is easy to explain in *abjad* notation). The arc of the *tasyīr* in 35 years will be:

1;30,23° * 35 = [1ˢ] 22;43°

The *tasyīr* will attain 22;43° of Sagittarius [210° + 52;43° = 262;43°], which is the longitude of the star *ᶜAyn al-Ramī*, which will be one of the *qawaṭiᶜ*. *ᶜAyn al-Ramī* is $\nu^1 + \nu^2$ Sagit., for which the *Almagest* gives a longitude of 255;10°. For Ibn ᶜAzzūz the longitude should be

255;10° + 6;48° = 261;58°

6. *Conclusions*

There is no doubt that HOROSCOPES 1 & 2 were cast by Ibn ᶜAzzūz retrospectively in order to check the validity of the new mean motion tables of his *Muwāfiq Zīj*. It is also clear that he was mainly interested in HOROSCOPE 2 (although he occasionally used horoscopes 1, 3 and 4). HOROSCOPE 2 is the radix of all his *tasyīr* computations and it has been cast far more carefully than HOROSCOPE 1. I do not know, however, whether the first horoscopes (not extant, apparently) he cast in relation to the battle of El Salado, in which he used mean motion tables derived from

---

[35] In fol. 65 v, Ibn ᶜAzzūz says that a conjunction will stay in the same triplicity 13 consecutive times in ca. 250 years. 239 years seems more accurate: using the *Muwāfiq* computer programme I find that the next Saturn-Jupiter conjunction with change of triplicity (219;46,41°) takes place on 20 August 1544, at about 16 hours after midday.

the tradition of Ibn Isḥāq, were also retrospective, and to what extent Ibn ᶜAzzūz had cast a horoscope before the battle because he had been asked to do so by the circles of power surrounding *amīr* Abū l-Ḥasan ᶜAlī. The problem is of particular interest, since the scholar Ibn Marzūq (1310-1379), who fought in the battle, wrote an hagiographic portrait of Abū l-Ḥasan, one chapter of which is dedicated specifically to Abū l-Ḥasan's rejection of Astrology - something that was a consequence of his extreme orthodoxy.[36] The question remains open but, if the answer was affirmative, it would not be the first instance in which an Islamic ruler adopted an official attitude of rejection while at the same time employing a private astrologer to inform him about the development of future events of interest to him: such is the case of the Andalusian dictator al-Manṣūr ibn Abī ᶜĀmir (981-1002) who was responsible for the selective burning of the books of the library of al-Ḥakam II (961-976) - including the books on Astrology - but who nevertheless employed an astrologer to cast the horoscope of the birth of his son, ᶜAbd al-Malik al-Muẓaffar.[37]

ACKNOWLEDGEMENTS: The present paper has been prepared within a research programme on "Astronomical tables and theory in al-Andalus and the Maghrib between the twelfth and the fourteenth centuries", sponsored by the Dirección General de Investigación Científica y Técnica of the Spanish Ministry of Education and Culture. John North's computer programme HOROSC and Benno van Dalen's CALH (for the conversion of dates) have been extensively used. The computer programme for the computation of planetary longitudes with the parameters of the *Muwāfiq Zīj* owes its existence to the joint efforts of Prof. E.S. Kennedy, Dr. Honorino Mielgo and my research graduate student Josep Casulleras. Information about manuscripts was given to me by my research graduate students Mònica Rius and Hamid Berrani. Prof. Aḥmad Shawqī Bīnbīn, Keeper of the Ḥasaniyya Library, generously offered microfilms of several manuscripts and Prof. Fuat Sezgin sent me information which was not available in Barcelona. A previous draft of this paper was read by Professors E.S. Kennedy, David Pingree, Jan P. Hogendijk and John North (!). My gratitude to all of them.

---

[36] See Muḥammad ibn Marzuq al-Tilimsānī, *al-Musnad al-ṣaḥīḥ al-ḥasan fī ma'āthir wa-maḥāsin mawlā-nā Abī l-Ḥasan*, ed. M.J. Viguera (Algiers, 1981), pp. 438-444; Spanish translation and commentary by M.J. Viguera, *El* Musnad: *hechos memorables de Abū l-Ḥasan, sultán de los Benimerines* (Madrid, 1977), pp. 361-366.

[37] J. Samsó, *Las Ciencias de los Antiguos en al-Andalus* (Madrid, 1992), p. 78.

APPENDIX: THE COMPUTATION OF PLANETARY LONGITUDES

HOROSCOPE 1 (11 March 1305) (Unit: degree)

Planet	mean long.	markaz	eq. cn.	markaz 2	mean an.	anom. 2	eq. anom.	true long.
Sun	346;31,45 (0;0,1)	267;19,31	1;52	-	-	-	-	348;23,45
Moon	173;10,53 (0;0,23)	Double elong. [13;18,16]	[1;57,44]	-	[110;51]	112;49,2 (0;0,18)	[-4;47]	168;23,45 (-0;0,8)
Saturn	177;26,54 (-0;5,1)	[296;20,31]	[5;42,58]	302;[3],26 (-0;0,3)	[169;4,51]	163;21,56 (0;0,3)	[1;56,14]	185;4,27 (-0;1,39)
Jupiter	168;20,30 (-0;0,19)	[7;31,7]	[-0;39,36]	6;52,27 (0;0,56)	[178;11,15]	178;50,55 (0;0,4)	[0;15,59]	167;56,? (rc. 167;56,53)
Mars	194;2,52 (-0;0,21)	[71;53,29]	[-10;28,34]	61;25,51 (0;0,56)	[152;28,53]	162;57,31 (0;0,4)	[25;3,1]	208;32,21 (-0;4,58)
Venus	34[6];31,45 (0;0,1)	[267;18,31]	[1;59]	269;[1]8,31 (0;1)	[50;41,20]	48;[4]2,21 (0;0,1)	[20;7,16]	8;37,56 (-0;0,5)
Mercury	346;3[1],45 (0;0,1)	[145;42,22]	[-1;44,53]	143;58,32 (0;1,3)	[343;22,59]	345;7,56 (0;0,4)	[-4;13,27]	340;31,57 (-0;1,28)

[38]The number corresponding to the minutes is doubtful in the MS: it may be a 3 or a 4 [39]MS 11^s 11;31,45° [40]38' in the MS
[41]12' in the MS [42]MS 11^s 16;38,45°

HOROSCOPE 2 (23 March 1305) (Unit: degree)

Planet	mean long.	markaz	eq. cn.	markaz 2	mean an.	anom. 2	eq. anom.	true long.
Sun	358;[9],59[43] (0;2,11)	278;57,45	1;50,2	-	-	-	-	0;0,1
Moon	328;45,16 (0;0,4)	Double elong. [301;10,34]	[8;24,57]	-	[265;6,59]	256;42,22 (0;0,20)	[5;29,39]	334;14,58 (0;0,3)
Saturn	177;55,[3]8[44] (0;0,1)	[296;49,15]	[5;41,32]	302;38,46 (0:7)	[180;19,21]	17[4];26,52[45] (-0;10,57)	[0;40,30]	184;6,22 (-0;11,18)
Jupiter	169;19,23 (-0;0,19)	[8;30]	[-0;44,30]	7;46,15[46] (0;0,45)	[188;50,36]	189;35,21[47] (0;0,15)	[-2;7,40]	166;27,9 (-0;0,4)
Mars	200;14,30 (-0;0,8)	[78;5,7]	[-10;53,20]	67;12,43 (0;0,56)	[157;55,29]	168;49,43 (0;0,54)	[18;36,21]	208;26,11 (0;28,40)
Venus	358;9,59 (0;2,11)	[278;57,45]	[1;58]	28[0];54,44[48] (-0;0,1)	[57;58,7]	56;1,7 (0;1)	[23;0,29]	23;7,23 (0;1,5)
Mercury	358;9,[59][49] (0;2,11)	[157;20,36]	[-1;10,58]	156;10,41 (0;1,3)	[20;3,56]	2[1];14,33[50] (-0;0,21)	[6;0,4]	2;59,15 (0;0,10)

[43] 20' in the manuscript. 9' corresponds to Venus' mean longitude. [44] 18" in the manuscript. [45] 177o in the manuscript.
[46] This is the manuscript value for the second anomaly. [47] This is the manuscript value for the second *markaz*.
[48] In the manuscript I read 9^s ?;54,44°. [49] 7" in the manuscript. [50] 20° in the manuscript.

XI

AN OUTLINE OF THE HISTORY OF MAGHRIBĪ ZIJES FROM THE END OF THE THIRTEENTH CENTURY

1. *The Andalusian Tradition in Maghribī Zijes: Ibn Isḥāq and his School*

Nothing is known about the earliest known Maghribī zij, Ibn Abī l-Rijāl al-Qayrawānī's *Ḥall al-ᶜaqd wa-bayān al-raṣd* (beginning of the eleventh century), which seems to have been lost. Two centuries later, Abū l-ᶜAbbās ibn Isḥāq al-Tamīmī al-Tūnisī (*fl.* Tunis and Marrakesh *c.* 1193–1222) left an unfinished set of tables which survive in a unique manuscript of Hyderabad, discovered in 1978 by D. A. King.[1] The predominant influence in Ibn Isḥāq's zij was that of the Andalusian school represented by Ibn al-Zarqālluh (d. 1100), Ibn al-Kammād (*fl.* Cordova *c.* 1115) and Ibn al-Hā'im (*fl.* 1205). This influence continued during the thirteenth and fourteenth centuries through several "editions" of the zij of Ibn Isḥāq such as the one prepared by the anonymous compiler of the aforementioned collection extant in the Hyderabad manuscript (*c.* 665 A.H./1266–680 A.H./1281), the *Minhāj* of Ibn al-Bannā' of Marrakesh (1256–1321),[2] and the two zijes composed by the Tunisian-Andalusian astronomer Muḥammad ibn al-Raqqām (d. 1315).[3] Andalusian influence is also present in two other fourteenth-century zijes, written by two astronomers of Constantine, in the Central Maghrib, who were active in Fez: the one compiled by Abū l-Ḥasan ᶜAlī ibn Abī ᶜAlī al-Qusanṭīnī, the canons of which were written in verse,[4] and the *al-Zīj al-Muwāfiq* of Abū l-Qāsim ibn ᶜAzzūz al-Qusanṭīnī (d. 1354),[5] partially based on observations made in Fez with an armillary sphere *c.* 1344.

All the aforementioned zijes share a certain number of characteristics among which we should mention that their mean motion tables are sidereal, and that they contain tables based on the theory of trepidation which enable the user to calculate the amount of precession for a given date and, thus, obtain the tropical longitudes of heavenly bodies. Trepidation also implies a variation in the obliquity of the ecliptic and these zijes also include tables, based on the model designed by Ibn al-Zarqālluh, which uses cycles that regulate the diminution and the expected future increase of the obliquity of the ecliptic.

2. *New Sources on Trepidation Theory in the Maghrib*

Dr Mercè Comes[6] and I have analysed three new sources dated between the fifteenth and the early seventeenth century. They shed some light on the progressive decline of the belief in the theory of trepidation in the Maghrib and on the reasons for the diffusion of Eastern zijes in this part of the Islamic world. These sources are, on the one hand, the *Kitāb al-adwār fī tasyīr al-anwār*, written by Abū ᶜAbd Allāh al-Baqqār in 821/1418,[7] and, on the other, two commentaries on the poem on time-keeping written in 1391 by al-Jadarī:[8]

(1) An anonymous one, which bears the title of *Natā'ij al-afkār fī sharḥ Rawḍat al-azhār* ("Results of thoughts towards an explanation of the Flower Garden").[9] Its author seems to have worked in Tilimsān (Tlemcen) *c.* 1515, and probably was a disciple of al-Ḥabbāk,[10] whom he calls *mawlayya wa-sayyīdī* (i.e. "my lord").[11] It is interesting to note that our anonymous author mentions, among other sources, the observations made in Barcelona by Abū Kursūm al-Yahūdī,[12] who is none other than Jacob Corsuno (active in Barcelona between 1378 and 1380), the author of the final version of the *Tables of Barcelona*.[13]

(2) A second commentary is the *Qaṭf al-anwār min Rawḍat al-azhār*, written by Abū Zayd ᶜAbd al-Raḥmān b. ᶜUmar b. Aḥmad al-Sūsī al-Jazūlī al-Buᶜaqīlī, Ibn al-Muftī (d. 1611),[14] extant in MS Cairo K7584 (112v–155r).[15] The author lived in Marrakesh and both this city and Fez are mentioned in the text, but the main interest of Ibn al-Muftī was al-Sūs al-Aqṣā and, in particular, Tārudant, for which he gives a latitude of 30;15° and computes a table of oblique ascensions.[16]

These sources give some evidence that observations were made in the Maghrib in the thirteenth and fourteenth centuries. Ibn ᶜAzzūz al-Qusanṭīnī speaks about his own observations made in Fez *c.* 1344 with an armillary sphere in order to correct Ibn Isḥāq's mean motion tables, and al-Baqqār also talks, vaguely, about Fāsī observations — meridian altitudes of the Sun and other celestial bodies made with an astrolabe, a quadrant or even a large-sized instrument — and of a careful determination of the latitude of the city. These observations raise doubts on values of trepidation computed with the zijes belonging to the Andalusian tradition. The *Natā'ij al-afkār* states that al-Jadarī considered that the amount of precession for his time (1391–92) was 10°, an amount calculated with the trepidation table in the zij of Ibn Isḥāq which has a maximum of 10;24°. The author of the *Natā'ij* adds that, according to the observations made by Ibn Abī 'l-Shukr al-Maghribī in Damascus in 1259, precession at the end of the fourteenth century should be about 12°, or slightly more. After Ibn Abī 'l-Shukr, a certain Abū 'l-Ḥasan ᶜAlī b. Yūnus al-Balansī al-Ḥākimī (!) made observations in Cairo in 732/1331 and obtained that the amount of precession for that date was approximately 13°.[17] As a conclusion, the *Natā'ij* states that the estimations of the *iqbāl* (accession) are not correct and there are disagreements between computation and observation when one tries to establish the meridian altitude of the Sun and other celestial bodies. There must exist another motion in addition to accession and recession, although it is difficult to be more precise. This is why our commentator, following Ibn Abī 'l-Shukr, states that precession for his time is 13;40° and that, using this amount, he obtains a good agreement with observation.

Similar critical remarks can be found in the *Qaṭf al-anwār*: precession in the time of al-Jadarī was 12° but the difference was, perhaps, not perceptible to that author. When the *Qaṭf* was written (*c.* end of the sixteenth century?) precession reached 13° and some astronomers claimed that it was 14°.[18] Far more rich in information is al-Baqqār's *Adwār* (1418): the author has computed the value of trepidation for his own time and obtained 10°, minus a few minutes, with Ibn al-Zarqālluh's tables, and 10;10° with Ibn Isḥāq's zij. When this amount is used to obtain the tropical longitudes of the Sun or the planets using the (sidereal) tables of Ibn Isḥāq and his followers, one easily detects the presence of an error in the results: this is particularly noticeable when the Sun or the celestial body is near the equinoxes, and not so much when its longitude is near one of the two solstices. The difference, in the case of the Sun, amounts to 2°, as has been established in observations made in Fez. Therefore, one should either add a second motion to trepidation or calculate trepidation tables with a maximum higher than 12°.

On the other hand, al-Baqqār saw zijes computed by Eastern astronomers who observed in Damascus and who disagree with the theory of trepidation. Al-Baqqār was able to determine that the mean longitudes of the Sun for the end of year 810/1407–8 exceeded the solar mean sidereal positions calculated in agreement with the observations of Ibn Isḥāq by 12;15,6°. One of these zijes is the *Tāj al-azyāj* of Ibn Abī 'l-Shukr al-Andalusī, who lived in Damascus, whose mean solar positions for 810/1407–8 exceed those of Ibn Isḥāq by 12;16,45°. All this agrees with Ibn Abī 'l-Shukr's tables of constant precession, from which al-Baqqār gives several numerical values. Values of precession calculated with these Eastern zijes have an obvious interest for Ibn al-Baqqār, for they agree perfectly with his own estimations, based on observations of meridian altitudes of the Sun and other celestial bodies, and our author has serious doubts about the truth of trepidation theory. He will, however, continue using the sidereal tables of the Zarqāllian-Ibn Isḥāq tradition because he needs them for astrological and magical purposes, but he will add 12° to the sidereal positions when an astronomical problem is involved.

Trepidation is obviously related to the secular diminution of the obliquity of the ecliptic.[19] The *Natā'ij al-afkār* mentions the standard historical values of the obliquity and quotes an obliquity of 23;31° used by Ibn al-Shāṭir (*fl.* Damascus *c.* 1350)[20] and by al-Mizzī (*fl.* Damascus, d. *c.* 1350).[21] As for determinations made in the Maghrib, Ibn Isḥāq states that a man from Miknāsa (Meknès) observed the obliquity in 602/1205–6 and obtained 23;32,30°: this parameter is extremely interesting because it is the one used not only by Ibn Isḥāq himself,[22] but also by the Alfonsine astronomers (the declination table calculated for this maximum in the *Libro del relogio de la piedra de la sombra* seems to derive from the corresponding table of Ibn Isḥāq)[23] and by an astronomer of a very different milieu, al-Sanjūfīnī.[24] The same result was obtained by Ibn Hilāl[25] with his observations made in Ceuta. Another observation was made in 704/1304–5 in Marrakesh — the latitude of which is 31;45,23°[26] — by al-Ḥakīm al-Mirrīkh (?), who obtained 23;26,57°. Finally a certain Ibn al-Tarjumān said that the obliquity of the ecliptic, at the end of the seventh century (699 A.H./

1299–1300) is 23;26°. All these observations, made in the thirteenth century, have the obvious interest of invalidating the geometrical model designed, in the eleventh century, by Ibn al-Zarqālluh, to calculate the value of the obliquity for a given date:[27] this model had been used, with adaptations in the parameters,[28] by all the Maghribī zijes of Ibn Isḥāq's school, but sooner or later it obliged an increase in the value of the obliquity which disagreed with observations. Our author, therefore, decides to forget about the problem, accepts 23;30° — which he takes from Ibn Abī 'l-Shukr[29] — and recommends anybody who wants to determine the precise value of the obliquity to observe it using the *libna* (mural quadrant) described by Ptolemy in the *Almagest*.[30]

3. *The Introduction of Eastern Zijes in the Maghrib*

The situation described so far justifies the introduction of Eastern zijes in the Maghrib from the fourteenth century onwards. In them, mean motions were tropical, trepidation was substituted by constant precession and there were no tables to compute the obliquity of the ecliptic. This implied a complete change of mentality: a change which had already taken place in the Iberian Peninsula towards the end of the thirteenth century, with the Latin version of the Alfonsine Tables, in which the influence of al-Battānī was predominant. As for the Eastern zijes which became known in the Maghrib, one should underline the role played by those of Ibn Abī 'l-Shukr — frequently mentioned because of his estimation of the precession of the equinoxes — Ibn al-Shāṭir and Ulugh Beg.

Ibn Abī 'l-Shukr al-Maghribī (d. 1283) is the author of at least two zijes of which only one, the *Tāj al-azyāj*, seems to have been known in the Maghrib. I know of two manuscripts of this zij, and both were written in Maghribī script. The first is Escorial ar. 932 in which, at the end of the canons (f. 57v), we find a note stating that the author compiled this zij in Damascus in 656/1258[31] and that the copy was made in Tunis by Muẓaffar b. ᶜAbd Allāh, for his own use, in 797/1394, under the supervision of ᶜAbd al-ᶜAzīz b. Masᶜūd b. ᶜAbd al-ᶜAzīz al-Tilimsānī al-Mālikī, who had been *imām* and *muwaqqit* in the cities of Fez, Tunis, Jerusalem and Damascus.[32] This note gives information about one of the channels through which the *Tāj al-azyāj* may have been introduced in the Maghrib, and the chronology (end of the fourteenth century) is in good agreement with the remark made by the anonymous author of the *Natā'ij al-afkār* that "in the time of the author [*mu'allif* = al-Jadarī (1375–1416)] this zij [the *Tāj*] was well known and it had been diffused through the rest of the countries of the Maghrib".[33]

The Escorial manuscript of the *Tāj* seems to have been used in Tunis and Cairo.[34] There is, however, a second manuscript of the *Tāj*, preserved in the Arabic Department of the University of Barcelona,[35] which has not been described until now. This bears witness to the diffusion in the Maghrib (Tilimsān and Marrākesh) of the *Tāj*, which was still in use in the nineteenth century. The copy is unfortunately not dated, but it contains a number of marginal notes, written in a script different from that of the copyist, which have a certain interest: the Syriac names of the months of the solar year need translation, and a marginal note in f. 4r states that *Tišrīn al-awwal* is *Uktūbar*, *Kānūn al-Awwal* is *Dujanbar* and *Kānūn al-Thānī* is *Yannayr*. The author of the notes also explains that the *Tāj* gives tropical positions calculated from the equinox (*al-mabda' al-ṭabīᶜī*), which are not the same as the sidereal ones, computed from the first point of Aries (*al-mabda' al-dhātī*) (f. 15r). The radices of mean motions are given for the beginning of the Hijra for Damascus and Tilimsān (written by the copyist of the manuscript himself) and notes written at the end of each page give the difference between the two mean positions. There are tables of oblique ascensions calculated for Damascus (latitude 33;20°) (ff. 90v–91v), but also for latitudes 35° (ff. 86v–87r) (Tilimsān), 30° (ff. 92r–93r) and 36° (ff. 93v–94v) (Tunis?): all of them use Ibn Abī 'l-Shukr's value for the obliquity of the ecliptic (23;30°). The length of daylight is also given for latitudes 33;20°, 30° and 36° (ff. 95r, 95v, 96r). Marginal notes also give radices for the Sun, the Moon (longitude and anomaly) and the lunar nodes for the end of 948/1542 in Tilimsān (ff. 49v, 50v, 51v, 52v), and for the solar apogee for year 1281/1864 (f. 50r). The manuscript includes tables of the solar and lunar velocity copied from Ibn al-Bannā's *Minhāj* and from the zij of al-ᶜAṭṭār (?) (f. 90 r). Finally, a note at the end of the canons, in a script different from that of the copyist and the author of most of the marginal notes, states that the manuscript was the property of the *muwaqqit* (*al-muqaddam ᶜalā 'l-tawqīt*) ᶜAbd Allāh al-Sanhājī al-Dādisī in Marrākesh.

Our information about the introduction in the Maghrib of the *Jadīd Zīj* of Ibn al-Shāṭir (*fl.* Damascus, d. 1375) is less precise, mainly because the sources available are undated and probably late. King said, some twenty years ago, that there is evidence that this zij was known in Tunis in the late fourteenth century,[36] and I have the impression that it was known in other parts of the Maghrib as well: we have seen that al-Baqqār (*fl.* 1418) quotes an obliquity of the ecliptic of 23;31° which he ascribes to an unnamed Damascus astronomer and that this same parameter is mentioned in relation with Ibn al-Shāṭir by the author of the *Natā'ij al-afkār* (*c.* 1514). We also know of the existence of a late recension of the *Jadīd Zīj* for Algiers.[37] This work seems to have circulated mainly through recensions and abridgements made by different authors such as those made by Shihāb al-Dīn Aḥmad b. Ghulām Allāh, called al-Kawm al-Rīshī (d. 1432) for the coordinates of Cairo,[38] or that made by Muḥammad b. ᶜAlī b. Ibrāhīm, called Ibn Zurayq al-Khayrī or al-Jīzī (d. 1400), in Damascus.[39] In other instances, Ibn al-Shāṭir's zij has been used for timekeeping: an anonymous author used them to compute conjunctions and oppositions of the Sun and the Moon for the meridian of Tetuan,[40] and, in 1214/1799 a certain Muḥammad b. al-Ṭayyib b. al-Makkī al-Ajbarī al-Ḥasanī wrote a treatise with two tables in which he explained how to determine the hours using the zijes of Ibn al-Shāṭir and Ulugh Begh: he states that his method is original and nobody has used it before him, because his starting point was the tropical longitude of the Sun (*mawḍiᶜ al-shams al-ṭabīᶜī*) (!).[41]

The last Eastern zij introduced in the Maghrib was Ulugh Begh's *Zīj-i Jadīd*

(1393–1449). I have no evidence that this zij was known in the Maghrib before the end of the seventeenth century, but it is obvious that it became very popular during the eighteenth and nineteenth centuries. The Arabic translation of the introduction to this zij, made by Ḥasan b. Muḥammad, known as Qāḍī Ḥasan al-Makkī (*fl.* seventeenth century), reached Morocco, for the Ḥasaniyya Library preserves a manuscript of this work dated 1291/1874.[42] Far more interesting is, however, the fact that there were at least two Tunisian recensions of this zij prepared by Muḥammad al-Sharīf, called Sanjaq Dār al-Tūnisī and by ᶜAbd Allāh Ḥusayn Qusᶜa al-Tūnisī.[43] Both authors are undated but I have been able to study superficially a manuscript of Sanjaq Dār's *Zīj al-Sharīf* (MS. 1816 of the National Library in Tunis[44]) in which the mean positions of the Sun, Moon and planets are given, in intervals of thirty years, between 1080/1669–70 and 1290/1873–74; in addition, the positions of the lunar mansions are given, according to the observations of Ulugh Begh, for the end of year 1090/1679–80 (f. 36r) and the day, hour and minute of the spring equinox is given for each year between 1090/1679 and 1205/1790. Another manuscript of the same work, also extant in Tunis,[45] is dated 1107/1695–96.[46] All this evidence points to a work produced in the late seventeenth century: commentaries on the introduction of this zij are preserved in Cairo manuscripts dated 1150/1737–38, 1163/1749–50, 1169/1755–56.[47]

Sanjaq Dār's zij is computed for longitude 41;45° and contains tables of oblique ascensions for a latitude of 36;50° (f. 28r), for the division of the houses for the same latitude (ff. 28v–31r), for half daylight for the same latitude (f. 33v), lunar longitude at sunset for latitude 36;40° (f. 35r), lunar parallax in longitude and latitude also for 36;40° (f. 36v), and ascendants of anniversaries for the same latitude (f. 45v): 36;50° is the modern value for the latitude of Tunis and it is not attested in any other historical source, while 36;40° is one of the three values for the latitude of Tunis given by al-Khwārizmī.[48] Apart from this, it is interesting to note that the prologue of the *Zīj al-Sharīf* states that he is going to follow the *ḥabṭaq* method, which means that planetary equations are determined in a more convenient way using double-argument tables. This type of table is documented in the East from the time of Ibn Yūnus (d. 1009),[49] but I do not know of any instance in which they appear in the Maghrib before the *Zīj al-Sharīf*, in spite of the fact that Ibn al-Kammād (*fl.* Cordova 1116) used double-argument tables for the computation of time from mean to true syzygy[50] and for the calculation of solar eclipses.[51] In these equation tables one enters the table vertically with the anomaly of the Moon or the planet (tabulated from 0° to 360° with 6° intervals) and horizontally with the *zodiacal sign* of the *markaz* (the mean longitude of the planet computed from the apogee): the total equation (centre + anomaly) will be read directly at the intersection of the two and is to be added to the mean longitude of the planet. In this part of the zij, the solar equation is standard, although displaced 1;56° (which is also the maximum value of the undisplaced equation) and computed for 6° intervals (f. 10r). The author adds to this a set of displaced equations of the centre for all the planets, also computed for 6° intervals (f. 19v). This simplified set of tables computes mean motions to the precision of minutes, but the zij also contains a second set of mean motion tables for the Sun (f. 23r) and the Moon (ff. 24v–25r), computed to the precision of thirds, as well as a second table of the (displaced) solar equation (f. 24r) computed for each degree of the argument and to the precision of thirds. There is also a set of lunar equations (ff. 25v–27r), computed to seconds, which is not standard and deserves study.

4. *Conclusions*

Some information has been gathered during the last few years on the existence in the Maghrib of a group of zijes of Andalusian descent, the influence of which seems to have been predominant during the thirteenth and fourteenth centuries. To this one may add that the analysis of a number of new sources made by Mercè Comes and myself shows that observations were made in the Maghrib during the same period and that the new evidence raised doubts in the belief in trepidation. The situation being thus, we find a new contact with the East which — at least in the case of al-Andalus — had been interrupted in the eleventh century. This brought the *Tāj al-azyāj* of Muḥyī al-Dīn al-Maghribī and the *al-Zīj al-Jadīd* of Ibn al-Shāṭir to the late fourteenth-century Maghrib. The third important zij, Ulugh Begh's *Zīj-i Jadīd*, does not seem to have reached the Maghrib until the end of the seventeenth century. These Eastern astronomical tables computed tropical longitudes, favoured constant precession and did not seek to predict the obliquity of the ecliptic for future times. As a result, the planetary positions computed with them were far more accurate than those one could obtain from the zijes of Ibn Isḥāq's school. In spite of this the Andalusian tradition stayed alive until the nineteenth century and coexisted with the "new" Eastern zijes. The reason is clearly explained by the astrologer al-Baqqār: horoscopes are cast using sidereal longitudes. My impression is that astrologers used Ibn al-Bannā's *Minhāj* and other similar sources, while astronomers and consciencious *muwaqqit*s preferred oriental zijes. I wonder, however, whether there were also astronomers who computed their horoscopes using tropical longitudes: the introduction of double-argument planetary equation tables in Sanjaq Dār's *Zīj al-Sharīf* seems to point in this direction.

Acknowledgements

This paper has been written within a research programme on "Astronomical tables and theory in al-Andalus and the Maghrib between the twelfth and fourteenth century", sponsored by the Dirección General de Investigación Científica y Técnica of the Spanish Ministry of Education and Culture. D. A. King has been, as usual, extremely generous in sending us microfilms and photographs of manuscripts. He has also corrected a previous draft of this paper. M. Comes has drawn my attention to many items of interest. My gratitude to them both.

REFERENCES

1. See e.g. David A. King, "An overview of the sources for the history of astronomy in the medieval Maghrib", *Deuxième Colloque Maghrébin sur l'Histoire des Mathématiques Arabes* (Tunis, 1988), 125–57. See also a recent survey of this manuscript in A. Mestres, "Maghribī astronomy in the 13th century: A description of manuscript Hyderabad Andra Pradesh State Library 298", in J. Casulleras and J. Samsó (eds), *From Baghdad to Barcelona: Studies in the Islamic exact sciences in honour of Prof. Juan Vernet* (Barcelona, 1996), i, 383–443.
2. The canons were edited by J. Vernet, *Contribución al estudio de la labor astronómica de Ibn al-Bannā'* (Tetuán, 1952). The solar tables were studied by J. Samsó and E. Millás, "Ibn al-Bannā', Ibn Isḥāq and Ibn al-Zarqālluh's solar theory" in J. Samsó, *Islamic astronomy and medieval Spain* (Aldershot, 1994), no. X (35 pp.). For the planetary tables see J. Samsó and E. Millás, "The computation of planetary longitudes in the *zīj* of Ibn al-Bannā'", forthcoming in *Arabic sciences and philosophy*.
3. E. S. Kennedy, "The astronomical tables of Ibn al-Raqqām, a scientist of Granada", *Zeitschrift für Geschichte der Arabisch-Islamischen Wissenschaften,* xi (1997), 35–72.
4. E. S. Kennedy and David A. King, "Indian astronomy in fourteenth century Fez: The versified Zīj of al-Qusunṭīnī", *Journal for the history of Arabic science*, vi (1982), 3–45, reprinted in D. A. King, *Islamic mathematical astronomy* (London, 1986), no. VIII (2nd rev. edn, Aldershot, 1993).
5. J. Samsó, "Andalusian astronomy in 14th century Fez: *al-Zīj al-Muwafiq* of Ibn ᶜAzzūz al-Qusanṭīnī", *Zeitschrift für Geschichte der Arabisch-Islamischen Wissenschaften*, xi (1997), 73–110.
6. See her paper "Some new Maghribī sources dealing with trepidation", presented at the XXth International Congress of History of Science (Liège, July 1997).
7. MS Escorial ar. 916, ff. 237v–264v. The significant passage on trepidation is in ff. 238r–242r. On this work see Juan Vernet, "Tradición e innovación en la ciencia medieval", *Oriente e occidente nel medioevo: Filosofia e scienze* (Rome, 1971), 741–57, reprinted in Vernet, *Estudios sobre historia de la ciencia medieval* (Barcelona-Bellaterra, 1979), 173–89 (see pp. 188–9). Two other manuscripts of the same work (not seen) in Rabat Ḥasaniyya 826 and 5372: see Muḥammad al-ᶜArabī al-Khaṭṭābī, *Fāhāris al-Khizāna al-Ḥasaniyya*, iii (Rabat, 1983), 430–1, nos 526 and 527.
8. See Kennedy and King, "Indian astronomy" (ref. 4), 9; King, "An overview" (ref. 1), 131–2 and 144.
9. David King was the first to draw attention to this work — see Kennedy and King, "Indian astronomy" (ref. 4), 9; King, "An overview" (ref. 1), 131–2 and 144 — which is extant in MSS Cairo K 4311 (ff. 2r–48r, copied in 1183/1769–70) and London British Library Or. 411 (ff. 21v–55r, copied in 1082/1670). He kindly provided photographs of these two manuscripts.
10. Mathematician and astronomer from Tlemcen who died in 867/1463: see H. Suter, *Die Mathematiker und Astronomen der Araber und ihre Werke* (Leipzig, 1900), no. 435, p. 177. See also D. A. King, *A survey of the scientific manuscripts in the Egyptian National Library* (Winona Lake, Indiana, 1986), 140, F28; and Driss Lamrabet, *Introduction à l'histoire des mathématiques maghrébines* (Rabat, 1994), 117, no. 445.
11. MS Cairo 4311, f. 36r; London, BL Or 411, f. 47v.
12. MS Cairo K4311, f. 5r. I have been unable to find this reference in the London MS.
13. J. M. Millás Vallicrosa, *Las tablas astronómicas del Rey Don Pedro el Ceremonioso* (Madrid and Barcelona, 1962); J. Chabás, "Astronomía andalusí en Cataluña: Las tablas de Barcelona", *From Baghdad to Barcelona* (ref. 1), i, 477–525.
14. Carl Brockelmann, *Geschichte der Arabischen Literatur* (2 vols, Leiden, 1943, 1949; 3 vols of supplements, Leiden, 1937, 1938 and 1942), Sii, 217; H. P. J. Renaud, "Additions et corrections à Suter", *Isis*, xviii (1932), 179–80 (no. 535); Lamrabet, *Introduction* (ref. 10), 144, no. 511.
15. King, *Survey* (ref. 10), 142, F43; King, *Fihris al-makhṭūṭāt al-ᶜilmiyya al-maḥfūẓa bi-Dār al-Kutub al-Miṣriyya*, i (Cairo, 1981), 352.
16. K7584, ff. 122v, 124r and v. The value 30;15° for the latitude of Tārudānt (modern value 30;31°)

does not appear in any source quoted by E. S. and M. H. Kennedy, *Geographical coordinates of localities from Islamic sources* (Frankfurt, 1987), 335. See also f. 139v.

17. I have not been able to identify him. The implication seems to be the famous Ibn Yūnus (d. 958–59), who was also called Abū 'l-Hasan ᶜAlī. D. A. King ("Ibn Yūnus", *Dictionary of scientific biography*, xiv, 574–80, p. 578) states that there are numerous later zijes compiled in Egypt, Persia and Yemen that use materials derived from Ibn Yūnus's *Ḥākimī Zīj*.
18. MS K7584, f. 119r.
19. MS K4311, f. 13r and v; MS BL Or 411, f. 27v. See also K4311, f. 15v and BL Or, ff. 28v–29r.
20. MS K4311, f. 13r calls him Ibn Shāhir; MS BL Or 411, f. 27v has Ibn Shāṭir. Ibn al-Shāṭir uses an obliquity of 23;31° in his *al-Zīj al-Jadīd*: *cf.* E. S. Kennedy, "A survey of Islamic astronomical tables", *Transactions of the American Philosophical Society*, n.s., xlvi (1956), 123–75, see p. 163.
21. MS K4311, f. 13r calls him Abū ᶜAbd Allah al-Raqqām b. Abū 'l-ᶜAbbās Aḥmad known as al-Mazzān; MS BL Or 411, f. 27v has Abū ᶜAbd Allāh Muḥammad b. Abū 'l-ᶜAbbas Aḥmad known as al-Mizzī. See Suter, *Mathematiker* (ref. 10), no. 406, p. 165; King, *Survey* (ref. 10), 63–64, C34.
22. Mestres, "Maghribī astronomy" (ref. 1), 418, Table 54. Ibn al-Muftī, the author of the *Qaṭf*, claims that Ibn Isḥāq obtained 23;33° through observation and that Ibn al-Banna' also used this parameter in the *Minhāj*: K7584, f. 120r.
23. M. Comes, "A propos de l'influence d'al-Zarqālluh en Afrique du Nord: L'apogée solaire et l'obliquité de l'écliptique dans le *zīdj* d'Ibn Isḥāq", *Actas del II Coloquio Hispano-Marroquí de Ciencias Históricas* (Madrid, 1992), 147–59.
24. On Sanjūfīnī's zij see E. S. Kennedy, "Eclipse predictions in Arabic astronomical tables prepared for the Mongol Viceroy of Tibet", *Zeitschrift für Geschichte der Arabisch-Islamischen Wissenschaften*, iv (1987–88), 60–88; E. S. Kennedy and J. P. Hogendijk, "Two tables from an Arabic astronomical handbook for the Mongol Viceroy of Tibet", *A scientific humanist: Studies in memory of Abraham Sachs* (Philadelphia, 1988), 233–4.
25. Identified by King ("An overview" (ref. 1), 131–2) with Abū ᶜAbd Allāh Muḥammad ibn Hilāl who lived in Ceuta in the first half of the fourteenth century. See also Lamrabet, *Introduction* (ref. 10), 98, no. 393.
26. This value for the latitude of Marrakesh is not to be found in any of the sources quoted by Kennedy and Kennedy, *Geographical coordinates* (ref. 16), 218. The modern value is 31;49°.
27. B. R. Goldstein, "On the theory of trepidation according to Thābit b. Qurra and al-Zarqāllu and its implications for homocentric planetary theory", *Centaurus*, x (1964), 232–47; J. Samsó, "Sobre el modelo de Azarquiel para determinar la oblicuidad de la eclíptica" in Samsó, *Islamic astronomy* (ref. 2), no. IX.
28. See Mercè Comes, "The accession and recession theory in al-Andalus and the north of Africa", *From Baghdad to Barcelona* (ref. 1), i, 349–64.
29. 23;30° is also used by Ibn al-Muftī, the author of the *Qaṭf*: K7584, f. 119v and 120r. Al-Baqqār, in his *Kitāb al-adwār* (f. 241r) mentions 23;30° (Ibn Abī 'l-Shukr) and 23;31°, which he attributes to one of the unnamed zijes made in Damascus (probably Ibn al-Shaṭir).
30. *Almagest* I,12. See G. J. Toomer, *Ptolemy's Almagest* (New York, 1984), 62–63.
31. According to the *Natā'ij al-afkār*, this zij is based on the observations made by this astronomer in Damascus in 657/1259 (Cairo K 4311, f. 4v). This date agrees with the statement we find in the text of the canons of the *Tāj* (MS Escorial 932, f. 22r–22v; MS Ar. Dept. of the University of Barcelona — on which see below — ff. 15v–16r): the star table is calculated for the first year of the reign of Hulāwūn (= Hulagu) which is 627 Yazdijird/ 1259. See G. Saliba, "An observational notebook of a thirteenth-century astronomer", *Isis*, lxxiv (1983), 388–401 (reprinted in Saliba, *A history of Arabic astronomy: Planetary theories during the golden age of Islam* (New York and London, 1994)). On p. 167 of the reprint Saliba conjectures that Ibn Abī 'l-Shukr served the Ayyubid ruler al-Malik al-Nāṣir of Damascus (1250–60) till at least 1257.
32. This is the author of the *Risalat al-Sayb fī ᶜamal al-jayb*, extant in MS Escorial ar. 918: see King,

Survey (ref. 10), 66, no. C46. The original work was written in Cairo in 795/1393 and contains a precession table copied from the *Tāj* (f. 91r). The *risāla* is the subject of a doctoral dissertation by Maravillas Aguiar, La Laguna, 1996: see "Las aplicaciones del cuadrante de senos en agrimensura a través de un tratado árabe oriental del siglo XIV", in C. Alvarez de Morales (ed.), *Ciencias de la naturaleza en al-Andalus: Textos y estudios*, iv (Granada, 1996), 93–113.

33. Cairo K 4311, f. 4v.
34. The mean motion tables have their *uṣūl* calculated for the beginning of the Hijra in Damascus but, in the case of the Sun, two interlinear notes give the *aṣl* for Tunis (f. 71v) and Cairo (f. 80v).
35. It was probably bought in Morocco by the late Professor J. M. Millás Vallicrosa. The manuscript has no title and does not mention the name of the author: it was identified by Dr M. Comes.
36. D. A. King, "Ibn al-Shāṭir", *Dictionary of scientific biography*, xii, 357–64, p. 362b.
37. King, "An overview" (ref. 1), 133. The recension for Algiers is extant in MS Cairo DM 533 (*c.* 1150/1737): see King, *Survey* (ref. 10), 62, no. C30, and 145, no. F66.
38. See King, *Survey* (ref. 10), 65, no. C41. This work, entitled *Kitāb al-Lumᶜa fī ḥall al-sabᶜa*, is extant in an undated Maghribī manuscript of the library of the late scholar Ḥasan Ḥusnī ᶜAbd al-Wahhāb, now in the National Library in Tunis: ᶜAbd al-Ḥafīẓ Manṣūr, *al-Fihris al-ᶜāmm li 'l-makhṭūṭāt. I. Raṣīd maktabat Ḥasan Ḥusnī ᶜAbd al-Wahhab* (Tunis, 1975), MS 18158 (pp. 393, 398). The Ḥasaniyya Library in Rabat possesses an undated Maghribī manuscript entitled *Nuzhat al-khāṭir fī talkhīs Zīj Ibn al-Shāṭir* (MS 2723) which Khaṭṭābī (*Fāhāris* (ref. 7), 382–3, no. 467) also attributes to al-Kawm al-Rīshī.
39. *al-Rawḍ al-ᶜĀtir fī Talkhīṣ Zīj Ibn al-Šāṭir*. On this author see Suter, *Mathematiker* (ref. 10), 173, no. 426; Brockelmann, *op. cit.* (ref. 14), ii, 157. This work seems to have been quite popular in the Maghrib but the dated MSS were copied in the nineteenth century: see, for example, Rabat General Library 1347D; Rabat Ḥasaniyya 1576, dated in 1255/1839 (Khaṭṭābī, *Fāhāris* (ref. 7), 273–6, no. 334); Rabat Ḥasaniyya 6292, undated (Khaṭṭābī, *Fāhāris*, 276–7, no. 335); Rabat Ḥasaniyya 5366, dated in 1265/1848 (Khaṭṭābī, *Fāhāris*, 277, no. 336); Rabat Ḥasaniyya 2802, dated in 1262/1845 (Khaṭṭābī, *Fāhāris*, 277–8, no. 337). Another Maghribī copy in Cairo TR 235,1 (King, *Survey* (ref. 10), 87, C116).
40. Rabat Ḥasaniyya 981, undated (Khaṭṭābī, *Fāhāris* (ref. 7), 167, no. 195).
41. Rabat Ḥasaniyya 8873, dated in 1214/1799 (Khaṭṭābī, *Fāhāris* (ref. 7), 223–4, no. 261). Other tabular materials derived from Ibn Abī 'l-Shukr, Ibn al-Shaṭir and other authors can be found in an anonymous and undated compilation extant in Rabat Ḥasaniyya 1433 (Khaṭṭābī, *Fāhāris*, 407–8, no. 496).
42. Khaṭṭābī, *Fāhāris* (ref. 7), 193–5, no. 227; see also King, *Survey* (ref. 10), 164, G99.
43. MS Cairo DM814 is a copy of this recension dated in 1325/1907–8: *cf.* King, *Survey* (ref. 10), 142, F46. A third (?), anonymous, Tunisian recension is preserved in two MSS of the Ḥasaniyya Library in Rabat: 2650 (undated) and 2148 (dated 1218/1803). See Khaṭṭābī, *Fāhāris* (ref. 7), 335–8, nos. 406–8.
44. Copy dated 1242/1826. Mercè Comes obtained a microfilm of this manuscript and drew my attention to it.
45. MS 18104 of the library of Ḥasan Ḥusnī ᶜAbd al-Wahhab: ᶜA.H. Manṣūr, *Fihris* (ref. 38), 398.
46. See also King, *Survey* (ref. 10), 143, F53; King also lists other manuscripts of the same work.
47. King, *Survey* (ref. 10), 143–4, F53, F54, F55. One of these commentaries, by Aḥmad b. Muḥammad Bū Daydaḥ al-Qādirī al-Qayrawānī, is also extant in Tunis, Ḥ. Ḥ. ᶜAbd al-Wahhāb Collection, no. 18104, dated 1301/1883–84: see ᶜA. H. Manṣūr, *Fihris* (ref. 38), 397.
48. Kennedy and Kennedy, *Geographical coordinates* (ref. 16), 362–3.
49. D. A. King, "A double argument table for the lunar equation attributed to Ibn Yūnus", *Centaurus*, xviii (1974), 129–46, reprinted in King, *Islamic mathematical astronomy* (ref. 4), no. V.
50. See a similar table in the *Zīj al-Sharīf*, f. 31v.
51. J. Chabás and B. R. Goldstein, "Andalusian astronomy: *al-Zīj al-Muqtabis* of Ibn al-Kammād", *Archive for history of exact sciences*, xlviii (1994), 1–41 (see pp. 14 and 23).

XII

Astronomical Observations in the Maghrib in the Fourteenth and Fifteenth Centuries

Argument

An Andalusian tradition of *zījes* seems to have been predominant in the Maghrib due to the popularity of the *zīj* of Ibn Isḥāq al-Tūnisī (fl. Tunis and Marrakesh *ca.* 1193–1222) and derived texts compiled in the fourteenth century. This tradition computed sidereal planetary longitudes and allowed the calculation of tropical longitudes by using trepidation tables based on models designed in al-Andalus by Abū Isḥāq ibn al-Zarqālluh (d. 1100). This tradition also used Ibn al-Zarqālluh's model to calculate the obliquity of the ecliptic, which implied that this angle had a cyclical period of oscillation between a maximum of 23;53° and a minimum of 23;33°: after reaching this minimum value the obliquity of the ecliptic was bound to increase. This paper argues that some new Maghribi sources give information on observations made in the Maghrib in the fourteenth and beginning of the fifteenth centuries that imply that precession had increased beyond the limits allowed by the Zarqāllian trepidation theory, while the obliquity of the ecliptic had diminished below the level accepted by astronomers who followed Ibn al-Zarqālluh. This explains the introduction in the Maghrib of Eastern *zījes*, which computed directly tropical longitudes and did not accept the cyclical variation of the obliquity. Information about observations of dawn and twilight made both in Egypt and in the Maghrib in the fourteenth and fifteenth centuries is also presented.

1. Introduction

The first important Maghribī astronomical document now extant is the *zīj* of Ibn Isḥāq al-Tamīmī al-Tūnusī (fl. Tunis and Marrakesh *ca.* 1193–1222), which the author seems to have left unfinished. Several recensions were made of this work towards the end of the thirteenth and beginning of the fourteenth century: Ibn al-Bannā' of Marrakesh (1256–1321) wrote his *Minhāj al-ṭālib fī-taʿdīl al-kawākib*,[1] and Muḥammad ibn al-Raqqām (d. 1315) prepared at least two "editions" of Ibn Isḥāq's

[1] The canons were edited by Vernet (1952); see Samsó and Millás 1994 and Samsó and Millás 1998, 259–286.

zīj entitled *al-Zīj al-shāmil fī tahdhīb al-kāmil* and *al-Zīj al-qawīm fī funūn al-taʿdīl wa-l-taqwīm.*[2] A third *zīj* of Ibn al-Raqqām is also extant in MS Rabat General Library 2461, pp. 153–289, and in a MS of the Tunis National Library. An incomplete copy has been preserved in Cairo DM 718 (fols. 3v–4r): see King 1986a, 84 (C100), 138 (F22). The relation between the latter (*al-Zīj al-mustawfī*) and the *zīj* of Ibn Isḥāq has not yet been studied. The anonymous author of *Natāʾij al-afkār* (on which see below) mentions *al-Zīj al-mustawfī*: see MS Cairo K 4311 fol. 2r, 13r, 37v–38r and British Library Or 411 fols. 27v, 48v. A third collection of materials derived from Ibn Isḥāq's *zīj* has been preserved in manuscript Hyderabad Andra Pradesh State Library 298, discovered in 1978 by D. A. King. According to Ibn Khaldūn, Ibn Isḥāq compiled his tables based on observations made by a Sicilian Jew who is referred to in the Hyderabad manuscript as Ghiyām ibn Rujjār, who is probably William II, son of William I, son of Roger II, who reigned in Sicily between 1166 and 1189 A.D. and was the patron of the unnamed Jewish astronomer. The analysis of the extant materials made by Angel Mestres (see Mestres 1996) does not seem to confirm Ibn Khaldūn's information and Mestres suggests that the Jewish astronomer did not provide Ibn Isḥāq with the results of his observations, but rather with Andalusian astronomical literature.

Concerning Maghribī astronomical observations, we feel on more secure ground with the information provided by the *Muwāfiq Zīj* of Abū l-Qāsim ibn [al-Ḥajjāj] ʿAzzūz al-Qusanṭīnī (fl. Fez 1344, d. Constantina 755/1354) (Samsó 1997, Samsó 1999). The prologue of that *zīj* reminds us of the observations made in his time by Ibn Isḥāq. Most of his contemporaries have used his mean motion tables, but modern astronomers have observed with their own eyes the existence of disagreements and errors regarding the amounts calculated with the tables, which affected the times of the conjunctions of the superior planets, the velocity of the motion of Mars, and the stations and retrogradations of Venus and Mercury. Ibn ʿAzzūz himself established the existence of such disagreements when he used *tasyīr* techniques to calculate the time at which important events of the past should have taken place, like the battle of El Salado (30th October 1340). The calculated times did not correspond to historical fact and Ibn ʿAzzūz considered the tables in use to be responsible for the mistake. Therefore, in order to correct the divergence existent in the famous *zīj*, he based his correction on extremely careful and precise observations made in Fez with an armillary sphere *ca.* 1344. My own analysis of the mean motion tables of the *Muwāfiq Zīj* seems to confirm, up to a certain extent, the words of Ibn ʿAzzūz in his prologue: the mean motions of the apogees, Saturn, Jupiter and Mars (longitude), as well as Venus (anomaly) could be original, or the result of a small correction of the parameters used by Ibn Isḥāq.

[2] See Kennedy 1997. A partial edition and commentary of the *Shāmil Zīj* has been prepared by Muḥammad ʿAbd al-Raḥmān (Institute for the History of Arabic Science, Aleppo) as a doctoral dissertation (*Ḥisāb aṭwāl al-kawākib fī l-zīj al-shāmil fī tahdhīb al-kāmil li-ibn al-Raqqām*), University of Barcelona, September 1996; it also contains an analysis of the materials drawn from *al-Zīj al-qawīm*.

Ibn ʿAzzūz bears witness not only to observations made by himself but also to the fact that modern [Maghribī] astronomers have also established, by visual observation, the existence of disagreements between observed and calculated positions. Some more information of this kind has been gathered recently by Dr. Mercè Comes[3] and me through the analysis of several new sources dated between the fifteenth and the early seventeenth centuries.[4] The following pages are intended to briefly describe these sources and to report on the information they contain.

2. The Commentaries on al-Jādarī

One of the most popular Maghribī treatises on timekeeping is the *urjūza* (a poem written in *rajaz* meter) entitled *Rawḍat al-azhār fī ʿilm waqt al-layl wa-l-nahār* (The Flower Garden on Timekeeping by Night and Day) written in Fez in 794/1391–92 by Abū Zayd ʿAbd al-Raḥman b. Abī Ghālib Muḥammad, known as al-Jādarī (King 1986a, 139 no. F26). This work, extant in many manuscripts, has been the object of a certain number of commentaries, of which I have read the following:

1) An anonymous one, which bears the title of *Natāʾij al-afkār fī sharḥ rawḍat al-azhār* (Results of Thoughts towards an Explanation of the Flower Garden), is interesting because of the information it contains.[5] Its author seems to have worked in Tilimsān (Tlemcen) and two *anni praesenti*,[6] at least, are mentioned in the commentary: 919/ 1513–14 and 920/ 1514–15. On the other hand, our anonymous author seems to have been a disciple of al-Ḥabbāk,[7] whom he calls *mawlāya wa-sayyidī* (my lord).[8] Among the authorities he quotes we find Ibn Isḥāq, Ibn al-Bannāʾ, Ibn al-Raqqām and Ibn Qunfudh al-Qusanṭīnī (d. 810/1407–08),[9] and our anonymous author states that the *zījes* of Ibn al-Bannāʾ, Ibn al-Raqqām, and Ibn Qunfudh are the most popular in the Maghrib in his own time. To these he also adds other Eastern

[3] See her paper, "Some new Maghribi sources dealing with trepidation," presented at the Twentieth International Congress of History of Science (Liège, July 1997).

[4] A summary of such information has appeared in my paper, Samso 1998.

[5] D. A. King was the first to attract attention to this work: see Kennedy and King 1982, 9 (reprinted in King 1986, no. 8); King 1988, especially 131–132 and 144. This source is extant in MSS Cairo K 4311 (fols. 2r – 48r, copied in 1183/ 1769–70) and London British Library Or. 411 (fols. 21v – 55r, copied in 1082/1670). David King kindly provided me with photographs of these two manuscripts.

[6] See Cairo K 4311 fols. 5r, 9v – 10r, 41r; London BL Or. fol. 51v.

[7] Mathematician and astronomer from Tlemcen who died in 867/1463: see Suter 1900, 177, no. 435. See also King 1986a, 140, F28; and Lamrabet 1994, 117 no. 445.

[8] MS Cairo 4311 fol. 36r; London BL Or. 411 fol. 47v.

[9] Cairo K 4311, fols. 5r and 8v; London BL Or. 411, fol. 27v. He mentions a *zīj* written by this author with the title *Tashīl al-ʿamal wa ʾl-ʿibāra fī taʿdīl al-kawākib al-sayyāra* which appears in the catalogue of Ibn Qunfudh's own works under the title *Tashīl al-ʿibāra fī taʿdīl al-sayyāra* (according to Ibn Qunfudh it contained 40 *bābs* and 60 *faṣls*). It is, therefore, a different work from the mini-*zīj* entitled *Tashīl al-maṭālib fī taʿdīl al-kawākib* (*Taysīr al- maṭālib. . .* in Ibn Qunfudh's catalogue): see Lévi-Provençal 1921, 133–134 (edition of Ibn Qunfudh's catalogue) and King 1986a, 139, no. F25.

astronomers such as Yaḥyā b. abī Manṣūr (fl. *ca.* 830), the Banū Amājūr (fl. *ca.* 885–933) and al-Bīrūnī (973–1048) of whom he mentions only the *Kitāb al-tafhīm fī awā'il ṣinā'at al-tanjīm*,[10] which seems to have been quite popular in the Maghrib.[11] It is also extremely interesting to note that our anonymous author mentions the observations made in Barcelona by Abū Kursūm al-Yahūdī,[12] who should be identified with Jacob Corsuno (active in Barcelona between 1378 and 1380), the author of the final version of the *Tables of Barcelona* (Millás Vallicrosa 1962; Chabàs 1992; Chabàs 1996). To these sources one may add the *Tāj al-azyāj* of Yaḥyā b. abī 'l-Shukr al-Maghribī (d. 1283).

2) A second commentary is the *Qatf al-anwār min rawḍat al-azhār*, written by Abū Zayd 'Abd al-Raḥmān b. 'Umar b. Aḥmad al-Sūsī al-Jazūlī al-Bu'aqīlī, Ibn al-Muftī (d. 1611) (Brockelmann 1943–49, II, p. 217; H.P.J. Renaud 1932, 179–180 (no. 535); Lamrabet 1994, p. 144 (no. 511), extant in MS Cairo K7584 (112v–155r) (King 1986b, p. 142 (no. F43); King 1981, p. 352). The author lived in Marrakesh and both this city and Fez are mentioned in the text,[13] but Ibn al-Muftī's main interest was al-Sūs al-Aqṣā and, in particular, Tārūdānt, for which he gives a latitude of 30;15° and computes a table of oblique ascensions.[14] Among the authorities quoted we should name al-Battānī, al-Sabtī, Ibn Isḥāq, Ibn al-Raqqām (d. 1315, *al-Zīj al-qawīm*), Ibn al-Bannā' (d. 1321, *Minhāj*, *al-Qānūn*),[15] Ibn abī 'l-Shukr, and Ibn Ḥabbāk.

3) A third commentary appears anonymously in MS Cairo K7584 (78v–111r), dated 1257/1841 (King 1986a, p. 139, no. F26). A second manuscript is Maktaba

[10] MS. Cairo K 4311, fol. 6r – 6v; London, BL Or. 411, fol. 22v. The passage deals with the length of the tropical year and it gives the estimations of Ptolemy, Yaḥyā b. Abī Manṣūr (observation made with an armillary sphere, obtaining 365;14,26,46,36d), and the Banū Amājūr (365;14,21,28d). An otherwise unknown Abū 'l-Ḥasan 'Abd al-'Azīz b. Aḥmad made observations with the instrument built by Abū Ḥāmid al-Ṣāghānī (d. 990) in Baghdad and obtained the same results as the Banū Amājūr: according to the text, all this is explained by al-Bīrūnī in the *Tafhīm*.

The length of the tropical year calculated on the basis of the mean motion tables of the *Ma'mūnī Mumtaḥan zīj* (ms. Escorial 927; facsimile edit. Frankfurt, 1986, 25 = fol. 13r) is 365;14,27,12,13d. Kennedy 1956, 30–31 gives other lengths of the tropical year related to the *Mumtaḥan* observations, none of which coincides with the one attributed to Yaḥya b. Abī Manṣūr by our commentator. As for the Banū Amājūr one can deduce from the data provided by Ibn Yūnus (Caussin de Perceval, 1804, 136) two parameters for the tropical year: 365;14,32,46,38,4d and 365;14,32,45,37,9d).

As far as the instrument built by al-Ṣāghānī in Baghdad is concerned, I have been unable to find any reference to it in the *Tafhīm*. Al-Bīrūnī's *Taḥdīd nihāyāt al-amākin li-taṣḥīḥ masāfāt al-masākin*, edited by P. Bulgakov in *Majallat ma'had al-makhṭūṭāt al-'arabiyya* (p. 100), mentions a ring with a diameter of six spans built by al-Ṣāghānī in the west part of Baghdad with which he determined the obliquity of the ecliptic and the local latitude. A similar instrument (?) was used by the same astronomer to determine the length of the seasons (al-Bīrūnī 1954–56, II, 659).

[11] Four MSS of that work are extant in the Ḥasaniya Library in Rabat, for example: see al-Khaṭṭābī 1983, 168–171.

[12] Ms. Cairo K4311, fol. 5r. I have been unable to find this reference in the London MS.

[13] K7584, fol. 146v, for example. For Marrakesh see also fol. 122v.

[14] K7584, fols. 122v, 124r and v. The value 30;15° for the latitude of Tārūdānt (modern value 30;31°) does not appear in any source quoted by E. S. and M. H. Kennedy 1987, 335. See also fol. 139v.

[15] Lamrabet (1994, 83–84) mentions three astronomical works by Ibn al-Bannā with the word *Qānūn* in the title: *Qānūn fī fuṣūl al-sana wa ma taḥtawī 'alayhi*, *Qānūn fī tarḥīl al-shams*, *Qānūn fī ma'rifat al-awqāt bi 'l-ḥisāb*.

Ḥamzawiyya (Ayt ʿAyāche) 80 (pp. 228–334) in which we find the name of the author: Abū Zayd ʿAbd al-Raḥmān al-Jānāti, known as al-Nafāwī.[16] The work has no title but its author seems to be working in Fez (lat. 33;40°,[17] sometimes rounded to 34°) (K 7584, fol. 104r; Ḥamzawiyya 80, 312). He accepts a constant precession established by Ibn al-Rassām or Ibn al-Raqqām and al-Sabtī (see below) of 1°/66 years. I have found two different statements on the value of precession for his own time: in one of them, precession has increased by 6° between the time of al-Jādarī and his own time (K7584, fol. 105r; Ḥamzawiyya 80, 315–316), which takes us to the end of the eighteenth century; in the other, which seems more reliable, the absolute value of precession for his time is 13°, 3° more than at the time of al-Jādarī (K7584, fols. 82v–83r; Ḥamzawiyya 80, 245), which corresponds to the end of the sixteenth century. The authorities quoted are Ibn al-Haytham (K7584, fol. 86v; Ḥamzawiyya 80, 258), Ibn al-Raqqām (d. 1315) (K7584, fol. 104r; Ḥamzawiyya 80, 313), Ibn al-Bannā' (d. 1321) (K7584, fol. 92v; Ḥamzawiyya 80, 243 (*al-Qānūn al-kabīr*), 273, 275, 289), Ibn Qunfudh (d. 1407) (K7584, fol. 86v), al-Ḥabbāk (d. 1463) (K7584, fol. 86v, 87v; Ḥamzawiyya 80, 259), Abū ʿAbd Allāh al-Harawī (?) (K7584, fol. 86v; Ḥamzawiyya 80, p. 259), Ibn Jaydūr (?),[18] Muḥammad al-Sanūsī (d. 1490), the author of a commentary on al-Ḥabbāk's *risāla* [*Bughyat al-ṭullāb*] (K4584, fol. 82v; Ḥamzawiyya 80, p. 243. Suter 1900, p. 221 n. 88) and, in relation to the question of the lunar mansions, early Eastern philologists such as Muḥammad b. Kunāsa (d. 824), Ibn Qutayba (d. 889), Abū Ḥanīfa al-Dīnawarī (d. 895) and Abū Isḥāq al-Zajjāj (d. 923) (K7584, fols. 105v–106r; Ḥamzawiyya 80, 317–319).

3. On Trepidation Theory

The information provided by these commentaries, which bear witness to a certain amount of astronomical activity in the Maghrib in the thirteenth and fourteenth centuries, deals with the theory of trepidation and with the determination of dawn and twilight. Trepidation is a topic which the Maghrib inherited from Andalusian astronomy, in which a fairly common belief is that its value was 0° in 581 AD, at the time of the birth of the Prophet,[19] a point that relates this theory to astrological historical cycles. We can add to this that al-Nafāwī's commentary states that the movable first point of Aries and the equinoctial point were together at the moment

[16] This author has been mentioned, though not identified, by Renaud 1934, 94. Renaud reads al-Nafarī and he is followed by Brockelmann 1943–49, II, 218. See also M. al-Mānūnī 1963.

[17] K.7584 fol. 97v; Ḥamzawiyya 80, p. 290. 33;40° for the latitude of Fez seems to derive from Ibn abī 'l-Shukr al-Maghribī: see Kennedy 1987, 117–118.

[18] K7584, fol. 87v; Ḥamzawiyya 80, 258. I presume that it is Ibn Haydūr al-Tādilī al-Fāsī (d. 1413): Lamrabet 1994, 110–113, no. 429.

[19] According to the *Brahmasphutasiddhanta* the sidereal and tropical longitudes of the Sun were equal in 580 AD. See J. Samsó, "Trepidation in al-Andalus in the eleventh century," in Samsó 1994, no. 8, 22; and also Samsó 1997, 107–110.

of Creation (K7584, fol. 83r.; Ḥamzawiyya 80, 245). Far more rich in information is the *Natāʿij al-afkār* which starts its treatment of the topic stating that al-Jādarī considers that the amount of precession for his time (1391–92) is 10°: the source of this value is the *zīj* of Ibn Isḥāq which (like those of Ibn al-Bannā', Ibn al-Raqqām and Ibn Qunfudh) contains a table which gives 10;24° as the maximum value of precession.[20] The author of the *Natā'ij* also adds that, according to the observations made by Ibn abī 'l-Shukr al-Maghribī in Damascus in 1259, precession at the end of the fourteenth century should be about 12°, or slightly more. After Ibn abī 'l-Shukr, a certain Abū 'l-Ḥasan ʿAlī b. Yūnus al-Balansī al-Ḥākimī (!) made observations in Cairo in 732/1331 and obtained that the amount of precession for that date was approximately 13°.[21] As a conclusion, the *Natā'ij* states that the estimations of the *iqbāl* (accession) are not correct,[22] and there are disagreements between computation and observation when one tries to establish the meridian altitude of the Sun and other celestial bodies. There must exist another motion to be added to accession and recession, although it is difficult to be more precise. This is why our commentator, following Ibn abī 'l-Shukr, states that precession for his time is 13;40° and that, using this amount, he obtains a good agreement with observation, as it happens with the table of solar tropical longitudes he has calculated for each day of the solar year using Ibn abī 'l-Shukr's tables.[23] Another passage in the commentary (K4311, fol. 40r; London BL Or 411, fols. 50 r and v) gives well known information on constant precession (1°/100 years according to Ptolemy, 1°/ 80 years according to the ancient Babylonians,[24] 1°/62 years according to al-Battānī and 1°/72 Persian years, which is the value used by Ibn abī 'l-Shukr). To this he adds another estimation by Abū ʿAbd al-ʿAzīz al-Rassām[25] (?) and al-Sabtī,[26] namely, 1°/66 years,[27] which is the amount accepted by al-Jādarī, while our commentator prefers Ibn abī 'l-Shukr's parameter.

[20] On the origin of this parameter see Samsó and Millás, "Ibn al-Bannā, Ibn Isḥāq and Ibn al-Zarqālluh's Solar Theory", reprinted in Samsó 1994, 10, 12–15. 10;24° is also attributed to Ibn Isḥāq and Ibn al-Bannā by Ibn al-Muftī: see K7584, fol. 119r.

[21] I have not been able to identify him. There seems to be some confusion here with the famous Ibn Yūnus (d. 958–59), who was also called Abu 'l-Ḥasan ʿAlī. D.A. King (1976, 578) states that there are numerous later *zījes* compiled in Egypt, Persia, and Yemen that use materials derived from Ibn Yunus' *al-Zīj al-ḥākimī*.

[22] Similar critical remarks can be found in the *Qaṭf al-'anwār*: precession in the time of al-Jādarī was 12° but the difference was, perhaps, not perceptible to that author. When the *Qaṭf* was written (ca. end of the sixteenth century?) precession reached 13° and some astronomers claimed that it was 14°: cf. K7584, fol. 119r.

[23] The remarks on the problem of precession can be found in ms. Cairo K4311, fols. 4v–5v. The solar table is extant in ms. BL Or. 411, fol. 24v.

[24] 1°/100 years and 1°/80 years are values quoted, without attribution, by Ibn al-Muftī in the *Qaṭf*: K7584, fol. 149r.

[25] According to K4311, fol. 40r; London BL Or 411, fol. 50r has ʿAbd Allāh b. al-Raqqām. K7584 (fol. 104r) also has ʿAbd Allāh Muḥammad b. Abī Yaʿqūb Ibrāhīm al-Raqqām, author of *al-Zīj al-mustawfī*.

[26] A certain al-Sabtī appears as the author of tables reproduced in ms. Hyderabad 298 of the *zīj* of Ibn Isḥaq: see Mestres 1996, 383 n. 3. A reference to al-Sabtī, also in relation to this value of precession appears in K7584, fol. 104r.

[27] Mentioned, without attribution, by Ibn al-Muftī in the *Qaṭf*: K7584, fol.149r.

A second source containing interesting information on trepidation theory is the *Kitāb al-Adwār fi tasyīr al-anwār*, written by Abū ʿAbd Allāh al-Baqqār in 821/1418.[28] This author begins by explaining the history of trepidation theory, emphasizing the prominent role played by Abū Isḥāq al-Zarqāllūh (d. 1100), who appears to be the first to treat trepidation theory mathematically. According to al-Baqqār, the maximum value of trepidation according to Ibn al-Zarqāllūh was 10°, a parameter close to that found in Ibn al-Zarqāllūh's two first models of trepidation[29] and it was Abū 'l-ʿAbbās b. Isḥāq who increased this value slightly by a few minutes.[30] Al-Baqqār has computed the value of trepidation for his own time (821/1418) and obtained 10° minus a few minutes with Ibn al-Zarqāllūh's tables, and 10;10° with Ibn Isḥāq's *zīj*. If this amount is added to the sidereal longitudes of the Sun and the planets, computed with the tables of Ibn Isḥāq, the results will be their tropical longitudes. According to al-Baqqār, one should not do this in the case of Venus, in which, he maintains, there seems to be an error in the motion in anomaly of the planet in the tables of Ibn Isḥāq and his followers, as al-Baqqār has shown in his *Maqālāt iṣlāḥ kawkab al-Zuhra*. For Venus, one should calculate directly its tropical longitude with al-Battānī's *zīj*. If one checks, then, these longitudes by observing the meridian altitudes of the Sun and the planets with an astrolabe, a quadrant of a circle, a solar quadrant or a large instrument for observation, it is easy to detect the presence of an error in the longitude of the celestial body, which is particularly noticeable when the Sun or the celestial body is near the equinoxes, and not so when its longitude is near one of the two solstices. The difference, in the case of the Sun, amounts to 2°, as has been established in observations made in Fez, after a careful determination of the latitude of the city. Precession, for 1418, should be 12°; this raises doubts about trepidation theory and, obviously, one should either add a second motion to trepidation or calculate trepidation tables with a maximum higher than 12°.

Al-Baqqār continues his exposition with a harsh criticism of Ibn al-Raqqām's rather careless treatment of the problem of trepidation. Ibn al-Raqqām's *zījes* include a table of tropical longitudes of the fixed stars for the end of year 680 H/1281–82.[31] Our author calculated the value of trepidation for that year, using Ibn al-Raqqām's own tables (maximum 10;24° like Ibn Isḥāq and Ibn al-Bannā') and obtained 9;26°.

[28] MS Escorial ar. 916, fols. 237v–264v. The significant passage on trepidation is in fol. 238r – 242r. On this work see Vernet 1971, reprinted in Vernet 1979, 173–189 (see 188–189). Two other manuscripts of the same work (not seen) in Rabat Ḥasaniyya 826 and 5372: see Khaṭṭābī 1983, 430–431 (nos. 526 and 527).

[29] J. Samsó, "Trepidation in al-Andalus in the 11th century," in Samsó 1994, no. 8.

[30] Actually Ibn Isḥāq, followed by Ibn al-Bannā' and by Ibn al-Raqqām, uses a maximum trepidation of 10;24°, a parameter which is implicit in Ibn al-Zarqālluh's third model: see Samsó & Millás, "Ibn al-Bannā, Ibn Isḥāq and Ibn al-Zarqālluh's Solar Theory" in Samsó 1994, no 10, 12–15.

[31] As a matter of fact, I have only been able to find this table in Ibn al-Raqqām's *Qawīm Zīj* (Ms. Rabat General Library 260, 100–103) where it is said that the positions of the stars were "observed" (*marṣūda*) in that year. D. A. King drew my attention to the fact that al-Marrakushi's *al-Mabādiʾ wa 'l-ghāyāt* also contains a table of the right ascensions of 210 stars for year 680 H/ 1281–82. See J. J. and L. A. Sédillot 1984, 276–284.

Then he has subtracted that amount from the tropical longitude of Regulus in Ibn al-Raqqām's star table (19;16°), the difference being 9;50° which should be the sidereal longitude of Regulus (*al-mawḍiʿ al-dhātī*), while the sidereal star tables established by the ancients (*al-qudamāʾ*) give Regulus a longitude of 9;8° or 9;18°.[32] This implies that the value of precession for 680/1281–82 should be 10;8° (= 19;16°–9;8°), which is the amount one gets – using *zījes* derived from the "observations" of Ibn Isḥāq – for year 819/1416–17. Al-Baqqār studied the horoscope cast by Ibn al-Raqqām for the birth of his son in 685/1286–87 and saw that the value of trepidation used was 10°.

Al-Baqqār also saw *zījes* computed by Eastern astronomers who made observations in Damascus and who disagreed with the theory of trepidation; he was able to determine that the mean longitudes of the Sun for the end of year 810/1407–08 exceed the solar mean sidereal positions calculated according to the "observations" of Ibn Isḥāq by 12;15,6°. One of these *zījes* is the *Tāj al-azyāj* of Ibn abī ʾl-Shukr al-Andalusī, who lived in Damascus at the time of the compilation of that *zīj*, whose mean solar positions for 810/1407–08 exceed those of Ibn Isḥāq by 12;16,45°. All this agrees with Ibn abī ʾl-Shukr's tables of constant precession, from which al-Baqqār gave several numerical values. These values of precession calculated with these Eastern *zījes* were obviously of interest to Ibn al-Baqqār, for they agreed perfectly with his own estimations, based on observations of meridian altitudes of the Sun and other celestial bodies, and our author had grave doubts about the truth of trepidation theory. Nonetheless, he continued using the sidereal tables of the Ibn al-Zarqāllūh-Ibn Isḥāq tradition because he needed them for astrological and magical purposes, but he added 12° to the sidereal positions when an astronomical problem was involved.

Trepidation is obviously related to the secular decrease in the obliquity of the ecliptic.[33] The *Natāʾij al-afkār* mentions the standard values of the obliquity established by Ptolemy (23;51°); the author of the *Mumtaḥan* (23;33°) (the same value was used by Ibn al-Bannā' and Ibn al-Raqqām), al-Battānī (23;35°) (also adopted by ʿAbd al-ʿAzīz al-Rassām (?) and by Ibn Qunfudh). Far more interesting is the fact that the author quotes an obliquity of 23;31° used by Ibn al-Shāṭir (fl. Damascus *ca.* 1350)[34]

[32] Ibn al-Bannā' has 9;8° in his *Minhāj*: see J. Vernet 1952, 108.

[33] K4311, fol. 13r and v; ms. BL Or 411, fol. 27v. See also K4311, fol. 15v and BL Or fols. 28v – 29r where the author reminds that according to Abū Jaʿfar b. Aḥmad, called al-Kammād al-Qurṭubī the motion of trepidation and the motion which produces the variation of the obliquity of the ecliptic are similar (*mutashābihatān*) because both are the result of the motion of the ecliptic. This similarity is denied by Abu ʾl-Ḥasan ʿAlī b. ʿAbd al-Ḥaqq al-Ghāfiqī [Ibn al-Hāʾlim] in his *Kitāb al-kāmil fī ʾl-taʿālīm*, who was followed in this respect by Ibn Isḥāq: see, on this question, J. Samsó 1992, 320–326. The author adds that 343 years have passed between the time of Ibn Isḥāq and his own time: if we accept 1514 as the approximate date of our commentary, this places Ibn Isḥāq in 1171, a date which seems slightly early.

[34] K4311, fol. 13r calls him Ibn Shāṭir; London BL Or 411, fol. 27v has Ibn Shāṭir. Ibn al-Shāṭir uses an obliquity of 23;31° in his *al-Zīj al-jadīd*: cf. Kennedy 1956, 41. 23;31° seems to have also been used by Ibn al-Shāṭir in his prayer tables: cf. King 1978, 79.

and by al-Mizzī (fl. Damascus, d. *ca.* 1350).[35] As for determinations made in the Maghrib, Ibn Isḥāq states that a man from Miknāsa (Meknès) observed the obliquity in 602/1205–06 and obtained 23;32,30°: this parameter is extremely interesting because it is the one used not only by Ibn Isḥāq himself (Mestres 1996, 418, table 54),[36] but also by the Alfonsine astronomers (the declination table calculated for this maximum in the *Libro del Relogio de la Piedra de la Sombra* seems to derive from the corresponding table of Ibn Isḥāq) (see Comes 1992) and by an astronomer of a very different milieu, al-Sanjūfīnī.[37] The same result was obtained by Ibn Hilāl[38] with his observations made in Ceuta. Another observation was made in 704/1304–05 in Marrakesh – the latitude of which is 31;45,23°[39] – by al-Ḥakīm al-Mirrīkh (?), who obtained 23;26,57°. Finally a certain Ibn al-Tarjumān said that the obliquity of the ecliptic, at the end of the seventh century H (699 H/ 1299–1300) is 23;26°. All this set of observations, made in the thirteenth century, have the obvious interest of invalidating the geometrical model designed, in the eleventh century, by Ibn al-Zarqāllūh, to calculate the value of the obliquity for a given date: in that model, the obliquity oscillated between 23;53° and 23;33°.[40] Ibn Isḥāq, who used an obliquity of 23;32,30°, was forced to change his limits and computed a new table, based on Ibn al-Zarqāllūh's model, in which the obliquity oscillated between 23;52,30° and 23;32,30° (see M. Comes 1992 and A. Mestres 1996, 413). Other adjustments must have been made, for our commentator states that some scientists have established that the obliquity of the ecliptic oscillated between 23;51° and 23;35°. In spite of these attempts to defend the existence of a period of oscillation at the end of which the obliquity would increase, astronomers obviously realized that, towards the beginning of the fourteenth century, the observed obliquity was below 23;30° and its downward trend showed no sign of stopping. Our author decides to ignore the problem, accepts 23;30° – which he takes from Ibn abī ʾl-Shukr[41] – and recommends anybody who wants to determine the precise value of ε to observe it using the *libna* (mural

[35] K4311, fol. 13r calls him Abū ʿAbd Allāh al-Raqqām b. Abī ʾl-ʿAbbās Aḥmad known as al-Mazzān; London BL or. 411, fol. 27v has Abū ʿAbd Allāh Muḥammad b. Abī 'l-ʿAbbās Aḥmad known as al-Mizzī. See Suter 1900, 165 (no. 406); King 1986a, 63–64 (C34). Al-Mizzī's prayer tables use an obliquity of 23;33°: cf. King 1978, 78.

[36] Ibn al-Muftī, the author of the *Qaṭf*, claims that Ibn Isḥāq obtained 23;33° through observation and that Ibn al-Bannāʾ also used this parameter in the *Minhāj*: see K7584, fol. 120r.

[37] On this *zīj* see Kennedy 1987–88; and Kennedy and Hogendijk 1988, 233–234.

[38] Identified by King (1988, 131–132) with Abū ʿAbd Allāh Muḥammad Ibn Hilāl who lived in Ceuta in the first half of the fourteenth century. See also Lamrabet 1994, 98, no. 393.

[39] This value for the latitude of Marrakesh is not to be found in any of the sources quoted by the Kennedys (1987, 218). The modern value for that latitude is 31;49°.

[40] See Goldstein 1964 and Samsó, "Sobre el modelo de Azarquiel para determinar la oblicuidad de la eclíptica," in Samsó 1994, no. 9.

[41] 23;30° is also used by Ibn al-Muftī, the author of the *Qaṭf*: K7584 fol. 119v. and 120r. Al-Baqqār, in his *Kitāb al-adwār* (fol. 241r) mentions 23;30° (Ibn abī ʾl-Shukr) and 23;31°, which he attributes to one of the unnamed *zīj*es made in Damascus (probably Ibn al-Shāṭir).

quadrant) described by Ptolemy in the *Almagest* (*Almagest* I, 12. See G.J. Toomer 1984, 62–63).

4. Dawn and Twilight

The third point of interest of the *Natāʾij* concerns the determination of the beginning of dawn (*fajr*) and the end of twilight (*shafaq*) (See Cairo K 4311 fol. 34v–37r; London BL Or. fol. 46r–48r. See also the commentary by al-Nafāwī in K7584, 102v–104r, and Ḥamzawiyya 80, 308–313). This phenomenon is due to vapors (*abkhira*) rising from the earth and this leads us to a possible source of that idea: the Andalusian astronomer Ibn Muʿādh al-Jayyānī (d. 1093) whose *Liber de crepusculis* (extant only in Latin and Hebrew versions) (see Goldstein 1977; Smith 1992; and Goldstein and Smith 1993) considers that dawn and dusk are caused by the reflection of sunlight on moist vapors that rise from the earth.[42] There are other points of coincidence, such as the fact that Ibn Muʿādh and the author of the *Natāʿij* distinguish the two phenomena by color: white for dawn and red for twilight. The *Natāʾij* remarks that astronomers do not agree on the precise moment that dawn begins or that twilight ends. A group of ancient astronomers (*ṭāʾifa min al-mutaqaddimīn*) considers that both phenomena take place when the Sun reaches a negative altitude of 18°, while some of the moderns (*al-mutaʾakhkhirūn*) ascribe 20° to dawn and 16° to twilight. Other modern authors made observations during several consecutive years and reached the conclusion that a depression of 18° corresponds to a phase of yellow color and 20° to a moment of darkness. They stated that the solar depression is variable and that it depends on atmospheric conditions such as the clarity of the atmosphere (*ṣafāʾ al-jaww*), the strength or weakness of the vapors, the thickness or thinness of the air, the presence or absence of the Moon, and the visual acuity of the observer. They also established that *fajr* corresponds to 19° and *shafaq* to 17°, but these parameters are only approximate[43] and it is difficult to be more precise. A certain Abū 'l-Qāsim b. ʿAbd Allāh b. ʿAbd al-Raḥmān Ḥasan al-Qurashī al-Ṣiqillī (?) says, in his book *al-Intiqaʾ min al-yawāqīt fī ʿilm al-mawāqīt*, that he made observations in Cairo and Alexandria and reached the conclusion that the solar depression is approximately 18° except when it is in Taurus, Gemini and Cancer, when it reaches 21°. Other authorities quoted by our commentator are ʿAbd al-ʿAzīz b. al-Rassām (?), already mentioned in relation to the obliquity of the ecliptic, who says, in his *Risāla ʿalā 'l-rubʿ al-mujayyab*, that some modern astronomers claim to have established by observation that the *naẓīr* of the

[42] The source could also be one of the parallel treatises written by Muʾayyad al-Dīn al-ʿUrḍī (d. 1266) and Quṭb al-Dīn al-Shīrāzī (d. 1311) but their similarities with our commentary are not so clear (see Saliba 1987).

[43] The *Qaṭf* (K7584, fol. 145v) quotes two parameters: 18° for both *fajr* and *shafaq*, and 17° (*shafaq*) and 19° (*fajr*). The same values appear in al-Nafawī's commentary: K7584, fol. 103r – 103v, and Ḥamzawiyya 80, 310.

degree of the Sun was 20° high at the beginning of the *fajr* and 19° high at the end of the *shafaq*: only God knows the truth but 20° seems to be better than 19° or 18°. Finally ʿAbd Allāh al-Ḥabbāk (d. 1463) uses 16° for the *shafaq* and 18° for the *fajr*, following, in this respect, the opinion of his teacher ʿAlī b. Qāsim al-Fakhkhār/al-Najjār.

5. Conclusions

The history of astronomy in the Maghrib is still to be written, but recent research proves the existence of a certain amount of astronomical activity during the thirteenth and fourteenth centuries. The starting point is the unfinished *zīj* of Ibn Isḥāq which has a clear Andalusian descent and is characterised by the use of mean motion tables for the computation of sidereal longitudes, a belief in trepidation and in the existence of cycles which regulate the decrease and the expected future increase of the obliquity of the ecliptic. There is no evidence that Ibn Isḥāq ever made astronomical observations, but other sources give information which show that other astronomers did observe in order to check the computed planetary positions obtained with Ibn Isḥāq's *zīj*. This is the case of Ibn ʿAzzūz al-Qusanṭīnī, who speaks about his own observations made in Fez *ca.* 1344 with an armillary sphere in order to correct Ibn Isḥāq 's mean motion tables. Al-Baqqār also talks, vaguely, about Fāsī observations – meridian altitudes of the Sun and other celestial bodies made with an astrolabe, a quadrant, or even a large-sized instrument – and of a careful determination of the latitude of the city. The information gathered on the determination of the beginning of dawn and the end of twilight is even less precise, although it seems clear that several attempts were made to observe the altitude of the *naẓīr* of the degree of the Sun at these two moments of the day and throughout the solar year: unfortunately, only one concrete reference is made to observations of this kind made in Cairo and Alexandria, and there is no clear evidence in the manuscripts I have read that similar observations were made in the Maghrib.

The sources are more positive about observations of the obliquity of the ecliptic: the distinctive 23;32,30° used by Ibn Isḥāq, Alfonso X and al-Sanjūfīnī seems to be the result (?) of an observation made in Meknes in 1205 and the values approximated to seconds for the latitude of Marrakesh (31;45,23°) and of the obliquity of the ecliptic (23;26,57°) – obtained one century later by a certain al-Ḥakīm al-Mirrīkh (?) – make me think of the possibility that a large instrument was used. This new evidence raises doubts about the belief in trepidation because, in spite of the adjustments in the parameters which we find in Maghribī *zījes* (see Comes 1996), the fact is that the observed precession of the equinoxes is much larger than the values which can be computed with trepidation tables, and the obliquity of the ecliptic stubbornly continues to fall below the limits fixed by tables of varying obliquity. The same kind of evidence led the Alfonsine astronomers to combine trepidation with constant precession and to forget entirely about tables for the computation of the obliquity of the ecliptic in the Latin version of the *Alfonsine Tables*: the former Castilian canons were far more traditional.

Acknowledgments

This paper has been written within a research program on "Astronomical tables and theory in al-Andalus and the Maghrib between the twelfth and fourteenth centuries," sponsored by the Dirección General de Investigación Cientifica y Técnica of the Spanish Ministry of Education and Culture. D.A. King has been, as usual, extremely generous in sending me microfilms and photographs of manuscripts. He has also corrected a previous draft of this paper. M. Comes has drawn my attention to many items of interest. My gratitude to them both.

References

Muḥammad ʿAbd al-Raḥmān. 1996. "Ḥisāb aṭwāl al-kawākib fī l-zīj al-shāmil fī tahdhīb al-kāmil li-ibn al-Raqqām". PhD dissertation, University of Barcelona.

Bīrūnī, al., abū al-Rayḥān. 1954–1956. *al-Qānūn al-masʿūdī.* Hyderabad.

Bīrūnī, al., abū al-Rayḥān. 1962. *Tahdīd nihāyāt al-amākin li-taṣḥīḥ masāfāt al-masākin.* In *Majallat maʿhad al-makhṭūṭāt al-ʿarabiyya*, edited by P. Bulgakov. Cairo 8.

Brockelman, Carl. 1943–49. *Geschichte der arabischen Litteratur.* 2 vols. plus 3 supplements, 2nd edition. Leiden: E. J. Brill.

Caussin de Perçeval, Jean Jacques Antoine. 1804. "Le livre de la grande Table Hakémite". *Notices et Extraits des Manuscrits de la Bibliothèque Nationale* vol. VII, an XII.

Chabàs i Bergon, Josep. 1992. *L'Astronomia de Jacob ben David Bonjorn.* Barcelona: Institut d'Estudis Catalans.

Chabàs i Bergon, Josep. 1996. "Astronomía andalusí en Cataluña: las Tablas de Barcelona". In Samsó and Casulleras 1996, vol. 1, 477–525.

Comes, Mercé. 1992. "A propos de l'influence d'al-Zarqāllūh en Afrique du Nord: l'apogée solaire et l'obliquité de l'écliptique dans le *zīdj* d'Ibn Isḥāq". In *Actas del II Coloquio Hispano-Marroquí de Ciencias Históricas*, 147–159. Madrid.

Comes, Mercé. 1996. "The Accession and Recession Theory in al-Andalus and the North of Africa". In Samsó and Casulleras 1996, vol. 1, 349–364.

Goldstein, Bernard R. 1964. "On the Theory of Trepidation according to Thābit b. Qurra and al-Zarqāllu and its Implications for Homocentric Planetary Theory". *Centaurus* 10:232–247.

Goldstein, Bernard R. 1977. "Ibn Muʿādh's Treatise on Twilight and the Height of the Atmosphere". *Archive for History of Exact Sciences* 17:97–118.

Goldstein, B. R. and A. Mark Smith. 1993. "The Medieval Hebrew and Italian Versions of Ibn Muʿādh's '*On Twilight and the Rising of Clouds*'". *Nuncius* 8:611–643.

Kennedy, Edward S. 1956. "A Survey of Islamic Astronomical Tables". *Transactions of the American Philosophical Society* 46–2:123–175.

Kennedy, Edward S. 1987–88. "Eclipse Predictions in Arabic Astronomical Tables Prepared for the Mongol Viceroy of Tibet". *Zeitschrift für Geschichte der Arabisch-Islamischen Wissenschaften* 4:60–88.

Kennedy, Edward S. 1997. "The Astronomical Tables of Ibn al-Raqqām, a Scientist of Granada". *Zeitschrift für Geschichte der Arabisch-Islamischen Wissenschaften* 11:35–72.

Kennedy E. S. and David A. King. 1982. "Indian Astronomy in Fourteenth Century Fez: the Versified *Zīj* of al-Qusunṭīnī." *Journal for the History of Arabic Science* 6:3–45.

Kennedy, E. S. and Mary Helen Kennedy. 1987. *Geographical Coordinates of Localities from Islamic Sources.* Frankfurt am Main: Institut für Geschichte der Arabisch-Islamischen Wissenschaften.

Kennedy, E. S. and Jan P. Hogendijk. 1988. "Two Tables from an Arabic Astronomical Handbook for the Mongol Viceroy of Tibet". *A Scientific Humanist. Studies in Memory of Abraham Sachs.* Edited by Erie Leichty et al., 233–242. Philadelphia: S. N. Kramer Fund.

Khaṭṭābī, Muḥammad al-ʿArabī al-. 1983. *Fahāris al-khizāna al-ḥasaniyya.* Vol. III. Rabat.

King, David A. 1976. "Ibn Yūnus". *Dictionary of Scientific Biography.* Vol. XIV, 574–580. New York: Scribners.

King, David A. 1978. "Astronomical Timekeeping in Fourteenth-Century Syria". In *Proceedings of the First International Symposium for the History of Arabic Science*, vol. 2, 75–84. Aleppo: Institute for the History of Arabic Science.

King, David A. 1981. *Fihris al-makhṭūṭāt al-ʿilmiyya al-maḥfūẓa bi-Dār al-kutub al-miṣriyya.* Vol. I. Cairo: General Egyptian Book Organization, in collaboration with the American Research Center in Egypt and the Smithsonian Institution.

King, David A. 1986a. *A Survey of the Scientific Manuscripts in the Egyptian National Library.* Winona Lake, Indiana: Eisenbrauns, Publications of the American Research Center in Egypt, 5.

King, David A. 1986b. *Islamic Mathematical Astronomy.* London: Variorum Reprints, London. Second revised edition by Variorum, Aldershot, 1993.

King, David A. 1988. "An Overview of the Sources for the History of Astronomy in the Medieval Maghrib". In *Deuxième Colloque Maghrébin sur l'Histoire des Mathématiques Arabes*, 125–157. Tunis: Université de Tunis – Institut Supérieur de Formation Continue – Association Tunisienne des Sciences Mathématiques.

Lamrabet, Driss. 1994. *Introduction à l'Histoire des Mathématiques Maghrébines.* Rabat: Imprimerie al-Maʿārif al-jadīda.

Lévi-Provençal, Evariste. 1921. *Les manuscrits arabes de Rabat (Bibliothèque générale du Protectorat Français au Maroc).* Paris.

Mānūnī, Muḥammad al-. 1963. "Maktabat al-zāwiya al-ḥamziyya. Ṣafḥa min tārikhiha". *Tiṭwān* 8:97–177.

Mestres, Angel. 1996. "Maghribī Astronomy in the 13th century: a Description of Manuscript Hyderabad Andra Pradesh State Library 298". In Samsó and Casulleras 1996, vol. 1, 383–443.

Millás Vallicrosa, J. M. 1962. *Las tablas astronómicas del Rey Don Pedro el Ceremonioso.* Madrid-Barcelona: Consejo Superior de Investigaciones Cientifices.

Renaud, H. P. J. 1932. "Additions et corrections à Suter". *Isis* 18:166–183.

Renaud, H. P. J. 1934. "Un prétendu catalogue de la bibliothèque de la grande mosquée de Fès, daté de 1268 Hég. (1851–1852 de J.C.)". *Hespéris* 18:76–99.

Saliba, George. 1987. "The Height of the Atmosphere According to Muʿayyad al-Dīn al-ʿUrḍī, Quṭb al-Dīn al-Shīrāzī and Ibn Muʿādh". In *From Deferent to Equant: a Volume of Studies in the History of Science in the Ancient and Medieval Near East in Honor of E. S. Kennedy*, edited by D.A. King and G. Saliba, 445–465. New York: New York Academy of Science.

Samsó, Julio. 1992. *Las Ciencias de los Antiguos en al-Andalus.* Madrid: Mapfre.

Samsó, Julio. 1994. *Islamic Astronomy and Medieval Spain.* Aldershot: Variorum.

Samsó, Julio. 1997. "Andalusian Astronomy in 14th Century Fez: *al-Zīj al-Muwāfiq* of Ibn ʿAzzūz al-Qusanṭīnī." *Zeitschrift für Geschichte der Arabisch-Islamischen Wissenschaften* 11:73–110.

Samsó, Julio. 1998. "An Outline of the History of Maghribī *Zīj*es from the End of the Thirteenth Century". *Journal for the History of Astronomy* 29,2:93–102.

Samsó, Julio. 1999. "Horoscopes and History: Ibn ʿAzzūz and his retrospective horoscopes related to the battle of El Salado (1340)." In *Between Demonstration and Imagination. Essays in the History of Science and Philosophy Presented to John D. North.* Edited by Lodi Nauta and Arjo Vanderjagt, 101–124. Leiden-Boston-Köln: Brill.

Samsó, J. and Casulleras J., eds. 1996. *From Baghdad to Barcelona. Studies in the Islamic Exact Sciences in Honour of Prof. Juan Vernet*, 2 vols. Barcelona: University of Barcelona.

Samsó J. and E. Millás. 1994. "Ibn al-Bannā', Ibn Isḥāq and Ibn al-Zarqālluh's Solar Theory". First published in Samsó 1994.

Samsó J. and E. Millás. 1998. "The Computation of Planetary Longitudes in the *Zīj* of Ibn al-Bannā'". *Arabic Sciences and Philosophy* 8:259–286.

Sédillot, J. J. and L. A. 1984. *Traité des instruments astronomiques des Arabes*, 2 vols. Reprint Frankfurt: Institut für Geschichte der Arabisch-Islamischen Wissenschaften.

Smith, A. Mark. 1992. "The Latin Version of Ibn Muʿādh's Treatise '*On Twilight and the Rising of Clouds*'". *Arabic Sciences and Philosophy* 2:83–132.

Suter, Heinrich. 1900. "Die Mathematiker und Astronomen der Araber und ihre Werke". *Abhandlungen zur Geschichte der mathematischen Wissenchaften, 10*, Leipzig. Reprint in Frankfurt: Institut für Geschichte der Arabisch-Islamischen Wissenschaften, 1986.

Toomer, Gerald J. 1984. *Ptolemy's Almagest*. New York: Springer-Verlag.

Vernet, Juan. 1952. *Contribución al estudio de la labor astronómica de Ibn al-Bannā'*. Tetuan: Editora Marroqui.

Vernet, Juan. 1971. "Tradición e innovación en la ciencia medieval". In *Oriente e Occidente nel Medioevo: Filosofia e* Scienze, 741–757. Roma: Accademia dei Lincei.

Vernet, Juan. 1979. *Estudios sobre Historia de la Ciencia Medieval*. Barcelona- Bellaterra.

XIII

On the Lunar Tables in Sanjaq Dār's *Zīj al-Sharīf*

1 Introductory Remarks

Nothing is known about the characteristics of the earliest known Maghribī *zīj*, Ibn Abī l-Rijāl al-Qayrawānī's *Ḥall al-ʿaqd wa-bayān al-raṣd* (beginning of the eleventh century), which seems to have been lost. Two centuries later, Abu'l-ʿAbbās Ibn Isḥāq al-Tamīmī al-Tunisī (fl. Tunis and Marrakesh ca. 1193–1222), left an unfinished set of tables which survive in a unique manuscript of Hyderabad, discovered in 1978 by D. A. King.[1] The predominant influence in Ibn Isḥāq's *zīj* was that of the Andalusian school represented by Ibn al-Zarqālluh (d. 1100), Ibn al-Kammād (fl. Cordova 1116–17) and Ibn al-Hāʾim (fl. 1205). This influence continued along the thirteenth and fourteenth centuries through several "editions" of the *zīj* of Ibn Isḥāq such as the one prepared by the anonymous compiler of the aforementioned collection extant in the Hyderabad manuscript (ca. 665 H./1266–680 H./1281), the *Minhāj* of Ibn al-Bannāʾ of Marrakesh (1256–1321),[2] and the two *zīj*es composed by the Tunisian-Andalusian astronomer Muḥammad ibn al-Raqqām (d. 1315).[3] Andalusian influence is also present in two other fourteenth century *zīj*es, written by two astronomers of Constantine, in the Central Maghrib, who were active in Fez: the one compiled by Abu'l-Ḥasan ʿAlī ibn Abī ʿAlī al-Qusanṭīnī, the canons of which were written in verse,[4] and the *Zīj al-Muwāfiq* of Abu'l-Qāsim ibn ʿAzzūz al-Qusanṭīnī (d. 1354),[5] partially based on observations made in Fez with an armillary sphere ca. 1344.

All the aforementioned *zīj*es share a certain number of characteristics among which we should mention that their mean motion tables are sidereal, and that they contain tables based on the theory of trepidation that enable the user to calculate the amount of precession for a given date and, thus, obtain the tropical longitudes of heavenly bodies. Trepidation implies a variation in the obliquity of the ecliptic and these *zīj*es also include tables, based on the model designed by Ibn al-Zarqālluh, which implies the existence of cycles that regulate the diminution and the expected future increase of the obliquity of the ecliptic. The analysis of a limited number of new sources dated between the fifteenth and the early seventeenth centuries (three commentaries on the poem on timekeeping written in 1391 by al-Jadhārī,[6] and the *Kitāb al-adwār fī tasyīr al-anwār*, written by Abū ʿAbd Allāh al-Baqqār in 821/1418)[7] give some evidence that observations were made in the Maghrib in the 13th and 14th centuries. The result of these observations was that astronomers realized that the observed precession of the equinoxes was much larger than the values that could be computed with trepidation tables and that the obliquity of the ecliptic stubbornly continued to diminish below the limits fixed in obliquity tables. The situation being thus, we find a new contact with the East which—at least in the case of al-Andalus—had been interrupted in the eleventh century. This brings to the Maghrib of the late fourteenth century the *Tāj al-azyāj* of Muḥyī al-Dīn al-Maghribī (d. 1283) and the *Zīj al-Jadīd* of Ibn al-Shāṭir (d.1375), and there is evidence of adaptations of these *zīj*es for their use in specific cities of the Maghrib. These *zīj*es compute directly tropical longitudes, are based on constant precession, reject the existence of cycles regulating the obliquity of the ecliptic and they offer results that agree with observations much better than those computed with the tables of the Andalusian school. In spite of this the Andalusian tradition stayed alive until the nineteenth century and coexisted with the "new" Eastern *zīj*es. The reason is clearly explained by the astrologer al-Baqqār: horoscopes were cast using sidereal longitudes and my impression is that astrologers used Ibn al-Bannā's *Minhāj* and other similar sources, while astronomers and conscienscious *muwaqqit*s prefered oriental *zīj*es.[8]

The last Eastern *zīj* which was introduced in the Maghrib was Ulugh Begh's *Zīj-i Sulṭānī* (1393–1449),[9] usually called *al-Zīj al-Jadīd* in Maghribī sources. I have no evidence that this *zīj* was known in the Maghrib before the end of the seventeenth century, but it is obvious that it became very popular during the eighteenth and nineteenth centuries. The Arabic translation of the introduction to this *zīj*, made by Ḥasan b. Muḥammad, known as Qāḍī Ḥasan al-Makkī (fl. 17th c.) reached Morocco, for the Ḥasaniyya Library preserves a manuscript of this work dated in 1291/1874.[10] Interestingly, however, there were, at least, two Tunisian recensions of this *zīj* prepared by Muḥammad al-Sharīf, called Sanjaq Dār al-Tūnisī and by ʿAbd Allāh Ḥusayn Quṣʿa b. Muḥammad b. Ḥusayn al-Ḥanafī al-Tūnisī.[11] Both authors are undated but MS 16650 of the Tunis National Library (Khaldūniyya collection) contains a copy of Quṣʿa's recension—under the title *Ghunyat al-ṭālib fī taqwīm al-kawākib*—where it is stated that the work (not the copy) was finished on Thursday 22nd Shawwāl 1091 H./15 November 1680 (which was a Friday), and that the tables have been adapted to the longitude of Tunis (41;45° from the western meridian).[12]

As for Sanjaq Dār's *Zīj al-Sharīf*—also called *al-Zīj al-Mukhtaṣar fī ʿilm al-taʿdīl wa l-taqwīm*—I have been able to study two manuscripts of this work, extant in MSS 1816 of the National Library in Tunis[13] (MS Ta hereafter) and 18104 of the library of the late Tunisian scholar Ḥasan Ḥusnī ʿAbd al-Wahhāb, now also in the Tunis National Library[14] (MS Tb hereafter). MS Tb is dated in 1107/1695–1696 (fol. 62 r).[15] In this *zīj* the mean positions of the Sun, Moon and planets are given, in intervals of thirty years, between 1080/ 1669–1670 and 1290/1873–1874; on the other hand, the positions (?) of the lunar mansions are given, according to the observations of Ulugh Begh, for the end of year 1090/ 1679–1680 (MS Ta, fol. 36r; MS Tb, fol 90 r) and the day, hour and minute of the spring equinox is given between years 1090/1679 and 1205/1790. All this evidence points to a work made in the late seventeenth century,[16] and this agrees with the presumed date for Quṣʿa's *Ghunya*: commentaries on the introduction of this *zīj* were written towards the end of the seventeenth or the beginning of the eighteenth century. One of them was written by Aḥmad b. Muḥammad Bū Daydaḥ al-Qādīrī al-Qayrawānī (fl. before 1150/1737–1738), who praised, in his introduction, the importance of Sanjaq Dār's *zīj* but added that this work was difficult to understand and to use. For that reason commentaries had been written by his masters *al-ḥājj* Abū ʿAbd Allāh Muḥammad al-Qalī and, before him, by Abu 'l-Ḥasan ʿAlī b. Māmī al-Ḥanafī, known as Karbāṣo (or Karbāṣa) (before 1163/1749–1750).[17] Al-Qālī's commentary was lost in the time of al-Qadīrī, while the work of Karbāṣo contained many mistakes and al-Qadīrī wrote, for that reason, his *Ḥāshiya ʿalā sharḥ al-Sharīf al-Tunisī Sanjaq Dār li-zīj al-Sulṭān Ulugh Beg,*[18] which, apparently, is not a very interesting work.

Sanjaq Dār's *zīj*, like Quṣʿa's *Ghunya*, is computed for 41;45° of longitude and it contains tables of oblique ascensions for a latitude of 36;50° (MS Ta, fol. 28 r; MS Tb, fol. 82 r), id. for the division of the houses for the same latitude (MS Ta, fols. 28 v–31 r; MS Tb, fols. 82 v–85 r), id. of half of daylight for the same latitude (MS Ta, fol. 33 v; MS Tb, fol. 87 v), lunar longitude at sunset for a latitude 36;40° (MS Ta, fol. 35 r; MS Tb, fol. 89 r), lunar parallax in longitude and latitude also for 36;40° (MS Ta, fol. 36 v; MS Tb, fol. 90 v) and ascendants of anniversaries for the same latitude (MS TA, fol. 45 v; MS Tb, fol. 98 r)): 36;50° is the modern value for the latitude of Tunis and it does not appear attested in any other historical source, while 36;40° is one of the three values for the latitude of Tunis given by al-Khwārizmī[19] and it is systematically used by the compiler of the Hyderabad recension of the *zīj* of Ibn Isḥāq. Apart from this, it is interesting to note that the prologue of the *Zīj al-Sharīf* states that the author is going to follow the *ḥabṭaq* method, which means that planetary equations are computed in a simplified way using double argument tables. This type of tables is documented in the East from the time of Ibn Yūnus (d. 1009),[20] but I do not know of any instance in which they appear in the Maghrib before the *Zīj al-Sharīf* for the computation of lunar or planetary equations. In spite of this, Ibn al-Kammād (fl. Cordova 1116) used double argument tables for the computation of time from mean to true syzygy[21] and for the calculation of solar eclipses,[22] and the Hyderabad recension of Ibn Isḥāq's *zīj* contains a set of double argument planetary latitude tables, based on Ptolemaic parameters, attributed to an otherwise unknown Ibn al-Bayṭār.[23] In the equation tables of the *Zīj al-Sharīf* one enters the table in the vertical sense with the mean anomaly of the Moon or the planet (tabulated from 0° to 360° with 6° intervals) and in the horizontal sense with the *zodiacal sign* of the *markaz* (the double elongation in the case of the Moon, and the mean longitude of the planet computed from the apogee): the total equation (center + anomaly) will be read directly in the intersection of the two and will be added to the mean longitude of the planet.

The present chapter intends to begin the study of this set of double argument equation tables with the case of the Moon, which seems particularly accessible. The *Zīj al-Sharīf* contains two different sets of tables for the computation of the solar and lunar longitudes: on the one hand, mean motions of the Sun, Moon, solar apogee, lunar nodes, and double elongation calculated to the precision of minutes (MS Ta, fols. 10 r and v; MS Tb, fols. 63 v–64 r); a table of the solar equation (MS Ta, fol. 10 r; MS Tb, fol. 63 v), also calculated to the precision of minutes and with an interval of 6° of the argument (tabular maximum 3;52° for arguments 264°–270°, the table being obviously displaced vertically 1;56°); the aforementioned double argument table for the lunar equation to the precision of minutes (MS Ta, fols. 11 r and v; MS Tb, fols. 65 v–66 r).

The second set of solar and lunar tables is far more precise. The solar mean motion tables (MS Ta, fol. 23 r; MS Tb, fol. 78 r) give the mean motion of the Sun and of the solar apogee (to the precision of thirds), for hours, days, lunar months, lunar years *mabsūṭa*, and the positions of the *markaz* (solar longitude from the apogee) for the end of years 1080–1290 H. in 30-year intervals. Here, as in the rest of the *zīj*, the system of intercalation is the same as that used by Ulugh Beg, in which years 2, 5, 7, 10, 13, 15, 18, 21, 24, 26, and 29 of the 30-year cycle are leap years (*kabīsa*). The corresponding solar equation table (MS Ta, fol. 24 r; MS Tb, fol. 78 r) is calculated for every degree of the argument from 0° to 359°, to the precision of thirds, it has a vertical displacement of 1;55,53,12°,[24] and it reaches a tabular maximum of 3;51,46,24° for an argument of 268°. As for the Moon, the mean motion tables (MS Ta, fols. 24 v–25 r; MS Tb, fols. 78 v–79 r) give the corresponding mean motions in longitude (*wasaṭ*), anomaly (*khāṣṣa*), double elongation (*markaz*) and nodes (*jawzahar*) for the same periods, computed to the precision of thirds (longitude) or seconds (the rest). Three other tables (MS Ta, fols. 25 v–26 v; MS Tb, fols. 79 v–80 v) tabulate more or less standard lunar equations which will be described in detail below. It is easy to see that—with the exception of the double argument equation tables of the first set and the lunar equations of the second—the first set is just the result of a rounding of the second one to the precision of minutes.

2 Mean Solar and Lunar Motions[25]

All the mean motion values derive from Ulugh Beg's *Zīj-i Sulṭānī.*[26]

- *Precession/motion of the apogees*: the analysis of the table of single years and that of positions for 1080–1290H. gives two different results

  0;0,0,8,27,14,19 (years)

  and a value between

  0;0,0,8,27,14,*24,31,41,45,32*

  and

  0;0,0,8,27,14,*28,52,55,30,50*

  for the table of periods. This corresponds, precisely, to a precession of 1° in 70 Persian years.
- *Sun*: two slightly different parameters appear to have been used.

  0;59,8,11,10,28,20° (days, months, positions 1080–1290H.)

  0;59,8,11,10,28,37° (single years)
- *Lunar longitude*: the different sets of tables are mutually compatible and the mean motion parameter used lies between

  13;10,35,1,47,53,*43,49,40,23,58*°

  and

  13;10,35,1,47,53,*45,38,5,22,28*°
- *Lunar anomaly*: the underlying parameter is

  13;3,53,55,54,24°
- *Double elongation*: the underlying parameter is

  24;22,53,*23,46,8,59,46,47,36*°

It is easy to check that this daily parameter does not correspond to the double value of the difference between the mean motion in longitude of the Moon and that of the Sun. For the computation we begin subtracting the daily motion of the apogee from the rounded value of the lunar mean motion in longitude:

13;10,35,1,47,53,45° (±0,1) – 0;0,0,8,27,14,27° (±0,2) =
13;10,34,53,20,39,18° (±0,3).[27]

and then,

13;10,34,53,20,39,18° (± 0,3) – 0;59,8,11,10,28,20° =
12;11,26,42,10,10,58° (± 0,3)

The corresponding mean motion in double elongation will be

24;22,53,*24,20,21,56*° (± 0,6)

This inconsistency is already present in Ulugh Beg's tables and it may be the reason (?) of the incoherence we find in the tables of positions for years 1080–1290. Table 10.1 collects all the information on positions of the solar center (col. 1), solar apogee (col. 2), lunar longitude (col. 4), and double elongation (col. 7): the values transcribed are those of the two manuscripts of the *Zīj al-Sharīf*. A control of errors has been made in all the cases: amounts between parentheses in col. 1 correspond to the difference (expressed in thirds) between the tabular and the recomputed value. Columns 3, 5, 6, 8 have been calculated from the corresponding tabular values and column 9 contains line-by-line differences in column 8.

Table 10.2 corresponds to positions also of the solar center (*markaz*, col. 1), solar apogee (col. 2), lunar longitude (col. 4), and double elongation (col. 7) for years 841 H.–871 H., at one year intervals, as they appear in Ulugh Beg's *Zīj-i Sulṭānī*. An asterisk (*) marks the leap-years (*kabīsa*). Here, once more, we find a disagreement between the values of the double elongation computed from the solar and lunar positions and those appearing in the table. It is easy to check, however, that the positions in the *Zīj al-Sharīf* derive from those in the *Zīj-i Sulṭānī*. To establish this, I have compared two sets of positions: those corresponding to 841 H. *nāqiṣa* (which means midday of the last day of 840) and those corresponding to the last day of 1080: the interval between these two dates should be 85048 days but the actual interval used for the recomputation is one day less (?). On the other hand a correction has been introduced to account for the difference in geographical longitude between Samarqand (longitude 99;16° in Ulugh Beg's *Zīj*) and Tunis (41;45° in the *Zīj al-Sharīf*): the difference in longitude (57;31°) corresponds to $3^h\ 50^m\ 4^s$ or $0;9,35,10^d$. The positions used in the two *zīj*es are:

	Solar *markaz*	Solar apogee	Lunar longitude	Double elongation
841	18;26,0,13°	90;30,4,48°	115;51,56,28°	25;12,49°
1080	321;32,2,24°	93;49,47,58°	51;1,29,2°	2;26,56°

For n = number of revolutions in each case, we can see that:

• *Solar* markaz:
18;26,0,13° + 0;59,8,11,10,28,20 * 85047;9,35,10^d = 360° * n + 321;32,2,27,9°

• *Solar apogee*:
90;30,4,48° + 0;0,0,8,27,14,26° * 85047;9,35,10^d = 93;49,47,57,28°

• *Lunar longitude*:
115;51,56,28° + 13;10,35,1,47,53,45° * 85047;9,35,10^d = 360° * n + 51;1,29,2,25°

• *Double elongation*:
25;12,49° + 24;22,53,23,46,9° * 85047;9,35,10^d = 360° * n + 2;26,55,2°

Table 10.1
Positions in the *Zīj al-Sharīf*

	(1)	(2)	(3) = (1) + (2)	(4)	(5) = (4) – (3)	(6) = (5) * 2	(7)	(8) = (7) – (6)	(9)
	Sun (center)	Apogee	[Solar Long.	Lunar Long.	[Elongation	[Double el.	Double el. (tab.)		Diff.
1080	321;32,2,24	93;49,47,58	55;21,50,22	51;1,29,2	355;39,38,40	351;19,17,20	2;26,56	11;7,39	
1110	359;31,30,21	94;14,45,53	93;46,16,14	89;18,12,39	355;31,56,25	351;3,52,50	2;9,51	11;5,58	0;1,41
1140	37;30,58,18(+1)	94;39,43,48	132;10,42,6	127;34,56,17	355;24,14,11	350;48,28,22	1;52,44[1]	11;4,16	0;1,42
1170	75;30,26,13	95; 4,41,42	170;35,7,56	165;51,39,54	355;16,31,58	350;33,3,56	1;35,40	11;2,36	0;1,40
1200	113;29,54,9(–1)	95;29,39,36	208;59,33,45	204; 8,23,32	355;8,49,47	350;17,39,34	1;18,34	11;0,54	0;1,42
1230	151;29,22,5(–1)	95;54,37,31	247;23,59,36	242;25, 7, 9	355;1,7,33	350;2,15,6	1;1,29	10;59,14	0;1,40
1260	189;28,50,2(–1)	96;19,35,26	285;48,25,28	280;41,50[2],46	354;53,25,18	349;46,50,36	0:44,22[3]	10;57,31	0;1,43
1290	227;28,17,58(–1)	96;44,33,20	324;12,51,18]	318;58,34,24	354;45,43,6]	349;31,26,12]	0:27,18	10;55,52	0;1,39

1. MS Tb 45"
2. Ms. Ta 56"
3. MS Tb 24"

Table 10.2
Positions in Ulugh Beg's Zīj-i Sulṭanī

	(1)	(2)	(3) = (1) + (2)	(4)	(5) = (4) – (3)	(6) = (5) * 2	(7)	(8) = (7) – (6)	(9
	Sun (Center)	Apogee	[Solar long.	Lunar long.	[Elongation	[Double el.	Double el.(tab.)		Diff.
841	18;26,0,13	90;30,4,48	108;56,5,1	115;51,56,28[1]	6;55,51,27	13;51,42,54	25;12,49	11;21,6	
842	7;20,18,19	90;30,54,41	97;51,13,0	100;18,37,5[2]	2;27,24,5	4;54,48,10	16;15,51	11;21,3	0;0,3
843*	357;13,44,16	90;31,44,42	87;45,28,58	97;55,52,43[3]	10;10,23,45	20;20,47,30	31;41,47	11;21,0	0;0,3
844	346;8,2,12	90;32,34,35	76;40,36,47	82;22,33,20	5;41,56,33	11;23,53,6	22;44,49	11;20,53	0;0,7
845	335;2,20,7	90;33,24,27	65;35,44,34	66;49,13,57	1;13,29,23	2;26,58,46	13;47,51	11;20,52	0;0,1
846*	324;55,46,14	90;34,14,29	55;30;0,43	64;26,29,35	8;56,28,52	17;52,57,44	29;13,47	11;20,49	0;0,3
847	313;50,4,10	90;35,4,21	44;25,8,31	48;53,10,11	4;28,1,40	8;56,3,20	20;16,49	11;20,46	0;0,3
848*	303;43,30,17	90;35,54,22	34;19,24,39	46;30,25,50	12;11,1,11	24;22,2,22	35;42,45	11;20,43	0;0,3
849	292;37,48,13	90;36,44,15	23;14,32,28	30;57,6,26	7;42,33,58	15;25,7,56	26;45,47	11;20,39	0;0,4
850	281;32,6,9	90;37,34,9	12;9,40,18	15;23,47,3	3;14,6,45	6;28,13,30	17;48,49	11;20,36	0;0,3
851*	271;25,34,16	90;38,24,9	2;3,58,25	13;1,2,41	10;57,4,16	21;54,8,32	33;[1]4,45[4]	11;20,36	0;0,0
852	260;19,50,[5]11	90;39,14,2	350;59,4,13	357;27,43,18	6;28,39,5	12;57,18,10	24;17,46	11;20,28	0;0,8
853	249;[14][6],8,7	90;40,3,54	339;54,12,1	341;54,23,54	2;0,11,53	4;0,23,46	15;20,49	11;20,25	0;0,3
854*	239;7,36,14	90;40,53,56	329;48,30,10	339;31,39,33	9;43,9,23	19;26,18,46	30;46,45	11;20,26	–0;0,1
855	228;1,5[4][7],10	90;41,43,48	318;43,37,58	323;58,20,9	5;14,42,11	10;29,24,22	21;49,47	11;20,23	0;0,3
856*	217;55,[22][8],7	90;42,33,50	308;37,55,57	321;35,35,[4]8[9]	12;57,39,51	25;55,19,42	37;15,43	11;20,23	0;0,0
857	206;49,36,[10]13	90;43,23,42	297;32,59,55	306;2,16,25	8;29,16,30	16;58,33,0	28;18,45	11;20,12	0;0,9
858	195;43,54,8	90;44,13,34	286;28,7,42	290;28,57,2	4;0,49,20	8;1,38,40	19;21,47	11;20,8	0;0,4
859*	185;37,20,15	90;45,3,36	276;22,23,51	288;6,12,39	11;43,48,48	23;27,37,36	34;47,43	11;20,5	0;0,3
860	174;31,38,11	90;45,53,29	265;17,31,40	272;32,53,16	7;15,21,36	14;30,43,12	25;50,45	11;20,2	0;0,3
861	163;25,56,7	90;46;43,22	254;12,39,29	256;59,33,52	2;46,54,23	5;33,48,46	16;53,48	11;19,59	0;0,3

862*	153;19,22,14	90;47,33,23	244;6,55,37	254;36,49,31	10;29,53,54	20;59,47,48	32;19,43	11;19,55	0;0,4
863	142;13,40,10	90;48,23,15	233;2,3,25	239;3,30,7	6;1,26,42	12;2,53,24	23;22,45	11;19,52	0;0,3
864	131;7,58,6	90;49,13,8	221;57,11,14	223;30,10,44	1;32,59,30	3;5,59,0	14;25,48	11;19,49	0;0,3
865*	121;1,24,12	90;50,3,9	211;51,27,21	221;7,26,22	9;15,59,1	18;31,58,2	29;51,43	11;19,45	0;0,4
866	109;55,42,8	90;50,53,2	200;46,35,10	205;34,6,59	4;47,31,49	9;35,3,38	20;54,46	11;19,42	0;0,3
867*	99;49,8,15	90;51,43,3	190;40,51,18	203;11,22,37	12;30,31,19	25;1,2,38	36;20,41	11;19,38	0;0,4
868	88;43,26,11	90;52,32,56	179;35,59,7	187;38,3,14	8;2,4,7	16;4,8,14	27:23,43	11;19,35	0;0,3
869	77;37,44,7	90;53,22,49	168;31,6,56	172;4,43,50	3;33,36,54	7;7,13,46	18;26,46	11;19,32	0;0,3
870*	67;31,10,14	90;54,12,50	158;25,23,4	169;41,59,29	11;16,36,25	22;33,12,50	32;52,41	11;19,28	0;0,4
871	56;25,28,10	90;55,2,43	147;20,30,53]	154;8,40,5	6;48,9,12	13;36,18,24]	24;55,44	11;19,26	0;0,2

1. 4^s 25;51,56,11 in the Aleppo ms.
2. 4^s in the Aleppo ms.
3. 4^s in the Aleppo ms.
4. 4' in the Aleppo ms.
5. 50 in the Alepo ms. The correct value should be 52".
6. [14] is the correct value: the Aleppo ms. has 40.
7. 52" in the Aleppo ms.
8. 48" in the Aleppo ms.
9. 18 thirds in the Aleppo ms.
10. 36" in the Aleppo ms. The correct value should be 40".

3 Solar and Lunar Equations

As I have previously stated, the *Zīj al-Sharīf* contains two displaced tables of the solar equation, the first being the result of a rounding, to the approximation of minutes, of the second one, which was copied from Ulugh Beg's *Zīj-i Sulṭānī*. Table 10.3 contains excerpts of the aforementioned second solar equation table of the *Zīj al-Sharīf*: the amounts between parentheses correspond to the differences, in thirds, between tabular and recomputed values, an eccentricity of 2;1,20^{p} having been used for the recomputation.[28]

The set of lunar equation tables also derive from Ulugh Beg's *Zīj-i Sulṭānī*. The lunar equation of the center, called *taʿdīl awwal* ("first equation") in the *Zīj al-Sharīf* (excerpts in table 10.4), although displaced vertically 13;15,34°, is a standard table calculated for an eccentricity of 12;33,22^{p}, the radius of the deferent being 60^{p}. The four tables (see excerpts below in tables 10.5, 10.6,

Table 10.3
Solar Equation

0	1;55,53,12°	180	1;55,53,12°
10	1;36,24,49	190	2;16,41,50 (+1)
20	1;17,28,37 (+1)	200	2;36,48,32
30	0;59,36,8	210	2;55,33,19 (+2)
40	0;43,17,44	220	3;12,19,28
50	0;29,1,47	230	3;26,35,19
60	0;17,14,5	240	3;37,55,7 (+1)
70	0;8,17,7	250	3;45,59,46 (+1)
80	0;2,29,14	260	3;50,37,13
		268	3;51,46,24
		269	3;51,[45],29[1]
90	0:0,3,57	270	3;51,[4]2,27[2]
		271	3;51,37,19
92	0;0,0,0		
100	0;1,9,11	280	3;49,17,10
110	0;5,46,38 (–1)	290	3;43,29,17
120	0;13,51,17 (–1)	300	3;34,32,19
130	0;25,11,5	310	3;22,44,37
140	0;39,26,57	320	3;8,28,40
150	0;56,13,17	330	2;52,10,16
160	1;14,57,52	340	2;34,17,47 (–1)
170	1;35,4,34 (–1)	350	2;15,21,35

1. 45' is legible in MS Tb fol. 78 r.
2. 42' is also legible in MS Tb, fol. 78 r.

Table 10.4
Lunar Equation of the Center

0	13;15,34°	180	13;15,34°
10	14;44,3	190	9;43,4 (–1)
20	16;[1]2;2[8][1]	200	6;30,10 (–1)
30	17;40,8 (+1)	210	3;51,33 (–1)
40	19;6,57 (+1)[2]	220	1;54,[4]3[3]
50	20;31,57	230	0;40,26
60	21;53,58	240	0;5,1 (–1)
		246	0;0,0
70	23;11,11	250	0;2,34
80	24;21,6	260	0;26,32
90	25;20,20	270	1;10,[4]8[4]
100	26;4,36	280	2;10,2
110	26;28,34	290	3;19,57
114	26;31,8		
120	26;26,7 (+1)	300	4;37,10
130	25;50,42	310	5;59,11
140	24;36,25	320	7;24,13 (+1)
150	22;39,35 (+1)	330	8;51,0 (–1)
160	20;0,58 (+1)	340	10;18,48
170	16;48,4 (+1)	350	11;47,5

1. 16;12,20° in MS Tb, fol. 79 v.
2. 19;6,55° in MS Tb, fol. 79 v.
3. 43" are legible in MS Tb fol. 79 v.
4. 48" are clearly legible in MS Tb, fol. 79 v.

10.7, 10.8) designed for the computation of the equation of anomaly are not so standard:[29] the first, called *taʿdīl thānī* (second equation), is a table displaced vertically 7;37,28°, but, if we subtract this constant from the tabular values, we will discover that the two halves of the table are not symmetrical. The solution to the difficulties posed by this table can be found in the instructions, given in the canons, for the computation of the lunar equation of anomaly (MS Ta, fol. 3v; MS Tb, fols. 56 v–57 r):[30]

- With the mean motion tables obtain the mean longitude (λ_m) and the mean anomaly (α_m) of the Moon as well as the *markaz* (double elongation, *2f*).
- Enter the table of the lunar equation of the center (*taʿdīl awwal*) with *2f* and obtain the equation of the center (η).
- Add $\eta + \alpha_m = \alpha_v$ (true anomaly, *al-khāṣṣa al-muʿaddala*).
- Enter with α_v the table of the "second equation" (*taʿdīl thānī*) and obtain γ.

Table 10.5
Taʿdīl Thānī ("Second Equation")
First Table for the Computation of the Lunar Equation of Anomaly

0	7;37,28°	180	7;37,28°
10	6;27,24 (–1)	190	8;34,7 (+1)
20	5;18,48 (–1)	200	9;28,32 (+1)
30	4;13,7	210	10;18,38 (+1)
40	3;11,49	220	11;2,38
50	2;16,23 (–1)	230	11;39,5[1]
60	1;28,22 (–1)	240	12;6,59
70	0;49,[1]7[2] (–2)	250	12;25,43 (+2)
80	0;2[4],40[3]	260	12;34,59 (–1)
		265	12;36,10 (+1)
90	0;3,54	270	12;3[5],3[4] (+1)
98	0;0,0 (–6)		
100	0;0,1[8][5]	280	12;26,13 (+1)
110	0;10,53 (–2)	290	12;[9],10 (+1)[6]
120	0;36,23 (–2)	300	11;44,39
130	1;16,57 (–1)	310	11;13,39 (+1)
140	2;12,0 (–1)	320	10;37,6
150	3;20,13	330	9;56,8 (+1)
160	4;39,21 (–1)	340	9;11,47
170	6;6,21	350	8;25,11

1. 11;39,35° in MS Tb, fol. 80 r.
2. 0;49,47° in Ta (fol. 26 r); 0;49,17° in Tb (fol. 80 r).
3. 0;20,40° in MS Tb, fol. 80 r.
4. 12;34,3 in MS Tb, fol. 26 r; 12;35,3° in MS Ta, fol. 80 r.
5. 0;10,13° in MS Tb, fol. 80 r.
6. 12;10,9° in MS Ta, fol. 26 r; 12;9,10° in MS Tb, fol. 80 r.

- Enter with α_v the table of the "variation" (*ikhtilāf*) and obtain $\Delta\gamma$.
- Enter with the *markaz* (*2f*) the first table of the "minutes of the anomalies" (*daqāʾiq al-ḥiṣaṣ*) if $0° < \alpha_v < 180°$ and obtain m_1. If $180° < \alpha_v < 360°$, then do the same with the second table of the "minutes of the anomalies" and obtain m_2.
- Multiply $m \cdot \Delta\gamma$.
- Add $\gamma + m \cdot \Delta\gamma$ and you will obtain the "corrected equation" [of anomaly] (*taʿdīl muḥkam*).
- The true longitude of the Moon in its "inclined sphere" (*falak māʾil*) will be: $\lambda_v = \lambda_m + \gamma + m \cdot \Delta\gamma$.

Instructions are given, after this, to calculate the equation of time and to obtain the true longitude of the Moon on the ecliptic.

Table 10.6
Ikhtilāf al-Qamar ("Variation of the Moon")
Second Table for the Computation of the Lunar Equation of Anomaly

0	0;0°	90	2;35,59 (–1)
10	0;22,21 (+1)	100	2;39,39 (–1)
		102	2;39,49
20	0;44,21 (+1)	110	2;38,20
30	1;5,41 (–1)	120	2;31,34 (+2)
40	1;26̀,1	130	2;18,54 (+1)
50	1;44,54	140	2;0,18 (+1)
60	2;1,55 (+1)	150	1;36,4 (–2)
70	2;16,29 (+1)	160	1;7,3
80	2;28,3 (–1)	170	0;34,28 (–1)

Table 10.7
Daqā'iq al-Ḥiṣṣa ("Minutes of the Anomaly")
First Function of Interpolation for the Computation of the Lunar Anomaly

0/360	60;0'	90/270	33;12'
30/330	56;46 (–1)	120/240	17;24 (+1)
60/300	47;24 (+1)	150/210	4;49 (+2)
		179/181	0;1 (–1)

Table 10.8
Daqā'iq al-Ḥiṣṣa ("Minutes of the Anomaly")
Second Function of Interpolation for the Computation of the Lunar Anomaly

0/360	0;0'	90/270	26;48'
30/330	3;14 (+1)	120/240	42;36 (–1)
60/300	12;36 (–1)	150/210	55;11 (–2)
		179/181	59;59 (–3)

Following the logic of the instructions I have just summarized, we can see that the table of the "second equation" (see table 10.6) computes two different functions:

- For $0° < \alpha_v < 180°$, the funcion involved is the lunar equation of anomaly for the minimum distance of the center of the lunar epicycle from the center of the Earth ($\gamma_{R\text{-}e}$). The table is displaced vertically 7;37,28° and, as the equation of anomaly is negative for $0° < \alpha < 180°$, it gives:

$$7;37,28° - \gamma_{R\text{-}e}.$$

The table can be recomputed using a radius of the epicycle of 6;17,46°,[31] an eccentricity of 12;33,22^p and a radius of the deferent of 60^p. The choice of the constant of displacement is inadequate and it corresponds to an error in the computation of the maximum value of the table, which should be 7;37,34° instead of 7;37,28°. The mistake was already present in Ulugh Beg's *zīj* and 7;37,28° is explicitely mentioned by Mīram Chalabī, in his commentary on Ulugh Beg's canons,[32] as the amount for the displacement and for the maximum equation.[33]

The table of the "variation" (*ikhtilāf*) is a standard table of differences between the equation of anomaly for minimum ($\gamma_{\text{R-e}}$) and for maximum ($\gamma_{\text{R+e}}$) distances:

$$\gamma_{\text{R-e}} - \gamma_{\text{R+e}}.$$

The interpolation function involved for the aforementioned values of the true anomaly (m_1) decreases monotonically from 60′ (for $2f = 0°$) to 0′ (for $2f = 180°$). It can be recomputed using the expression:

$$m_1 = (max\ \gamma_{2f} - max\ \gamma_{R\text{-}e})/(max\ \gamma_{R\text{-}e} - max\ \gamma_{R+e})$$

in which $max\ \gamma_{R\text{-}e} = 7;37,28°$, and

$$max\ \gamma_{R+e} = 4;58,42°.$$

It is easy to see the logic of the system for the computation of the lunar equation of anomaly at syzygies in which $2f = 0°$, $m_1 = 60'$ and $\gamma(\alpha_v) = \gamma_{R+e}$:

$$7;37,28° - \gamma(\alpha) = 7;37,28 - \gamma_{R\text{-}e} + 60'(\gamma_{R\text{-}e} - \gamma_{R+e}) = 7;37,28° - \gamma_{R+e}.$$

At quadratures, $2f = 180°$, $m_1 = 0'$ and $\gamma(\alpha_v) = \gamma_{R\text{-}e}$:

$$7;37,28° - \gamma(\alpha) = 7;37,28 - \gamma_{R\text{-}e} + 0'(\gamma_{R\text{-}e} - \gamma_{R+e}) = 7;37,28° - \gamma_{R\text{-}e}.$$

• For $180° < \alpha_v < 360°$, the funcion involved is the lunar equation of anomaly for the maximum distance of the center of the lunar epicycle from the center of the Earth (γ_{R+e}). The table is also displaced vertically 7;37,28° and, as the equation of anomaly is positive for $180° < \alpha < 360°$, it gives:

$$7;37,28° + \gamma_{R+e}.$$

The interpolation function involved for the aforementioned values of the true anomaly (m_2) increases monotonically from 0′ (for $2f = 0°$) to 60′ (for $2f = 180°$). It can be recomputed using the expression:

$$m_2 = (max\ \gamma_{2f} - max\ \gamma_{R+e})/(max\ \gamma_{R\text{-}e} - max\ \gamma_{R+e}).$$

Again, at syzygies, $2f = 0°$, $m_2 = 0'$ and $\gamma(\alpha_v) = \gamma_{R+e}$:

$$7;37,28° + \gamma(\alpha) = 7;37,28 + \gamma_{R+e} + 0'(\gamma_{R\text{-}e} - \gamma_{R+e}) = 7;37,28° + \gamma_{R+e}.$$

At quadratures, $2f = 180°$, $m_2 = 60'$ and $\gamma(\alpha_v) = \gamma_{R\text{-}e}$:

$$7;37,28° + \gamma(\alpha) = 7;37,28 + \gamma_{R+e} + 60'\ (\gamma_{R\text{-}e} - \gamma_{R+e}) = 7;37,28° + \gamma_{R\text{-}e}.$$

4 ḤABṬAQ TABLES OF THE COMBINED LUNAR EQUATIONS

The *Zīj al-Sharīf* contains, as we have seen, a set of double argument tables to calculate the lunar equation of anomaly (MS Ta, fols. 11 r and v; MS Tb, fols. 65 v and 66 r): see samples below, in tables 10.9 and 10.10. The arguments are the *markaz* (double elongation), at intervals of 30°, and the mean anomaly (at intervals of 6°): 720 values of the equation of anomaly are computed and I have recalculated all of them. On the whole, the calculator did a good job and errors have usually an amount of 1′, with the only exception of the equations calculated for a double elongation of 240°, in which errors are systematic and reach a maximum of ± 8'.[34] It has been established that these *ḥabṭaq* tables have been calculated using the lunar equation tables that I have just described and that derive from Ulugh Beg's *Zīj-i Sulṭānī*. For the recomputation of the *ḥabṭaq* tables I have used Benno van Dalen's *Table Analysis* and, especifically, the sub-programme called *Table calculator*. The procedure used for the recomputation has been the following one:

Table 10.9
Ḥabṭaq Table for the Lunar Equation of the Anomaly for 0° < α < 180°

Markaz (double elongation)							
Mean anomaly	0	60	120	180	240	300	330
0	6;35 (+1)	5;44	4;53	6;5	7;37	7;13	6;54
12	5;40 (+1)	4;47	3;45	4;44	6;23 (+2)	6;11	5;57
24	4;49	3;55	2;45	3;28	5;10 (+3)	5;12	5;3
36	4;4	3;11	1;54	2;20	4;2 (+4)	4;17	4;15 (+1)
48	3;27	2;37	1:16	1;23	3;1 (+5)	3;30	3;33
60	2;59	2;15	0;53	0;39	2;10 (+7)	[2];51[1]	3;1
72	2;43	2;6	0;46	0;10	1;30 (+7)	2;23	2;39
84	2;39	2;11	0;57 (–1)	0;0 (+5)	1;4 (+8)	2;8	2;30
96	2;4[8][2]	2;31	1;28	0;10	0;54 (+8)	2;6 (–1)	2;35
108	3;11	3;6	2;17 (–1)	0;41	1;2 (+8)	2;20	[2];53[3]
120	3;47	3;56	3;25	1;34 (+1)	1;28 (+7)	2;49	3;24 (–1)
132	4;34 (–1)	4;57	4;47	2;47 (+1)	2;13 (+6)	3;32 (–1)	4;9
144	5;32	6;8	6;20	4;17	3;16 (+5)	4;29	5;5
156	6;36 (–1)	7;24	7;56 (–1)	6;0	4;34 (+4)	5;36	6;9
168	7;44 (–1)	8;41	9;33 (–1)	7;49	6;2 (+1)	6;50	7;49

1. MS Ta 3;51°
2. MS Ta 2;43°
3. MS Ta 3;53°

Table 10.10
Ḥabṭaq Table for the Lunar Equation of the Anomaly for 180° < α < 360°

	Markaz (double elongation)						
Mean an.	0	60	120	180	240	300	330
180	8;52	9;54	11;3	9;38	7;37 (–1)	8;7	8;29
192	9;55 (–1)	10;59	12;19	11;[1]9[1] (+1)	9;12 (–3)	9;22	9;[3]6[2] (–1)
204	10;51	11;53	13;20	12;46 (+1)	10;41 (–5)	10;31	10;37
216	11;36 (–1)	12;33	14;2	13;55 (+1)	11;59 (–6)	11;31	11;28
228	12;10	12;59	14;24	14;43	13;2 (–7)	12;[1]7[3]	12;7
240	12;30	13;9	14;28	15;9	13;47 (–8)	12;50 (+1)	12;32 (–1)
252	12;36	13;5	14;14	15;14	14;13 (–8)	13;7 (+1)	12;44
264	12;30 (+1)	12;47	13;45	15;0	14;21 (–8)	13;9 (+1)	12;42
276	12;11	12;17	13;2	14;28	14;15[4] (–3)	12;57 (+1)	12;27
288	11;41	11:36	12;7	13;41	13;45 (–7)	12;32 (+1)	12;0
300	11;2	10;47	11;3	12;41	13;5 (–6)	11;55	11;23
312	10;16	9:51	9;53	11:31 (–1)	12:13 (–5)	11;10 (+1)	10:39 (+1)
324	9;24	8;51	8;39 (+1)	10;14	11;12 (–4)	10;17 (+1)	9;47
336	8;29	7;49	7;22	8;52 (–1)	10;7	9;18	8;51
348	7;32 (+1)	6;46	6;6	7;28 (–1)	8;53	8;16	7;53

1. MS Ta 11;59°.
2. MS Ta 9;56.
3. 12;7 in MS Ta, in which 17’ appears in a marginal correction.
4. 14;15° in MS Ta; 14;11° in MS Tb.

1. For 0° < α_v < 180°.

1.1 Enter a table $T1(c_m)$ of the lunar equation of center η as a function of the mean centrum, for e = 12;33,22^p, displaced vertically 13;15,34°, for arguments comprised between 0° and 330°, with intervals of 30°. The actual values entered were those that appear above in table 10.4.

From here on all the steps are given for one particular value of c_m.

1.2 Enter a table $T2(c_m)$ of the function of interpolation m_1 for arguments 0, 30, 60...360°. The values entered are those of table 10.7 above.

1.3 Add

$$\eta + \alpha_m = \alpha_v$$

to obtain the true lunar anomaly by adding, for each particular value of c_m,

$$\alpha_m + T1(c_m), \text{ for } \alpha_m = 0, 6, 12...174°.$$

The result obtained will be table $T3(\alpha_m)$.

1.4 Calculate a table $T4(\alpha_m)$ of the equation of anomaly for minimum distance (γ_{R-e}), the arguments being the true anomalies obtained from $T3(\alpha_m)$, for each particular value of c_m. The table has to be displaced 7;37,28° and we must, therefore, calculate

$$7;37,28° - \gamma_{R-e}.$$

The expression used is:

$$7;37,28-(atan((6;17,46*\sin(T3))/(47;26,37 + 6;17,46*\cos(T3)))),$$

in which $T3$ means $T3(\alpha_m)$.

1.5 Calculate a table $T5(\alpha_m)$ of the equation of anomaly for maximum distance (γ_{R+e}), also displaced 7;37,28°, again using as arguments the values of $T3(\alpha_m)$, for each particular value of c_m:

$$7;37,28 - (atan((6;17,46*\sin(T3))/(72;33,22+6;17,46*\cos(T3)))),$$

$T3$ being $T3(\alpha_m)$.

1.6 The final table for each value of the mean anomaly, and still for our particular value of c_m, will be:

$$T4 + ((T5\text{-}T4)*T2),$$

in which

$T2$ is $T2(\alpha_m)$,
$T4$ is $T4(\alpha_m)$,
$T5$ is $T5(\alpha_m)$.

2. For $180° < \alpha_v < 360°$

2.1 As in 1.1 above: $T1(c_m)$.

2.2 Enter a table $T2(c_m)$ of the function of interpolation m_2 for arguments 0, 30, 60...360°. The values entered are those of table 10.8 above.

2.3 As in 1.3 above for α_m = 180, 186, 192...354°:

$T3(\alpha_m)$, for each particular value of c_m.

2.4 Calculate 7;37,28 – γ_{R+e} for the values of $T3(\alpha_m)$, using the same expression as above in 1.5:

$T4(\alpha_m)$.

2.5 Calculate 7;37,28 – γ_{R-e} for the values of $T3(\alpha_m)$, using the same expression as above in 1.4:

$T5(\alpha_m)$.

2.6 As in 1.6 above, calculate

$$T4 + ((T5-T4)*T2).$$

ACKNOWLEDGMENTS

The present chapter has been prepared within a research program on "The circulation of astronomical ideas in the Mediterranean between the twelfth and fourteenth centuries," sponsored by the Dirección General de Investigación Científica y Técnica of the Spanish Ministry of Education and Culture. Benno van Dalen's programs CALH (for the conversion of dates) and TA ("Table Analysis"), as well as Honorino Mielgo's ATMM (for the analysis of mean motion tables) have been extensively used. Information about manuscripts in the National Library of Tunis and the Ṣabīḥiyya Library of Salé (Morocco) was given to me by Dr. Mercè Comes and by my research graduate student Hamid Berrani. Benno van Dalen read two successive drafts of this chapter and corrected some errors I had made. He also tried to improve my hopeless mathematical inconsistencies and sent me photocopies of Sédillot's publications on Ulugh Beg's *zīj*. My gratitude to all of them.

NOTES

1. See f. ex. David A. King, "An Overview of the Sources for the History of Astronomy in the Medieval Maghrib." *Deuxième Colloque Maghrébin sur l' Histoire des Mathématiques Arabes*. Tunis, 1988, pp. 125–157. See also a recent survey of this manuscript in A. Mestres, "Maghribī Astronomy in the 13th Century: A Description of Manuscript Hyderabad Andra Pradesh State Library 298," in J. Casulleras and J. Samsó (eds.), *From Baghdad to Barcelona. Studies in the Islamic Exact Sciences in Honour of Prof. Juan Vernet*. Barcelona, 1996, I, 383–443. A complete edition of the canons of the Hyderabad compilation, together with a commentary and a partial edition of the numerical tables was presented by Angel Mestres as a Ph.D. dissertation (University of Barcelona, January 2000).

2. The canons were edited by J. Vernet, *Contribución al estudio de la labor astronómica de Ibn al-Bannāʾ*. Tetuán, 1952. The solar tables were studied by J. Samsó and E. Millás, "Ibn al-Bannāʾ, Ibn Isḥāq and Ibn al-Zarqālluh's Solar Theory" in J. Samsó, *Islamic Astronomy and Medieval Spain*. Variorum. Aldershot, 1994, no X (35 pp.). For the planetary tables see J. Samsó and E. Millás, "The Computation of Planetary Longitudes in the *Zīj* of Ibn al-Bannāʾ," *Arabic Sciences and Philosophy* 8 (1998), 259–286.

3. See E. S. Kennedy, "The Astronomical Tables of Ibn al-Raqqām, a Scientist of Granada," *Zeitschrift für Geschichte der Arabisch-Islamischen Wissenschaften* 11 (1997), 35–72. On these *zīj*es a doctoral dissertation by Muḥammad ʿAbd al-Raḥmān (Institute for the History of Arabic Science, Aleppo), *Ḥisāb aṭwāl al-kawākib fī l-Zīj al-Shāmil fī Tahdhīb al-Kāmil li-Ibn al-Raqqām*, was presented in the University of Barcelona (September 1996).

4. E. S. Kennedy and David A. King, "Indian Astronomy in Fourteenth Century Fez: the Versified Zīj of al-Qusunṭīnī," *Journal for the History of Arabic Science* 6 (1982), 3–45.

Reprint in D. A. King, *Islamic Mathematical Astronomy*, Variorum Reprints, London, 1986, no. VIII (second revised edition by Variorum, Aldershot, 1993).

5. J. Samsó, "Andalusian Astronomy in 14th Century Fez: *al-Zīj al-Muwāfiq* of Ibn ʿAzzūz al-Qusanṭīnī," *Zeitschrift für Geschichte der Arabisch-Islamischen Wissenschaften*, 11 (1997), 73–110. See also J. Samsó, "Horoscopes and History: Ibn ʿAzzūz and his retrospective horoscopes related to the battle of El Salado (1340)," in Lodi Nauta and Arjo Vanderjagt (eds.), *Between Demonstration and Imagination. Essays in the History of Science and Philosophy Presented to John D. North*, Brill, Leiden-Boston-Köln, 1999, 101–124.

6. See Kennedy and King, "Indian Astronomy," p. 9; King, "Overview," pp. 131–132 and 144.

7. See Juan Vernet, "Tradición e innovación en la ciencia medieval," *Oriente e Occidente nel Medioevo: Filosofia e Scienze*, Accademia dei Lincei, Roma, 1971, pp. 741–757; reprint in Vernet, *Estudios sobre Historia de la Ciencia Medieval*, Barcelona-Bellaterra, 1979, pp. 173–189 (see pp. 188–189). See now Montse Díaz-Fajardo, *La teoría de la trepidación en un astrónomo marroquí del siglo XV. Estudio y edición crítica del* Kitāb al-adwār fī tasyīr al-anwār *(parte primera) de Abū ʿAbd Allāh al-Baqqār.* Barcelona, 2001.

8. See J. Samsó, "An Outline of the History of Maghribī Zījes from the End of the Thirteenth Century." *Journal for the History of Astronomy* 29 (1998), 93–102; see also Samsó, "Astronomical Observations in the Maghrib in the Fourteenth and Fifteenth Centuries," *Science in Context* 14 (2001), 165–178.

9. See L. P. E. A. Sédillot, *Prolegomènes des Tables Astronomiques d'Oloug-Beg.* 2 vols., Paris, 1847 and 1853.

10. Muḥammad al-ʿArabī al-Khaṭṭābī, *Fahāris al-Khizāna al-Ḥasaniyya* vol. III (Rabat, 1983), pp. 193–195 (no. 227); see also D. A. King, *A Survey of the Scientific Manuscripts in the Egyptian National Library.* Winona Lake, Indiana, 1986, p. 164 (G99). MSS 11420 and 12616 of the National Library contain versions of Ulugh Beg's *zīj* for the coordinates of Cairo (long. 55° from the western meridian).

11. Ms. Cairo DM814 is a copy of this recension dated in 1325/1907–1908: cf. King, *Survey* p. 142 (F46). A third (?), anonymous, Tunisian recension is preserved in two mss. of the Ḥasaniyya Library in Rabat: 2650 (undated) and 2148 (dated in 1218/1803). See Khaṭṭābī, *Fahāris* 335–338 (no. 406–408). Ekmeleddin Ihsanoğlu *et al., Osmanli Astronomi Literatürü Tarihi* (*History of Astronomy Literature during the Ottoman Period*). Istanbul, 1997, p. 314 (no. 175) and pp. 347–348 (no. 213).

12. Another copy of the same *zīj* is extant in MS 5990 of the same library. The copy was finished in 1229 H./1814 by Muḥammad b. ʿAbd Allāh al-Khayyārī.

13. Copy dated in 1242/1826. Mercè Comes obtained a microfilm of that manuscript and called my attention to it.

14. See ʿAbd al-Ḥafīẓ Manṣūr, *al-Fihris al-ʿāmm li 'l-makhṭūṭāt. I. Raṣīd maktabat Ḥasan Ḥusnī ʿAbd al-Wahhāb*, Tunis, 1975, p. 398.

15. See also King, *Survey,* p. 143 (F53) who lists other manuscripts of the same work: ms. Cairo Ṭalʿat Riyāḍa 319,1 (pp. 1–16, ca. 1300 H.) contains the mean motion tables of this *zīj*. A complete copy is in ms. Paris B.N. ar. 2536 (48 fols., ca. 1150 H.).

16. The incomplete copy extant in MS Tb (fol. 104 r) gives an example of the computation of the solar longitude and the date used is the 16th Jumādā I 1099 H/ 19.3.1688.

17. Driss Lamrabet, *Introduction à l'histoire des mathématiques maghrebines* (Rabat, 1994), p. 143 (no. 506), mentions Ibn Māmī and places him tentatively after the sixteenth century. One copy (dated 1163 H/ 1749–1750) of his work is extant in Cairo N. L. (King, *Survey* p. 143, F54).

18. Tunis Nat. Library, col. Ḥ. Ḥ. ʿAbd al-Wahhāb 18104, dated in 1301/1883–1884: see ʿA. Ḥ. Manṣūr, *Fihris* p. 397, and in Tunis Nat. Library MS 2770. Another copy of the same work is extant in MS 1042 of the Ṣabīḥiyya Library in Salé (Morocco). Two copies of this work, dated in 1150/1737–1738 and in 1169/1755–1756, are also extant in Cairo N. L.: see King, *Survey* p. 144, F55. I have another reference to a summary of Sanjaq Dār's *Mukhtaṣar*, mixed with materials derived from Ibn al-Shāṭir's *zīj*, in MS Tunis N. L. 5608. Finally, the Ṣabīḥiyya Library also contains two summaries (*Mukhtaṣars*) of Ulugh Beg's *zīj* in MSS 1167 and 1168, the author being Muḥammad b. Abī l-Fatḥ al-Ṣūfī.

19. E. S. Kennedy and M. H. Kennedy, *Geographical Coordinates of Localities from Islamic Sources* (Frankfurt, 1987), pp. 362–363.

20. D. A. King, "A Double Argument Table for the Lunar Equation Attributed to Ibn Yūnus," *Centaurus* 18 (1974), 129–146. Reprinted in King, *Islamic Mathematical Astronomy* no. V. For other double argument tables for the computation of lunar and planetary equations see D. A. King, "On the Astronomical Tables of the Islamic Middle Ages," *Colloquia Copernicana* 13 (1975), 37–56 (cf. pp. 44–45, 55), reprinted in *Islamic Mathematical Astronomy* no. II; Claus Jensen, "The Lunar Theories of al-Baghdādī," *Archive for History of Exact Sciences* 8 (1971–1972), 321–328; Mark J. Tichenor, "Late Medieval Two-Argument Tables for Planetary Longitudes," *Journal of Near Eastern Studies* 26 (1967), 126–128, reprinted in E. S. Kennedy, Colleagues and Former Students, *Studies in the Islamic Exact Sciences* (Beirut, 1983), 126–128; G. Saliba, "The Double Argument Lunar Tables of Cyriacus," *Journal for the History of Astronomy* 7 (1976), 41–46 and "The Planetary Tables of Cyriacus," *Journal for the History of Arabic Science* 2 (1978), 53–65.

21. See a similar table in the *Zīj al-Sharīf* MS Ta fol. 31 v; MS Tb, fol. 85 v.

22. J. Chabás and B. R. Goldstein, "Andalusian Astronomy: *al-Zîj al-Muqtabis* of Ibn al-Kammâd," *Archive for History of Exact Sciences* 48 (1994), 1–41 (see pp. 14 and 23).

23. I owe this information to Angel Mestres.

24. This displacement is explicitely mentioned by Maḥmūd b. Muḥammad b. Qāḍīzādah al-Rūmī, known as Mīram Chalabī (d. 1524) in his commentary to the *zīj* of Ulugh Beg: cf. Sédillot II (1853), p. 140.

25. Mean motions have been calculated using Honorino Mielgo's ATMM. See

H. Mielgo, "A Method of Analysis for Mean Motion Astronomical Tables," in J. Casulleras and J. Samsó (eds.), *From Baghdad to Barcelona. Studies in the Islamic Exact Sciences in Honour of Prof. Juan Vernet* (Barcelona, 1966), I, 159–179.

26. I have checked ms. Aleppo, Waqfiyya 1307. A microfilm of this manuscript was obtained from the Institute for the History of Arabic Science (Aleppo), microfilm no. 507.

27. I am following here Benno van Dalen's notation: the two digits after the ± refer to the last two digits of the parameter.

28. This eccentricity is mentioned by Mīram Chalabī in his commentary of Ulugh Beg's canons: see Sédillot II (1853), p. 142.

29. Mīram Chalabī mentions an equivalent eccentricity of $10;23^{p}$ for a radius of the deferent of $49;37^{p}$. See Sédillot II (1853), p. 147.

30. The same set of instructions appears in Ulugh Beg's canons: see Sédillot II (1853), pp. 138–153.

31. Mīram Chalabī mentions a radius of the epiycle of $5;12^{p}$ for a radius of the "inclined sphere" of 60^{p}. He seems to be making a mistake here: $5;12^{p}$ is probably a rounded value and it corresponds to a radius of the deferent of $49;37^{p}$. $6;17,18^{p}$ would be the corresponding epicycle radius for a deferent radius of $60^{p.}$ See Sédillot II (1853), p. 158.

32. See Sédillot II (1853), p. 151.

33. We have seen that Mīram Chalabī also ascribes to Ulugh Beg a radius of the epicycle of $5;12^{p}$ (for a deferent radius of $49;37^{p}$), equivalent to $6;17,18^{p}$ (for $R = 60^{p}$), instead of our $6;17,46^{p}$. With this radius the maximum value of the equation of anomaly for minimum distance would be:

$$\gamma_{max} = \text{atan}\,(6;17,18/(60–12;33,22)) = 7;33,0°.$$

34. Benno van Dalen, after reading a draft of this chapter, suggested that the errors practically disappear if one assumes that Sanjaq Dār made a mistake and used interpolation coefficients 20;24 (instead of 17;24) and 39;36 (instead of 42;36). He is absolutely right. After recalculating the column for mean anomaly 240°, using these erroneous coefficients, the only differences (in the sample values) are:

12	6;23(+1)	216	11;59(–1)
168	6;2(–1)	276	14;15(+4)
180	7;37(–1)	336	10;7(+3)
192	9;12(–1)	348	8;53(+1)
204	10;41(–1)		

XIV

Abraham Zacut and José Vizinho's *Almanach Perpetuum* in Arabic (16th–19th C.)

1. Introduction

The recent publication by José Chabás and Bernard R. Goldstein of a detailed study of the astronomical works of Abraham Zacut (1452–1515) (Chabás & Goldstein, 2000) represents the first serious attempt to evaluate these works and place them within the context of Iberian astronomy at the end of the Middle Ages. Some twenty years ago Goldstein himself presented an important collection of new materials on Zacut (Goldstein, 1981) and thus laid the foundations for a new approach to this important figure after the pioneering study of F. Cantera (1931 and 1935). One of the conclusions Chabás and Goldstein have reached is that, in spite of the assertion appearing in the colophon of the canons of the *Almanach Perpetuum*[1], these canons are not a translation from Hebrew; they are entirely independent from Zacut's *Ḥibbur*, and there is no evidence of the participation of Abraham Zacut in their compilation, which should probably be ascribed to José Vizinho (Chabás & Goldstein, 2000, pp. 95–98). This explains, therefore, the title of this paper.

Among the topics which have attracted the attention of Chabás and Goldstein are the Arabic versions of the *Almanach* made in the sixteenth and seventeenth centuries (Chabás & Goldstein, 2000, pp. 163–164, 170–171), which imply the indirect introduction in the Arab world of the *Alfonsine*

Tables and of other materials derived from the research done by Jewish astronomers who flourished in Southern France in the fourteenth century (Jacob ben David Bonjorn and, also indirectly, Levi ben Gerson). It might therefore be useful to offer a preliminary survey of the manuscripts accessible to me of a part of this tradition: that related to the diffusion of the *Almanach* in the Maghrib from the seventeenth century onwards.

2. The Canons Written in the Mashriq by Mūsā Jālīnūs (912 H/1506–07 AD)

One should bear in mind, however, that the *Almanach* was already known in the Muslim East in the sixteenth century as a result of the version of the canons prepared by the Jewish physician Mūsā Jalīnūs in 912 H/1506–07 AD[2]. He was commissioned to do this work in 911 H/ 1505–06 by a certain ᶜAbd al-Raḥmān, who held the important post of judge of the [Ottoman] army (*al-Qāḍī bi 'l-ᶜaskar*) (MS Escorial 966, fol. 1v. See Nagy, 1978). A superficial reading of these canons and tables has led me to the conclusion that Mūsā Jālīnūs was probably quite alien to Spanish and Maghribī culture. He does not use the standard Andalusī and Maghribī names of the months of the Julian year, but pure Arabic transliterations of the Latin names. It is also surprising that the name of Salamanca, whose meridian is used systematically in Zacut's tables, was probably entirely unknown to him: throughout his canons he repeats that the tables' positions are calculated for the meridian of Toledo,[3] although the tables are exactly the same as in the printed version of the *Almanach.* In spite of this, Mūsā Jālīnūs seems to have understood correctly the use of the tables of the *Almanach*, is aware of the fact that the lunar cycle used by Zacut corresponds to a period of 31 Julian years *and two days* (MS Escorial 966 fol. 3r: see Vernet, 1979, pp. 343 and 349) and had information on the *Alfonsine Tables*: he states that "the Christian King of the Maghrib called Alfonso" (*al-malik al-naṣrānī al-maghribī al-musammā bi-Alfūnsh*) compiled two small tables which allow the easy computation of the ascendant of any anniversary (*taḥwīl*, MS Escorial 966 fol. 10r). He is clearly refering to tables edited under number 11 in Poulle 1984, p. 130.

3. The Maghribī Translation by al-Ḥajarī (ca. 1624 A.D.)

The Maghribī tradition is entirely different and much later. The introduction of the *Almanach* in the Maghrib is the result of a translation by a Morisco exile called Aḥmad b. Qāsim b. Aḥmad b. al-Faqīh Qāsim b. al-Shaykh al-Ḥajarī al-Andalusī (1570– after 1640) who left Spain in 1599 and settled in Marrākush where, after 1608, he became the secretary and interpreter from Spanish of Sultan Mawlāy Zaydān b. Aḥmad al-Manṣūr (d. 1627) and of his two sons, sultans Abū Marwān ᶜAbd al-Malik b. Zaydān (1627–1630) and al-Walīd b. Zaydān (1630–1635) (see Koningsveld, al-Samarral, & Wiegers, 1997; Mannūnī, 1963–64). We know that during his stay in Marrākush he studied astrology with the *faqīh* Aḥmad al-Maṣyūb al-Fāsī (d. 1613) (Koningsveld, al-Samarral, & Wiegers, 1997, pp. 190–192; Lamrabet, 1994, p. 142, no. 496). We do not know the date of his translation of the *Almanach* although it has been suggested that he must have been working on it around 1624 due to the existence of an autograph letter addressed by him to the famous Arabist Jacob Golius in which he asks him about certain astronomical terms (Koningsveld, al-Samarral, & Wiegers, 1997, pp. 43–44).

Whatever the case, al-Ḥajarī's translation is extant in several manuscripts. Two are well known: MS Milan Ambrosiana 338 (C82), dated in 1086 H/ 1675 A.D., carefully described by Griffini (1916, pp. 88–106), and MS Ar. Vatican 963 (Levi della Vida, 1935, pp. 101–102), apparently a copy of the former. In 1983 Khaṭṭābī published an excellent catalogue of the astronomical manuscripts of the Rabat Hassaniya Library in which he described items apparently related to al-Ḥajārī's text and it seemed appropriate to verify their contents. It is clear that MS Rabat Hassaniya 8184 also contains al-Ḥajarī's translation of the canons (Khaṭṭlābī, 1983, pp. 284–286, no. 344) in 21 unnumbered pages (which I have been able to examine), followed by 262 pp. of tables (not seen, except for a few samples): this manuscript seems late and the table of the lunar longitude which corresponds to the third year of the cycle includes a worked example for the year 1816 A.D. Another copy, with slight differences, is extant in MS Hassaniya 1433, fols. 5r–9v (Khaṭṭābī, 1983, pp. 286–287, no. 345), followed (fols. 9v–10r) by an extra chapter on lunar eclipses copied from ᶜAbd al-Raḥmān al-Fāsī's *risāla* (see below). The same MS 1433 (fols. 11v–15v) (Khaṭṭābī, 1983, p. 231, no. 270) contains a summary of al-Ḥajarī's translation, unimportant from a textual point of view but interesting for other reasons. A marginal note (fol. 11v) gives a worked example for 1822 and the text was probably written in Fez: the difference in geographical longitude between Fez and Salamanca is given as 0;46° and the corresponding time difference is $0;3,4^{h}$ (fols. 14v–15r).[4] An incomplete abridgement of the same text (dealing only with the ascendant and division of the houses, longitudes of the Sun, Moon and lunar nodes and latitudes of Venus and Mercury) appears in MS Hassaniya 1331 (pp. 61–65) (Khaṭṭābī, 1983, p. 231, no. 271).

Another manuscript which I have been able to examine in full is Cairo National Library DM 1081 (King, 1981, pp. 139–141; King, 1986, nos. F31, F33 and F52, pp. 140 and 143) which contains three *risāla*s related to the use of Zacut's *zīj*. I will deal here first with the second one (pp. 9–19) identified by King as the translation by al-Ḥajarī (spelt al-Ḥajdarī on p. 19). This identification is correct, although we are dealing here with a version revised by an unknown compiler who acknowledges indirectly his intervention in the text in its colophon (p. 19):

> This is the end of the text as it was found, glory to God. The written canons were extremely corrupt. The text from which we copied was almost illegible and we could not have read it without God's help – let Him be exalted. We contented ourselves with a simple copy of the original when there was no other solution, but we made our best efforts in the transcription and we tried to establish the correct meaning. When we had no other alternative, we just copied the text as it was. Our Lord provides [us with everything] and knows [everything]

A cursory reading of this text, compared to MS Milan Ambrosiana 338 and Rabat Hassaniyya 8184 and 1433, gives me the impression that the author of this recension has begun by correcting al-Ḥajarī's Arabic which – understandably in an author who spent the first thirty years of his life in the Spain of the beginning of the seventeenth century – was by no means faultless. Besides he sometimes has difficulty in understanding certain technical aspects of Zacut's tables: such is the case of the square matrix of 9 integers which appears in each table of the 31-year cycle which allows the computation of lunar longitude (Chabás & Goldstein, 2000, p. 113), which the anonymous author of this recension entirely misunderstands[5]. On other occasions he seems to be unable to identify certain names: this is the case of the chapter in which the *Almanach Perpetuum* states that, although they have computed tables for solar-lunar conjunctions and oppositions in agreement with the method of Poel (Jacob ben David Bonjorn of Perpignan) (see Chabás, 1988,

1991, 1992; Chabás, Roca & Rodríguez, 1992), they want to explain how to compute them using the tables of King Alfonso (Albuquerque, 1986, p. 82). In MS Milan Ambrosiana 338, as well as in Rabat Hassaniya 8184 (p. 9 in my own consecutive numeration) Poel has become *Fa'.l* and King Alfonso is *Sulṭān Alfunsh* (Griffini, 1916, p. 97), while in MS Cairo DM 1081 (p. 14) Poel has disappeared and the Castilian king becomes *Sulṭān al-Rūm* without further identification. In a similar way, the final chapter of the *Almanach* quotes the pseudo-ptolemaic *Centiloquio* (Albuquerque, 1986, p. 100) (*Karpós*): obviously al-Ḥajarī's knowledge did not allow him to identify this work with the standard Arabic title of *Kitāb al-Thamara* and the Ambrosiana MS merely gives a transliteration of the Spanish *Centiloquio* by *al-Sintiluqī*[6], while the anonymous author of the Cairo recension, who does not understand this peculiar coinage, refers only to Ptolemy and does not give any other precision. Finally, as the canons of the *Almanach* are not very systematic in the numbering of the chapters (Chabás & Goldstein, 2000, pp. 96–97), it is no surprise that such numbers in the Cairo MS are not always the same as in the MSS of the Ambrosiana and Rabat. There are many more examples but I believe that the aforementioned evidence is sufficient to establish that MS Cairo DM 1081, pp. 9–19, contains a recension of the Arabic text of Zacut & Vizinho's canons which is not another copy of al-Ḥajarī's translation, but rather a revision of the same text.

4. Maghribī Texts on the Use of Zacut's Zīj

4.1 *ᶜAbd al-Raḥmān al-Fāsī (1631–1685)*. This is, so far, all I know about al-Ḥajarī's MSS. It is interesting to remark that Zacut and Vizinho's *Almanach*, in al-Ḥajarī's translation, attracted the attention of several Maghribī astronomers from the second half of the seventeenth century onwards. Consequently a series of commentaries and reelaborations of this text appeared, in which the authors tried to explain how to compute planetary longitudes and latitudes using cycles (*bi-l-adwār*). One of the earliest dated is ᶜAbd al-Raḥmān al-Fāsī (Fez, 1631–1685) (Renaud, 1932, p. 182, no. 541; Brockelmann, 1938, pp. 694–695, and 1949, p. 612; Levi-Provençal, 1960; Lamrabet, 1994, pp. 151–153, no. 536): the third introduction to the *Almanach* extant in ms. Cairo DM 1081 (pp. 20–28) is attributed by the copyist to him (MS Cairo DM 1081 p. 20; King, 1986, p. 140, no. F31). This attribution is not beyond all possible doubt, for the text begins dealing with the problem of converting Hijra dates into the Christian calendar and gives an example for year 1113/1701 A.D., some seventeen years after the death of the supposed author. It seems, however, that we should accept it for, as we have seen, MS Hassaniya 1433 (fols. 9v–10r) contains a quotation on lunar eclipses from a text by Abū Zayd Sīdī ᶜAbd al-Raḥmān al-Fāsī which can be found in Cairo DM 1081 p. 25. The title of al-Fāsī's work is *Tuḥfat al-muḥtāj fī ᶜilm al-taᶜdīl wa 'l-azyāj* ("A present for those who need to learn the computation of true longitudes and the use of *zīj*es") and another (worse) manuscript of the same *risāla*, also anonymous, is MS Hassaniyya 1433 (fols. 1r–4v) (Khaṭṭābī, 1983, pp. 153–154, no. 178). ᶜAbd al-Raḥmān al-Fāsī says that he read the *Risāla Zakūtiyya* in a manuscript annotated by ᶜAbd Allāh b. ᶜAbd al-Qādir Abī Shaykh al-Lakhmī (fl. 1668)[7]: our author often quotes ᶜAbd Allāh b. ᶜAbd al-Qādir's notes and he calls him *ṣāḥib al-ṭurar* ("the author of the notes") but the *Kanz al-asrār* (MS Rabat General Library D2027, p. 84) of Muḥammad al-Muᶜṭī Marīn (see below) also ascribes to him an independent *risāla* on Zacut's *zīj*. A second source used by ᶜAbd al-Raḥmān al-Fāsī is a *risāla* on the same topic written by the *faqīh* and *muᶜaddil* Sīdī ᶜAbd Allāh Aṣnāk al-Marrākushī (?). Al-Fāsī decided to assemble in one text the materials he had gathered in the two aforementioned sources and this is why the colophon of both manuscripts states that this is the end of the *Risālat al-risālatayn al-madhkūratayn* ("The epistle [based] on the two aforementioned epistles") (MS Cairo DM 1081, p. 28; MS Hassaniya 1433, fol. 4v). To this he added instructions for calculating the Christian date from the date in the Muslim calendar, for the *Almanach Perpetuum* is entirely based on the Julian calendar. For that purpose he begins with a long quotation of the *Minhāj al-ṭālib fī taᶜdīl al-kawākib* of Ibn al-Bannā' (1256–1321) (Vernet, 1952, pp. 19–20) which explains the procedure for calculating the *rūmī* date with the era of Alexander and, from here (using an equivalence given by the *ṣāḥib al-ṭurar*) the corresponding Julian date from A.D. This is followed by the aforementioned example of conversion of the 23rd of Shawwāl 1113/11th March (Julian) 1702 A.D for which al-Fāsī (?) uses a direct procedure.

4.2 *ᶜAbd Allāh Aṣnāk al-Marrākushī (fl. ca. 1655).* ᶜAbd al-Raḥmān al-Fāsī is careful to state the sources of his quotations and, thus, he distinguishes between, for example, *al-mutarjim ᶜan/ᶜalā risālat mu'allif al-jadāwil* ("the translator of the canons of the author of the tables"), the *ṣāḥib al-ṭurar* (often quoted in his full name) and, finally, the *Risāla ᶜarabiyya* (the Arabic canons) which should be identified with the work written by his third source: ᶜAbd Allāh Aṣnāk al-Marrākushī, who was also dead at the time of the composition of the *Tuḥfa*. Al-Fāsī's quotations have led me to identify this source in the contents of MS Hassaniya 1331 (pp. 53–61) (Khaṭṭābī, 1983, pp. 231–232, no. 271): some materials from the same source also appear in MS Cairo 1081 (pp. 1–2), which corresponds to the beginning of the first of the three *risāla*s extant in the Cairo MS. This source contains a useful collection of worked examples for the computation of solar-lunar conjunctions oppositions, as well as the longitudes of Saturn, Mars, Venus and Mercury. The dates used by the author correspond to 1652, 1656 and 1657, which is a further proof of the early interest Moroccan astronomers had in al-Ḥajarī's translation. It is possible that Aṣnak's text was written in Marrākush, for the time difference between the locality and Salamanca is given as $17^{m}8$. One of the chapters of this *risāla* (MS Hassaniya 1331, p. 58) deals with the division of the houses of the horoscope explaining the dual longitude method (based on a trisection of the arc of the ecliptic between the cusps), a method which all known Islamic sources attribute to Maghribī astronomers (North, 1986, pp. 40–42; Kennedy, 1996, p. 540 and *passim*). An example is given, in which the longitudes of the first six houses are:

I	215°	IV	309°
II	246;20°	V	337;40°
III	277;40°	VI	6;20°

From these data the calculated latitude of the place (using North's programme HOROSC) is around 33°, a value which seems to fit Fez better than Marrākush. In any case it is interesting to remark that Aṣnak is one of the few authors – amongst those examined here – who avoids using Zacut's tables for the computation of the ascendant and the division of the houses, a set of tables that was calculated for Salamanca and should not be used for other latitudes.[9]

Aṣnak's text is followed, in MS Hassaniya 1331, by an abridgement of al-Ḥajarī's translation (pp. 61–65), which might be a part of Aṣnak's *risāla*. However, one must bear in mind that this MS is a *majmūᶜ* which contains materials from other sources, like quotations from al-Fāsī's *Tuḥfa*, including the example for a date conversion for year 1113/1702 (p. 51). A colophon on

p. 65 explains the history of al-Ḥajarī's translation and it is followed, on the same page, by a chronological note in which it is stated that if we add 585 to the Hijra years we will obtain the A.D. years: this rule would obviously be correct for c. 1205 H./1790 A.D. The MS was, then, used in the second half of the eighteenth century and it contains (p. 67) twelve verses of an *urjūza* on the use of Zacut's *zīj* by the *shaykh* Sīdī ᶜAbd al-ᶜAzīz al-Wazkānī, who can probably be identified as Abū ᶜAbd Allāh Muḥammad b. ᶜAbd al-ᶜAzīz b. ᶜAbd al-Salām al-Wazzānī al-Wazkānī (or his father) who was alive in 1183/1769 (King, 1986, no. F58; Lamrabet, 1994, p. 157, no. 557.).

4.3 *Muḥammad al-Muᶜṭī (d. 1808) and his source ᶜAbd al-Karīm Agbāl (unknown date between 1655 and 1797).* Zacut's tradition thus continued in the Maghrib in the eighteenth century. A well known astronomer, Abū 'l-Rabīᶜ Sulaymān b. Aḥmad al-Fishtālī al-Fāsī (d. 1793) (Renaud, 1932, p. 183, no. 543; Brockelmann, 1938, p. 709; Lamrabet, 1994, pp. 158–159, no. 565; Calvo, 1994) wrote a *Risālat al-anwār fī 'l-taᶜdīl bi 'l-adwār* (not seen)[10] and the interest endured in the next century, for Abū Isḥāq Ibrāhīm b. Muḥammad al-Tādilī al-Ribāṭī (d. 1894) (Lamrabet, 1994, pp. 164–165, no. 594) studied one of the chapters of the *al-Zīj al-Zakūṭī* with his master, the physician and astronomer of Rabat Muḥammad al-Raṭal. Another source of information can be found in a *risāla* entitled *Kanz al-asrār wa-fayḍ al-anwār fī taᶜdīl al-nayyirayn wa 'l-khamsa al-mutaḥayyira bi 'l-adwār* ("Treasure of secrets and abundance of lights on the computation of the true positions of the Sun, Moon and five planets using cycles") written in 1211/1797 by Muḥammad al-Muᶜṭī b. Aḥmad al-Ṭayyib b. Muḥammad[11] Marīn al-Najjār al-Ribāṭī (d. 1808)[12]. This work was finished in the *zāwiya* of Wazzān, NW of Fez and near al-Qaṣr al-Kabīr, an institution which played an important role in eighteenth century Morocco (see Lourido, 1978, pp. 270–275); this points to another area of diffusion of al-Ḥajarī's translation, apart from Fez and Marrākush. We have already seen that ᶜAbd Allāh al-Lakhmī was a *muwaqqit* in al-Qaṣr al-Kabīr (in the seventeenth century) and that ᶜAbd al-ᶜAzīz al-Wazkānī was also called al-Wazzānī. In this *risāla* Muḥammad al-Muᶜṭī mentions (p. 84) a list of astronomers who had written works on Zacut's tables. Among them we find an unidentified *risāla* written by the Imām al-Ḥ.mānī al-Andalusī, which is – according to Muḥammad al-Muᶜṭī – the best of the whole collection: I wonder whether al-Ḥ.mānī is just a corruption of al-Ḥajarī. Two other sources quoted are already known to us: ᶜAbd al-Raḥmān al-Fāsī and Sīdī ᶜAbd Allāh b. Sīdī ᶜAbd al-Qādir Abī Shaykh al-Lakhmī, who wrote a commentary on the *Rawḍat al-azhār.*

A fourth source is new: the unidentified *faqīh* and *muᶜaddil* Sīdī ᶜAbd al-Karīm, known as Agbāl, who must have lived some time between the second half of the seventeenth century[13] and 1797, by which time it is known that he was already dead. Agbāl's work is extant in MS Rabat General Library D2014 (pp. 1–55) and it has a descriptive title: *Risāla fī kayfiyyat al-taᶜdīl bi 'l-zīj alladhī waḍaᶜa-hu Ibrāhīm al-Yahūdī al-maᶜrūf bi-Azkūṭ li-taᶜdīl al-kawākib al-sayyāra* ... ("Epistle on how to compute with the *zīj* calculated by the Jew Abraham, known as Azkūṭ, to obtain the true longitudes of the planets ...").[14] Once more it seems that this character was active in the North of Morocco because he states (p. 1) that Zacut's *zīj* had been calculated for his own city, Salamanca, at the extreme limits of the Christian lands (*bi-aqṣā bilād al-Rūm*), whose longitude is 25;46° and latitude 41;19°. According to the author, this longitude is similar to that of Ceuta, Tanger, Aṣīla, al-Qaṣr [al-Kabīr] or Fez, for which he gives a longitude of 24;52°, not documented in other sources. In spite of this, he gives (p. 14) a time correction for the computation of lunar longitude of 17^{m} which is the value given by Aṣnak, probably for Marrākush.

Agbāl wrote his *risāla* after reading many other works of the same kind, all of which are excessively brief. Agbāl's *risāla* is not as concise but it contains a certain number of errors which are difficult to understand: for example, on p. 3 he says that Zacut's *zīj* was calculated for Alexander's era, from which he obtained the Christian era: this is followed by an incomplete rule to perform this kind of operation. He also has difficulty (pp. 19–21) in understanding the function of the two tables of lunar latitude in Zacut's *Almanach* (Albuquerque, 1986, pp. 221 and 223; Chabás & Goldstein, 2000, pp. 130–131) and confuses the argument of latitude with the lunar anomaly; in Arabic the term *ḥiṣṣa* can refer to either (pp. 21–24). He also refers to tables to calculate the longitude of Mercury structured in Arabic (?) and *ᶜajamī* months and to tables of right ascension, included in Zacut's *zīj*, computed from Aries 0°: the tables of right ascension in the *Almanach* (Albuquerque, 1986, p. 222) have the usual origin in Capricorn 0°. Far more interesting is the fact that he mentions a table for the velocity of Mars which reaches a maximum of 0;39°/day (p. 40): the *Almanach Perpetuum* (Albuquerque, 1986, pp. 381–386) contains only one double argument table which produces directly the velocity of Mercury and it has been argued, convincingly, that Zacut's source was Judah ben Asher (d. 1391) whose *Ḥuqqot shamayim* include double argument tables of this kind for all five planets[15]. I do not think, however, that Agbāl is referring here to this tradition, but rather to a different one attested to in tables related to both the Toledan and the Alfonsine corpora (Goldstein, Chabás & Mancha, 1994) as well as in a set of tables calculated ca. 1344 in Fez by Ibn ᶜAzzūz al-Qusanṭīnī (Samsó, 1997, pp. 88–91, 104–105). These tables are not double argument and they compute two different functions, whose composition gives the planetary velocity as a final result: the arguments of the two functions are the true centre and the true anomaly of the planet. For the case of Mars, the maximum value of the first function is 38;40′ in the Alfonsine tradition (38;30′ in Ibn ᶜAzzūz's *zīj*), which agrees with the 39′ mentioned by Agbāl.

Let us return now to Muḥammad al-Muᶜṭī's *Kanz al-asrār* which is a fairly long text (18 chapters) preserved, as we have already seen, in MS Rabat General Library D2027 (pp. 83–118): this MS has been copied by two Maghribī hands (one for pp. 83–92, an another for pp. 93–118). The author gives a competent account of the use of the tables of the *Almanach*[16] and, in addition to the four aforementioned sources, and Aṣnak's *Risāla ᶜarabiyya* (pp. 89, 102), he also quotes (pp. 101–102) Ibn Muᶜādh's *Tabulae Jahen* for the limits of solar eclipses for the latitude of Jaén[17] and for another unspecified latitude (probably Damascus) which he takes from an otherwise unknown *Yasāra mukhtaṣara min Zīj ᶜAlā' al-Dīn ibn al-Shāṭir al-Dimashqī* (p. 103), a summary of Ibn al-Shāṭir's *zīj* (on the diffusion of this latter work in the Maghrib, see Samsó, 1998).

Like many other authors, Muḥammad al-Muᶜṭī begins by posing the chronological problem (pp. 84–87) and deals with the Christian era whose beginning corresponds to Saturday 1st of January, seven days after Jesus' birth, in a village called B.'.l.n.ī (*Bālanī*? from Sp. Belén), near Jerusalem. January is the third (actually the fourth) month of year 312 of Alexander's era, which precedes A.D. by 311 years and 3 months. He gives a correct rule for date conversion and uses Wednesday 22nd April 1797, three hours and thirty minutes after midday, as an example for the correction of the hour as a result of the difference in geographical longitude.

The *risāla* ends with a rule for the visibility of the new moon, based on the Indian condition of visibility (the difference between the descension of the Moon, at moonset, and the sun, at sunset, should reach a minimum of 12°, see King, 1994). There seems to be a mistake in the formulation of the extant text because instead of applying a correction of 2/3 (a standard value which corresponds roughly to the tangent of the latitude of Baghdad but also to that of Fez) of the lunar latitude to the lunar longitude in order to obtain a modified lunar longitude, this correction is applied to the difference in descensions between the Moon and the Sun, which does not seem to make much sense.

5. Conclusion

This is the provisional end of my survey. No spectacular results have been obtained but the information gathered provides a good example of the transmission of astronomical ideas from Spain and Southern France to both ends of the Mediterranean and of a survival of a tradition until very late. It is also interesting to remark that, as Mūsā Jālīnūs' version was relatively unproductive, this was the result of the work of only one man, the Morisco exile al-Ḥajarī, whose efforts, unfortunately, were not followed up by other scholars who might have put the Arab world in contact with the new European astronomy from the sixteenth century onwards. Another interesting topic for further study is to see how Zacut's tradition is mixed with other kinds of materials derived from Andalusī-Maghribī sources (the names of Ibn Muᶜādh, Ibn al-Kammād, Ibn al-Bannā', Ibn al-Raqqām appear often in the manuscripts) and also from the Eastern tradition of Muḥyī al-Dīn al-Maghribī and Ibn al-Shāṭir.

Acknowledgements

This paper was written as a part of a research project on "The circulation of astronomical ideas in the Mediterranean between the twelfth and the nineteenth centuries", sponsored by the Spanish Ministry of Education and Culture (reference BHA 2000-0722). Some years ago, my master Prof. Juan Vernet gave me his own annotated copy of MS Escorial 966 which I have used here. Bernard R. Goldstein sent me all the information he had about MSS Ambrosiana 338 and Vatican 963 and he lent me his microfilm of MS Cairo DM 1081 (which had been given to him by David A. King). By doing so Prof. Goldstein followed a tradition which began more than thirty years ago:

whenever he wanted me to do a particular job he was not very keen on doing himself, he made sure I had the materials I required. I can offer two good examples of this: why on earth should I be the author of the *Dictionary of Scientific Biography* articles on Levi ben Gerson and al-Biṭrūjī? He has done the same thing again and I hope to have fulfilled his wishes. I owe all the Rabat MSS used here to the efforts of my postgraduate student Hamid Berrani and to the kindness of Professors Aḥmad Shawqī Binbine (Director of the Hassaniya Library) and Aḥmad Tawfīq (Director of the Rabat General Library). José Chabás and David King read a draft of this paper, corrected some mistakes and offered useful suggestions. My gratitude to all of them.

BIBLIOGRAPHY

Albuquerque, Luís de

1986: Facsimile edition of Abraham Zacut's *Almanach Perpetuum* (Leiria, 1496). Lisbon.

Brockelmann, Carl

1938: *Geschichte der Arabischen Litteratur. Zweiter Supplementband.* Leiden, E.J. Brill.

1949: *Geschichte der Arabischen Litteratur.* Vol. II. Leiden, E.J. Brill.

Calvo, Emilia

1994: "On the Construction of Ibn Bāṣo's Universal Astrolabe (14th c.) According to a Moroccan Astronomer of the 18th Century", *Journal for the History of Arabic Science* 10, pp. 53–67.

Cantera, F.

1931: "El judío salmantino Abraham Zacut. Notas para la historia de la Astronomía en la España Medieval", *Revista de la Academia de Ciencias Exactas, Físico-Químicas y Naturales de Madrid* 27.

1935: *Abraham Zacut. Siglo XV.* Madrid, *s.d.* (1935).

Chabás, José

1988: "Une période de récurrence de syzygies au XIVe siècle: le cycle de Jacob ben David Bonjorn", *Archives Internationales d'Histoire des Sciences* 38, pp. 243–51.

1991: "The Astronomical Tables of Jacob ben David Bonjorn", *Archive for the History of Exact Sciences* 42, pp. 279–314.

1992: "L'influence de l'astronomie de Lévi ben Gershom sur Jacob ben David Bonjorn", in Gad Freudenthal (ed.), *Studies on Gersonides. A Fourteenth-Century Jewish Philosopher-Scientist.* Brill. Leiden-New York-Köln, pp. 47–54.

Chabás, José, Roca, Antoni and Rodríguez, Xavier

1992: *L'Astronomia de Jacob ben David Bonjorn.* Barcelona.

Chabás, José and Goldstein, Bernard R.

2000: *Astronomy in the Iberian Peninsula: Abraham Zacut and the Transition from Manuscript to Print, Transactions of the American Philosophical Society* 90, Pt. 2, Philadelphia.

Goldstein, Bernard R.

1981: "The Hebrew Astronomical Tradition: New Sources", *Isis* 72, pp. 237–251.

Goldstein, Bernard R., Chabás, José and Mancha, José Luís
1994: "Planetary and Lunar Velocities in the Castilian Alfonsine Tables", *Proceedings of the American Philosophical Society* 138, no. 1, pp. 61–95.
Griffini, E.
1916: *Lista dei manoscritti arabi nuovo fondo della Biblioteca Ambrosiana di Milano, Rivista degli Studi Orientali* 7.
Kennedy, E.S.
1996: "The Astrological Houses as Defined by Medieval Islamic Astronomers", in J. Casulleras and J. Samsó (eds.), *From Baghdad to Barcelona*, Barcelona, vol. 2, pp. 535–78.
Kennedy, E.S. and M.H.
1987: *Geographical coordinates of localities from Islamic sources*, Frankfurt.
Khaṭṭābī, Muḥammad al-ᶜArabī al-
1983: *Fahāris al-Khizāna al-Ḥasaniyya* vol. III. Rabat.
King, David A.
1981: *Fihris al-makhṭūṭāt al-ᶜilmiyya al-maḥfūẓa bi-Dār al-Kutub al-Miṣriyya*, vol. I, Cairo.
1986: *A Survey of the Scientific Manuscripts in the Egyptian National Library*, Winona Lake, Indiana.
1994: "Ru'yat al-hilāl", in *Encyclopédie de l'Islam* VIII, fasc. 141–2, Leiden-Paris, pp. 669–70.
Koningsveld, P.S. van, al-Samarral, Q., and Wiegers, G.A.
1997: *Aḥmad ibn Qāsim al-Ḥajarī, Kitāb Nāṣir al-Dīn ᶜalā 'l-Qawm al-Kāfirīn (The Supporter of Religion against the Infidel)*, C.S.I.C. and A.E.C.I., Madrid.
Lamrabet, Driss
1994: *Introduction à l'Histoire des Mathématiques Maghrébines*, Rabat.
Levi della Vida, Giorgio
1935: *Elenco dei Manoscritti Arabi Islamici della Biblioteca Vaticana. Vaticani Berberiniani Borgiani Rossiani*, Città del Vaticano.
Lévi-Provençal, E.
1960: "ᶜAbd al-Raḥmān b. ᶜAbd al-Ḳādir al-Fāsī", *Encyclopédie de l'Islam*, Leiden-Paris, vol. 1, p. 88.
Lourido, Ramón
1978: *Marruecos en la segunda mitad del siglo XVIII. Vida interna, política, social y religiosa durante el sultanato de Sīdī Muḥammad b. ᶜAbd Allāh (1757–1790)*, Madrid, Instituto Hispano-Arabe de Cultura.
al-Mannūnī, Muḥammad
1963–64: "Ẓāhira taᶜrībiyya fī 'l-Maghrib ayyām al-Saᶜdiyyīn", *Revista del Instituto de Estudios Islámicos* (Madrid) 11–12, pp. 329–58.
Nagy, Gy. Káldy
1978: "Ḳāḍī ᶜAskar" in *Encyclopédie de l'Islam*, Leiden-Paris, vol. 4, p. 392.
North, John
1986: *Horoscopes and History*, London.
Poulle, Emmanuel
1984: *Les Tables Alphonsines avec les canons de Jean de Saxe*, Paris.
Renaud, H.P.J.
1932: "Additions et corrections à Suter", *Isis* 18, pp. 166–183.
Samsó, Julio
1992: *Las Ciencias de los Antiguos en al-Andalus*, Madrid, Mapfre.

1997: "Andalusian Astronomy in 14th Century Fez: *al-Zīj al-Muwāfiq* of Ibn ᶜAzzūz al-Qusantīnī", *Zeitschrift für Geschichte der Arabisch-Islamischen Wissenschaften* 11, pp. 73–110.

1998: "An Outline of the History of Maghribī Zijes from the End of the Thirteenth Century", *Journal for the History of Astronomy* 29, pp. 93–102.

1998–99: "Abraham Zacuto en el Magrib: sobre la presunta cristianización del astrónomo judío y la islamización de su discípulo José Vizinho", *Anuari de Filologia. Estudis Hebreus i Arameus. Homenatge a la Dra. Teresa Martínez Sáiz* XXI, secció E, Número 8, pp. 155–65.

Vernet, Juan

1952: *Contribución al estudio de la labor astronómica de Ibn al-Bannā'*, Tetuán.

1979: "Una versión árabe resumida del *Almanach Perpetuum* de Zacuto", in Vernet, *Estudios sobre Historia de la Ciencia Medieval*, Barcelona-Bellaterra, pp. 333–51.

NOTES

1. Albuquerque, 1986, p. 100: "Aquí se acaba la reçela [Ar. *risāla*] de las tablas tresladadas de abrayco en latin et de latin en noestro vulgar romançe per mestre jusepe vezino deçipolo del actor de las tablas". On the difficulties Maghribī astronomers had to understand this colophon see Samsó, 1998–99.
2. Extant in MS Escorial 966: the year 912 H appears in the colophon of the canons (fol. 12v). On the other hand the text uses as an example for the computation of the solar longitude and the longitude of Venus the 14th August 1505 in which a lunar eclipse took place (Esc. 966 fols. 2v and 8v). See J. Vernet (1979).
3. Esc. 966 fol. 3r, 4r, 7v, 8v. In fols. 10v–11r he gives instructions for calculating the ascendant and dividing the houses using the tables of the *Almanach* and states that these tables can only be used in places with latitude 41;30°: this latitude does not fit Toledo or Salamanca exactly (for which the latitude used by Zacut is 41;19°).
4. The longitude of Salamanca used by Zacut is 25;46° and 25° is a standard value for the longitude of Fez in the Andalusī-Maghribī tradition: see E.S. & M.H. Kennedy, 1987, pp. 117–118.
5. Cairo DM 1081 p. 11. At the end of the page (right margin) there is an explanatory note followed by the remark: "The meaning of this was explained by ᶜUmar Khawāja Tuḥamī Afan[dī], interpreter of English (*tarjumān al-inklīz*) in the fortress of Algiers (*maḥrūsa al-Jazā'ir*)".
6. Griffini, 1916, p. 99. MS Escorial 966 contains, after the recension of Mūsā Jālīnūs, a second set of more elaborate canons for the use of the *Almanach* (fols. 13v–18v): in fol. 17 v the *Centiloquio* is translated by *al-Mi'a Kalima* ("The hundred words").
7. He was a *muwaqqit* in al-Qaṣr al-Kabīr and the author of a commentary on the *Rawḍat al-azhār*, written in Fez in 794/1391–92 by al-Jadarī. This commentary is extant in MSS 4151 and 7077 of the Ḥasaniyya Library (Khaṭṭābī, 1983, pp. 139–141, nos. 162–163). The explicit of this work in ms. 4151 states that the commentary was finished after midday prayer of Friday 7 Rabīᶜ II 1079 [/3 September (Julian) 1668, which was a Thursday]. Lamrabet, 1994, p. 156 (no. 552) dates this work in 1748 (?), which seems a mistake. ᶜAbd Allāh b. ᶜAbd al-Qādir was apparently dead at the time of the composition of the *Tuḥfa*.
8. MS Hassaniya 1331, p. 53; Cairo DM 1081, p. 24, according to the *Risāla ᶜarabiyya*,

but al-Fāsī says that he has found a marginal note in this place written by one of the good scholars (*bi-khaṭṭ baᶜḍ al-fuḍalā'*): 17^m corresponds to Marrākush and surroundings, while the correction for Fez is only 8^m (end of quotation). According to al-Fāsī's opinion the correction for Fez should only be 3^m, for the difference in longitude between the city of the author of the tables and Fez is 0;46°. A time correction for Marrākush of 17^m could correspond to a longitude for that city of 21;20° (E.S. & M.H. Kennedy, 1987, p. 218), for which the calculated value would be $17;44^m$. As for Fez, a time difference of 8^m does not fit exactly any documented geographical longitude of that city (E.S. & M.H. Kennedy, 1987, pp. 117–118): with a longitude of 24°, the time difference would be $7;4^m$. A time difference of 3^m fits a longitude for Fez of 25° and it is approximately the same as the one used in the summary of al-Ḥajarī's translation extant in MS Hassaniya 1433 (see above).

9. Mūsā Jālīnūs (in MS Escorial, fol. 10v–11r) explains that these tables should not be used for latitudes different from that for which they have been computed and the same kind of remark can be found in MS Rabat General Library D2027 (p. 88), which contains a *risāla* by al-Muᶜṭī (see below). In MS Cairo DM 1081 p. 21 we find a marginal note with a corrupt rule allowing the correction of Zacut's values for other latitudes. Finally, also in MS Cairo DM 1081, p. 34, an appendix gives instructions for calculating the ascendant and for dividing the houses according to the standard method.
10. According to Mannūnī (1963–64, p. 353) this *risāla* is extant in MS Rabat General Library 1468K, pp. 278–303. I failed to find it during a visit to the Library in March 2002. The manuscript number is apparently wrong and the librarians were unable to find any reference to this work by al-Fishtālī in any of the manuscripts in the Collection.
11. In the colophon of the MS. Rabat General Library 2027D (p. 118) this part of the name is given as al-Ṭayyib b. Muḥammad b. Muḥammad b. Muḥammad.
12. MS. Rabat General Library 2027D, pp. 83–118. In p. 118 the author states that he finished his epistle in the Zāwiya of Wazzān half an equal hour after sunset of Sunday 2nd of Dhū-l-Ḥijja (according to the calendrical computation, *bi-ḥisāb al-ᶜalāma*) or the 1st of Dhū-l-Ḥijja (according to the actual vision of the new moon, *bi-ḥisāb al-ru'ya*) of year 1211 H., 17th May 1797 A.D. On the author see also Lamrabet, 1994, p. 159 (no. 570) who reads Moreno (*M.rīnū*) instead of Marīn. There is also another astronomer called al-Masnāwī Moreno al-Ribāṭī (Lamrabet, 1994, p. 159, no. 566).
13. Muḥammad al-Muᶜṭī states in the *Kanz* (MS Rabat General Library D2027, p. 102) that Sīdī ᶜAbd al-Karīm Agbāl wrote his *risāla* on the *Risāla ᶜarabiyya* and we have already seen that this latter source should be identified with Aṣnak's work, probably written between 1650 and 1660.
14. MS Rabat General Library D2014 contains Agbāl's canons followed by a copy of the edition of the *Almanach Perpetuum* printed in Venice 1502 (15th July) by Petrus Liechtenstein Coloniensis (on this edition see Chabás & Goldstein, 2000, p. 162). Both the manuscript and the printed text have their pages numbered in pencil by a modern hand following the Arabic order (from right to left). The Latin titles and subtitles as well as the arguments of the tables (names of the months, for example) have been translated into Arabic between the lines. Arabic (and Hebrew) notes and comments have been added to the printed text. In p. 455 a note in Arabic states that the book was the property of Sīdī Muḥammad b. Aḥmad al-Qusanṭīnī al-Manṣūrī.
15. Chabás & Goldstein, 2000, pp. 50 and 145. A reference to Zacut's table can be found in the *Kanz al-asrār* of Muḥammad al-Muᶜṭī (MS Rabat General Library D2027, pp.

116–117). An Arabic version of the table appears, for example, in MS Escorial 966 (fols. 176r–178v) and in MS Cairo DM 1081, pp. 314–319.

16. With occasional corrections. Such is the case of the computation of the latitude of Jupiter which uses, as one of the arguments, the anomaly of the planet: Zacut (Albuquerque, 1986, p. 93) considers that no correction in the anomaly is necessary after the completion of the first cycle of 86 years, while Muḥammad al-Muᶜṭī (p. 109) says that research (*istiqrā'*) has established that a correction of 0;7° per cycle should be subtracted.
17. It corresponds to chapter 22 of the Latin text of the *Tabulae Jahen* (see Samsó, 1992, pp. 152–166). The same quotation appears in MS Hassaniya 1433 (fol. 14r) and Cairo DM 1081 (p. 5): these two latter texts are narrowly related. Muḥammad al-Muᶜṭī also gives Zacut's limits for the latitude of Salamanca, as quoted by Agbāl (p. 102) and another set of limits for Fez, "according to some [astronomers]": from 5^s 17;48° to 6^s 12;12° and from 11^s 17;48° to 0^s 12;12°.

XV

On the Arabic translation of the colophon of the *Almanach Perpetuum*

The canons of the Spanish version of the *Almanach Perpetuum* end with a colophon which Maghribī readers seem to have found difficult to understand to the:

> Aquí se acaba la reçela [Ar. *risāla*] et las tablas tresladadas de abrayco en latin et de latin en noestro vulgar romançe per mestre jusepe vezino deçipolo del actor de las tablas[1].

This could be translated as:

> This is the end of the epistle and of the tables translated from Hebrew into Latin and from Latin into our colloquial Romance language by master Jusepe Vezino, disciple of the author of the tables.

The main problem seems to have been the identification of what a Romance language is and the extent to which this language is different from Latin. Thus, in MS Rabat Ḥasaniyya 8184 (p. 21)[2] - which contains al-Ḥajarī's Arabic translation of the canons - we read, written in

[1] Facsimile edition (Lisbon, 1986), p. 100.

[2] Muḥammad al-ᶜArabī al-Khaṭṭābī, *Fahāris al-Khizāna al-Ḥasaniyya* vol. III (Rabat, 1983), pp. 284-286 (no. 344). The same words reappear in MS Ḥasaniyya 1331 (p. 65): Khaṭṭābī, *Fahāris* p. 231, no 271.

incorrect Arabic which can easily be misunderstood, the following translation of the colophon:

ترجمة من عبراني الى لغة اللتين في لسان رَمْنَص وهي
اللغة العجمية المتصرّفة في بلاد سبانية وهي بلاد
الاندلس على يد المعلّم يوشب تلميذ المؤلّف للجداول
...

> Translation from Hebrew into the Latin language in (*sic*) the language of *Ramnaṣ* (*sic*), which is the non-Arabic (*ᶜajamiyya*) language used in the land of *Sbāniyya*, which is the same as al-Andalus, by master Yūshab, disciple of the author of the tables...

Here Romance has been transformed into *Ramnaṣ*. On the other hand there seems to be some confusion between Latin and Romance. The translator is, probably, unaware of the fact that the first edition of the *Almanach* (Leiria, 1496, in the press of Abraham Samuel Dortas) was printed twice, once with the canons in Latin and, again, in Spanish, both versions apparently due to Vizinho himself. In any case, in both prints, the tables were exactly the same, with their headings in Latin.[3]

The confusion becomes greater in the explicit of MS Cairo DM 1081 (p. 19) where the reference to the Spanish version has disappeared and Spanish is identified with Latin:

انتهت الرسالة للجداول المترجمة من عبراني الى لغة
اللتين ومن اللتين الى اللسان العرب [كذا] واللّتين هي
اللغة العجميّة المتصرّفة في بلاد اسبانية وهي بلاد
الاندلس على يد المعلّم يوشب تلميذ المؤلّف زكوط
جامع الجداول وترجمها من لسان الرمُونص عبيد ربّه
واسير ذنبه [كذا] الراجي عفو ربّه احمد بن بلقاسم بن
الفقيه قاسم بن الشيخ الجحدري [الحجدري] الاندلسي.

> End of the canons on [the use of] the tables, translated from Hebrew into Latin and from Latin into Arabic. "Latin" is the non-Arabic [*al-ᶜajamiyya*] used in the land of Spain, which is al-Andalus. [The translation from Hebrew] was made by master Yushab, disciple of the

---

[3] Luís de Albuquerque, *Introduçao* to the facsimile edition of the *Almanach* (Lisbon, 1986), p. 24.

> author Zacut, who compiled the tables. The translation from Romance [*Ramūnṣ* in the Arabic text] was made by the little servant of his Lord [*ᶜubayd Rabbi-hi*] and prisoner of his own sins - who hopes to obtain mercy from his Lord - Aḥmad b. B.l-Qāsim[4] b. al-Shaykh al-Ḥajdarī [or al-Jaḥdarī] al-Andalusī.

I have found the same colophon, with small variants, in other MSS such as Ḥasaniyya 1433[5] where it appears twice. In fol. 1r we read a correct interpretation, for it states: "according to the canons of the *zīj* written by its author [the name is not mentioned] in Hebrew, later translated into Latin and, from Latin to Romance". In fol. 9v, however, the reference to the Latin translation has been omitted and we read "End of the canons of the tables, translated from Hebrew [blank in the MS] and Latin into the Romance language [...]" but it adds: "the *r.m.n.ṣ.* is the little servant of God and prisoner of his own sins... Aḥmad b. Qāsim..."

انتهى الرسالة للجداول مترجمة من عبرانيّ [بياض في المخطوط] واللتين في لسان رمنص...الرمنص عبيد لامه [كذا، اللّه¿] واسير ذنبه ...احمد ابن قاسم...

Here *R.m.n.ṣ* has been identified with the translator himself. A similar, peculiar interpretation reappears in a marginal gloss added, probably, by a reader of MS Ḥasaniyya 8184 (p. 21), in which *R.m.n.ṣ* (= Zacut) is the Christian master of a mysterious Yūsuf al-Andalusī (= José Vizinho):

ذكرَ في رسالة اخرى ونقلها كذلك المعلّم يوسف الاندلوسي [كذاً] من عند معلّمه وكان نصرانيّا اسمه [¿] رمنص ومن عند المعلّم [ي]وسف المذكور ترجمها باللغة العربيّة [ال]عدل احمد بن قاسم الاندلسي عرف بالحجري

> Mentioned in another epistle also translated by master Yūsuf al-Andalūsī [*sic*] from his master who was a Christian named *R.m.n.ṣ*. And from [the text written by] the aforementioned Yūsuf

4 Probably a corruption of Abī 'l-Qāsim > Bā'l-Qāsim. The correct form should be Aḥmad b. al-Qāsim. A similar confusion appears in MS Ḥasaniyya 8184 (p. 21) where I read the name of the author of the translation as Qāsim b. Aḥmad b. al-Faqīh Qāsim *b.l* al-šayj (instead of Abī-l-Šayj) al-Ḥaŷarī al-Andalūsī (*sic*).

5 Khaṭṭābī, *Fahāris* pp. 286-287 (no. 345).

> the *ᶜadl*[6] Aḥmad b. Qāsim al-Andalusī, known as al-Ḥajarī, translated it into Arabic.[7]

The confusion increases in one of the recensions of the canons due to the otherwise unknown ᶜAbd al-Karīm b. ᶜAlī Aghbāl (fl. some time between 1624 and 1797). This work is extant in MS D2014 of Rabat's *al-Khizāna al-ᶜĀmma* and it bears the title of *Risāla... fī kayfiyyat al-taᶜdīl bi-l-Zīj alladhī waḍaᶜa-hu Ibrāhīm al-Yahūdī al-maᶜrūf bi-Azkūṭ* [sic]... ("Epistle... on how to compute true planetary positions using the astronomical tables compiled by Ibrāhīm al-Yahūdī, known as Azkūṭ"). In p. 2 of the aforementioned MS, Aghbāl states that he has written his own recension on the basis of several epistles on the same topic. They all derive, ultimately:

من رسالة مؤلّف الزيج وكانت اوّلا مكتوبة بالقلم العبراني ثمّ كُتِبَت بخطّ اللطين ثمّ نقلت منه بخطّ روم سبانية ووجدت بيد نصرانيّ اسمه رمنص وأخذها من عند المعلّم يوسف الاندلوسي [كذا] وهو اوّل من ترجمها بالعربيّة في مدينة مرّاكش

> From the canons of the author of the *zīj* which were, first, written in Hebrew letters (*qalam*), later written in Latin script (*khaṭṭ*) and, then, transformed into the writing (*khaṭṭ*) of the Christians (*rūm*) from Spain (*Sbāniyya*). I found [it] in the handwriting of a Christian (*naṣrānī*), whose name was *R.m.n.ṣ*, who had copied it from Master Yūsuf al-Andalūsī [*sic*] who was the first translator [of the work] into Arabic, in the city of Marrākush.

We may see here that the author uses words like *qalam* and *khaṭṭ*, whose standard meaning is "writing" or "script", in the sense of "language". Far more interesting is to realize that the "Christian" *R.m.n.ṣ* has become a mere copyist or transmitter of the Arabic text, while Yūsuf al-Andalusī (= José Vizinho) has become the author of the first translation, made in Marrākush, of the canons into Arabic. Al-Ḥajarī has completely disappeared from the scene. The misinformation given by Aghbāl has led

---

[6] An *ᶜadl* is a reliable witness and the term is also applied to designate a notary. It is probably a reminiscence of al-Ḥajarī's work as an official translator of sultan Mawlāy Zaydān.

[7] Khaṭṭābī, *Fahāris* p. 286.

certain scholars to add a second Western translation (by Yūsuf al-Andalusī) of the canons compiled by Vizinho, which were translated in Morocco only once by al-Ḥajarī.[8] A last echo of all these confusions can be found in a later source, Muḥammad al-Muᶜṭī (d. 1808), usually better informed, who mixes up the figure of Zacut with that of José Vizinho, for he mentions the author of the *zīj* as Yūsuf (instead of Abraham or Ibrāhīm) al-Isrā'īlī al-Salamankī, known as Zakūṭ, who compiled it for the longitude of Salamanca:[9]

رسالة على زيج يوسف الإسرائيلي السلمنكي المعروف بزكوط
الذي وضعه على طول سلمنكة

We may see, therefore, that the Portuguese Jew José Vizinho, who seems to have been the author of the canons of the *Almanach*, extracted from the Hebrew text of Zacut's *Ha-ḥibbur ha-gadol*, has become Yūsuf al-Andalusī, a Muslim from Marrākush who authored the first translation of the canons into Arabic. On the other hand the name of the author of the *Ḥibbur*, Abraham Zacut, often disappears and is replaced by a mysterious Christian called *R.m.n.ṣ*, who is identified with the master of Yūsuf al-Andalusī and appears also as the translator of the text from Castilian into Arabic or as a mere copyist or transmitter of the Arabic text. I do not know how far this identification of the Jew Abraham Zacut with a Christian called *R.m.n.ṣ* is related to the fact that the Arabic MS 338 of the Ambrosiana Library (Milan),[10] which contains al-Ḥajarī's translation of the *Almanach*, bears two different titles: on the one hand *Zīj Zakūṭū* and, on the other, *Zīj al-Naṣrānī* or *al-Zīj al-Naṣrānī* ("Astronomical tables of the Christian" or "Christian Astronomical Tables"), probably due to the necessary use of the Julian calendar and of the era of Christ's birth.

---

[8] Muḥammad al-Mannūnī, "Ẓāhira taᶜrībiyya fī 'l-Maghrib ayyām al-Saᶜdiyyīn", *Revista del Instituto de Estudios Islámicos* (Madrid), 11-12 (1963-64), 329-358. See pp. 348-358.

[9] In his *Kanz al-asrār wa-fayḍ al-anwār fī taᶜdīl al-nayyirayn wa-l-khamsa al-mutaḥayyara bi-l-adwār* ("Treasure of secrets and affluence of lights for the computation of the positions of the two luminaries and the five planets using cycles") extant in MS Rabat al-Khizāna al-ᶜĀmma 2027D (pp. 83-118). See p. 83.

[10] E. Griffini, "Lista dei manoscritti arabi nuovo fondo della Biblioteca Ambrosiana di Milano", *Rivista degli Studi Orientali* 7 (1916), pp. 88-106.

This second title appears on pages written in Eastern *naskhī* script[11] and Griffini attributes the "Christian" title to the presumed copyist, the Turkish *aghā* Muḥammad b. Aḥmad aghā Arḍ-rūmī (= Erzerūmī), who wrote the work, probably in the Maghrib, in 1086 H/ 1675. Another possibility is to ascribe the second title to one of the Yamanī owners of the manuscript, among whom we find the Egyptian astronomer Yūsuf b. Yūsuf al-Maḥallī, who was in Yemen in 1143-1147 H/ 1730-1734. David King has the suspicion that the attribution of the copy to Arḍ-rūmī may be unreliable and that the manuscript might have been copied in the Yemen.[12] The title *Zīj al-Naṣrānī* also appears in MS Ar. Vatican 963, which seems to be a copy of the Ambrosiana MS. In this second MS we also find (fol. 38) *Zīj Kazzawṭūh* [sic] *al-Naṣrānī* and, immediately below, a reference to *Kassawṭuh al-Naṣrānī*.

---

[11] Two different copyists have collaborated in this MS: one writes in Maghribī and the other in Eastern script. The two copyists seem to have worked together, for there are folios with one page written by an Eastern hand and the other written by a Maghribī.

[12] David A. King, *Mathematical Astronomy in Medieval Yemen. A Biobibliographical Survey* (American Research Center in Egypt, Undena Publications, Malibi, 1983), pp. 7 (n. 16) and 45-46.

XVI

IN PURSUIT OF ZACUT'S *ALMANACH PERPETUUM* IN THE EASTERN ISLAMIC WORLD

1. *Introduction*

In two previous papers[1] I have studied the broad lines of a Maghribī astronomical tradition which began ca. 1624 when a Morisco exile called Aḥmad b. Qāsim b. Aḥmad b. al-Faqīh Qāsim b. al-Shaykh al-Ḥajarī al-Andalusī (1570- after 1640)[2] translated the canons of the *Almanach Perpetuum* into Arabic, probably in Marrakesh. These canons had been written by a Portuguese Jew, José Vizinho, on the basis of the *ha-Ḥibbur ha-Gadol* compiled by Abraham Zacut (1452-1515) for the coordinates of Salamanca[3]. The *Almanach Perpetuum* was printed in Leiria, in 1496[4] and new editions appeared in the sixteenth century: al-Ḥajarī must have used one of them for his translation[5]. The *A.P.* was easier to handle than a standard *zīj* and this is the reason for its success in the Maghrib, where the Zacutian tradition remained until the second half of the nineteenth century; its tables were copied and recopied and several Maghribī scholars of the seventeenth and eighteenth centuries wrote new sets of canons to simplify their use. This was partly due to the fact that al-Ḥajarī's Arabic – understandably in an

[1] Samsó, 1998-99 and 2003.

[2] For biographical details see van Koningsveld, al-Samarrai, and Wiegers, 1997. New evidence on al-Ḥajarī's activities as an official translator in Morocco in García Arenal, Rodríguez Mediano & El Hour, 2002, pp. 337-339, 367-372, 373-376: edition of the original Arabic text and al-Ḥajarī's Spanish translation of three documents (1616) for sultan Mawlāy Zaydān (d. 1627).

[3] See Chabás & Goldstein, 2000.

[4] I am using here the facsimile edition published by Albuquerque, 1986 which I will quote as *A.P.* followed by the page number of the facsimile.

[5] The 15th and 16th c. editions were printed in 1496, 1498, 1502, 1525 and 1528. We know that at least one printed copy of the *A.P.* circulated in the Maghrib: MS Rabat General Library D2014 contains the canons written by ʻAbd al-Karīm Aghbāl (unknown date between 1655 and 1797) followed by a copy of the edition of the *Almanach Perpetuum* printed in Venice 1502 (15th July) by Petrus Liechtenstein Coloniensis (on this edition see Chabás & Goldstein, 2000, p. 162).

author who spent the first thirty years of his life in the Spain of the end of the sixteenth century and the beginning of the seventeenth century – was by no means faultless and he did not seem to have a thorough knowledge of the Arabic technical vocabulary.[6] Indeed, readers had difficulty in understanding certain procedures they needed to use to perform certain computations. Thus MS Cairo DM 1081 (pp. 9-19) contains a corrected version of al-Ḥajarī's translation but it seems that the correction was insufficient for, at the end of chapter 19 (p. 17, on the determination of the latitude of Mars) an interlineal note in Maghribī script, apparently different from that of the copyist, says: *Hādhā 'l-bāb lā yakādu yufham kalāmu-hu li-anna-hu fī ghāyat al-taʿqīd wa lā yuḥaqqaq bi-hi ʿamal wa-llāhu aʿlam* ("This chapter is almost incomprehensible because it is extremely complicated and cannot be applied for a calculation, but God knows best"). A similar remark appears on p. 18 (ch. 22, on the determination of the true place of Mercury) and in other parts of the same MS.

2. *The* Almanach Perpetuum *in the Mashriq.*
2.1 *Istanbul*

This Maghribī tradition documents the use of the *A.P.* in Morocco, mainly in Fez and Marrakesh, but also in the north of the country: the MSS contain references to Ceuta, Tanger, Aṣīla, al-Qaṣr [al-Kabīr] and the *zāwiya* of Wazzān, NW of Fez and near al-Qaṣr al-Kabīr. It is also possible that it was known in Algiers.[7] In this paper I would like to analyse its diffusion in the Mashriq where the Zacutian Islamic tradition actually began, for the first recension of its canons was written in Arabic by the Jewish physician Mūsā Jalīnūs in 912 H/ 1506-07 AD[8]. The work was commissioned in 911 H/ 1505-06 by a certain ʿAbd al-Raḥmān, who held the important post of judge of the [Ottoman] army (*al-Qāḍī bi 'l-ʿaskar*). It seems therefore that the work was done in Istanbul, although the only extant manuscript does not say so. In any case, this early version was not as important as al-Ḥajarī's translation which, as we will see, reached Cairo and the Yemen.

[6] In chapter 3 (MS Milan Ambrosiana 338, fols. 3v-4v, and Rabat Hassaniyya, 1433, fol. 2v) "Revoluçion de los años del mundo" is translated by *Adwār sinīn [sic] al-dunyā* (not *taḥāwīl sinī al-ʿālam*) and "Revoluçion de las natividades" by *Adwār al-mawālīd*.

[7] For details see Samsó, 2003.

[8] Extant in MS Escorial 966. See Vernet, 1979. On this author see now Ihsanoğlu, 1997, I, 224-225, no 102.

2.2 *Cairo*

This Eastern diffusion of the *A.P.* is documented in three manuscripts which I will try to analyse here: Cairo DM 1081[9], Milan Ambrosiana Ar. 338 (C82)[10] and Vatican 963[11]. The first of these three MSS, Cairo DM 1081, is written in Maghribī script and it contains a whole set of numerical tables which, in one case at least, seems to be more complete than those of the edition *princeps*. Chabás & Goldstein (2000, p. 122) have remarked that the table of lunar parallax in *A.P.* (pp. 215-216) is incomplete: Capricorn is missing, and Cancer appears repeated.[12] In MS Cairo DM 1081 there is a complete table on pp. 144 (March-August, Aries-Virgo) and 145 (September-February, Libra-Pisces).

This MS also contains three different collections of Maghribī canons which include materials (pp. 1-2) from the *Risāla ʿarabiyya* by the *faqīh* and *muʿaddil* Sīdī ʿAbd Allāh Aṣnāk al-Marrākushī (fl. ca. 1655), the aforementioned revised version of al-Ḥajarī's translation (pp. 9-19), and the *Tuḥfat al-muḥtāj fī ʿilm al-taʿdīl wa 'l-azyāj*, also called *Risālat al-risālatayn* (pp. 20-28) by ʿAbd al-Raḥmān al-Fāsī (Fez, 1631-1685). In spite of its Maghribī origin, this MS bears witness to the use of *A.P.* in Cairo in the nineteenth century. The numbers of the pages appear in Eastern ciphers (pp. 1-152; I have added numbers for pp. 153-329). One extra folio appears before p. 1 which I label pp. -1/0. On p. 0 there is the mark of property of the only owner of this MS we know of: ʿAlī al-Khashshāb al-Dimyāṭī al-Falakī who owned it in 1239 H/ 1823-24. The same mark of property and date is repeated in p. 20[13]. The MS has some notes written in Turkish[14] and many others in Arabic

[9] King, 1986 pp. 140 and 143, nos. F31, F33 and F50; King, 1981, I, pp. 139-141.

[10] Very carefully described by Griffini, 1916, pp. 88-106.

[11] Levi della Vida, 1935, pp. 101-102. This MS has been foliated in modern European typed characters from fol. 13r. The text of al-Ḥajarī's translation begins on fol. 12v. The manuscript also has six more folios containing a wealth of notes scribbled by the users, which will be the basis of my analysis here. I have numbered these folios backwards, from folio 13r, and the first folio with inscriptions, in my counting system, is fol. 6r.

[12] The same in Mūsā Jālīnūs version in MS Escorial 966 fol. 92r and v.

[13] See King, 1983, p. 117 (D120): al-Khashshāb has not been identified, but he is the author of two small texts extant in Cairo. One of them is a short treatise (6 fols.) on the equation of time and lunar eclipses (Cairo DM 261, dated 1293/1876); the second (1 page on fol. 2r) is a calculation of the qibla in Cairo and London (*Lundra*) (MS K4011, 2, dated 1285/1868-9).

[14] See pp. 69, 103.

by an Eastern hand[15]. At least two of these notes are due to the owner al-Khashshāb (pp. 103 and 105).

The Cairo MS is not dated and we only know that it was copied before 1823. A peculiar characteristic appearing on p. 49 could point to a very early date. This page reproduces the *Jadwal ta'dīl adwār al-shams* (*Tabula equationis solis* in *A.P.* p. 123). The arguments in *A.P.* reach 34 cycles (136 years: 1476 + 136 = 1612) and a Maghribī user of the tables has stretched the arguments to 38 cycles. Could this imply that the table was used between 1613 and 1628?

2.3 *Yemen*

2.3.1 MS Cairo DM 1081

Ms. Cairo DM 1081 could also bear witness to a possible connection with Yemen which is clearly documented in the two other manuscripts. On p. 0 there are two corrections in longitude: the longitude of Salamanca is given as 25;46° (the same value as in *A.P.*) and the correction to apply to the motion of the Sun is given twice, but I am not sure that I have read them correctly. One of the corrections might be 0;7,46° which, assuming a mean solar motion per hour of 0;2,28° would imply a difference in time of 3;8,55^{h}, which corresponds to a longitude difference of 47;13,47°: the longitude of the place in which it was presumably used would be 25;46° + 47;14° = 73°. This could correspond to Ṣan'ā' (?). In fact, in MS Vatican 963, fol. 30r, a marginal note states that the longitude of Ṣan'ā' is 63;30°[16] but seems to ascribe to Salamanca a longitude of 15;45° (not 25;46°), the difference in longitude between the two places being 47;45°, not far away from the computed difference (47;13,47°) in the Cairo MS. In fact, using modern coordinates, the longitude difference between Salamanca and Ṣan'ā' is 49;54°, the difference in time being 3;19,36^{h}.

2.3.2 MS Ambrosiana Ar. 338 (C82)

The Yemeni connection of the Cairo MS is a mere hypothesis and we are on more secure ground with the Ambrosiana MS Ar. 338 (C82), which has been considered by King[17] to be a Yemeni copy of the Maghribī version of *A.P.*, written in Yemeni script. The copy of the manuscript is attributed to Muḥammad b. Aḥmad Āghā Arḍ Rūmī (from Erzurum) who finished the tables on a Sunday in Rabī' I 1086

[15] See pp. 11, 20, 26, 51, 59, 60, 103, 105, 121, 140, 143, 151.

[16] A common value in Kennedy & Kennedy, 1987, pp. 300-301.

[17] King, 1983, p. 7 n.16, and pp. 45-47.

H (from 15th May to 13th June 1675)[18]. The same date is repeated at the end of the canons but, in this case, the month is Rabīʿ II[19]. In fact there are two copyists; one of them, who copied part of the numerical tables, writes in Maghribī script[20]: the copyists seem to have worked together, for there are folios with one page written by an Eastern hand and the other written by a Maghribī[21]. The situation is, therefore, somewhat confusing for we have the name of a copyist who, apparently, is an Ottoman Turk, and a MS most of which appears written in Yemeni script, with a few folios copied by a Maghribī who worked together with his Yemeni colleague. It is possible that this MS was copied from the author's (i.e. al-Ḥajarī's) personal copy: a note at the top of fol. 62v, written in Eastern script, points out a deficiency in the "author's copy" (*nuskhat al-muʾallif*).[22]

The Yemeni connection of the Ambrosiana MS is, however, absolutely clear, due to the fact that the MS bears a mark of property of Yūsuf al-Maḥallī in 1157 H/ 1744-45.[23] This scholar has been tentatively identified by King as Yūsuf b. Yūsuf al-Jamālī, called Kalarji[24], whose astronomical activity is documented in Cairo in 1113 H/ 1701-2, 1127 H/ 1715 and 1133 H/ 1720-21. In 1143 H/ 1730-31 Yūsuf al-Maḥallī was in Ṣanʿāʾ where he copied astronomical MSS and compiled a set of ephemerides (*Taqwīm al-sana*) for the solar year 1146-47 H/ 1733-34, which he dedicated to the Yemeni Sultan al-Manṣūr Abū 'l-ʿAbbās Ḥusayn. The same folio contains a second mark of property (with the name of the owner repeated several times): the book belonged to a certain al-Sayyid Aḥmad b. Sharaf al-Dīn al-Dakī the 12th Ṣafar 1245 H/ 31st July 1829. The same name reappears on fol. 0v. On fol. 1v we

[18] Fol. 148v. See Griffini, 1916, p. 105. According to Griffini p. 105 (my microfilm is illegible here) the name of the copyist Muḥamma[d ibn Aḥmad Āghā ...] appears at the bottom of fol. 1 r. A.D. equivalent dates are always Julian unless I state otherwise.

[19] Fol. 20v: from 14th June 1675 to 12th July 1675. See Griffini, 1916, p. 99 who considers that the tables were finished in Rabīʿ I and the canons in Rabīʿ II.

[20] Fols. 49r-49v, 60r-68v, 69v-70v, 72r-85v, 100r-104r, 110r-118v.

[21] See fol. 69r (Eastern), 69v (Western), 104r (Maghribī), 104v (Eastern).

[22] In fol. 12r we find a remark which lacks this precision: in the middle of a text related to the computation of the lunar parallax, the copyist adds *wa hādhā min aṣl al-nuskha. Hākadhā yūjad* ("This was taken from the original of the copy. *Sic*").

[23] In fol. -1r. The MS has two unnumbered folios at the beginning which I label -1/0. On this author see King, 1983, pp. 45-47.

[24] Cf. King, 1986, p. 108 (D61). He was a disciple of Riḍwān Efendi (fl. 1123/1711) on whom see King, 1986, pp. 107-108 (D58) and Ihsanoğlu, 1997, I, pp. 377-384 (no 246).

find it in a more complete form, as al-Sayyid Aḥmad b. Sharaf al-Dīn al-Raṣid (sic)... al-Raqqām b. (or Abū) Muḥammad.

The manuscript contains three notes of computations which document its use in the 18th and 19th c. On fol. -1v we find an example of the computation of the solar longitude for 30th (*sic* thalāthūn) Jumādā II 1201 which corresponds (according to the text) to 9th March 1788. In fact the latter Julian date corresponds to 13th Jumādā II 1202. On fol. 71r there is a computation for 1165 Yazdigird/1795-96 AD. Finally, on fol. 0v, there is a reference to Saturday 8th Jumādā I 1297 which, according to the text, corresponds to 6th April 1880, although it adds that the aforementioned Saturday was 17th April. In fact 8th Jumādā I 1297 is 5th April 1880.

2.3.3 MS Vatican 963

The script of this MS is also Yemeni according to D.A. King (private communication) and we will see that this origin can easily be established from multiple internal references. Levi della Vida considered that it is a copy of MS Ambrosiana Ar. 338 and this is probably true, but we must bear in mind that the Vatican MS does not contain the appendix of Andalusī-Maghribī tables of the Ambrosiana MS (see below § 5) and that, unlike the latter, it contains three different sets of canons for the use of *A.P.*: those of al-Ḥajarī (fols. 13v - 28v), a second set (fol. 29r - 34v) which should be identified as the *risāla* written by ʿAbd Allāh Aṣnāk al-Marrākushī (fl. ca. 1655) extant in MS Rabat Hassaniyya 1331 (pp. 53-61) and, partially, in MS Cairo DM 1081 (pp. 1-2)[25]. A reference, in Aṣnāk's text, to the difference in geographical longitude between Salamanca and Marrākush (fol. 30r), has led a reader to write a marginal note stating that the longitude of Ṣanʿāʾ is 63;30° and the difference in longitude between Salamanca and Ṣanʿāʾ is 47;45°.[26] Aṣnāk's canons finish on fol. 34v with the explicit *Intahā mā wujida min hādhā 'l-zīj* ("the end of what was found of that *zīj*"). There follows (fol. 35r - 36v) a third set of incomplete canons, which I am not able to identify.[27]

The title page is fol. 38r, on which the book is called *Zīj Kazzūṭūh*

[25] Cf. Samsó, 2003.

[26] In fol. 36r another marginal note gives the latitude of Ṣanʿāʾ as 14;30°, a common value: see Kennedy & Kennedy, 1987, pp. 300-301.

[27] They deal with the computation of the ascendent and the division of the houses, entrance of the Sun in the zodiacal signs, lunar node, lunar latitude, latitudes of Venus and Mercury, solar and lunar eclipses.

al-Naṣrānī and *Kassawṭūh al-Naṣrānī*. On fol. 12r we find a cancelled mark of property of a former owner of the MS: Ṣalāḥ al-Dīn b. Sharaf al-Dīn b. Ṣalāḥ Ibrāhīm b. Muḥammad b. Ibrāhīm b. ʻAlī b. al-Imām Sharaf al-Dīn Hibat Allāh. A second note states that the aforementioned owner, here called Ṣalāḥ b. Sharaf al-Dīn al-Qāsim, sold the manuscript to Ḥusayn b. Aḥmad b. Ismāʻīl al-Mukarramī on the 9th of Ṣafar 1145 H/ 20th July 1732. The new proprietor is described as the humble servant of "our lord (*sayyidunā*) Hibat Allāh, son of our lord Ibrāhīm, son of our lord ʻAlī, son of my lord (*sayyidī*) Hibat Allāh". When Ḥusayn b. Aḥmad died his heirs agreed in giving the manuscript to its copyist (*rāqimu-hā*) Muḥammad b. ʻAbd Allāh b. Sulaymān. This took place in the month of June, which corresponds to Muḥarram 1178 H (1st Muḥarram 1178 = 19th June 1764) (fol. 6r).

It is clear, therefore, that the manuscript was copied before 1732, when it was bought by Ḥusayn al-Mukarramī. The MS contains a considerable number of marginal computations which mention dates, most of them corresponding to the period between 1715 and 1734. These references document a very active use of the tables during this period in which the MS was probably in the possession of the aforementioned Ṣalāḥ al-Dīn b. Sharaf al-Dīn. The list of the dates of these computations follows, arranged in chronological order:

Fol. 38r:	1st Muḥarram 1114 H/ 16th May 1702.
Fol. 38r:	1128 H/ 1715.
Fol. 91r:	1st Muḥarram 1129/ 4th December 1716.
Fol. 38r:	2028 Alexander/ 1716-17.
Fol. 6v:	1st Muḥarram 1131 H/ 12th November 1718.
Fol. 11v:	1st Dhū-l-Hijja 1131 H/ 3rd October 1719.
Fol. 7r:	13th Jumādā I 1133 H/ 28th February 1721.
Fol. 6v:	1st Ādhār 2032 Alexander/ 1st March 1721.
Fol. 6v:	1st Ādhār 2033 Alexander/ 1st March 1722.
Fol. 8v:	19th Rajab 1134 H/ 23th April 1722.
Fol. 35r, 52v:	1136 H/ 2035 Alexander/ 1723-24.
Fol. 7v:	1st Muḥarram 1137 H/ 8th September 1724.
Fol. 11v:	13th Kiyahk (Coptic) 2038 Alexander/ 9th December 1726.
Fol. 57v:	11th Kānūn I 2038 Alexander/ 11 December 1726.
Fol. 9v:	29th Jumādā II H/ 14th November 1734.
Fol. 14r:	1146 H/ 1734.
Fols. 7v, 8r:	2082 Alexander/ 1770-71.

The MS contains, however, two references to seventeenth century dates. One of them corresponds to an observation, dated 14th Sha'bān 1047 H/ 21st December 1637 (fol. 7r) (see below § 6). The other appears on fol. 7v where we find a set of computations involving 1671 AD. I do not consider them significant for dating the MS. 1637 seems too early for a Yemeni copy of al-Ḥajarī's translation which was probably finished ca. 1624. On the other hand on fol. 9v we find a reference to the *Zīj al-Muthannā*, compiled in 1081 H/ 1670 (see below § 4). But both dates should be rejected if we accept Levi della Vida's opinion that MS Vatican 963 is a copy of MS Ambrosiana Ar. 338 (dated in 1675). I believe that the reference to the observation of 1637 was copied from an earlier source and that the computations for 1671 are the result of a systematic error of 100 years: 1771 is probably the correct date because it agrees with year 2082 of Alexander, which also appears on the same page.

3. *Problems of cultural adaptation*

This Maghribī tradition poses some problems of cultural adaptation to the Eastern user. For example, the tables in MS Cairo DM 1081 (pp. 35-329) are written in Western ciphers, as stated in a marginal note on p. 35 which contains a small table with the equivalence between Western and Eastern ciphers.[28] Other difficulties are related to the calendar used by both *A.P.* and al-Ḥajarī[29]: a solar calendar and the AD era. This era was well known to a Morisco like al-Ḥajarī but it had no relation to the Islamic astronomical tradition: its appearance in the *zīj* of al-Khwārizmī-Maslama, or in the *Toledan Tables*, is, to a certain extent, a surprise[30] and may be due to a later interpolation by the Latin translators. In fact, Ibn al-Zarqālluh's *Almanac*, which uses the same

[28] Griffini, 1916, p. 101 remarked that MS Ambrosiana 338, fols. 65r-68v, reproduces a table of luni-solar conjunctions and oppositions and that the years (1478-1508) are written in Maghribī numerals. Note that the table for syzigies in the *A.P.* begins in 1478, whereas the tables for solar and lunar positions begin in 1473. The same table reappears in Vatican 963, fols. 83r and ff., where the first four years of the cycle (1478-1481) are copied twice, using both Maghribī and Eastern ciphers. Mūsā Jālīnūs avoided this kind of difficulty by using the *abjad* in MS Escorial 966 (fols. 19v - 191r).

[29] A strange calendarical table in MS Vatican 963, fol. 38v, seems related to this problem. It mentions eras such as the Jewish era, Jalālī, Birth of the Prophet and that of Jesus, but the numbers quoted do not seem to make much sense. It also gives the names of the Arab, Latin, Coptic, Persian and Syriac months.

[30] See Suter, 1914, p. 109; Neugebauer, 1962, pp. 82-84. This era appears however in a few Andalusī texts related to folk-astronomy: cf. Samsó, 2001, pp. 74-76.

technique for the computation of solar and planetary longitudes as *A.P.*, is based on the era of Alexander[31]. This latter era is the one used by most of the Western and Eastern scholars interested in the Zacutian tradition: the three MSS under consideration contain many examples which reduce the radix date of *A.P.* (1st March 1473) to the corresponding date of Alexander's era (1st Ādhār 1784) and use *A.P.* on this basis[32]. This explains the note at the top of the table for the computation of solar longitude in MS Cairo DM 1081 p. 41, written in Eastern script, which states that these tables were calculated *ʿalā 'l-dahr al-rūmī al-Iskandarī* (according to the *Rūmī* calendar and Alexander's era). On p. 42 the Eastern superscription about Alexander's era is repeated but the text adds that one should subtract 12 days from the days of the table to obtain the correct result: this is probably due to the difference between the Gregorian and the Julian dates, the latter being the one obviously used in *A.P.* Another difficulty for Eastern scholars is the use, in al-Ḥajarī's translation and the Maghribī tradition, of the old Latin names of the Julian months. In the three MSS considered we find many instances in which the copyist or a reader has added the names of the Syriac months to the Latin ones.[33]

4. *Two worked examples using* A.P.

Vatican MS fol. 9v [8v according to Levi della Vida]

This page contains a most interesting prologue which is not found in any other manuscript of the Arabic version of the *Almanach Perpetuum.* The beginning of this text is in rhymed prose (*sajʿ*) and it says that this *zīj* is called *Zīj al-Naṣrānī* and that its author follows a most simple method that nobody else has followed before or after him. It is based on the Christian Era. The language used is not very correct (*wa-khuṭbatuhu allatī laysat bi 'l-lisān al-faṣīḥ*). There are no copies of this *zīj* in places other than this country (*illā fī hādhihi 'l-diyār*), which means Yemen. Some Yemeni scholars who were experts in this art asked the author of the prologue to examine this book and to give them some simple examples of its use. He began to work on it and he

[31] See Millás, 1943-50, pp. 72-237.

[32] Both MSS Ambrosiana 338 (fol. 20v) and Vatican 963 (fol. 27v) give a rule to calculate the Rūmī date (era Alexander) from the Islamic one and, then, the date of the Christian era.

[33] See MS Cairo DM 1081 pp. 41, 47-48, 152. In pp. 280, 281 and 287 the names of the months are given in their Latin, Syriac and Egyptian forms. Syriac and Latin months appear together in MS Ambrosiana 338, fols. 24 v and ff., 108r, and in MS Vatican 963, fol. 39r-44v.

struggled for a long time with the computation (*taqwīm*) of lunar positions. He is going to present his results and he will not bother with the rest of the planets because this would require writing another book.

Example of a computation of the solar longitude (*mithāl taqwīm al-shams*), with this *zīj*, for midday of Thursday 29th Jumādā II of year 1147 H which corresponds to 14th Tishrīn II 2046 of Alexander [Thursday 14th November 1734 AD]. He subtracts:

2046 - 1783 = 263

[1783 is the year he uses as Alexander's radix of the *Almanach Perpetuum*, 1472 AD complete: the actual radix is 1st March 1473/ 1st Ādhār 1784].

Then he divides:

263 : 4 = 65.

The remainder is 3. This means that he must enter the table corresponding to the third of the four years of the solar cycle. In this table [*A.P.* p. 120] he looks for the solar longitude which corresponds to the 14th Tishrīn II, which is November, and he obtains correctly

8^s 1;3,10°.

Then he enters the *Jadwal taʿdīl al-adwār* [*Tabula equationis solis, A.P.* p. 123] and obtains a correction of 1;54,47°

[The *Tabula equationis solis* calculates the correction in solar longitude using as argument the number of cycles – periods of 4 years – elapsed since epoch. The value of this correction amounts approximately to 0;1,46° per cycle and

34 cycles	1;0,0°
31 cycles	0;54,43°,

the result being 1;54,43°][34].

The solar longitude for the aforementioned date will be:

8^s 1;3,10° + 1;54,47° = 8^s 2;57,57°.

The author of the prologue notes that this result exceeds what could be obtained from the *Zīj al-Muthannā* by about 11 minutes. This might be due to the difference in longitudes, for the calculated result corresponds to the geographical longitude of the place for which the *zīj* was computed [i.e. Salamanca].

[34] Chabás & Goldstein, 2000, p. 107 draw attention to the existence of slight differences in the *Tabula equationis solis* as it appears in the different editions of the *A.P.* J. Chabás (private communication) tells me that a correction of 1;54,46° or 1;54,50° could be obtained for 65 solar cycles using the editions of 1502 or 1525.

Commentary: The *Zīj al-Muthannā* was compiled in 1081/1670 by ʿAbd Allāh b. ʿAbd Allāh al-Sarḥī, called al-Muthannā, and it became very popular in the Yemen[35]. The argument based on the longitude difference is valid: we have already seen (§ 2.3.3) that a note on fol. 30r establishes that the difference in longitude between Salamanca and Ṣanʿāʾ is 47;45° (49;54° with modern coordinates), the time difference being $3;11^h$. This may explain a difference in excess of about 0;8° for the Sun.

It is interesting to remark that the result of the computation with the *A.P.* is extremely accurate for Ṣanʿāʾ. Using the programme E.Z. Cosmos, for 25th November 1734, Gregorian (14th November Julian), I obtain the following equatorial coordinates for the Sun:

Right ascension $16;3,33^h$,
declination - 20;46,31°,
from which I calculate a solar longitude of 242;56,31°.

The prologue continues with an *example of the computation of the lunar longitude (mithāl taqwīm al-qamar)* for the same date and hour.[36] The author operates again with a difference between the year of the computation and the radix date of *A.P.* of 263 years. As the lunar cycle used by Zacut is 31 years, he divides:

263 : 31 = 8,

the remainder being 15. Unlike the case of the sun, he considers he has to operate with *complete years* and he enters table number 14 of his version of *A.P.* Following Zacut's instructions (*A.P.* p. 77) he subtracts 9 days every four lunar cycles. The subtraction should therefore be of 18 days and

14th November - 18d = 28th October.

In table 14 of his version of the *A.P.* (fol. 63v) he reads 7^s 11;58° in front of the 28th October. To this amount he adds a correction of 6^s 2° per cycle (*A.P.* p. 77). The result is

6^s 2° x 8 cycles = 48^s + 16°.

The correction is, then, 16° and he obtains:

7^s 11;58° + 16° = 7^s 27;58°.

A second correction is introduced: in the table of fol. 63v he reads that the

[35] See King, 1983, pp. 10 and 45.

[36] In the Vatican MS a small piece of paper is attached to fol. 69v. It gives the detail of the operations needed to compute the lunar longitude (0^s 16;57°) for an unspecified date of the same year: 2046 Alexander [/1734]. It is easy to see that the date in question is 2nd October.

correction which corresponds to the 28th October is 34' (*A.P.* p. 158 has 36', 4 and 6 being easily confused in Arabic *abjad*). He multiplies:

34' x 8 cycles = 4;32°.

The final value of the lunar longitude will be:

7^s 27;58° + 4;32° = 8^s 2;30°.

According to the text of the prologue, this result is more accurate if we calculate in this way than if we follow the canons (*khuṭba*) of al-Naṣrānī which say that we must enter the table corresponding to the remainder of the subtraction (in this case table 15, instead of 14). He has established his procedure after an adequate consideration (*imtiḥān*). In any case the result he has obtained exceeds the value calculated with the *al-Durr al-Yatīm* by 1°, which may be due to the difference in geographical longitude. It has taken him a great deal of time to obtain these results and he has given up doing the same with the rest of the planets.

Commentary: the final result obtained by the author of the prologue is fairly good. With the programme E.Z. Cosmos, for the midday of Ṣanʿāʾ of 25th November (Gregorian) 1734 I obtain the following equatorial coordinates of the Moon:

right ascension: 16;1,0^h,

declination: -18;40,38°,

from which I calculate:

longitude: 8^s 1;56,32°,

latitude: 1;57,53°,

the longitude being slightly above (half a degree) the computation of the text.

The author of the prologue has not checked this result against a computation with *Zīj al-Muthannā*, as in the case of the Sun, but against another work called *al-Durr al-Yatīm*. This title corresponds to that of a set of auxiliary tables for compiling ephemerides computed by the Egyptian astronomer Shihāb al-Dīn Abū 'l-ʿAbbās Aḥmad b. Rajab b. Ṭaybughā (1365-1447).[37] As for the author's remark that the difference of 1° between his computation with *A.P.* and what he obtains with *al-Durr al-Yatīm* may be due to the difference in geographical longitude, we have already seen that the time difference between Ṣanʿāʾ and Salamanca amounts, using the coordinates we find in the same MS (fol. 30r), to 3;11^h. Assuming a lunar mean motion in longitude of 0;32,56°/hour, the mean motion in 3;11^h would amount to 1;44,50°.

[37] Analysed by David A. King and E.S. Kennedy, 1980.

The results obtained are due to two different corrections of the *A.P.*:

1. The choice of table 14 (instead of table 15) of the lunar cycle. This is based on the assumption that between 14th Tishrīn II 2046 (date of the computation) and 1 Ādhār 1784 (radix of the *A.P.* using Alexander's era) there is a difference of 2046 - 1783 = 263 years. The actual difference amounts to 262 incomplete years. If we use 262 for the calculation of the number of the lunar cycle, we obtain:

262 : 31 = 8,

the remainder being 14. The choice of table 14 is, therefore, entirely appropriate and in agreement with the instructions of *A.P.* It is in the case of the Sun where he has actually corrected the procedure established by the *A.P.* for:

262 : 4 = 65,

the remainder being 2. He should have used table 2, instead of 3, for the Sun. If he had done so he would have obtained 8^s 3;13,20° instead of 8^s 2;57,57°. As the solar longitude obtained from E.Z. Cosmos is 8^s 2;56,31°, his correction seems more accurate.

2. As we have seen, the author of the prologue reads on fol. 63v of the Vatican MS 7^s 11;58° in front of 28th October in table 14. In *A.P.* p. 158 we do not find the same amount but 7^s 24;58°, 13° more. This is not an isolated mistake but a systematic crude correction which appears throughout the set of the 31-year cycle of lunar tables of the Vatican MS as well as in the corresponding tables of the Ambrosiana MS[38], but not in the Cairo MS. The correction must have been introduced therefore sometime before 1675 (date of the Ambrosiana MS). Apart from the obvious remark that -13° corresponds approximately to one day of lunar motion, I cannot give any explanation for this correction. I will only say that it gives more accurate results: if I calculate the lunar longitude for the same day using the *A.P.* the final result I obtain is:

Computation with *A.P.*:	8^s 15;46°,
Vatican example:	8^s 2;30°,
computation from E.Z. Cosmos:	8^s 1;56,32°.

The difference:

8^s 15;46° - 8^s 2;30° = 13;16°,

in which 13° correspond to the systematic correction of -13° throughout the set of lunar tables, while 0;16° is the result of the error of the MS

[38] Vatican MS fols. 50r - 80v; Ambrosiana MS, fols. 30r - 60v.

in the second correction applied to the lunar longitude computation: 34' per cycle instead of 36'. As the number of cycles involved is 8, it is obvious that

0;2° x 8 = 0;16°.

A last remark should be an attempt to guess the identity of the author of the prologue on fol. 9v. The example used is for year 1734 AD and we have already seen many references to other years, not far away from 1734, in the first folios of the Vatican MS (see § 2.3.3). We have already seen that the owner of the MS, Ṣalāḥ b. Sharaf al-Dīn al-Qāsim, sold it to Ḥusayn b. Aḥmad b. Ismāʿīl al-Mukarramī in 1732 AD. The latter is, therefore, a likely candidate as the author of the prologue. One cannot forget, however, the possibility of ascribing it to Yūsuf ibn Yūsuf al-Maḥallī, whose activity is documented in Yemen in 1730-31 and 1733-34 in which he compiled a set of ephemerides for the solar year 1146-47 H/ 1733-34 which he dedicated to the Sultan al-Manṣūr Abū 'l-ʿAbbās Ḥusayn.[39] He was clearly interested in Zacut's tables for, in 1744-45, he owned the copy of the Arabic translation of *A.P.* extant in the Ambrosiana MS (§ 2.3.2). It seems quite possible that he was the author of the prologue. He might have become interested in works like *A.P.* and *al-Durr al-Yatīm* precisely when he was engaged in the preparation of a set of ephemerides for the sultan. Let us also remember that Yūsuf al-Maḥallī was the disciple of Riḍwān Efendi who compiled a set of planetary tables (*al-Durr al-naẓīm fī ṣināʿat al-taqwīm*) in the tradition of Ibn al-Majdī's *al-Durr al-Yatīm*, but based on the parameters of Ulugh Beg.[40] The observation, made on 23th April 1722, of an occultation of Saturn by the Moon (§ 6), can also be ascribed to Yūsuf al-Maḥallī if he was already in Ṣanʿāʾ in that year.

5. *Other Andalusī and Maghribī astronomical materials introduced in the Mashriq through these MSS*

The Andalusī astronomical tradition computes sidereal longitudes from which tropical longitudes can be obtained using trepidation tables. Chabás & Goldstein (2000) have clearly established that the work of Abraham Zacut has an Alfonsine descent. This implies that the astronomer from Salamanca is the last Iberian medieval link of a second astronomical tradition which follows Ptolemy, al-Battānī and the *aṣḥāb*

[39] King, 1983, pp. 45-46.

[40] King, 1986, p. 107.

al-Mumtaḥan in computing tropical positions directly and in using uniform precession. I have a strong suspicion that this tradition is basically Jewish, as it is followed by Maimonides and Abraham bar Ḥiyya (whose main astronomical source was al-Battānī), Abraham ben ʿEzra (although he translated Ibn al-Muthannā's commentary on al-Khwārizmī, he used al-Ṣūfī when he computed his *Tabulae Pisanae*), the authors of the *Alfonsine Tables* (Yehudah b. Mosheh and Isḥāq b. Sīd), Jacob ben David Bonjorn and, obviously, Zacut. The only exception would be the *Tables of Barcelona*, computed by Jacob Corsuno and strongly influenced by Ibn al-Kammād, although Chabás' analysis of the mean motions of the Sun and the planets in these tables[41] makes me think that this exception is a mere illusion.

Maghribī astronomers followed the traditional Andalusī school (sidereal mean motion tables, trepidation, a solar model with variable eccentricity, the Zarqāllian correction in the lunar model, etc.) during the thirteenth and fourteenth centuries, mainly due to the strong influence exerted by Ibn Isḥāq al-Tūnisī (fl. Tūnis and Marrākush ca. 1193-1222).[42] A few new observations made during these centuries introduced serious doubts about the validity of Andalusī astronomical principles and this justified the use of Eastern *zīj*es (Ibn Abī 'l-Shukr al-Maghribī, Ibn al-Shāṭir and Ulugh Beg) in the Maghrib from the fourteenth century onwards.[43] The introduction of the *Alfonsine Tables* through Zacut's *Almanach Perpetuum* towards the beginning of the seventeenth century followed the same pattern. In spite of this, the old Andalusī-Maghribī tradition remained alive until the nineteenth century and its echoes appear mixed with the Zacutian tradition both in the Maghrib and in the Mashriq. This survival explains the references in some texts to the fact that *A.P.* computes *ṭabīʿī* (tropical), and not *dhātī* (sidereal) positions: this is repeatedly stated by ʿAbd al-Raḥmān al-Fāsī (Fez, 1631-1685)[44] in ms. Cairo DM 1081 (pp. 20-28). Al-Ḥajarī does not seem to have had very clear ideas in this respect, for his translation of the title of chapter 4 (lunar position) is *Fī maʿrifat mawḍiʿ al-qamar al-ḥaqīqī al-dhātī* (sic) ("On the knowledge of the true *sidereal* position of the Moon").[45] A marginal note on the projection of rays and the

[41] See Chabás, 1996.

[42] See Mestres, 1996.

[43] See Samsó, 1998 and 2001.

[44] See the article by E. Lévi-Provençal in *Encyclopédie de l'Islam* I (Leyde-Paris, 1960), p. 88; King, 1986, p. 143 (F50).

[45] MS Ambrosiana 338 fol. 4v.

computation of a sidereal ascendent using the *Taʿdīl ḥarakat Raʾs al-Ḥamal* ("equation of the motion of the Head of Aries") appears in MS Vatican 963 (fol. 29r) in a passage in which Ibn Isḥāq is also mentioned. To finish with the topic of trepidation I should only say that MS Cairo DM 1081 (p. 326), after the last table for the latitude of Mercury, reproduces the star table of the *Minhāj* of Ibn al-Bannāʾ and states that the stellar positions are sidereal (*dhātī*).[46] The *Minhāj* could also be the source for some of the values of geographical coordinates appearing in the table of MS Cairo DM 1081 (pp. 328-329).[47]

Trepidation is not the only Andalusī-Maghribī topic which appears in the three MSS under consideration. Apart from the important collection of tables of this origin which appear in MS Ambrosiana 338 (on which see below), the following items in MS Cairo DM 1081 deserve comment:

The chapter on lunar eclipses in MS Cairo DM 1081 (p. 5) ends with a quotation from the *Tabulae Jahen* of Ibn Muʿādh (d. 1093)[48] for the limits of solar eclipses for the latitude of Jaén. It corresponds to chapter 22 of the Latin text of the *Tabulae Jahen.* The same quotation appears in MS Hassaniyya 1433 (fol. 14r) and in Muḥammad al-Muʿṭī's *Kanz al-asrār* (MS Rabat General Library D2027 pp. 101-102).[49]

MS Cairo DM 1081 (pp. 119-120) has tables of the lunar and solar velocity per hour which derive from the *Qawīm Zīj* of Ibn al-Raqqām (d. 1315), or from the *Shāmil Zīj* of the same author.[50]

Finally MS Cairo DM 1081 (pp. 5-6) contains quotations of Ibn ʿAzzūz (d. 1354)[51] on lunar parallax in latitude, lunar crescent visibility and the illuminated portion of the crescent.

The most important collection of Andalusī-Maghribī materials appears, however, in MS Ambrosiana 338. Griffini (1916) was the first to draw attention to them although in several of his identifications he was misled by a short note appearing at the end of fol. 141v which he edited[52] and I translate: "End of the *zīj* of Zakūṭū. The following

[46] The same table has been edited by Vernet, 1952, pp. 107-108 and studied by Comes, 1991.

[47] Vernet, 1952, p. 75.

[48] See Samsó, 1992, pp. 152-166.

[49] See on these sources Samsó, **2003(?)**.

[50] MS Rabat 260 pp. 90-91; MS Kandilli fols. 81r and v. See Kennedy, 1997, pp. 63-64; Goldstein, 1996, p. 185.

[51] See Samsó, 1997.

[52] Griffini, 1916, p. 104.

tables, namely the geographical one (*asmā' al-buldān*), the velocity of the two luminaries and the star table were copied from the *zīj* of Ibn al-Bannā'. The tables for the latitude of Venus and Mercury and the motions of the planets [in longitude] and anomaly have been copied from the *zīj* of Ibn 'Azzūz".

The supplementary tables added to *A.P.* seem to have a clear Maghribī origin. They have been copied by an Eastern hand but the *abjad* used is Maghribī.[53] One of these tables is obviously the table on lunar crescent visibility appearing in fol. 1r. These tables, however, do not correspond to the list of the aforementioned colophon: I cannot find any geographical table or tables for the motions of the planets in longitude or anomaly. The star table's source is clearly Ibn al-Raqqām. As for the tables of solar and lunar velocity, their source is not Ibn al-Bannā's *Minhāj*: they are the same as the ones in the *zīj* of al-Khwārizmī, although the source used by the compiler of the Ambrosiana MS could also be Ibn al-Kammād (active in Cordova in 1116-17)[54] or Ibn 'Azzūz[55]. The double argument tables for the latitude of Venus (fols. 113v-115v) are those of the Almanach Perpetuum (pp. 330-334). I am not sure about the source of the tables for the latitude of Mercury (fols. 137r- 141v) but it is not Ibn 'Azzūz's *Muwāfiq zīj*, in which the tables for the computation of planetary latitudes are taken from the *zīj* of al-Khwārizmī.[56]

This appendix of Maghribī tables does not begin immediately after the colophon of fol. 141v. On fol. 142r we find two tables taken from *A.P.* (p. 123): solar declination for an obliquity of the ecliptic 23;33° and a table for the correction of the solar longitude according to the number of cycles (*adwār*) since epoch. The table on the equation of time on fol. 142v also derives from *A.P.* (p. 124). The tables added, with an attempt to identify of the source, whenever possible, are listed here:

Ambrosiana MS 338, fol. 143r-143v:

Solar and lunar velocity from al-Khwārizmī's *zīj*[57]. The actual source used by the compiler could be Ibn al-Kammād or Ibn 'Azzūz.

[53] See fols. 144r, 144v, 145r, 145v, 146r, 147r.

[54] See Chabás & Goldstein, 1994.

[55] Samsó, 1997, p. 88.

[56] Samsó, 1997, p. 92.

[57] Suter, 1914, pp. 175-180 (tables 61-66); Neugebauer, 1962, pp. 105-107; Goldstein, 1996, pp. 183-184.

Ambrosiana MS 338, fol. 144r:
Table of shadows for g = 12 (*aṣābiʿ*) and g = 6;40 (*aqdām*). See Griffini p. 104.

Ambrosiana MS 338, fol. 144v:
Jadwal maʿrifat irtifāʿ al-sāʿāt al-zamāniyya ("On the knowledge of the [solar] altitude for each seasonal hour"): the argument of the table is the meridian solar altitude (*irtifāʿ al-zawāl*) from 1° to 90° (h_m). For each meridian altitude the table gives the solar altitude for the end of the 1st, 2nd, 3rd, 4th and 5th hours (h_1, h_2..., h_5). The table is, therefore, universal and seems to have been calculated in a rather crude way. A few sample values follow:

h_m	h_1	h_2	h_3	h_4	h_5
16° (*sic*)	4°	8°	11°	14°	15°
30	7	14	21	26	29
45	11	20	30	38	43
60	13	25	38	49	58
75	15	29	43	57	70
90	15	30	44	63	75

The *abjad* used is Maghribī (*ṣād* for 60).

Ambrosiana MS 338, fol. 145r:
Jadwal al-irtifāʿ wa-l-ẓill wa-l-aqdam [sic] ("Table of the altitude, shadow and feet")

Table of shadows for g = 12 (*al-ẓill al-mabsūṭ*) and g = 6;30 (*aqdām*). The same table appears in Ibn al-Raqqām's *Qawīm Zīj.*[58]

Ambrosiana MS 338, fol. 145v-146r:
Dhikr mawādiʿ al-kawākib al-thābita ṭabīʿiyya li-sanat 680 li-l-Hijra ("Tropical positions of fixed stars for year 680 H")

Year 680 H/ 1281-82 AD. List of 58 stars with their tropical longitude, latitude, mediation, declination, ecliptic degrees which rise and set together

[58] *Qawīm*, MS Rabat General Library 260, p. 89; see Kennedy, 1997, p. 63.

with the star, half the day arc and meridian altitude. The computed local latitude is 36;37° (Tunis). The longitudes are those of the star catalogue of the *Almagest* with an increase of 16;46° due to precession. The same table is preserved in Ibn al-Raqqām's *Qawīm Zīj*.[59]

Ambrosiana MS 338, fol. 146v:
Jadwal sāʿāt niṣf al-nahār al-muʿtadila li-ʿarḍ kull balad ("Table of equal hours for half the daylight and for all latitudes")

In spite of the title this table cannot be valid for all latitudes, for it gives the length of half daylight expressed in equal hours as a function of the solar longitude. This table is the same as the one in Ibn al-Raqqām's *Qawīm Zīj*[60]: length of half daylight for Granada whose latitude is 37;10°.

Ambrosiana MS 338, fol. 147r:
Jadwal niṣf qaws al-nahār li-ʿarḍ al-buldān li-Ibn Isḥāq ("Ibn Isḥāq's table of half the arc or daylight for the latitude of all places")

The argument is the solar longitude and it gives half the arc of daylight expressed in degrees and minutes. The extreme values are:

Cancer 0°: 108;55°

Capricorn 0°: 71;5°.

Using an obliquity of the ecliptic of 23;33°, the latitude obtained from half the maximum length of daylight is 36;38,33°, very near to the value used both by Ibn Isḥāq and Ibn al-Raqqām for the latitude of Tunis (36;37°). Ibn Isḥāq also uses 36;40°.[61] This table does not appear in the Hyderabad MS of Ibn Isḥāq's *zīj*, but it has been preserved in Ibn al-Raqqām's *Qawīm Zīj* in which a latitude 36;37° is mentioned[62]: like many other tables in this *zīj*, this one may have been copied from Ibn Isḥāq.

Ambrosiana MS 338, fol. 147v:
Jadwal taʿdīl azmān al-sāʿāt li-ʿarḍ al-buldān ("Time degrees of the [seasonal] hours for the latitude of all places")

This table seems unrelated to the one in fol. 147r. The argument is also the solar longitude and the extreme values are:

Cancer 0°: 18;11°

Capricorn 0°: 11;49°.

[59] MS Rabat General Library 260, pp. 100-103.

[60] MS Rabat General Library 260, p. 88; see Kennedy, 1997, p. 70.

[61] Mestres, 1996, p. 276.

[62] MS Rabat General Library 260, p. 161; Madrid Museo Naval fol. 41v. See Kennedy, 1997 p. 70.

Using again an obliquity of the ecliptic of 23;33°, the latitude obtained from half the maximum length of daylight (18;11° x 6 = 109;6°) is 36;53,52°. A similar table for the latitude of Tunis can be found in Ibn al-Raqqām's *Qawīm Zīj*[63]. A table which gives half the arc of daylight for the latitude of Granada appears in the same *zīj*[64] with the following extreme values:

Cancer 0°: 109;5° (Ambrosiana: 109;6°)

Capricorn 0°: 70;55° (Ambrosiana: 70;54°).

Ambrosiana MS 338, fol. 148r:
Jadwal mazāl [sic, for *manāzil*] *al-qamar*

Sidereal longitude of the lunar mansions. Occasional drawings of the constellations. An instruction at the top of the table states that one should enter the table with the "longitude of the star/planet (*kawkab*)" after having subtracted the value of the *iqbāl*.

MS Vatican 963 contains three tables related to the lunar mansions:

1) Fol. 166r: Unfinished table which is not to be found in Zacut. Its purpose is to establish a correspondence between the Julian date, the position of the Sun on the zodiac and the lunar mansion. 12 cases at the top of the table indicate the zodiacal sign, the lunar mansion and the name of the month (in its Latin form). Under each name we find three sets of ciphers which correspond to the zodiacal signs (from 1° to 30°), the lunar mansions (from 1 to 13 days), and the days of each month. The dates of the equinoxes are 8th March and 3rd September, while the solstices are 5th June and 2nd December. A spring equinox on 8th March may correspond to the early beginning of the twentieth century (?).

2) Fol. 166v: This table resembles the one on fol. 166r, although the names of the months have been omitted. Only two series of ciphers appear: the zodiacal degree and the days (1-12 or 1-13) for each lunar mansion. On top of the table we find the following legend: "Enter [the table] with the degree of each planet [*kawkab*] vertically [*ṭūlan*] and with the zodiacal sign horizontally [*ʿarḍan*]. Where both lines meet you will find the lunar mansion".

3) Fol. 8r: Unfinished table which seems to give positions of the lunar mansions in the 12 Syriac months of the solar year. It seems to be an attempt to adapt the same table in fol. 166r: the Latin names have been replaced by the Syriac ones.

Ambrosiana MS 338, fol. 1r (Griffini 1a):
Jadwal maʿrifat ruʾyat al-ahilla bi-l-ʿashiyyāt fī 'l-aqālīm al-sabʿ ("Knowledge

[63] MS Rabat General Library 260, p. 162.

[64] MS Rabat General Library 260, p. 166.

of the visibility of the lunar crescent in the evening in the seven climates")

The vertical argument are the zodiacal signs, while the horizontal argument corresponds to the seven climates. The table is known from several manuscripts and is described by King[65], who considers it early Andalusī (9th or 10th c. AD). This table is extant in the Ambrosiana MS and in the Museo Naval MS (fol. 59b) where it is stated that it was copied from the *Qawīm Zīj* of Ibn al-Raqqām: I cannot find it, however, in the Rabat MS of this *zīj*.

6. *Reports on two observations made in 1637 and in 1722*

Without any apparent relation to the *Almanach Perpetuum* or to the Andalusī-Maghribī tables associated to the Arabic version of the *A.P.*, MS Vatican 963 contains two reports of observations of planetary conjunctions made in Yemen in 1637 and 1722. They are interesting and deserve a translation and commentary in spite of the fact that they do not give many details. Reports of this kind are not very common in Arabic astronomical literature.[66]

1) Vatican MS 963, fol. 9r:

"*Faṣl*: there was a conjunction of Mars and Jupiter which could be observed (*bi-l-ru'ya*) and it agreed with computation. It took place at dawn on Wednesday 14 Sha'bān ... of year 1047 H. At dawn on that day Mars was concealing the planet Jupiter and there did not seem to be any difference in their latitudes:

Longitude (*taqwīm*) of Jupiter: 7^s 1;24,14°
Longitude of Mars: 7^s 1;15,10°
Anomaly (*khāṣṣa*) of Jupiter: 2^s 17;43,4°
Anomaly of Mars: 8^s 12;12,2°.

14 Sha'bān 1047 H corresponds to 21st December 1637 (31st December, Gregorian). With Tuckermann's tables (1964), which always use the Julian calendar, I obtain, by a linear interpolation, the following positions for the aforementioned date:

	Longitude	*Latitude*
Jupiter	7^s 1;39,47°	1;16,37°
Mars	7^s 2;9,14°	1;18,58°

This result can be checked with the computer programme E.Z. Cosmos

[65] King, 1987, pp. 197-207.

[66] See for example King & Gingerich, 1982.

with which I obtain for 31st December 1637 (Gregorian) at 5.00 in the morning for the meridian of Ṣanʿāʾ[67]:

	Right ascension	Declination
Jupiter	$13;59,28^h$	-10;55,2°
Mars	$14;0,27^h$	-10;53,49°

From which I calculate the longitudes and latitudes of the two planets:

	Longitude	Latitude
Jupiter	7^s 1;36,16°	1;13,13°
Mars	7^s 1;49,27°	1;19,21°

The two planets were, therefore, extremely close to each other and an observer might have believed that Jupiter was being occulted by Mars. The positions calculated were extremely accurate with an error of about -0;12,2° for the longitude of Jupiter and +0;34,17° for that of Mars.

The computation was not made with the *Almanach Perpetuum*, with which I have obtained the following results (in parentheses the differences between the recomputed values and those appearing in the text):

	Longitude	Anomaly
Jupiter	6^s 29;2,30° (-2;21,44°)	1^s 22;16° (25;27,4°)
Mars	7^s 1;16,0° (0;0,50°)	3^s 15;41° (3;28,53°)

I have argued in § 2.3.3 that this report was probably copied from an earlier source and does not bear any relation to the date in which the Vatican MS was copied.

2) Vatican MS 963, fol. 8v:

Another report of an observation: "There was a conjunction of the Moon and the planet Saturn during the night of Monday 19th of the month of Rajab 1134. The difference in latitude between the two planets was very small. The altitude of both planets, which were together (*jamīʿan*) was 52°. Both were in the sign of Sagittarius, as if they were (*kaʾanna-humā*) in the 17th degree of Sagittarius, but God knows best

[67] Sunrise took place at $6;32^h$. At $5;15^h$ the solar altitude was approximately at -18°.

... This conjunction was observed (*wa-hādhā 'l-qirān bi-l-ru'ya*): the latitude of Saturn was northern; the altitude of Qalb al-ʿAqrab was 48°, western; the altitude of *al-Simāk al-Rāmiḥ* was 53°, western. The Moon was at its maximum altitude: 52°".

19th Rajab 1134 corresponds to 23th April 1722 (4th May, Gregorian). Using the computer programme E.Z. Cosmos for the aforementioned Gregorian date at 2 o'clock in the morning, I find the following set of equatorial coordinates, from which I have calculated the corresponding ecliptical coordinates:

	Right ascension	*Declination*	*Longitude*	*Latitude*
Saturn	$17;4,24^h$	-21;11,28°	8^s 17;2,39°	1;41,5°
Moon	$17;4,42^h$	-21;58,13°	8^s 17;11,42°	0;54,57°

At the same hour, in Ṣanʿā', we find the following altitudes:

Saturn	53;3°
Moon	52;16°
Qalb al-ʿAqrab (Antares)	48;7°
al-Simāk al-Rāmiḥ (Arcturus)	51;38°

The data of the text are, therefore, fairly accurate. An occultation of Saturn by the Moon did almost take place: the difference in latitude between the two celestial bodies amounts to about three quarters of a degree; both are in the 17th degree of Sagittarius; the lunar altitude is 52° and the altitude of Qalb al-ʿAqrab is 48°. We only have an error of about 1° for the altitude of al-Simāk al-Rāmiḥ. The data of the report do not seem to be the result of a computation (as was the case in the first report): they are given to the precision of one degree, which suggests that the observation was probably made (by Yūsuf al-Maḥallī?) with some kind of instrument.

7. A brief conclusion

The Arabic translation of *A.P.* seems to be the result of a very curious mixture of several traditions. Western almanachs use Babylonian goal-year periods, adapted by a mysterious Hellenistic Awmātiyūs in the third or fourth century AD,[68] and revised by a Toledan astronomer, Ibn al-Zarqālluh, in the second half of the 11th c. On the other hand the author of the tables of *A.P.* was Abraham Zacut, a Jewish astronomer

[68] Cf. Samsó, 1992, pp. 166-171.

of the end of the 15th c., who used the *Alfonsine Tables*, calculated by two Toledan Jews of the 13th c. (Yehudah b. Mosheh and Isḥāq b. Sīd), under the patronage of Alfonso X (r. 1252-1284), a Christian king. To this one should add that the *Alfonsine Tables* were strongly influenced by al-Battānī's *zīj* and that Zacut introduced in the tables of *A.P.* materials derived from another Jewish tradition: that of Jacob Bonjorn of Perpignan (fl. 1361) and, indirectly, that of Levi ben Gerson (1280-1344). All this mixture was introduced in the Maghrib by a Morisco exile, al-Ḥajarī, and was surprisingly successful, both in the Maghrib and in the Mashriq, until the 19th c. This paper has tried to document the diffusion of this tradition in Cairo and, especially, in Yemen, through the analysis of three MSS: in two of them (Cairo and Ambrosiana) we have been able to see that *A.P.* was mixed with an Andalusī-Maghribī astronomical tradition in which the main influence seems to be that of Ibn al-Raqqām, a follower of Ibn Isḥāq, whose work reached the Mashriq at a very late date. The Vatican MS is the third and it has the interest of having been used extensively in the 18th c. and of preserving two interesting reports of observations made in 1637 and 1722. This Yemeni diffusion of *A.P.* could be due to the efforts of an 18th c. Egyptian astronomer, Yūsuf al-Maḥallī, active in Yemen ca. 1730: my suspicion is that he introduced al-Ḥajarī's translation from Egypt.

ACKNOWLEDGEMENTS: This paper was written as a part of a research project on "The circulation of astronomical ideas in the Mediterranean between the twelfth and the nineteenth centuries", sponsored by the Spanish Ministry of Education and Culture (reference BHA 2000-0722). Some years ago, my master Prof. Juan Vernet gave me his own annotated copy of MS Escorial 966 which I have used here. Bernard R. Goldstein sent me all the information he had about MSS Ambrosiana 338 and Vatican 963 and he lent me his microfilm of MS Cairo DM 1081 (which had been given to him by David A. King). José Chabás, Bernard R. Goldstein and David A. King have read a previous draft of this paper, corrected mistakes and offered useful suggestions. Bernard Goldstein is in fact the author of the title of the present paper. My gratitude to all of them.

BIBLIOGRAPHICAL REFERENCES

Luís de Albuquerque, Facsimile edition of Abraham Zacut's *Almanach Perpetuum* (Leiria, 1496). Lisbon, 1986.

José Chabás, "Astronomía andalusí en Cataluña: las Tablas de Barcelona", in J. Casulleras & J. Samsó (eds.), *From Baghdad to Barcelona. Studies in the Islamic Exact Sciences in Honour of Prof. Juan Vernet* (Barcelona, 1996), I, pp. 477-525.

José Chabás & Bernard R. Goldstein, "Andalusian Astronomy: *al-Zīj al-Muqtabis* of Ibn al-Kammād". *Archive for History of Exact Sciences* 48 (1994), 1-41.

José Chabás and Bernard R. Goldstein, *Astronomy in the Iberian Peninsula: Abraham Zacut and the Transition from Manuscript to Print* in "Transactions of the American Philosophical Society" Vol. 90, Pt. 2, Philadelphia, 2000, XII+196 pp.

Mercè Comes, "Deux echos andalous à Ibn al-Bannā' de Marrākush", in *Le patrimoine andalous dans la culture arabe et espagnole* (Tunis, 1991), pp. 81-94.

Mercedes García Arenal, Fernando Rodríguez Mediano & Rachid El Hour, *Cartas Marruecas. Documentos de Marruecos en Archivos Españoles (Siglos XVI-XVII).* Consejo Superior de Investigaciones Científicas (C.S.I.C.), Madrid, 2002.

Bernard R. Goldstein, "Lunar velocity in the Middle Ages: a comparative study", in J. Casulleras & J. Samsó (eds.), *From Baghdad to Barcelona. Studies in the Islamic Exact Sciences in Honour of Prof. Juan Vernet* (Barcelona, 1996), I, pp. 181-194.

E. Griffini, "Lista dei manoscritti arabi nuovo fondo della Biblioteca Ambrosiana di Milano", *Rivista degli Studi Orientali* 7 (1916), pp. 51-130.

Ekmeleddin Ihsanoğlu (ed.), *Osmanlı Astronomi Literatürü Tarihi (History of Astronomy Literature during the Ottoman Period).* Islâm Tarih, Sanat ve Kültür Araştırma Merkezi (IRCICA). 2 vols., Istanbul, 1997, CCVI + 1146 pp.

E.S. Kennedy, "The Astronomical Tables of Ibn al-Raqqām a Scientist of Granada". *Zeitschrift für Geschichte der Arabisch-Islamischen Wissenschaften* 11 (1997), 35-72.

E.S. & M.H. Kennedy, *Geographical coordinates of localities from Islamic sources.* Frankfurt, 1987.

David A. King, *Fihris al-makhṭūṭāt al-ʿilmiyya al-maḥfūẓa bi-Dār al-Kutub al-Miṣriyya.* 2 vols., Cairo, 1981-86.

David A. King, *Mathematical Astronomy in Medieval Yemen. A Biobibliographical Survey.* American Research Center in Egypt. Undena Publications. Malibu, 1983.

David A. King, *A Survey of the Scientific Manuscripts in the Egyptian National Library.* Winona Lake, Indiana, 1986.

David A. King, "Some early Islamic tables for determining lunar crescent visibility". In D.A. King & G. Saliba (eds.), *From Deferent to Equant: A Volume of Studies in the History of Science in the Ancient and Medieval Near East in Honor of E.S. Kennedy*. New York, 1987, pp. 185-225. Reprinted in King, *Astronomy in the Service of Islam*. Variorum, Aldershot, 1993, no II.

David A. King and Owen Gingerich, "Some Astronomical Observations from Thirteenth Century Egypt". *Journal for the History of Astronomy* 13 (1982), pp. 121-128. Reprinted in David A. King, *Islamic Mathematical Astronomy*. Variorum Reprints. London, 1986, no VII.

David A. King and E.S. Kennedy, "Ibn al-Majdī's Tables for Calculating Ephemerides". *Journal for the History of Arabic Science* 4 (1980), pp. 48-68. Reprinted in David A. King, *Islamic Mathematical Astronomy*. Variorum Reprints. London, 1986, no VI.

P.S. van Koningsveld, Q. al-Samarrai, and G.A. Wiegers, *Aḥmad ibn Qāsim al-Ḥajarī, Kitāb Nāṣir al-Dīn ʿalā 'l-Qawm al-Kāfirīn (The Supporter of Religion against the Infidels)*. C.S.I.C. and A.E.C.I., Madrid, 1997.

Giorgio Levi della Vida, *Elenco dei Manoscritti Arabi Islamici della Biblioteca Vaticana. Vaticani Barberiniani Borgiani Rossiani*. Città del Vaticano, 1935.

Angel Mestres, "Maghribī Astronomy in the 13th Century: a Description of Manuscript Hyderabad Andra Pradesh State Library 298", in J. Casulleras & J. Samsó (eds.), *From Baghdad to Barcelona. Studies in the Islamic Exact Sciences in Honour of Prof. Juan Vernet* (Barcelona, 1996), I, 383-443.

José María Millás Vallicrosa, *Estudios sobre Azarquiel*. Madrid-Granada, 1943-50.

O. Neugebauer, *The Astronomical Tables of al-Khwārizmī. Translation with Commentaries of the Latin Version edited by H. Suter supplemented by Corpus Christi College MS 283*. København, 1962.

Julio Samsó, *Las Ciencias de los Antiguos en al-Andalus*. Madrid, 1992.

Julio Samsó, "Andalusian Astronomy in 14th Century Fez: *al-Zīj al-Muwāfiq* of Ibn ʿAzzūz al-Qusanṭīnī". *Zeitschrift für Geschichte der Arabisch-Islamischen Wissenschaften* 11 (1997), pp. 73-110.

Julio Samsó, "An Outline of the History of Maghribī Zijes from the End of the Thirteenth Century". *Journal for the History of Astronomy* 29 (1998), 93-102.

Julio Samsó, "Abraham Zacuto en el Magrib: sobre la presunta cristianización del astrónomo judío y la islamización de su discípulo José Vizinho". *Anuari de Filologia. Estudis Hebreus i Arameus. Homenatge a la Dra. Teresa Martínez Sáiz* XXI, secció E, Número 8 (1998-99), pp. 155-165.

Julio Samsó, "La medición del tiempo en al-Andalus en torno al año 1000". In Luis Ribot García, Julio Valdeón Baruque, Ramón Villares Paz (eds.), *Año 1000, Año 2000. Dos milenios en la Historia de España*. Vol. I (Madrid, 2001), 71-92.

Julio Samsó, "Astronomical Observations in the Maghrib in the Fourteenth and Fifteenth Centuries". *Science in Context* (Cambridge, U.K.) 14 (2001), 165-178.

Julio Samsó, "Abraham Zacut and Jose Vizinho's *Almanach Perpetuum in Arabic* (16th-19th c.)". Forthcoming in Centaurus (2003).

H. Suter, *Die astronomischen Tafeln des Muḥammed ibn Mūsā al-Khwārizmī in der Bearbeitung des Maslama ibn Aḥmed al-Madjrīṭī und der latein. Uebersetzung des Athelhard von Bath auf Grund der Vorarbeiten von A. Bjørnbo und R. Besthorn in Kopenhagen herausgegeben und kommentiert.* København, 1914.

Bryant Tuckerman, *Planetary, Lunar and Solar Positions A.D. 2 to A.D. 1649 at five-day and ten-day Intervals*, Philadelphia, 1964.

Juan Vernet, *Contribución al estudio de la labor astronómica de Ibn al-Bannā'*, Tetuán, 1952.

Juan Vernet, "Una versión árabe resumida del Almanach Perpetuum de Zacuto" in Vernet, *Estudios sobre Historia de la Ciencia Medieval*, Barcelona-Bellaterra, 1979, pp. 333-351.

ADDENDA ET CORRIGENDA

I, 520: On al-Qalaṣādī's *Riḥla* see now M. Marín, "The making of a mathematician: al-Qalaṣādī (d. 891/1486) and his *Riḥla*", *Suhayl* 4 (2004). 295-310.

I, 521-22: Ibn ᶜAbdūn's treatise on practical geometry was edited by A. Djebbar, "al-Risāla fī l-Taksīr li-Ibn ᶜAbdūn: shāhid ᶜalā l-mumārasāt al-sābiqa li l-taqlīd al-jabarī al-ᶜarabī", *Suhayl* 5 (2005), 7-68 (of the Arabic section of the journal). The text, incomplete in the aforementioned vol. 5, is supplemented in *Suhayl* 6 (2006), 81-86.

I, 525: On the 9th c. Cordovan astrologers see now the new evidence furnished by Ibn Ḥayyān's *Muqtabis* II-1: Facsimile edition in J. Vallvé, *Ben Haián de Córdoba (m. 469 H/1076 J.C.) Muqtabis II (1). Anales de los Emires de Córdoba Alhaquem I (180-206/796-822) y Abderrahman II (206-232/822-847). Edición facsímil de un manuscrito árabe de la Real Academia de la Historia (Legado Emilio García Gómez)*. Madrid, 1999. Edition by M.ᶜA. Makkī, *al-Sifr al-thānī min Kitāb al-Muqtabis li-Ibn Ḥayyān al-Qurṭubī*. Riyāḍ, 2003. Spanish translation by M.ᶜA. Makkī and F. Corriente, *Crónica de los emires Alhakam I y Abdarrahman II entre los años 796 y 847 (Almuqtabis II.1)*. Zaragoza, 2001. Analysis of the information about the astrologers in M. Forcada, "Investigating the Sources of Prosopography. The Case of the Astrologers of Abd al-Rahman II". *Medieval Prosopography* 23, 2002, 73-100; Forcada, "Astronomy, Astrology and the Sciences of the Ancients in Early al-Andalus (2nd/8th - 3rd/9th centuries". *Zeitschrift für Geschichte der arabisch-islamischen Wissenschaften* 16 (2004-2005), 1-74; M. Rius, "La actitud de los emires hacia los astrólogos: entre la adicción y el rechazo", in Cristina de la Puente (ed.), *Identidades marginales. Estudios Onomástico-Biográficos de al-Andalus* vol. XIII (Madrid, 2003), 517-549.

III, 243 n. 51: On al-Khwārizmī's *zīj* see B. Van Dalen, "Al-Khwārizmī's astronomical tables revisited: analysis of the equation of time", in J. Casulleras and J. Samsó (eds.), *From Baghdad to Barcelona.*

Studies in the Islamic Exact Sciences in Honour of Prof. Juan Vernet (Barcelona, 1996) I, 195-252.

III, 242 n. 47 (and also **V**): On the *Toledan Tables* see the splendid edition prepared by F.S. Pedersen, *The Toledan Tables. A review of the manuscripts and the textual versions with an edition*. Historisk-filosofiske Skrifter 24:1-4. Det Kongelige Danske Videnskabernes Selskab. Copenhagen, 2002.

V: An edition of the complete text, with introduction, English translation and commentary is now available in J. Samsó and H. Berrani, "The Epistle on *Tasyīr* and the Projection of Rays by Abū Marwān al-Istijī". *Suhayl* 5 (2005), 163-242. The problem of the identification of *Zīju-nā al-muṣaḥḥaḥ* and, consequently, of the date of the *Toledan Tables*, is discussed again in pp. 166-167 as a result of the objections presented by M. Comes in "Ibn al-Hā'im's Trepidation Model", *Suhayl* 2 (2001), 291-408 (see pp. 318-322).

V, 302-03: on Ibn Mu^{c}ādh's treatise on the projection of rays see now J.P. Hogendijk, "Applied mathematics in 11th century Spain: Ibn Mu^{c}adh al-Jayyani and his computation of astrological houses and aspects". *Centaurus* 47 (2005), 87-114; J. Casulleras, "Ibn Mu^{c}ādh on the astrological rays". *Suhayl* 4 (2004) 385-402; Casulleras, *El tratado sobre proyección de rayos de Ibn Mu^{c}āḏ de Jaén (m. 1093. Edición, traducción y estudio*. Ph.D. diss. presented at the University of Barcelona in 2006.

V, 585: Thābit b. Qurra's *Kitāb al-shakl al-qaṭṭā^{c}* has been edited, translated and studied by Richard Lorch, *Thābit ibn Qurra, On the sector-figure and related texts*. Edited with translation and commentary. Islamic Mathematics and Astronomy, 108. Frankfurt, 2001.

V, 588-594: there is a recent edition of al-Bīrūnī's *Isti^{c}āb*: *Isti^{c}āb al-wujūh al-mumkina fī ṣan^{c}at al-asṭurlāb*. Nashrat Muḥammad Akbar. Mashhad, 1418 h. [2001].

VII: New materials on Jābir b. Aflaḥ's *Iṣlāḥ*, mainly related to the motions of the Sun and Moon and the Ptolemaic theory of eclipses have been presented by Josep Bellver, *Críticas a Ptolomeo en el s. XII: El caso del* Iṣlāḥ al-Maŷisṭī *de Ŷābir b. Aflaḥ*. Ph.D. diss., University of Barcelona, 2005.

VII, 208 n. 21: add A.I. Sabra, "One Ibn al-Haytham or two?", *Zeitschrift für Geschichte der arabisch-islamischen Wissenschaften* 15 (2002-2003), 95-108.

VIII, 259 n. 1: on Ibn al-Bannā' see M. Aballagh and A. Djebbar, *Ḥayāt wa mu'allafāt Ibn al-Bannā' (ma^ca nuṣūṣ ghayr manshūra). La vie et l'oeuvre d'Ibn al-Bannā (1256-1321).* Rabat, 1998.

VIII, 259 n. 2 (and **XIII, 302**): David King's *Overview* has been updated in King, "On the History of Astronomy in the Medieval Maghrib", *Études Philosophiques et Sociologiques Dédiées à Jamal ed-Dine Alaoui.* Faculté des Lettres et des Sciences Humaines Dhar El Mahraz - Fès, 1998, 27-61.

VIII, 260-261: on Andalusian and Maghribī *zīj*es see also D.A. King and J. Samsó, with a contribution by B.R. Goldstein, "Astronomical handbooks and tables from the Islamic world (750-1900): an interim report".- *Suhayl*, 2, 2001, 9-105 (see pp. 56-64).

VIII, 268-69 (and **IX, 82-83**): on the motion of the planetary apogees according to Ibn al-Zarqālluh and Ibn Isḥāq see now M. Díaz Fajardo, "Al-Zīŷ al-Mustawfà de Ibn al-Raqqām y los apogeos planetarios en la tradición andaluso-magrebí", *Al-Qanṭara* 26 (2005), 19-30.

VIII, 286: on the Zarqāllian correction of Ptolemy's lunar model see R. Puig, "The theory of the Moon in the *al-Zīj al-Kāmil fi'l-Ta^cālim* of Ibn al-Hā'im". *Suhayl* 1 (2000), 71-99.

IX, 77, end of n. 11: the two missing pages of Ibn Ḥabīb's *Kitāb fī l-nujūm* have been edited by P. Kunitzsch, "[c]Abd al-Malik ibn Ḥabīb's *Book on the Stars* (Conclusion)". *Zeitschrift für Geschichte der arabisch-islamischen Wissenschaften* 11 (1997), 179-188.

XI, 93 (and **XII, 167**): an analysis of the same sources in M. Comes, "Some new Maghribī sources dealing with trepidation". *Science and Technology in the Islamic World.* Turnhout, 2002, 121-141.

XI, 94: on al-Baqqār see M. Díaz Fajardo, *La teoría de la trepidación en un astrónomo marroquí del siglo XV. Estudio y edición crítica del* Kitāb al-adwār fī tasyīr al-anwār *(parte primera), de Abū [c]Abd Allāh al-Baqqār.* Barcelona, 2001; Chedli Guesmi, *El* Kitāb al-amṭār wa l-as[c]ār *de Abū [c]Abd Allāh al-Baqqār. Edición crítica y estudio.* Ph.D. diss. presented at the University of Barcelona in 2005.

XI, 94: on Abū Kursūm al-Yahūdī/ Jacob Corsuno a new reference appears in P. Kunitzsch, "A hitherto unknown Arabic manuscript of the *Almagest*". *Zeitschrift für Geschichte der arabisch-islamischen Wissenschaften* 14 (2001), 31-37: Isḥāq-Thābit's translation of the *Almagest* was copied in 1381 in Zaragoza by Aḥmad b. Aḥmad b. Salāma al-Ṣ.n[...]ānī al-Ḥājirī for his master and teacher Abū Isḥāq Ya[c]qūb ibn

Isḥāq ibn Ya^cqūb, known as Ibn al-Qursunuh al-Isrā'īlī, astronomer of King Peter (IV) of Aragon and Count of Barcelona.

On Muḥyī al-Dīn al-Maghribī see C. Dorce, "The *Tāj al-azyāj* of Muḥyī al-Dīn al-Maghribī (d.1283). Methods of computation". *Suhayl*, 3 (2002-2003), 193-212; Dorce, *El* Tāŷ al-azyāŷ *de Muḥyī al-Dīn al-Magribī*. Barcelona, 2002-2003.

INDEX OF NAMES AND SUBJECTS

This index contains the names of authors (both ancient and modern scholars) as well as place-names and main subjects. I have not included my own name or those of the co-authors of some of the papers.

INDEX OF MANUSCRIPTS

INDEX OF PARAMETERS AND NUMERICAL VALUES